Contributions to Political Science

The series Contributions to Political Science contains publications in all areas of political science, such as public policy and administration, political economy, comparative politics, European politics and European integration, electoral systems and voting behavior, international relations and others. Publications are primarily monographs and multiple author works containing new research results, but conference and congress reports are also considered. The series covers both theoretical and empirical aspects and is addressed to researchers and policy makers. All titles in this series are peer-reviewed. This book series is indexed in Scopus.

David Ramiro Troitiño
Editor

E-Governance in the European Union

Strategies, Tools, and Implementation

Springer

Editor
David Ramiro Troitiño
Tallinn University of Technology
Tallinn, Estonia

ISSN 2198-7289 ISSN 2198-7297 (electronic)
Contributions to Political Science
ISBN 978-3-031-56044-6 ISBN 978-3-031-56045-3 (eBook)
https://doi.org/10.1007/978-3-031-56045-3

This Springer imprint is published by the registered company Springer Nature Switzerland AG
The registered company address is: Gewerbestrasse 11, 6330 Cham, Switzerland

Introduction

This publication emanates from the endeavours of the Jean Monnet Chair on Digital Europe and Future Integration, presently overseen by Professor David Ramiro Troitiño. Prof. Troitiño also assumes the role of Deputy Director within the Jean Monnet Network on E-Governance and Digital Development. Additionally, he holds the position of Senior Researcher in EU Politics at Tallinn University of Technology (Estonia) and serves as a European Union specialist at Turku University (Finland).

His scholarly pursuits encompass European Union integration, digital policies, and e-governance. Prof. Troitiño has curated volumes in reputable journals such as IDP Revista de Internet Derecho y Política (Vol. 34, October 2021: 'Europe Facing the Digital Challenge'), CIBOD (Vol. 131, September 2022: 'The Digitalisation of the European Union: Repercussions and Expectations'), Revista Ayer (Vol. 129 (1), January 2023: 'Luces y Sombras de Europa Central y del Este en la Unión Europea'), and the Brazilian Journal of International Law (Vol. 20 (2), September 2023, 'The Digital Transformation of Mercosur: Influence and Cooperation of the European Union').

With a prolific academic output, Prof. Troitiño has authored 169 articles and chapters in international journals and high-quality monographs. Noteworthy among his contributions are publications in CIBOD, Revista de Occidente, and the Journal of European Studies. Furthermore, he has authored or co-edited seven books, including 'The EU in the 21st Century: Challenges and Opportunities for the European Integration Process' (Springer, 2020) and 'Digital Development of the European Union: An Interdisciplinary Perspective' (Springer, 2023).

Prof. Troitiño's leadership extends to the coordination of eight international projects, including 'Digital Single Market as a New Core of European Union Studies' (Jean Monnet Module) and 'Digital Single Market as a Key Element in EU-oriented Georgian Higher Education' (financed by the Estonian State). Presently, he serves as Deputy Director for four international projects, namely 'Digital Europe and Future Integration' (Jean Monnet Chair), 'Legal and Regulatory Governance of Artificial Intelligence Systems' (Jean Monnet Module), 'Baltic Chain' (Europe for

Citizens), and 'E-Governance and Digital Transformation in the European Union' (Jean Monnet Network).

The Jean Monnet Chair on Digital Europe and Future Integration directs its focus towards emerging technologies and their anticipated impact on the European integration process. Recognizing the digital future, the EU must adequately prepare for the transformative implications of digitization, which holds substantial societal development opportunities. Integration within the digital sphere assumes significance as it often transcends national sovereignty, offering avenues for deepening Union ties while mitigating potential opposition from stakeholders.

The Chair's project delineates three primary objectives:

1. Digital Single Market and EU integration.
2. E-governance and the EU demos.
3. Digital ethics.

Complementary to these priorities, the Chair includes two additional areas of teaching and research:

4. Cyber-security and EU integration.
5. New Technologies and Common Defence Policy in the EU, incorporating various complementary facets.

The Chair's analytical approach evaluates the positive potential consequences of integrating these new areas concerning the further development of the European Union. The Digital Europe and Future Integration (DEFI) initiative encompasses five courses, the establishment of five research groups aligned with project priorities, and an ambitious plan of activities, ultimately aiding the EU in its digital transformation.

Contents

e-Governance as a Future Option

David Ramiro Troitiño

Abstract The world is facing a new social revolution: digitalization. It will affect the whole socioeconomic structure and change the social paradigm of our societies. Therefore, we are facing a world change with such an influence as the implementation of agriculture in the Neolithic, the evolutions implemented by ancient Greeks, or the Industrial Revolution. It is a major change in humanity and those who evolve will succeed in a highly interconnected world. Consequently, the European Union must embrace digitalization in order to lead a new era. This publication presents different fronts where digitalization is a priority within the European Union.

Introduction

The European Union is facing a digital transition, reflecting the evolution of the modern culture as a logical step of the institutions adapting to modern society. Therefore, the supranational organization should speed up the digitalization process in order to connect with its own citizens, who are already implementing living in a digital environment. The European Union, as an organization including many nations and national states, based on a balance of importance between the Member States (Council in its different shapes), the citizens (European Parliament), and its own process of integration (European Commission), requires a constant effort adapting to the necessities of those relevant actors involved in the process of constructing a united, wealthy, and peaceful Europe.

e-Governance is a solution for the most relevant necessities in an interconnected world, such as the lack of funds, economic resources, or labor force. Any political organization needs to generate enough money (incomes) to cover the expenditures of the services it provides to its members. The society, including private and economic agents, shares its wealth to fund the communality of public policies and

D. Ramiro Troitiño (✉)
Jean Monnet Chair on Digital Development of the EU, Tallinn University of Technology, Tallinn, Estonia
e-mail: david.troitino@taltech.ee

D. Ramiro Troitiño (ed.), *E-Governance in the European Union*, Contributions to Political Science, https://doi.org/10.1007/978-3-031-56045-3_1

services (Kerikmäe & Dutt, 2014). Usually, this transfer of wealth, from the private to the public, is done through taxes allowing the members of the society to contribute according to their incomes to the common budget focusing on the common necessities. Nevertheless, if the funds are not enough, there are traditionally different options, such as lending money via public debt, reducing the quality and the extension of the services decreasing the cost, or increasing taxes to cover the expenditures. The digital tools provide a new option of cutting the cost without affecting the quality of the service, including less taxes. The digital services provided by governments can also be more effective in the use of resources available and workforce. To become more competitive means fewer resources are required and less workers involved in the services. The issue of funds in the case of the European Union goes beyond the capacity to afford quality public service because those against the European Union and the integration process usually complain about the waste of national money at the European level (Mooij, 2021). This is a common critic with not much ground to support it, but popular among those willing to stop the integration process. Therefore, an effective use of the available economic resources, increasing the quality of the public services provided by the European Union, and reducing the expenditures would fundamentally reduce nationalist criticism of the EU.

The European Union needs to make an effort to identify the fields where a digital approach will increase the satisfaction of the European citizens (Ramiro Troitiño, 2023). The mapping is a crucial task already undergoing under the promotion of the European Commission, whose priorities are:

- eGovernment for public administrations: Cross-border digital public services
- eGovernment in the Digital Single Market: Information on the EU's electronic exchange of social security information (EESSI), EU rules on social security coordination, public directory of social security institutions
- Electronic payments and invoicing: The EU's e-Invoicing directive, European initiatives on e-Invoicing, how to check for compatibility with EU rules, exchange of information on e-Invoicing
- Electronic customs: How the EU plans to replace paper-based customs procedures with electronic ones, EU legislation and initiatives related to electronic customs, strategic plan for electronic customs in the EU

European Union e-Governance: The Future of the European Integration

The publication focuses on the possibilities of the European Union to develop an efficient e-governance. The organization has a structural problem since its origins, the gap between the institutions and the citizens. The latter feel closer to their states and their level of loyalty is higher at the national level and at the European level. Nevertheless, this can change; different factors can influence a transition promoting multilevel identity and loyalty levels, adding the European level to the current local, regional, and national levels. Among these factors, digitalization is the most promising, because it abolishes the problem of distance, it is effective in solving the problems of the citizens, and it is cheaper, allowing us to reallocate funds to other priorities of the society (Oliievska et al., 2020).

In order to implement a digital society within the European Union, it is required to understand the influence of digitalization on the most successful theories of European integration, neofunctionalism. It is a theory widely followed that shows the way of the integration, and how we can prepare for further actions, a roadmap for the creation of a solid European organization. It is not the only theory involved in the building of Europe, but is the most influential. Therefore, the first chapter of this publication is focused on the relation between neofunctionalism and digitalization, proposing different aspects to combine both effectively in the continuous process of integrating Europe. The strategy of the European Union institutions is based on their essence, and linked with theories of integration, mainly the European Commission with neofunctionalism, Council with Intergovernmentalism, and European Parliament with federalism. Therefore, their attitude toward digitalization is different as they have different priorities and different approaches on building Europe. To present and discuss these options is fundamental to understand the process of digitalization and how a compromise between the three main institutions of the Union will affect them. In addition, the Member States of the European Union have different traditions, priorities, and levels of development, influencing their position toward digitalization and e-governance in the European Union. An analysis of the internal situation of the level of digital implementation in the European States allows us to understand how far e-governance can go in the European Union (Troitiño, 2022).

There are two fundamental issues regarding the digital revolution in the European Union, digital identity and the impact of digitalization on social policies because they are two pillars of the European spirit and what makes Europe different from other parts of the world. The European Union is the only organization in the world generating a high level of integration that embraces economy, social aspects, and politics. It has a general influence over the population and is creating a common body of citizens. Nevertheless, nationality is still the main vehicle to attract the loyalty of the people and there is no European nation as such (Rek, 2010). Therefore, the European Union has been built on the concept of citizenship, more effective to interact socially from a logical point of view, but weaker than the emotional connotations of nationality (Mulder, 2021). Nevertheless, e-Identity is a step forward to European digital citizenship because of its endless possibilities. Welfare policies are another pillar in the common identity of the Europeans and what makes Europe different from other parts of the world. Digital innovations will affect it as well and it is required to research its impact to understand the evolution of Europe. Both pillars are analyzed in this book from a wide perspective trying to find out obstacles for their digital implementation in the European Union and proposing some solutions. All these aspects have been researched by David Ramiro Troitiño and Viktoria

Mazur, in a common approach to these fundamental issues with the goal of integration in the horizon.

e-Democracy in the European Union is the next logical step after e-Identity. Once a common demos is generated by fostering the digital identity, a new structure must be created for allowing the common citizens to interact together and with the institutions representing them. e-Democracy provides the digital frame for the European Union to generate a stronger democracy in Europe, a part of its own identity. The obstacles and solutions are analyzed by Mateja Rek in an excellent work focusing on the European Union perspectives.

The digitalization and possibilities of e-governance are total, affecting all parts of the society, including economy. Therefore, it is a priority to adapt the European market to the digital economy. Consequently, Digital Single Market (Ježová, 2017) is a crucial part of this book, masterly presented by Daniela Jezova. A work complemented by the research of Pawan Dutt on "Digital competition law issues and interrelated aspects of law." Digital economic integration also requires an analysis of European Union contracts (Ayata, 2021) in digital environments, as Zeynep Ayata presents in this book. In relation to transparency and financial matters, Annelieke Mooji presents her research on "Transparency of political party financing through blockchain. Designing a blockchain system to generate transparency for EU finances," a crucial part for increasing the trust in the European system and adapt it to the modern necessities (Kerikmae and Troitiño, 2021). Data protection is a must in terms of e-governance, from the economic point of view, but from the political as well: a topic developed by three outstanding scholars from Olomouc university (Andraško et al., 2021).

In the international relations field, there is also a relevant impact in the digital revolution of the European Union. The organization can implement an effective digital diplomacy, allowing the institutions to interact with the rest of the world in a fast and secure way. There is the traditional reluctance for a common diplomacy because it is a symbol of the national states, but the current globalization and the responsibilities of the Union internationally will foster integration in such a fundamental field.

Politics, social aspects, and economy are complemented with a legal system, educational necessities, and IT systems for their digital implementations. Celso Coutela presents his research on European Education Area and Digital Education Action Plan (2021–2027): One more step toward the Europeanization of Education Policy, as a basic step toward a common digital integration (Cancela Outeda, 2010). "Europeanization the digital way and trans-European IT systems" based on the case of EESSI is developed by Evert-Jan Mulder. Finally, "e-Justice governance in the EU," authored by Elena Alina Onţanu, provides the readers and researchers with the global vision this book develops in terms of e-governance in the European Union. All the chapters are interconnected with the others but at the same time can be read independently, allowing the readers to focus on their most relevant area (Rashica, 2019), but at the same time, understanding e-governance as a global process affecting all the aspects of the European Union.

Conclusions

The priorities in terms of e-governance in the Union are focused on the Digital Single Market and areas associated with it, as payments and customs. Since the beginning of the European integration process, the implementation of a Common Market, with common customs and common trade policy, has been one of the most successful European initiatives. In addition, the economic integration has fostered integration in other fields, as the current society model based on capitalism allows an imbrication of economics with almost all the areas of the society (Hamulák, 2018). Nevertheless, the irruption of the digital economy generated a dysfunctionality between the European economy, highly integrated, and the digital economy, still nationally divided. Therefore, the EU priorities on e-governance focus on adapting the digital economy to the European Union's common economic frame, but this book presents other aspects relevant for a balance process of digital implementation.

References

Andraško, J., Hamuľák, O., & Mesarčík, M. (2021). The digital development of the European Union: data governance aspects of cooperative, connected and automated mobility. *IDP: Revista de Internet Derecho y Politica, 34*, 1–16.

Ayata, Z. (2021). Old abuses in new markets? Dealing with excessive pricing by a two-sided platform. *Journal of Antitrust Enforcement, 9*(1), 177–195.

Cancela Outeda, C. (2010). La eurorregión Galicia-Norte de Portugal: un escenario de cooperación territorial. *Razón y Palabra, 15*(74).

Hamulák, O. (2018). La carta de los derechos fundamentales de la union europea y los derechos sociales. *Estudios constitucionales, 16*(1), 167–186.

Ježová, D. (2017). Fundamental rights in the European Union—Perspective of the digital era. In: *Human rights in EU external relations: Between law and politics* (pp. 79–86). Vydavateľstvo UK, Univerzita Komenského.

Kerikmäe, T., & Dutt, P. K. (2014). Conceptualization of emerging legal framework of E-regulation in the European Union. In T. Kerikmäe (Ed.), *Regulating etechnologies in the European Union: Normative realities and trends* (pp. 7–32). Springer.

Kerikmae, T., & Troitiño, D. R. (2021). El mercado digital europeo y los acuerdos comerciales con Iberoamérica: Problemas y oportunidades de seguridad. In *La integración europea e iberoamericana II: Las relaciones de la Unión Europea (UE) y el Mercado Común del Sur (MERCOSUR) con el Sistema de Integración Centroamericano (SICA)* (pp. 139–155). Aranzadi Thomson Reuters.

Mooij, A. A. (2021). European Central Bank digital currency: The digital euro. What design of the digital euro is possible within the European Central Bank's legal framework?

Mulder, E. J. (2021). Living apart together? Discussing the different digital worlds in city government. In E. Estevez, T. A. Pardo, & H. J. Scholl (Eds.), *Smart cities and smart governance: Towards the 22nd century sustainable city* (pp. 289–302). Springer.

Oliievska, N., Troitiño, D. R., & Kerikmäe, T. (2020). Internal security: Terrorism and criminality fostering integration in the EU. In D. R. Troitiño, T. Kerikmäe, R. M. de la Guardia, & G. Á. Pérez Sánchez (Eds.), *The EU in the 21st century: Challenges and opportunities for the European integration process* (pp. 85–100). Springer.

Ramiro Troitiño, D. (2023). The European Commission, the Council, and the European Parliament: Differentiated theoretical frame for the digital revolution. In D. Ramiro Troitiño, T. Kerikmäe, & O. Hamuľák (Eds.), *Digital development of the European Union: An interdisciplinary perspective* (pp. 349–361). Springer.

Rashica, V. (2019). Digital diplomacy: aspects, approaches and practical use. *European Perspectives, 23*.

Rek, M. (2010). Europeanization of civil society sector in Central and Eastern Europe. *Innovative Issues and Approaches in Social Sciences, 3*(1), 160–186.

Troitiño, D. R. (2022). La estrategia de las instituciones de la Unión Europea ante el reto de digitalización. *Revista CIDOB d'Afers Internacionals, 131*, 17–40.

Digitalization, Neofunctionalism, and Integration in the European Union

Viktoria Mazur and David Ramiro Troitiño

Abstract This research focuses on the analysis of the general impact of digital integration in the European Union as a new way to deal with public services and public policies implementation. The perspective of the work is based on the long-term development of the European Union following the spillover effect of neofunctionalism integration theory. Consequently, the European Union is understood as a process, an initiative in progress that has not reached its final shape and requires the innovative approaches to keep the right track of development. As a result, the work explores the potential of digitalization fostering the European integration to a new level in the long process of achieving a stable integrated, wealthy, and peaceful area.

Introduction

The European Union is an organization in constant development founded on the idea of supranational management of common policies. The origins of the organization are linked with the Second World War and the idea of confrontation between national states in Europe. Key figures involved in the creation of the first European Communities, and leading forces in the integration process, identified the source of conflict between Europeans with the exacerbated nationalism and its monopoly over the concept of sovereignty. Therefore, to avoid further conflicts in Europe it was required to break the connection between nations and political power by creating a new entity above the nations of Europe focused on the necessities of the citizens regardless of their nationality. This was the theoretical frame for the creation of the European Communities based on integration, versus other options linked with cooperation keeping intact the concept of national sovereignty.

Obviously, it was not possible to implement this radical social change at once because of the power of nationalism among European states and nationals, whose

V. Mazur · D. Ramiro Troitiño (✉)
Jean Monnet Chair on Digital Development of the EU, Tallinn University of Technology, Tallinn, Estonia
e-mail: viktoria.mazur@taltech.ee; david.troitino@taltech.ee

D. Ramiro Troitiño (ed.), *E-Governance in the European Union*, Contributions to Political Science, https://doi.org/10.1007/978-3-031-56045-3_2

identification with the nation, from a political perspective, was, and still is, very strong. It is important to outline that the focus was not on attacking nationalism, but rather weakening its connection with politics, keeping nations on cultural aspects rather than political, in order to prevent confrontations between nations with the full support of the states they represented.

The necessity to build a new socio-political model based on common sovereignty, the concept of common citizenship and entailing different nationalities, required a frame for its gradual development. The formula chosen was neofunctionalism with elements of intergovernmentalism and federalism, as the main theoretical body for a progressive implementation of a new model substituting the previous national state model. Neofunctionalism established a frame to replace the previous politics with a new supranational style. As a starting point, areas of low politics should be integrated, but ensuring that these are key strategic economic sectors, as coal and steel, the first sector to be integrated in the European Communities. The importance is not politics because it attracts the attention of the nationals willing to fight back the process of integration due to their fear of weakening of the nation. In order to avoid a strong opposition of the integration process, neofunctionalism focuses on economic areas that will bring relevant benefits for the society as a whole, connecting the needs and expectations of the citizens (Hamulák, 2018). Therefore, issues such as culture or defence are not a priority in the integration process, but a consequence of the economic integration. Economy here plays a crucial role because as the more united an economic area is, the more economic actors will lobby for common rules and common management, directing the area naturally to a common decision-making procedure, a common authority representing all of the members of the organization regardless of their nationality.

Neofunctionalism also includes institutional issues as it promotes the creation of a high authority to oversee the integration process acting as a common institution for all the members, overseeing the common wealth rather than the national interest of each participant in the process. In addition, the common high authority is in charge of sponsoring further integration from a common perspective and for the benefit of the whole organization. Therefore, the high authority should be independent from the national states and their decisions respected by all of the actors involved in the process of integration. Consequently, it should provide ideas and directives for deeper integration.

Another relevant part of neofunctionalism is the spillover effect, based on the idea of integrating specific areas with the potential to bring benefits for the partners involved, but at the same time generating new necessities that will require further integration to properly address them. It is a natural process leading to a common integrated area. As an example of the spillover effect, we see the European Coal and Steel Community that established a common market for these products. It meant an important boost for the companies of the Member States working in this field. It gave them a common market with common rules that all the actors had to respect. Nevertheless, Member States had different policies to transport raw materials, with the consequent influence on the competitiveness of the companies as there were transport subsidies involved. Those companies affected pursued competition on equal terms in the whole market, pushing for deeper integration with common rules also in transport. It means that the actors involved in the sector that was integrated are going to become active players asking for deeper integration. Therefore, spillover effect creates a common integrated area step by step, without major conflicts with national states and nationalism, as a consequence of a necessity rather than an imposition. Nevertheless, spillover effect needs that the economies of the Member States are reasonably interdependent for its correct implementation. Spillover effect also needs political activism to give a push in the right direction because the Member States will bargain down to a lowest common denominator position (Troitiño, 2022).

According to neofunctionalism, deeper integration is a consequence of the socio-economic interest on its benefits. The greater these benefits, the more support there is for a common integration. The transfer of loyalty from the citizens of the national states to the Union will be a consequence of the search of the most effective route for the fulfilment of the material interest of the social groups. It accepts that politics are just a group-based activity, a competition between different groups to influence decision-making, and the Member States will be under pressure to fulfil the demands of these groups for deeper integration. As the integration deepens, the centre of decision-making will change gradually from the Member States to the common institutions, where the decisions for the whole organization are taken. The social and economic groups will try to influence the common institutions, changing their interest from the national to the supranational actors, shifting swiftly their loyalty from the national level to the common level. As a constant process, it includes gradually more policies, more actors, and more sectors in the integration process, and new institutions at the common level are needed. It means that political integration is a side effect of economic integration.

Additionally, this model of generating new necessities by partial integration implies the impossibility to keep the organization at a standstill unless the integration is reversed. If an area is integrated, it provides benefits for the society, but also generates new necessities. There are just two ways to address these new necessities, national solutions (regression in the integration) or further integration, but there is no option to stand still because the tensions generated by the previous integration require solutions to avoid a full collapse of the system. Therefore, the options are to dismantle the integration achieved or to proceed with further integration. This scheme normally leads to further integration, as the members of the society do not want to lose the benefits provided by the already implemented integration (Twizeyimana & Andersson, 2019). Therefore, they will support further integration to protect the acquired benefits rather than for political reasons.

As a critique of neofunctionalism, it is a theory that does not provide any empirical evidence to support its claims and forgets about key values such as liberty and justice that are mainly protected by the national states. Additionally, it does not take into consideration the feelings and emotions of the citizens as it approaches the whole integration from a pragmatic perspective. Nationals will not just transfer their loyalty from the national governments to the common level just because they will get bigger economic benefit. Being part of a nation provides citizens with a common emotional frame that is not logical, but it is very powerful and includes emotional attachment and feeling of belonging difficult to break. Finally, neofunctionalism cannot explain the different periods of stagnation in the integration process. The periods when integration halted completely cannot be explained by the spill-over effect.

Digital Integration and Neofunctionalism

According to neofunctionalism, there are basic steps to follow in order to narrow down the integration in the right direction. The main goal would be the creation of common digital sovereignty shared between the Member States without any distinction or barrier because of the nationality. A common citizenship means common rights and common duties of all citizens regardless of their nationality. Therefore, neofunctionalism aims to create same rights and duties in the digital world for the citizens affected by the process. Consequently, digital rights and duties are part of the process from a theoretical perspective, but allowing national differences based on exceptions is linked with major issues, as for example environment, protection of customers, or gender equality. These concessions must be as less restrictive as possible, regulated or approved by a common digital authority and overseen by a common legal digital frame in order to prevent the members of the organization to use them as national barriers. Overall, a common judicial system must supervise the correct implementation of the digital sovereignty with supreme powers over the national judicial systems.

Common digital sovereignty from the neofunctionalism approach helps to prevent the national confrontation in the digital platforms, generating a common space with shared responsibilities and separating the concept of nation and digital world. It follows the logic of what is shared among members cannot be used against each other, preventing digital confrontations between national states that could easily lead to major problems.

In addition, the creation of a common digital framework means a more powerful integrated areas in terms of importance compared with the implementation of a separate system in each of the members of the organization. The size matters in terms of controlling the high-tech companies that operate worldwide and escape the control of single states unless their relevance allows them to impose national rules. In the current world, there are too few states with such capacity, such as the USA or China. The former serves as the headquarters for many of these corporations and is a primary market for their operations. Therefore, Washington has the capacity to impose market rules and taxes on the activities of these companies because it has the power to do it thanks to a strong federal government and a free market economy with clear regulations on monopolies or tax evasion (Rashica, 2018). China perhaps is the only state standing on a similar level to the USA and bases its power on a state control economy and a huge market with tight connections with most of Asian countries and the rest of the world. Consequently, the Government of Beijing can control the big high-tech companies thanks to an efficient authoritarian system and to the size of the economy. Access to its market provides a huge network of clients and potential benefits (Mergel et al., 2019). The combination of a state control economy and sizeable market has led to the creation of national high-tech companies serving the national interest of the state, but it is a worldwide exception because only the Republic of China has this combination, authoritarian system–huge market, to generate its own high-tech companies competing in an intervened market with international corporations.

Neofunctionalism idea of common digital sovereignty can focus on different angles, depending on the area to be implemented, such as politics of market. The idea of common sovereignty requires a common body to manage this sovereignty, a common frame where to implement the common will. It can politically adopt many forms, as a federal structure with a common government dealing with the areas affected by the common sovereignty and leaving to each Member State the regulation and control of the areas excluded from the community. It can adopt the shape of a confederation, with a more restrictive understanding of the common interest, or intergovernmentalism based on cooperation with a very weak concept of communality beyond a common understanding of socio-economic challenges. This idea also applies to authoritarianism with an imposed communality controlled by a strong central power with the means to repress any misbehaviour (Gorwa, 2019). Nevertheless, digitalization allows a higher participant of the citizens in the political life via e-democracy and the civic participation in the public life. The control of the State can be maintained even if the possibilities provided by the digital progress are countless, but the access to information cannot be totally controlled. Therefore, in general, digitalization should lead to higher involvement of the citizens in public affairs through initiatives such as e-voting, or online consultations, reducing the controlled state policies.

The second pillar to achieve common digital sovereignty is the digital market. The creation of a common digital space with common rules and a reliable system to implement them and avoid any attempt to use shortcuts or just bend the rules looking for a particular benefit generates market capacity to have a strong and independent system able to face challenges from companies or even from other states and their respective models of digital economy linked with their political structure and a national interest. Therefore, the size of the market is pretty relevant in the implementation of common digital sovereignty based on domestic rules free from other international agents, being states or corporations. In order to implement a common digital market in an area wide enough, it is required to decrease gradually the national differences, create common rules, eliminate national barriers to trade, reduce the obstructive effect of national digital exceptions with the implementation of as less restrictive approach as possible, establish an efficient common management authority, and develop a common system to overview the right implementation of the common measures to protect them from national distortion or manipulation from any agent involved in the process (Ayata, 2018).

Common digital sovereignty has also an impact of the common identity of an area, as the nationals of the Member States should have the same rights and duties in the digital market without any exception based on their national background.

Most of daily life aspects are related somehow to the economy, and digital market is increasing in importance constantly (Brown & Marsden, 2023). Therefore, building a common digital market means building a common digital space where the citizens of the Member States will interact with equal rights regardless of their geolocation or any other variable. If there are no distinctions, the common digital identity will be reinforced, facilitating digital political integration.

A common digital market will increase the size of the national markets, allowing for a more competitive digital economy with better prices and conditions for the consumers, enforcing the support of the citizens to the common digital sovereignty. It facilitates a spillover effect, as the digital market brings clear benefits for companies and citizens, but generates new problems that previously have not existed, as the management of common rules, or the regulation of currently unforeseen issues. These new problems will require further integration from a digital perspective in order to solve the new issues or dismantling the digital market. The agents involved, citizens and companies, will not want to lose the benefits provided by the digital market and will accept digital integration in politics, which will take the shape of the best system for the area following the mentioned models, or even generating new models of digital political integration consequence of the innovation progress of the society (Di Gregorio et al., 2019). Therefore, the digital market will require an increasingly common management as it expands, integrating areas of low politics, such as data protection or customers rights, leading step by step to deeper digital integration, and finally the creation of a digital political communality. The new integrated areas need to have some key strategic importance for further integration, as data protection will probably lead to a common position on artificial intelligence as it is the main source for AI to work properly.

The digital integration should not solely rely on the spillover effect, without any supervision to push for the right direction in terms of benefits for the society. If the common digital market operates autonomously, it will pursue benefits that cannot be controlled by individual states with the exception for the USA or China, pushing for deeper integration but without state control. Digital geographical borders do not exist; the mobility in the digital world is almost absolute, or increasingly difficult to control. Therefore, it is required to build a common authority supervising the digital environment, economic and political to supervise the implementation of the rules decided by the Member States and to act as an independent agent in the digital integration protecting the common interest against private or national attempts to bend the rules for their own benefit. The common digital authority requires independence and autonomy to push for deeper digital integration in the right direction but requires some control from the Member States and the citizens.

The roadmap for establishing common digital spaces aligns with neofunctionalist ideas, but notable differences arise in applying this framework to analog and digital realms. Neofunctionalism advocates for integrating low politics, leaving crucial policies such as security and defense in the hands of Member States due to the expected resistance to integration in these fields. However, in the digital realm, both security and defense take precedence over low politics. This prioritization stems from the necessity in the digital economy and society for robust security to safeguard transactions against cyberattacks. Without a high level of trust in the system, stakeholders in digital development may hesitate to adopt innovations, fearing the potential threat of cyberattacks. Therefore, cybersecurity is a field that requires a common effort, with a common agency, protecting all the agents involved in the digital integration, market and citizens, economy and politics. If there is a high risk (there will be always a risk in the analog and digital spheres) for digital economic transactions, the digital market will constrain the reduction of the digital economic benefits, a regression in the economy (Mulder & Snijders, 2022). States can trust the efforts of companies to protect their customers, as they need to be trusted in order to attract customers in the digital business, but big high-tech companies can lead to the creation of digital monopolies and consequently worldwide giants with such power that most of the world states would be at risk of becoming digital banana republics following the frame generated by American Fruit Company in Central America at the beginning of the twentieth century. Therefore, digital integration needs to prioritize security over other areas, contrary to the principles defended by neofunctionalism. The creation of a strong common security implemented in the integrated area will foster digital integration in other areas and will not face a strong opposition from the agents involved as in the analog world.

Additionally, defence is a priority area for the security of the services provided to the citizens, the economic transactions and the external threats. The cyberattacks originated in Russia against Estonia during the crisis of the Bronze Soldier reflect the necessity to protect the digital environment from external attacks. This threat increases as the digital integration becomes deeper and more policies are involved. The digitalization of the society is a fact, not anymore a choice; therefore, protection is required in order to keep the system working and avoid external attacks that could lead to a crisis in the whole system and the consequent weakening position towards aggressive international actors. The case of Estonia was originated by domestic issues, moving the location of a statute of a Red Army soldier from the city centre of Tallinn, capital of the country, to another less visible location. The Red Army represents for national Estonians the occupation of the country by the Soviet Union and the repression of the local population with mass deportations to Siberia and the imposition of a Communist regime. On the other hand, national Russians saw the statue as a symbol of freedom against Nazi Germany, as Red Army fought hardly against the Wehrmacht forcing them to retreat from Estonian soil. This difference of interpretations led to diplomatic confrontation between the Russian Federation and Estonia that was mainly conducted by cyberattacks originated in Russia against the digital environment of Estonia, a country highly advanced in terms of e-governance. The country suffered a partial collapse for a few days until the situation could be reversed with the support of Western cyber agencies. It clearly shows that the benefits of digital integration can become a weakness if there is no security frame which is ready to protect the cyber sovereignty from external aggressions. Neofunctionalism approach would be inefficient in the case of digital integration as it clearly excludes defence and security from the priority areas (Kerikmäe et al., 2019).

The transfer of loyalty from the citizens of the national states to a common digital union will be a consequence of the search of the most effective route for the fulfilment of the interest of the social groups and the capacity to protect it from external and internal threats (defence and security). Therefore, the priority areas should provide relevant benefits for the citizens. The digital market is an example, as it generates synergies in a common area that provide relevant benefits in terms of quality or price for the customers, the citizens (Dutt & Kerikmäe, 2014). Other possibilities of digital integration can increase the satisfaction of the citizens, fostering further integration, as e-health. The creation of a digital health system, diverting patients to reduce the waiting time, increasing the access to the most innovative facilities, and online consultation are part of a digital policy that will increase the satisfaction of the citizens and help to increase the transfer of loyalty to the digital authorities managing these kinds of policies. Therefore, integration must focus on these areas before focusing on digital political integration.

Digital Integration in the European Union

The European Union is a process, as it has not reached its final shape and is constantly evolving from a modest origin to its current shape. Nevertheless, the process cannot stop until it presents a cohesive structure able to maintain itself, still far from now. Therefore, there is a lot to do in the European Union and theories of integration help to understand what next steps and the direction of the integration should be. The fathers of Europe, such as Jean Monnet or Spinelli, clearly were looking for a supranational organization to prevent new wars in the continent and provide peace and stability. The issue of shared sovereignty was present since the beginning following the simple idea of what is shared cannot be used against each other. Nevertheless, they had different visions on how to implement these ideas. Altiero Spinelli was an outstanding federalist focusing on the creation of a common European federation. Jean Monnet had a different vision thanks to his previous life experience, outlining his work in the League of Nations and the inoperative system based on cooperation that could not prevent the disaster of the Second World War. Despite his strong belief in a common organization in Europe, Monnet thought that the European society was still too attached to the nationalistic principles and was not ready for the implementation of a common Europe. Therefore, he initiated the integration as a process using neofunctionalism as the best frame to avoid opposition, or at least reduce it. Consequently, this theory of integration, based on the spillover effect, is a strategy on progressive steps towards a united Europe (Ramiro Troitiño, 2023).

According to neofunctionalism, there are basic steps to follow in order to narrow down the integration in the right direction. The implementation of a common sovereignty step by step, eliminating national differences in the political sphere, applies perfectly to the concept of digitalization, as distance is not anymore a problem. If we consider distance, especially in terms of cultural matters and ideas, a fundamental pillar for a common identity, as a basic element for the creation of a community with minimum similarities allowing them to implement a common management of public affairs, a common sovereignty, digitalization allows the integration of countless communities in a single one based on their capacity to access the Internet rather than the distance between them. The transportation revolution in the nineteenth century helped to create a new social reality eliminating local differences and allowing the creation of larger national states. Previous anathemas, such as loyalty to the king, were outdated and substituted by loyalty to the nation. Consequently, the current digital revolution would have a similar impact on the society, eliminating barriers and creating larger levels of identity leading to new political forms of common managements, to common sovereignty on higher levels. The implementation of common policies, including common access, common services, or common benefits, will enormously contribute to the creation of a common identity. It will not substitute current levels of identity, family, local, regional, or national, but will empower the European level of identity. Policies, such as e-health with a common management in, for example, eliminating waiting lists according to the different capacities of the Member States of the European Union, will accelerate a common identity. Nevertheless, at the current level of integration within the Union, it is difficult to implement a common digital system, but would be relatively easy to create minimum common digital standards, and from there, deepen the integration gradually.

Nevertheless, following neofunctionalism, the first steps on digital integration should be done in the field of the Digital Single Market, eliminating any barriers to digital trade. The integration of the digital economy will create benefits for companies and consumers, increasing the economic power of the Union itself, and helping to control the fair competence and social contributions (via taxes) of the participants on the digital market. Obviously, as far as the digital economy is more integrated, new problems will arise and deeper integration will be required to address the new necessities following the frame of the spillover effect. Even the European Union has a deeply integrated common market; in terms of digital economy there are still numerous barriers to trade, using online tools and services, generating a distortion between traditional and digital economies within the Union. In addition, this distortion reduces the capacity of business and consumers to fully embrace the benefits of digitalization, slowing down the process that needs inevitably to be implemented to face the new world challenges. The governments are also affected by these obstacles as they cannot increase the efficiency of their digital policies as they cannot really coordinate with other Member States generating synergies for the benefit of their citizens. Digitalization of the economy in the European Union will increase the trade, economic transactions, and the competitiveness of the European companies, allowing them to compete in the international market with the economic giants from the USA or China (Sachs, et al., 2019).

The Digital Single Market strategy was adopted on 6 May 2015 and is one of the European Commission's ten political priorities. It is made up of three policy pillars:

1. Improving access to digital goods and services

The Digital Single Market will lead to better access for consumers and business to online goods and services across the European Union. In addition, it will increase the protection of consumers, as they will be protected all over the European Union.

2. An environment where digital networks and services can prosper

   The Digital Single Market will create the right environment for digital networks and services by providing high-speed, secure, and trustworthy infrastructures and services supported by the right regulatory conditions from a stronger body, the EU, which is able to control the movement of economic agents thanks to its market power. High-tech companies will implement the common rules of the Union because they cannot afford to lose access to the European market, one of the most important in the world. The creation of digital infrastructure includes cybersecurity, data protection/e-privacy, the fairness, and transparency of online platforms.

3. Digital as a driver for growth

   The Digital Single Market Strategy will foster the growth potential of the European Digital Economy, so that every economic agent operating within the EU market can fully enjoy its benefits. The digital capacity and skills are important in order to achieve an inclusive society following the European model, notably different from other areas in the world. It is a basic element in Europe, beyond even the European Union, a balanced social system. Therefore, digitalization cannot forget it, and measures should implement to reassure equal opportunities in the digital world.

The creation of the Digital Single Market can be framed with the integration in low politics to avoid opposition from the actors involved. Therefore, the areas integrated in the digital economy should be strategic and with potential to lead to further integration. Low politics include those areas not essential for a State in terms of functionality from a theoretical point of view. Consequently, the Member States of the European Union will be more open to integrate these areas on the European level. Nevertheless, as the European Union was built on a theoretical frame based on separation of nation and state, culture and politics, in order to avoid nationalistic conflicts like WWII, low politics are those neither affecting significantly the identification of nation and state nor the functionality of the national state model of the Member States of the European Union. Policies as a traditional defence, including army and the national security forces, education, communication with national channels of dissemination, diplomacy and international relations, language, constitutional frame, or relation with minorities, are those policies essentially national that traditionally are part of the relation between nation and a state. Most of these policies are under threat in the current world affecting the National State model, and the digitalization process of the European Union could help to dismiss the negative impact of globalization, and at the same time, increase the integration in Europe toward a supranational structure. The EU can protect the nations politically from an integration perspective; it is a contradiction but can easily be explained; without integration the national states could disappear; with the supranational model, the nations are protected sharing their sovereignty and managing commonly politics. Such issues as immigration, changing the internal composition of the national states, growing inequality and global economy beyond the control of traditional states, minorities challenges, Balkanization or national disintegration, cultural globalization, global civic society, global risks out of the control of single states, and religious extremism are examples where the European Union could act more efficiently and help the nations to survive the current globalization. If the nations understand that their future in Europe depends on common management of common problems, they will accept the common sovereignty.

In terms of digitalization in the European Union, high politics linked with the nation that could be integrated include aspects such as common digital borders with the creation of common rules for e-residency, the creation of e-companies within the Union, common digital citizenship with rights and duties, common management of the free digital movement in all the territory of the Union, and especially those foreigners accessing digital residency within the EU. In terms of education, there is a necessity to rule online studies with a common frame as they are not linked anymore with a territory, but with the Internet. Therefore, the EU should create common rules for online studies to avoid distortions in the system, where nationals from one Member State apply for online education in other Member States because the rules are laxed or the requirements are different. This is an example of dysfunctionality in the system, as education titles issues within a Member State are accepted all over the Union to avoid discrimination because of the nationality. The Internet opens the door for shortcuts or directly taking advantage of the system.

Common digital sovereignty will increase the effectiveness to defend the European model of society from international giants such as China or the USA with alternative models, and from high-tech international corporations that escape from the control of the Member States individually. A common digital model in the European Union will increase the power of the Union and its capacity to interact equally with alternative international models and control the operations of international companies. The EU can protect the national models of its members from global threats with a common digital management. The problem of the digital market and international corporations is also related with taxes. The traditional model based on location cannot be implemented because the physical location is not relevant to provide an online service. Companies are registering their operations in the Member State of the Union with better fiscal conditions and pay their taxes there even if their main economic activity is in other parts of the market. It goes much further than the traditional tax evasion of international companies because there are no location elements in the digital world. Therefore, the European Union should address the problem that a full Digital Single Market will generate to the taxes, incomes of the Member States, beforehand. The creation of common European Taxes on the operations related to the Digital Single Market seems the better option for its effective implementation (Abraham et al., 2019). The Member States need to understand that otherwise it will generate strong inequalities inside the Union and a distortion to the market strong enough to threaten its own existence. Obviously, the Member States are traditionally against common taxes, with exceptions as common customs, because their own model of society depends on the incomes generated by, mainly, taxes. But digital economy is not an option; it is just a reality, and the Member States need to adapt to it or risk facing obsolescence.

Nevertheless, the EU actions on high politics, from a national perspective, are cautious, and timid, based on promotion of cooperation rather than integration. For example, the EU is fostering the collaboration between civic organizations located in different Member States. Digitalization provides with much more opportunities to create common projects and common cooperation. In a similar approach, the promotion of European culture supported by the European Union by different programmes, as creative Europe, looks for deepening the cooperation and distribution at the European level to balance the cultural globalization (Lindgren et al., 2019). In terms of digital diplomacy, there is a big room for digitalization, but national traditions are strong in the field and fiercely oppose integration. Other issues such as migration or religious extremism are complicated to integrate from a digital perspective, beyond administrative issues, because they are strongly related to physical movement of people and ideas (Rosenau, 2021).

In relation with low politics, trade (Common Digital Market) is the best option for digitalization within the EU. The creation of a common digital economic area includes the establishment of external common digital borders. All the participants in the Digital Single Market must accept a common management in their international trade relations with common rules and common management from the EU. In addition, a common digital trade policy should be founded within the Union. It should operate independently of the Member States and with the capacity to sign agreements related to digital trade with other partners of the world. Comitology needs to be avoided since the implementation of a Common Digital Policy to prevent the current dysfunctionality of the European Union in terms of international trade with a system implemented because of the pressures of the French president de Gaulle with the Luxembourg Compromise of 1966 to solve the Empty Chair crisis.

The market provides great opportunities for further digital integration in low politics, as the creation of a common policy of protection of consumers, with relevant implications for the process, or data protection and artificial intelligence. The algorithm working in the digital economy required massive inputs in data to work more efficiently (Mooij, 2021). Therefore, a common management of the European data and common protection from external companies will provide the European Union with a clear advantage as the capacity to generate data is bigger than in other parts of the world thanks to the high percentage of Internet users within the Union. It applies in the same way to the generation of artificial intelligence models that required massive data inputs and regulation (Ježová, 2017). Currently, the USA is the leading international actor in terms of AI regulation, and the EU needs to increase the integration in this field to protect its citizens, its Member States, and its model of society. The threat represented by AI is present and needs present common regulations: a field that definitely will require integration in the European Union to prevent real risks.

The process of digitalization with the European Union faces different realities that cannot be framed within neofunctionalism and make unpractical a strict implementation of this theory in the digital integration. The main issue in this regard is related to defence, a field that neofunctionalism advises to obviate in the integration process because it will generate an important opposition from the participants in the process (Cancela-Outeda, 2020). Nevertheless, in terms of digitalization, cybersecurity is a priority because without trust in the digital world, the European agents will not participate in the digital revolution, condemning Europe to underdevelopment. In this direction, the EU already counts with specific agency working on it. The European Union Agency for Cybersecurity (ENISA) contributes to EU cyber policy by enhancing the liability of ICT products, services, and processes with cybersecurity certification schemes (Andraško et al., 2021). This agency cooperates with Member States and EU bodies and helps Europe to prepare for the cyber challenges of tomorrow. Its powers are still reduced, but it should be the embryo for the implementation of a real common cybersecurity agency without major opposition from Member States (Finger & Pécoud, 2003). Here is a clear differentiation on the resistance of Member States to create a common police force to deal with European crimes that go beyond the national borders because of the symbolic national importance of security forces. A common cybersecurity is needed to prevent the system from collapsing and should be a priority for the EU. ENISA is just the beginning but should not become the EUROPOL of the digital world, an information centre for collaboration between national security forces, and must evolve to a real and effective cybersecurity force for the European Union.

Cyber defense and cybersecurity represent distinct aspects of digital security. It is a coordinated act of resistance that guards information, systems, and networks from cyberattacks by implementing protective procedures such as firewalls, network detection and response (NDR), and endpoint detection and response (EDR) to identify, analyze, and report incidents that occur within a network. It has become a problem in the European Union already because the international treats are already a reality and Europe has focused its efforts on NATO, another organization not belonging to the European Union and under the auspices of USA. At the 2023 NATO Summit in Vilnius, NATO endorsed a new concept to enhance the contribution of cyber defense on three cyber levels—political, military, and technical—ensuring civil–military cooperation at all times through peacetime, crisis, and conflict, as well as engagement with the private sector, as appropriate. It obviously oversteps the prerogatives of the European Union and threatens its viability in the digital world. The NATO Cyber Security Centre (NCSC) is located at Supreme Headquarters Allied Command Europe (SHAPE) in Mons, Belgium, and protects NATO's own networks by providing centralized cyber defense support. This capability evolves on a continual basis and maintains pace with the rapidly changing threat and technology environment. NATO has also established a Cyberspace Operations Centre in Mons, Belgium. The Centre supports military commanders with situational awareness to inform the Alliance's operations and missions. It also coordinates NATO's operational activity in cyberspace, ensuring freedom to act in this domain and making operations more resilient to cyber threats (Rek, 2007). The NATO Cooperative Cyber Defense Centre of Excellence is a multinational and interdisciplinary cyber defense hub located in Tallinn, Estonia, which does research, training, and exercises in four core areas: technology, strategy, operations, and law. Therefore, the operations of NATO in cyber defense are a reality and the European Union will need to decide how its relations with NATO will be conducted. It can follow a traditional approach established during the Cold War, leaving the European defense in the hands of NATO, or generate an alternative model with European cybersecurity. Events like the war in Ukraine suggest that NATO is still the main protection shield of Europe and it will continue in the digital world being the same (Ramiro Troitiño et al., 2023).

The last relevant element according to neofunctionalism in the implementation of an integrated digital model in the EU is related to the institutions. The theory suggests the creation of a common authority to manage, supervise, and lead the integration process. The current institution representing this role is the European Commission. It seems unlikely that the creation of a different and autonomous institution within the Union to deal with digital integration is possible. The model followed so far, and probably in the future, is the creation of specific agencies, as ENISA, with specific objectives for digitalization, within the European Commission. They are bodies set up by the EU to carry out specific technical, scientific, or administrative tasks. They are divided into four groups: decentralized agencies carrying out technical, scientific, or managerial tasks that help the EU institutions to make and implement policies. Therefore, the creation of new EU agencies to address the integration in the fields mentioned in this research is expected.

Conclusions

The transfer of loyalty from the citizens of the national states to the Union will be a consequence of the search of the most effective route for the fulfilment of the material interest of the social groups, according to neofunctionalism. Digitalization will foster it, as it is clearly more effective than other models addressing the problems of the citizens. Digitalization, neofunctionalism, and integration in the European Union are clearly connected and the model is still valid in most of the policies involved in the process. Especially, it is important that the creation of the European Digital Market will generate a crucial spillover effect fostering deeper integration in the digital sphere. Nevertheless, there are important differences in relation to high and low politics. Neofunctionalism recommends to avoid high politics in the integration process, but digitalization requires the integration of crucial policies as cybersecurity. In addition, digitalization and globalization require common actions to protect the nations' members of the organization that are under threat.

The complexity of the digital integration suggests that the European Union will not follow a single path in its digital integration, but several theories simultaneously, as traditionally done with neofunctionalism, federalism, and intergovernmentalism. Nevertheless, the main role will be played by neofunctionalism due to its versability and practical implementation.

References

Abraham, R., Schneider, J., & Vom Brocke, J. (2019). Data governance: A conceptual framework, structured review, and research agenda. *International Journal of Information Management, 49*, 424–438.

Andraško, J., Mesarčík, M., & Hamuľák, O. (2021). The regulatory intersections between artificial intelligence, data protection and cyber security: challenges and opportunities for the EU legal framework. *AI & Society*, 1–14.

Ayata, Z. (2018). Does big innovation lead to big change: European Union competition law put to the test through big data. *Banka Huk. Dergisi, 34*, 203.

Brown, I., & Marsden, C. T. (2023). *Regulating code: Good governance and better regulation in the information age*. MIT Press.

Cancela-Outeda, C. (2020). The post-crisis European Union before the political union: Coordinates and keys of the future institutional architecture. In D. Ramiro Troitiño, T. Kerikmäe, R. M. de la Guardia, & G. Á. Pérez Sánchez (Eds.), *The EU in the 21st century: Challenges and opportunities for the European integration process* (pp. 117–133). Springer.

Di Gregorio, M., Fatorelli, L., Paavola, J., Locatelli, B., Pramova, E., Nurrochmat, D. R., May, P. H., Brockhaus, M., Sari, I. M., & Kusumadewi, S. D. (2019). Multi-level governance and power in climate change policy networks. *Global Environmental Change, 54*, 64–77.

Dutt, P. K., & Kerikmäe, T. (2014). Concepts and problems associated with eDemocracy. In T. Kerikmäe (Ed.), *Regulating eTechnologies in the European Union: Normative realities and trends* (pp. 285–324). Springer.

Finger, M., & Pécoud, G. (2003). From e-government to e-governance? Towards a model of e-governance. *Electronic Journal of E-government, 1*(1), 52–62.

Gorwa, R. (2019). What is platform governance? *Information, Communication & Society, 22*(6), 854–871.

Hamulák, O. (2018). La carta de los derechos fundamentales de la union europea y los derechos sociales. *Estudios constitucionales, 16*(1), 167–186.

Ježová, D. (2017). EU digital single market—Are we there yet?. *AD ALTA*, 99–102.

Kerikmäe, T., Troitiño, D. R., & Shumilo, O. (2019). An idol or an ideal? A case study of Estonian E-Governance: Public perceptions, myths and misbeliefs. *Acta Baltica Historiae et Philosophiae scientiarum, 7*(1).

Lindgren, I., Madsen, C. Ø., Hofmann, S., & Melin, U. (2019). Close encounters of the digital kind: A research agenda for the digitalization of public services. *Government Information Quarterly, 36*(3), 427–436.

Mergel, I., Edelmann, N., & Haug, N. (2019). Defining digital transformation: Results from expert interviews. *Government Information Quarterly, 36*(4), 101385.

Mooij, A. (2021). The European Central Bank's monetary policy and Central Bank Digital Currency: Can the ECB lawfully introduce a digital euro under its monetary mandate? *Irish Journal of European Law, 23*, 163–188.

Mulder, E. J., & Snijders, D. (2022). Playing the telephone game in a multilevel polity: On the implementation of e-government services for business in the EU. *Government Information Quarterly, 39*(2), 101526.

Ramiro Troitiño, D. (2023). Mapping E-governance in the EU. In D. Ramiro Troitiño, T. Kerikmäe, & O. Hamuľák (Eds.), *Digital development of the European Union: An interdisciplinary perspective* (pp. 303–317). Springer.

Ramiro Troitiño, D., Kerikmäe, T., & Hamuľák, O. (2023). The digital future of the European Union. In D. Ramiro Troitiño, T. Kerikmäe, & O. Hamuľák (Eds.), *Digital development of the European Union: An interdisciplinary perspective* (pp. 3–6). Springer.

Rashica, V. (2018). The benefits and risks of digital diplomacy. *Seeu Review, 13*(1), 75–89.

Rek, M. (2007). Organised civil society in the multilevel system of European governance. In F. Adam (Ed.), *Social capital and governance. Old and new members of the EU in comparison* (pp. 151–173). LIT.

Rosenau, J. N. (2021). Governance in the Twenty-first Century. In *Understanding global cooperation* (pp. 16–47). Brill.

Sachs, J. D., Schmidt-Traub, G., Mazzucato, M., Messner, D., Nakicenovic, N., & Rockström, J. (2019). Six transformations to achieve the sustainable development goals. *Nature Sustainability, 2*(9), 805–814.

Troitiño, D. R. (2022). The European Union facing the 21st century: The digital revolution. *TalTech Journal of European Studies, 12*(1), 60–78.

Twizeyimana, J. D., & Andersson, A. (2019). The public value of E-Government—A literature review. *Government Information Quarterly, 36*(2), 167–178.

The Strategy of the European Institutions on Digital Integration

David Ramiro Troitiño and Viktoria Mazur

Abstract Political will and societal support are required within the European Union to improve the situation of the organization addressing current problems and future challenges with innovative approaches based on terms of efficiency. Therefore, e-governance is a priority for the EU institutions, but what they tackle is implementation from different perspectives according to their essence and goals. The European institutions are key actors in the development and implementation of a system of e-governance in the European level. Nevertheless, it is a process facing numerous challenges, as the position of the Member States (not always favouring further integration). E-governance requires a strong political support for its implementation, and consequently the attitude of the EU institutions is crucial. This research analyses the positions of the European Commission, the European Parliament, and the Council, representing three different perspectives, as intergovernmentalism, federalism, and neofunctionalism, to understand the strategy on e-governance of each institution and their common interaction with the development of a common approach.

Introduction

In the contemporary era, the digital landscape has become a pivotal aspect of global progress, influencing various facets of society, economy, and governance. The European institutions have recognized the significance of digital integration and have formulated comprehensive strategies to harness its potential. This chapter delves into the strategy of European institutions on digital integration, exploring the objectives, challenges, and potential impacts of their initiatives from a theoretical approach based on the three main institutions of the Union and the three main theories of European Integration. The chapter investigates the correlation between

D. Ramiro Troitiño (✉) · V. Mazur
Jean Monnet Chair on Digital Development of the EU, Tallinn University of Technology, Tallinn, Estonia
e-mail: david.troitino@taltech.ee; viktoria.mazur@taltech.ee

D. Ramiro Troitiño (ed.), *E-Governance in the European Union*, Contributions to Political Science, https://doi.org/10.1007/978-3-031-56045-3_3

the European Commission (EC), the European Parliament (EP), and the Council with intergovernmentalism, neofunctionalism, and federalism under the prism of digitalization. The frame is complemented with the main objectives of the integration within the EU from digital elements, such as:

- Digital Single Market (DSM): Currently, the main priority of European institutions is the establishment of a Digital Single Market. This involves removing barriers to digital trade and ensuring seamless cross-border access to online services. The DSM aims to foster innovation, drive economic growth, and enhance competitiveness by creating a unified digital space within the European Union (EU).
- Digital Skills and Education: Recognizing the importance of a skilled workforce in the digital age, European institutions focus on promoting digital literacy and associated education. Initiatives are in place to equip citizens with the necessary skills to navigate the digital landscape, fostering a digitally competent society.
- Data Protection and Privacy: Ensuring the privacy and protection of personal data is a key aspect of the strategy. The General Data Protection Regulation (GDPR) is a cornerstone in this regard, providing a robust framework for the responsible handling of personal information and granting individuals greater control over their data.
- Innovation and Research: European institutions foster innovation in the digital sector. Funding programmes, such as Horizon Europe, support research and development initiatives, encouraging collaboration between academia, industry, and start-ups to drive technological advancements.

The investigation narrows down the narrative by including one more element, the challenges in digital integration, because they really have an impact on the priorities of the EU institutions. Therefore, the digital revolution, as well as the European integration in general, faces the problem of integrating such a vast area in terms of diversity, as the European Union comprises diverse Member States with varying levels of integration, and in this case, digital infrastructure and economic development (Budd and Harris, 2009). Harmonizing digital policies and standards across this diversity poses a significant challenge. In addition, as all these issues are related to digitalization, there are significant cybersecurity concerns. The interconnected nature of digital systems makes them vulnerable to cyber threats. European institutions must address cybersecurity concerns to safeguard critical infrastructure and ensure the secure functioning of digital services in order to attract citizens and economic agents to the European digital platforms. In addition, there is a relevant challenge within Europe: the digital divide. Despite efforts to promote digital inclusivity by the EU institutions, a digital divide persists in the European society, with disparities in access to technology and digital skills. Bridging this gap is essential to ensure that the benefits of digital integration are accessible to all citizens in Europe. We are dealing with a world with high rates of digital access or interaction, but still, there are some groups that remain in the analog world and need to be attracted to the digital platforms to increase the effectiveness of the new systems. The EU, as it is based on solidarity and is following some principles based on social equality, cannot leave any group behind in the digitalization process; therefore, the EU institutions must take it into consideration in their digital strategies.

The Essence of the Council, the Commission, and the European Parliament, Intergovernmentalism, Neofunctionalism, and Federalism at Work

The institutional frame of the European Union was already designed at an early stage of the integration process with a clear functional intention based on further development of the organization. Jean Monnet, the architect of the first European Communities, proposed a model based on integration, rather than cooperation. His previous experience in the League of Nations, and the following failure of this international organization in preventing the Second World War, drove him towards a new model where the good intentions of the League were reinforced with real power to implement the common decisions. Jean Monnet needed to address several challenges finding an institutional model entailing integration and common decision-making. At the same time, he was aware of the power of the national states in Europe and the necessity of giving them voice in the integration process as main actors. His core intentions were to bring closer to the common organization those sceptics who thought of the national sovereignty as the last level of common management, to incorporate nationalism in the form of cooperation to help the process of deepening the integration. In addition, he had to bring closer the people of Europe to his dream of unity. Indeed, the European citizens, after a devastating war, were still under the influence of national paradigms. Therefore, the creation of a common sovereignty had to be done gradually to avoid rejection.

Consequently, the European Coal and Steel Community (ECSC), established in 1951, marked a historic milestone in the journey towards European integration. Formed with the objective of promoting economic cooperation and preventing another devastating war, the ECSC introduced innovative institutional structures that laid the foundation for the European Union. It included a High Authority, serving as the executive body of the ECSC, representing a ground-breaking departure from traditional intergovernmental structures. Composed of independent experts, the High Authority was tasked with overseeing the common market for coal and steel. It held significant powers, including the ability to propose legislation, supervise markets, and resolve disputes. The establishment of a supranational executive marked a departure from traditional state-centric governance and set the precedent for future European institutions. Currently, this role has mostly been adopted by the European Commission, and it represents the common management of Europe, integration in the decision-making and management. Working in tandem with the High Authority, the Special Council of Ministers represented the member states within the ECSC. Comprising ministers from each participating nation, this Council played a crucial role in decision-making, providing a platform for intergovernmental cooperation (Finger and

Sultana, 2012). The interplay between the supranational High Authority and the intergovernmental Council laid the groundwork for the unique institutional balance that would later characterize the European Union. Nevertheless, the Council, still a key institution within the Union, represents cooperation, the consensus in decision-making, common agreements where no measure could be implemented without the explicit agreement of all the Member States. Therefore, it is a clear attempt to attract the States to the process of integrating Europe keeping intact their national sovereignty. Finally, the Common Assembly, the precursor to the European Parliament, was the ECSC's parliamentary institution. Unlike traditional parliaments, its members were not directly elected by citizens but appointed by national legislatures. Nevertheless, the Common Assembly provided a forum for dialogue and cooperation among representatives from Member States (Ježová, 2020). This early experiment in parliamentary cooperation foreshadowed the later development of a directly elected European Parliament. There was no room for a real European Parliament as there was no European demo, and there was no European citizenship. Nevertheless, Jean Monnet included the Common Assembly with clear intentions to increase gradually its powers in a process of progress in the integration. The institutions of the European Coal and Steel Community played a pioneering role in the evolution of European integration. By introducing a supranational executive, a parliamentary assembly, and a judicial institution, the ECSC fostered cooperation while respecting the sovereignty of Member States. The legacy of these institutions endures in the institutional architecture of the European Union, showcasing the enduring impact of the ECSC in shaping the course of European history and helping to include the three main European integration concepts in it, neofunctionalism, intergovernmentalism, and federalism. These institutions evolved to the current Council, Commission, and Parliament, with their own essence and their own priorities.

The Council of the European Union, commonly known as the Council of Ministers, stands as a key institution within the EU's complex institutional framework. Unlike the European Commission, which represents the supranational interests of the Union, the Council is intergovernmental, comprising representatives from each Member State's government. This intergovernmental nature is rooted in the principle of national sovereignty, reflecting the necessity to provide a balance between different actors and interests within the Union. The Council's evolution can be traced back to the Treaty of Paris in 1951, which established the ECSC. Over the years, subsequent treaties, such as the Treaty of Rome (1957) and the Single European Act (1986), expanded the Council's powers and broadened its scope. The Maastricht Treaty (1992) marked a significant turning point, transforming the European Community into the European Union and enhancing the Council's role in the decision-making process. The Council is composed of representatives from the national governments of the Member States, with the composition varying depending on the policy area under consideration. Different configurations of the Council exist, such as the General Affairs Council, the Economic and Financial Affairs Council, and the Foreign Affairs Council. The rotating presidency further emphasizes the intergovernmental character, with each Member State undertaking the role of presiding over the Council for a specified period, with the main power of influencing the working agenda of the Council. Decision-making within the Council typically involves negotiations and consensus-building among Member States. The principle of unanimity prevails in certain policy areas, requiring all Member States to agree for a decision to be adopted. In other cases, qualified majority voting is employed, reflecting a balance between supranational and intergovernmental decision-making structures (Rek, 2019). While intergovernmental cooperation in the Council ensures respect for national sovereignty, it also poses challenges. Divergent national interests, particularly during economic crises or geopolitical tensions, can hinder the swift adoption of policies. The need for consensus may lead to compromises that dilute the effectiveness of proposed measures (Georgios and Nikolaos, 2021). Additionally, the rotating presidency may introduce variations in leadership styles, potentially impacting the Council's efficiency. Despite challenges, intergovernmental cooperation in the Council presents opportunities for Member States to actively engage in the decision-making process. The Council serves as a platform for diplomatic dialogue, enabling states to articulate and defend their positions. The Council of the European Union, as an intergovernmental institution, plays a crucial role in shaping the policies and direction of the European Union. Its historical evolution, composition, decision-making processes, and challenges highlight the delicate balance between supranational and intergovernmental dynamics. While intergovernmental cooperation can be challenging, it offers Member States the opportunity to actively contribute to the European project, ensuring that decisions are informed by diverse perspectives and interests. As the EU continues to evolve, understanding the role of the Council in intergovernmental cooperation remains essential for comprehending the complexities of European governance.

Intergovernmental cooperation stands as a cornerstone of international relations and within the European Union, representing the collaborative efforts among sovereign states to address shared challenges and pursue common objectives. The key characteristics of intergovernmental cooperation are:

Sovereignty retention: At the heart of intergovernmental cooperation lies the principle of sovereignty retention. Participating states willingly engage in collaboration while retaining control over their domestic policies and decisions.

Diplomacy and negotiation: Diplomacy serves as the primary tool for intergovernmental cooperation. Negotiations and diplomatic channels provide the means for states to discuss issues, find common ground, and reach agreements that benefit all parties involved.

Bilateral and multilateral agreements: Cooperation can take various forms, ranging from bilateral agreements between two nations to multilateral initiatives involving multiple countries. The number of participating states and the scope of cooperation can vary based on the issue at hand.

Ad hoc nature: Intergovernmental cooperation is often ad hoc, established for specific purposes or to address particular challenges. This flexibility allows states to tailor their collaboration to the evolving needs of the international landscape.

Intergovernmental cooperation is mainly used internationally for increasing the interoperability of different zones that focus on trade agreements, such as Progressive

Agreement for Trans-Pacific Partnership (CPTPP) or the United States–Mexico–Canada Agreement (USMCA); security alliances, like the North Atlantic Treaty Organization (NATO), where member states coordinate defence efforts to ensure collective security against common threats; environmental treaties such as the Kyoto Protocol and the Paris Agreement where States came together to commit to reducing emissions, promoting sustainability, and mitigating climate change; and humanitarian and developmental initiatives, mainly led by the United Nations (UN) and its specialized agencies to address humanitarian crises, promote development, and uphold human rights on a global scale. Therefore, the importance of cooperation is huge, and it is essential to understand the current international relations. Nevertheless, it lacks effectiveness when implementation is not respected by the partners, reducing its impact and outlining the importance of convergence of interest in terms of cooperation (Cancela Outeda & González Cacheda, 2021). This approach has worked good in the European Union, providing with new progress in terms of integration as a first step uniting the Member States in a common goal before the action or policy is fully communalized. Therefore, it is important within the Union because it balances national interests within the framework of intergovernmental cooperation. The flexible nature of intergovernmental cooperation presents opportunities for states to adapt to changing circumstances and address emerging issues (Troitiño, 2023). This adaptability allows for the continuous evolution of collaborative initiatives. Nevertheless, the power imbalances among participating states may lead to unequal contributions or benefits, posing challenges to effective collaboration and raising questions about the fairness of the cooperative arrangements. In addition, intergovernmental cooperation often relies on voluntary compliance, and there may be limited mechanisms to enforce agreements. The absence of robust enforcement mechanisms can impact the effectiveness of collaborative efforts.

The next crucial institution within the European Union analysed in this research is the European Commission. It exemplifies the essence of neofunctionalism through its supranational character. Unlike intergovernmental institutions, the Commission operates independently of national governments, representing the collective interests of the European Union. Its role in proposing legislation, enforcing EU policies, and safeguarding the general European interest positions it as a key driver of integration, aligning with neo-functionalist principles. The Commission's involvement in various policy areas demonstrates the spillover effect described by neofunctionalism. Initially, as High Authority, tasked with managing the European Coal and Steel Community, the Commission's responsibilities expanded over time, encompassing areas such as competition policy, environmental regulation, and consumer protection. This evolution reflects the spillover from economic cooperation to broader policy domains, validating neo-functionalist predictions. Neofunctionalism, as articulated by scholars such as Ernst Haas, emphasizes the spillover effect and the role of supranational institutions in driving integration (Millard, 2017). The spillover effect suggests that cooperation in one policy area will create a domino effect, spilling over into other domains. Neofunctionalism also underscores the importance of supranational institutions, like the European Commission, in facilitating this process by taking on roles traditionally held by nation-states. The Commission's mediating role between Member States and its proactive stance in proposing policies contributes to the deepening of integration. Neofunctionalism suggests that supranational institutions, like the Commission, act as mediators, resolving conflicts and fostering cooperation. The Commission's ability to bridge national interests and propose initiatives that serve the collective European interest aligns with neo-functionalist expectations. The European Commission and neofunctionalism share a symbiotic relationship that has shaped the trajectory of European integration. The Commission's role as a supranational actor, its expanding responsibilities, and its mediating function contribute to the realization of key neo-functionalist principles. As the EU continues to evolve, understanding the dynamic interplay between the European Commission and neofunctionalism provides insights into the ongoing process of European integration and the role of supranational institutions in shaping the European Union.

The third pillar of the institutional frame of the European Union is the European Parliament, representing the citizens of the Union. As federalist ideas have gained prominence in discussions about the future of European integration, the role of the European Parliament in the context of integration has rocketed. The European Parliament traces its roots back to the ECSC Common Assembly, an empty institution but with symbolic power. Over the decades, the Parliament has evolved from a consultative body with limited powers to a directly elected legislative institution. The Maastricht Treaty in 1992 marked a significant turning point by granting the Parliament increased legislative powers and budgetary responsibilities. The European Parliament plays a crucial role in the legislative process, co-deciding on EU laws along with the Council of the European Union. The direct election of its members enhances the democratic legitimacy of the EU, representing the citizens at the supranational level. This legislative function contributes to the federalist discourse by fostering a shared decision-making process between European institutions and Member States. Federalist visions for the EU often emphasize the need for stronger supranational institutions. The European Parliament, as a directly elected body with legislative powers, aligns with federalist aspirations by serving as a check on both the European Commission and the Council (Misuraca and Viscusi, 2013). A stronger Parliament enhances the federalist principle of shared sovereignty, distributing powers between the central authority and Member States. Despite its federalist potential, the European Parliament faces challenges that stem from intergovernmental dynamics. The Council's role, representing Member States, can sometimes hinder the realization of a more federalist European Union. Tensions between federalist ideals and the intergovernmental nature of certain policy areas, such as foreign affairs and defence, may limit the Parliament's ability to fully embody federalist principles. The European Parliament plays an essential role in shaping the federalist discourse within the European Union. Its legislative functions, democratic legitimacy, and potential to serve as a counterbalance to intergovernmental forces contribute to the federalist vision of a more integrated and united Europe. As the EU continues to evolve, the role of the European Parliament remains central in determining the extent to which federalist aspirations can be realized in the complex landscape of European governance.

Digital Strategy of the Council

In the ever-evolving digital landscape, the Council of the European Union has embraced a collaborative approach to a digital strategy, recognizing the power of cooperation in harnessing the potential of emerging technologies. The foundations of the Cooperative Digital Strategy of the Council are rooted in the spirit of interinstitutional collaboration. Recognizing the interconnectedness of EU institutions, the strategy encourages active cooperation with the European Commission, the European Parliament, and other relevant bodies. This collaborative approach ensures a cohesive and harmonized digital vision across the EU. A common vision does not mean a common digital policy, but at least, it provides a common starting point for further common actions. The Member States' participation is central to the cooperative digital strategy, as it is based on the active involvement of the Member States. The Council facilitates a collaborative framework where Member States contribute to the formulation of similar digital policies, share best practices, and coordinate efforts to address common challenges (Ramiro Troitiño, 2023a). This inclusive approach ensures that the digital strategy reflects the diverse perspectives and needs of all EU members, but does not address the common challenges properly, especially regarding common actions to protect the Union from digital threats. The key components of cooperative digital strategy are as follows:

- Common standards and regulations: The cooperative digital strategy prioritizes the development and adoption of common standards and regulations. This facilitates a harmonized digital market, fostering interoperability and reducing barriers to cross-border digital activities. Common rules enhance predictability and create a level playing field for businesses and citizens across the EU.
- Shared digital infrastructure: Recognizing the importance of digital infrastructure, the cooperative strategy promotes the development and sharing of common digital resources. This includes collaborative initiatives to build secure and resilient digital networks, cloud services, and other critical infrastructure components that bring benefits to all Member States.
- Joint research and innovation: The cooperative digital strategy encourages joint research and innovation efforts among Member States. Collaborative projects, supported by shared funding mechanisms, aim to drive technological advancements, address digital challenges, and position the EU as a global leader in digital innovation.
- Digital skills collaboration: Addressing the digital skills gap is a key component of the cooperative strategy. Member States collaborate on educational initiatives, training programmes, and knowledge-sharing platforms to enhance digital literacy and skills across the EU. This collective approach ensures that citizens and businesses are equipped to navigate the digital landscape.

The Council of the EU in all its wingspan and with the limitations and opportunities given by its cooperationist essence is looking for a transformative impact of the European society without raising controversial concerns that could slow down the process. Therefore, the focus is on issues such as enhancing the competitiveness of the EU in the global digital economy. By fostering collaboration in research, innovation, and skills development, the EU can position itself as a hub for cutting-edge technologies, attracting investments and promoting economic growth. Collaboration in establishing common standards and regulations contributes to a resilient and secure digital ecosystem. By sharing cybersecurity best practices and collectively addressing vulnerabilities, the EU can create a robust digital environment that protects critical infrastructure and citizen data. Such controversial issue as cybersecurity is basic for a common digital environment and, perhaps, is one of the areas where the Council can agree on a high degree of integration to increase its functionality. In addition, the Council prioritizes digital inclusion by collaborating on initiatives that bridge the digital divide; the EU fosters social cohesion and prevents the emergence of digital inequalities among Member States. Therefore, the focus is on disparities between States rather than between citizens in this digital area. On international relations, the digital initiatives of the Council focus on presenting a unified front on the global stage. This collaborative digital strategy allows the EU to engage in international discussions, shape global digital governance standards, and assert its values in the evolving digital order.

Digital Strategy of the European Commission

In the rapidly evolving landscape of the digital age, the European Commission has embarked on a comprehensive Digital Strategy that mirrors the principles of neofunctionalism—an influential theory in the context of European integration. The European Commission's Digital Strategy exhibits a multifaceted approach that integrates various policy areas. By addressing issues such as digital infrastructure, data governance, artificial intelligence, and digital skills, the strategy acknowledges the interconnected nature of the digital domain. This mirrors the neofunctionalism's notion that progress in one policy area can create ripple effects across others, contributing to a broader integration process. Therefore, there is a connection between all these policies, a bridge facilitating the spread of the integration. Therefore, the EU Commission presents a horizontal approach instead of the vertical priorities of the Council, levelling the most relevant policies of the EU from a digital prism. Neofunctionalism emphasizes the role of supranational institutions in driving integration. Similarly, the European Commission, as a supranational entity, takes a leading role in the Digital Strategy. It proposes legislation, sets standards, and coordinates efforts among Member States to ensure a cohesive approach to digital challenges. The supranational governance structure aligns with the neo-functional idea that independent institutions facilitate integration beyond the national level. The Digital Strategy envisions spillover effects by addressing not only immediate digital concerns but also by influencing broader socio-economic aspects. For example, initiatives on digital skills contribute to workforce development, impacting employment and social cohesion. This aligns with the neofunctionalism principle that integration in one area can lead to positive consequences in others, fostering a more interconnected and unified European landscape. The Commission Digital Strategy advocates for a common European approach to digital challenges. Whether it's in data governance, artificial intelligence, or connectivity, the strategy promotes shared standards and cooperative frameworks. This echoes the neo-functional idea that supranational institutions encourage states to pool their resources and work together for common goals, transcending narrow national interests. The main priority of the European Commission, in terms of digitalization, seems corelative to the Council, as it is focused on economic development and increasing the effectiveness of the economy. At the core of the European Commission's digital development strategy is the creation of a Digital Single Market (DSM), a vision aimed at removing barriers to the free flow of data and digital services within the EU. By harmonizing regulations and promoting cross-border digital interactions, the DSM seeks to unlock the full economic potential of the digital realm (Andraško et al., 2021). The European Single Market is one of the most successful innovations implemented by the European Union, becoming the central core of the organization in practical matters. The European Single Market stands as a testament to the ambitious vision of fostering economic integration among European Union Member States. Envisioned as a cornerstone of the European project, and heir of the Common Market, the Single Market aimed to eliminate barriers to trade and created a seamless and competitive common economic environment. The European Single Market officially came into existence on 1 January 1993. Its primary objective was to remove obstacles to the free movement of goods, services, capital, and labour. To attain this goal, it necessitated the harmonization of regulations, standards, and policies across the Member States. Key components include the free movement of goods, services, capital, and people, as well as the harmonization of technical standards and the establishment of a competition policy. It responds to basic integration approach, what is shared cannot be used against each other; war needs a strong economy to support the operations; if the economy is shared in a common organization, war becomes unlikely due to economic restraints (Ramiro Troitiño, 2023b). Therefore, integrating the economy, analog or digital, provides economic benefits, as the Council outlines, but also provides benefits for the peace, which is the main target of the Union and a priority for the Commission.

The Digital Single Market is the adaptation of the Single Market to the digital economic burst. Therefore, the adaptation is not an option, but a necessity. Therefore, the Commission has worked to facilitate cross-border e-commerce by addressing issues such as geo-blocking and ensuring fair competition. Initiatives like the Single Digital Gateway provide businesses and consumers with seamless access to information and services, fostering a more integrated and competitive digital market. In addition, recognizing the value of data as a driver of innovation and economic growth, the Commission has focused on creating a European data economy. This involves initiatives to enhance data sharing, improve data infrastructure, and establish common European data spaces, thereby fostering a collaborative and dynamic digital ecosystem. Moreover, fostering innovation increases the European possibilities to develop and implement a digital model compatible with the European values and organization of the society. Therefore, the Commission places a strong emphasis on promoting digital innovation to ensure the EU's global competitiveness and resilience in the digital age through programmes like Horizon Europe. These programs support research and innovation in key digital technologies, including artificial intelligence, cybersecurity, and high-performance computing, aiming to position the EU at the forefront of technological advancements, driving economic growth and societal progress. Digital Innovation Hubs play a crucial role in the Commission's strategy by providing support to businesses and public entities in their digital transformation journey. These hubs offer expertise, infrastructure, and networking opportunities, fostering a collaborative environment for innovation across Member States. It complements the public policies and research by interacting with private agents, normally more agile responding external stimulus.

The European Commission also works on cybersecurity, a constant to the three European institutions analysed in this research. It is actively involved in shaping digital governance frameworks and enhancing cybersecurity measures because without trust in the system, the participation of the citizens and companies will be reduced, influencing negatively the digital development of the EU. Therefore, security is basic on the functionality of the market, and a priority for all the European institutions involved in the integration. European Digital Identity is a part of the priorities of the Commission as the main gate to access the Digital Market, to empower citizens and businesses in their digital interactions. This initiative aims to enhance online trust and streamline digital processes across borders (Hamulák, 2018). But, following the Spillover effect, it will bring a common digital identity among the EU citizens, increasing their identification, and their loyalty, to the European integration process. Therefore, it is a double purpose digital initiative. The Cybersecurity Act empowers the European Union Agency for Cybersecurity (ENISA) and establishes a framework for cybersecurity certification by setting common standards and strengthening cooperation. Consequently, the Commission aims to enhance the overall cybersecurity resilience of the EU.

Another similar priority with other institutions is the digital divide. The Commission faces the task of ensuring that digital benefits are accessible to all citizens, regardless of their geographical location or socio-economic background. It follows the same logic, according to the European model of society, states, or supranational organizations, the society is responsible for all its members; no one can leave behind voluntary (Saxena, 2005). It encompasses disparities in access to the Internet, computers, smartphones, and other digital devices, as well as variations in technology literacy and skills. Several factors contribute to the digital divide, including:

- Infrastructure: Disparities in the availability of physical infrastructure, such as reliable internet connections, in different geographical areas.
- Economic factors: Affordability of digital devices and Internet services can be a barrier for individuals or communities with lower socio-economic status.
- Educational factors: Differences in digital literacy skills and education levels can affect one's ability to effectively use technology.
- Geographical factors: Rural areas may face challenges in terms of infrastructure development, leading to limited access to digital services.

- Social factors: Age, gender, and other social factors can influence access to and use of technology.

The digital divide has important implications for individuals and communities. Those on the wrong side of the divide may face limitations in accessing educational resources, employment opportunities, healthcare services, and civic participation. Bridging the digital divide is a goal for the European institutions in general.

In the realm of digital priorities, the European Commission adopts a distinctive perspective centred on regulatory harmonization. The European Commission is the executive branch of the European Union responsible for proposing legislation, implementing decisions, upholding EU treaties, and managing the day-to-day business of the EU. The EC holds regulatory powers in various areas (Kerikmäe & Dutt, 2014). It is important to note that while the European Commission has significant regulatory powers, the legislative process involves collaboration with the European Parliament and the Council of the European Union. Decisions are often made through a complex system of checks and balances to ensure democratic representation and accountability. Nevertheless, achieving regulatory harmonization across diverse Member States remains an ongoing challenge. Balancing the need for common standards with respect for national autonomy requires adept navigation by the Commission to ensure effective digital governance. The European Commission's digital development initiatives underscore the commitment to harnessing the transformative power of digitalization for the benefit of the entire EU (Rashica, 2019). By fostering harmonization, national differences are eliminated, paving the way for a common understanding of the digital world from a wide perspective in order to extract as much benefit as possible for the scale of the European actions. In addition, there are no national traditions linked with digital aspects; perhaps there are national priorities, but no cultural aspects associating with national and digital aspects. Therefore, the actions of the Commission find less obstacles from the Member States if a common action will be more effective than individual initiatives.

Digital Strategy of the European Parliament

As the directly elected legislative body representing EU citizens, the European Parliament plays a pivotal role in shaping the digital future of the Union. The European Parliament, in its legislative capacity, contributes to shaping the regulatory framework for digital policies. This includes laws related to data protection, cybersecurity, digital markets, and the governance of emerging technologies (Ayata, 2021). A federalist approach ensures that these regulations strike a balance between common EU standards and the autonomy of Member States in implementing and enforcing digital laws. As the democratic body of the Union, directly elected by European citizens to address common issues at the European level, digital democracy and citizen engagement play a central role in the digital priorities of the European Parliament. Digitalization provides new avenues for citizen engagement and participation in the democratic process. The European Parliament, through digital platforms and technologies, can enhance direct communication with citizens, seeking their input on legislative matters and policy decisions (Shahin and Finger, 2008). This fosters a sense of digital democracy, aligning with federalist principles that emphasize the involvement of citizens in the decision-making process. Digital Democracy Initiatives promoted by the EP are:

- Online Consultations and Platforms: The European Parliament has leveraged digital platforms to facilitate online consultations and engage citizens in policy discussions. Initiatives like the "Have Your Say" platform enable citizens to express their views on specific topics, ensuring a broader range of voices in the decision-making process.
- E-Participation Tools: The Parliament has embraced various e-participation tools to involve citizens in legislative processes. Platforms like the European Citizens' Initiative allow citizens to directly propose legislative actions, enhancing the participatory nature of democracy in the digital age.
- Digital Transparency and Accessibility: Digital democracy involves ensuring transparency and accessibility. The European Parliament has implemented measures to make legislative information easily accessible online, providing citizens with the tools to track legislative processes, access documents, and stay informed about parliamentary activities.
- Social Media Engagement: The Parliament actively utilizes social media platforms to connect with citizens. Through official accounts and campaigns, members of the European Parliament (MEPs) engage in real-time discussions, share information, and seek input on various issues, fostering a more direct and immediate form of digital democracy.

Regarding cross-border Digital Connectivity, the European Parliament plays a role in initiatives aimed at promoting it. This includes efforts to harmonize digital infrastructure, eliminate digital barriers, and facilitate the seamless flow of data and services across Member States. Federalism in this context involves coordinating actions to achieve common goals while respecting the diversity of national digital ecosystems.

On a federal approach, subsidiarity is a key element of this theory. Subsidiarity is a principle often associated with federalism, particularly in the context of governance and decision-making, aiming to ensure that decisions are made at the most local level possible, with higher levels of government intervening only when necessary. In a federal system, power is divided between a central (supranational), state (national), and regional (provincial) governments. Subsidiarity is intended to prevent unnecessary centralization of power and to promote local autonomy. The principle implies that decisions should be made at the level of government that is the closest to the citizens and is most capable of addressing the issue effectively. In relation to subsidiarity in Digital Governance, the European Parliament, in collaboration with Member States, should ensure that digital policies respect national competencies and only intervene at the EU level when necessary to address shared challenges.

On the other hand, the EP is very involved in common standards for digital rights, as part of common standards for citizen rights, because the EP is the representative of the EU citizens. Digital federalism involves establishing common standards for digital rights and protections through legislation, such as the General Data Protection Regulation (GDPR), aiming to create a robust framework that safeguards citizens' digital rights while allowing for flexibility in implementation at the national level. In the same direction, EP digital strategy emphasizes equal opportunities for all Member States and citizens in the digital realm (Troitiño et al. 2022). The European Parliament, recognizing the diversity of digital capacities among nations, works towards digital inclusion, ensuring that all citizens have access to digital services and opportunities, regardless of their geographical location; a common point with the other two institutions analysed.

Ensuring Digital Sovereignty is essential for the chamber entailing the European sovereignty; balancing the pursuit of common digital goals with the preservation of national sovereignty is crucial. The European Parliament must ensure that digital policies contribute to the EU's collective strength without conflicting with the Member States, as the free participation of states and citizens must be a reality to avoid the future collapse of the organization.

Conclusions

The cooperative digital strategy of the Council of the European Union exemplifies a forward-looking and inclusive approach to digital transformation. By fostering collaboration among EU institutions and Member States, this strategy not only positions the EU as a global digital leader but also ensures that the benefits of the digital revolution are shared by all citizens and businesses across the European Union. As the cooperative digital strategy unfolds, it will continue to shape the digital future of the EU, emphasizing the transformative power of unity in navigating the complexities of the digital age.

The European Commission's Digital Strategy exemplifies a neo-functionalist approach to European integration in the digital era. By recognizing the interconnectedness of digital policy areas, promoting supranational governance, and anticipating spillover effects, the strategy aligns with the foundational principles of neofunctionalism. The EU navigates the tough challanges and the bright opportunities presented by the digital revolution. Consequently, the Digital Strategy serves as a testament to the enduring relevance of neofunctionalism in understanding and shaping.

The European Parliament, guided by federalist principles, plays a central role in navigating this digital transformation. By respecting subsidiarity, establishing common standards, and fostering digital inclusion, the Parliament contributes to a vision of digital federalism that aligns with the principles of unity, diversity, and shared progress within the European Union.

Combining the priorities of the European Council, European Commission, and European Parliament requires a collaborative and coordinated approach, as these institutions play distinct yet interconnected roles in the European Union. Each institution has its specific functions, and aligning priorities involves negotiation, compromise, and a shared commitment to the overarching goals of the EU. There are common grounds, such as cybersecurity, interoperability of systems, or digital divide that will allow a common digital approach. Other fields as harmonization or digital sovereignty present a clear battlefield for the EU institutions. Nevertheless, the main conductor for the agreement will not be European but international. The digital world escapes the control of the European national authorities; consequently, just a common action will be effective to interact safely in the digital world. In addition, the power of states as the USA or China will lead to an expansion of their own digital models to those weak areas in the planet in terms of digitalization. Therefore, if the EU wants to implement a model based on the European standards, on the European values and way of life, it would need to unite creating a digital European frame, strong enough to face the international challenges. The priorities of the European institutions here described will converge to a common position to face effectively international challenge, protect the Member States, the citizens, and all the European agents, and foster deeper integration.

References

Andraško, J., Hamuľák, O., & Mesarčík, M. (2021). The digital development of the European Union: data governance aspects of cooperative, connected and automated mobility. *IDP: Revista de Internet, Derecho y Politica, 34*, 1–16.

Ayata, Z. (2021). Old abuses in new markets? Dealing with excessive pricing by a two-sided platform. *Journal of Antitrust Enforcement, 9*(1), 177–195.

Budd, L., & Harris, L. (Eds.). (2009). *E-governance: managing or governing?* Routledge.

Cancela Outeda, C., & González Cacheda, B. (2021). Mecanismos digitales para la participación en partidos políticos de la CPLP. *População e Sociedade*. https://doi.org/10.52224/21845263

Finger, M., & Sultana, F. N. (Eds.). (2012). *E-governance, a global journey* (Vol. 4). IOS Press.

Georgios, K., & Nikolaos, V. (2021). Reinstating Greek e-governance: A framework for e-government benchmarking, improvement and government policies. *Вопросы государственного и муниципального управления, 6*, 103–127.

Hamulák, O. (2018). La carta de los derechos fundamentales de la union europea y los derechos sociales. *Estudios constitucionales, 16*(1), 167–186.

Ježová, D. (2020). Sharing economy in digital single market EU—A phenomena with future potential. *European Studies—The Review of European Law, Economics and Politics, 7*(1), 218–236.

Kerikmäe, T., & Dutt, P. K. (2014). Conceptualization of emerging legal framework of E-regulation in the European Union. In T. Kerikmäe (Ed.), *Regulating etechnologies in the European Union: Normative realities and trends* (pp. 7–32). Springer.

Millard, J. (2017). European strategies for e-governance to 2020 and beyond. In A. Ojo & J. Millard (Eds.), *Government 3.0—Next generation government technology infrastructure and services: Roadmaps, enabling technologies & challenges* (pp. 1–25). Springer.

Misuraca, G., & Viscusi, G. (2013). Managing e-Governance: a framework for analysis and planning. In *Developing e-government projects: Frameworks and methodologies* (pp. 204–224). IGI Global.

Ramiro Troitiño, D. (2023a). The European Commission, the Council, and the European Parliament: Differentiated theoretical frame for the digital revolution. In D. Ramiro Troitiño,

T. Kerikmäe, & O. Hamuľák (Eds.), *Digital development of the European Union: An interdisciplinary perspective* (pp. 349–361). Springer.

Ramiro Troitiño, D. (2023b). EU Elections and internet voting (i-voting). In D. Ramiro Troitiño, T. Kerikmäe, & O. Hamuľák (Eds.), *Digital development of the European Union: An interdisciplinary perspective* (pp. 319–333). Springer.

Rashica, V. (2019). Digital diplomacy: aspects, approaches and practical use. *European Perspectives, 23*.

Rek, M. (2019). Media education in Slovene preschools: A review of four studies. *CEPS Journal, 9*(1), 45–60.

Saxena, K. B. C. (2005). Towards excellence in e-governance. *International Journal of Public Sector Management, 18*(6), 498–513.

Shahin, J., & Finger, M. (2008, December). The operationalisation of e-governance. In *Proceedings of the 2nd international conference on theory and practice of electronic governance* (pp. 24–30).

Troitiño, D. R. (2023). *Digital development of the European Union: An interdisciplinary perspective*. Springer.

Troitiño, D. R., de la Guardia, R. M., & Sánchez, G. A. P. (2022). *The European Union and its political leaders*. Springer.

The Members of the EU and e-Governance, Analysis, and Institutional Support

Viktoria Mazur and David Ramiro Troitiño

Abstract The investigation focuses on a general analysis of the domestic situation of each Member State of the European Union in terms of e-governance. The internal situation of each individual Member State is different, from the digital approach of Estonia to other States with minimum connection with e-governance. Therefore, the general analysis is required to understand the internal situation of each Member State and the implications it has in the position of the national governments towards the development of e-governance at the EU level. Therefore, analysing the current situation will allow the creation of common standards, foster the integration in digital aspects in the European Union, and allow a concrete mapping for further common developments.

Introduction

The European Coal and Steel Community (ECSC) emerged as a core milestone in the post-World War II era, signifying the beginning of a new approach to European cooperation. Founded in 1951, the ECSC was aiming to unite states through economic integration, fostering stability, and preventing future conflicts. The original members, Belgium, France, Germany, Italy, Luxembourg, and the Netherlands, embarked on a journey of collaboration that would shape Europe nowadays and in the future. In the aftermath of World War II, Europe laid in ruins, both physically and economically. The devastating consequences of the war prompted a reevaluation of traditional geopolitical strategies and top visionary leaders such as Jean Monnet to explore alternative paths to ensure peace and prosperity. The ECSC was born out of this vision, spearheaded by key figures such as Altiero Spinelli, Robert Schuman, or even Winston Churchill as a promoter, but not a participant. This novel

V. Mazur · D. Ramiro Troitiño (✉)
Jean Monnet Chair on Digital Development of the EU, Tallinn University of Technology, Tallinn, Estonia
e-mail: viktoria.mazur@taltech.ee; david.troitino@taltech.ee

D. Ramiro Troitiño (ed.), *E-Governance in the European Union*, Contributions to Political Science, https://doi.org/10.1007/978-3-031-56045-3_4

approach included six Member States, the original members of the European Communities, because of several reasons. The integration process was seen as a peace system to avoid wars in Europe, and main contenders in continental Europe were France and Germany, two countries with the power to drag other countries into their conflicts. The power, influence, and economic muscle of both states made them the central States in European affairs, especially as the UK was more interested in its own colonial world. Therefore, the European integration process was built around these two countries, France and Germany, which are still currently the main members of the European Union. Indeed, they cannot impose their will on the other partners, but their influence is relevant; their participation in the European Union is indispensable. Therefore, their essence in terms of digital national strategies and the implementation of a common digital policy within the European Union is a fundamental requirement, not the only one, but still an essential requirement among others.

Additionally, there were other four Member States in the original ECSC, Belgium, the Netherlands, Luxembourg, and Italy. Belgium, having endured the ravages of war, recognized the necessity of collective efforts to rebuild and prevent future conflicts. The country joined the ECSC with a commitment to shared prosperity and a vision of a united Europe. Despite its small size, Luxembourg played a significant role in the formation of the ECSC as the Grand Duchy recognized the potential for collaboration in the coal and steel sectors to promote economic development and regional solidarity (Ayata & Önay, 2021). The Netherlands, having experienced occupation during the war, sought a path to lasting peace and prosperity. Joining the ECSC allowed the Netherlands to participate in a collective effort to rebuild Europe and prevent future conflicts. In addition, the BENELUX countries had already started a process of deep cooperation among them and could not afford to lose access to the French and German markets in case of the creation of a European market. Therefore, there was not a one unique reason for these countries to participate in the European integration process, but several, as economic reasons but also idealistic targets, as the establishment of a stable peace system. The contribution of these Member States to the digital revolution of the Union is significant, mainly coming from their size and their capacity to adopt new technologies and new solutions. Italy, grappling with the aftermath of fascism and war, saw the ECSC as a means to reestablish its standing among other European nations. By participating in the community, Italy aimed to contribute to regional stability and economic growth.

The original members of the European Coal and Steel Community undertook a historic initiative that transcended national interests and historical grievances. Their visionary commitment to economic integration not only revitalized war-torn economies but also laid the foundation for a united Europe. The legacy of the ECSC lives on in the form of the European Union, a testament to the transformative power of collaboration and shared ideals. These original members have still a predominance in European affairs due to their political, economic, and moral stature, with special position, as mentioned, for France and Germany. Both countries are the heart of the organization, the leaders of the process, never challenged. The

UK could have become a leading partner but was never interested in that position. Nevertheless, France, a former world power defeated in WWII, was unable to compete with the USSR or the USA in the context of the Cold War. Therefore, France saw the European integration as a way to reassure its independence and use the other partners for her own political benefits. West Germany, a miraculous economic power, saw Europe as a redemption for WWII and as an economic market for the German products. Therefore, both accepted their roles as France the political leader of the Union and Germany the economic motor of the integration. This predominance persisted in time, but decreased in intensity due to consecutive enlargements; nevertheless, the two countries are crucial for the digitalization of the EU.

The European Communities entailed continental Western states because of the conditions to join the organization, as holding a democratic political regime disabled Greece, Spain, and Portugal, the concept of integration did not match with the British conception based on cooperation, and the countries attached to the British economy, such as Ireland or Denmark. BREXIT will have an impact on the European Union in the long term, and it is relevant in terms of digital policies. The UK is one of the more digitalized economies in Europe, but their model will not impact the European Union anymore. The UK, particularly London, is a global tech hub. The city attracts tech start-ups, entrepreneurs, and investors, making it a centre for digital innovation and technology-driven businesses. The UK has a well-developed e-commerce sector, and its financial technology (fintech) industry is particularly strong. The country has a diverse digital services sector, including software development, digital marketing, and online content creation. These contribute significantly to the country's digital economy, and the UK government has implemented various initiatives to support the growth of the digital economy, including investments in digital infrastructure and programmes to enhance digital skills. The UK places a strong emphasis on cybersecurity, given the increasing importance of digital security. The country has a robust cybersecurity industry, and it actively participates in global efforts to combat cyber threats. Nevertheless, BREXIT has meant the digital isolation of the country in terms of integration in a wider area, the European one, reducing the impact of its alternative model, more similar to the USA, on the EU's digital development. Therefore, this self-isolation will increase the influence of France and Germany on the digitalization of the European Union (Mooij, 2021).

In addition, the neutrality of countries like Sweden, Finland, or Austria blocked them to join an organization seen by the USSR as an economic tool of the capitalistic countries against the workers of the world, protected by the Communist regime of Russia. There were also economic conditions based on market economy, incompatible with the vision of state economy implemented in central and east Europe. Nevertheless, these obstacles were removed gradually; the UK's withdrawal from the British-sponsored European Free Trade Association led to the enlargement of the UK, Ireland, and Denmark, even when the British were never truly involved in the idea of integration and became the paladin of cooperation within the organization until their withdrawal. European Communities were enlarged with less developed countries (in comparation with the original members) and included the spiritual soul of Europe, Greece, and two of the countries with higher internationalization such as Spain and Portugal. The end of the Cold War meant the enlargement of the neutral countries, free from the Soviet restraints. The democratization of central and east Europe opened the European Union to newly independent countries that had to rebuild from the ground up their institutional frameworks: opportunity used by Estonia to build a successful model of e-governance (Potnis, 2010). In addition, new enlargements are expected from the Balkan area, where Croatia took the lead, but Serbia, Montenegro, and Macedonia could become the next Member States of the Union. Ukraine needs reforms in all aspects of the society, economy, and political structure to finalize a long-term negotiation process, also affected by the war. Therefore, no immediate results are expected from Ukraine candidacy, as well as from Turkey, whose Islamist government distances the country from Europe, from the principles of the French Revolution, and from the guidelines implemented by Mustafa Kemal. Therefore, there are many different Member States within the European Union, with different traditions, with different priorities, and with different levels of digital implementation. This investigation focuses on those more relevant to the process integrating Europe from a political perspective, such as France, an economic perspective, such as Germany, the level of digitalization, such as Estonia, or based on their impact in the decision-making of the Council. This institution represents the Member States within the European institutional frame but is not the only forum where the states can collaborate and promote different actions at the European level, as the Franco-German meetings promoted by Charles de Gaulle, or the implementation of international agreements in the EU like Schengen area, or the grouping of countries according to particular interest as Visegrad countries (Rose, 2005).

The states selected for this investigation are Germany and France, because of their historical weight within the European Union. The level of digitalization in both countries is neither high nor low in the context of the whole Union, but the power of their governments provides these two countries with a special relevance not equalized by any other Member State of the EU. The Netherlands has been chosen as a representative of those countries leading digitalization in Europe with outstanding digital performance, not only in Europe, but also globally. Then Estonia is selected because of being representative of the second group of Europe, in terms of digital development, and because of the high level of governmental digital policies, making this country an example in terms of e-governance (Rashica, 2019). Finally, its neighbour Latvia has been chosen as a representative of those states more modest in terms of digital development and implementation within the European Union. Therefore, these countries are representatives of the European Union and its internal composition. A deeper analysis focusing on each Member State requires a longer investigation for a correct examination. Nevertheless, a deep analysis of all the states members of the Union is not the target of this research, but merely an overview of their general priorities and positions in terms of digitalization and European Integration.

Digitalization in Europe

Digitalization has become a pervasive force reshaping the fabric of societies, economies, and governance across the globe. In Europe, the wave of digital transformation has been particularly impactful, ushering in unprecedented changes that touch every aspect of life. It has been a key driver of economic growth in Europe, fostering innovation, efficiency, and competitiveness. The adoption of digital technologies by businesses has led to the creation of new markets and business models. e-commerce, for example, has experienced exponential growth, providing consumers with unprecedented access to goods and services. Start-ups and small businesses have thrived in the digital era, leveraging online platforms to reach global audiences. Moreover, digitalization has propelled the rise of Industry 4.0, where automation, artificial intelligence, and the Internet of Things (IoT) are integrated into manufacturing processes (Ramiro Troitiño, 2023a). This has enhanced productivity, reduced costs, and improved the overall efficiency of industries. European countries have been at the forefront of these technological advancements, positioning themselves as global leaders in various sectors.

The impact of digitalization extends beyond the economic realm, profoundly influencing social dynamics in Europe. The widespread use of social media has revolutionized communication, connecting people across borders and fostering new forms of social interaction. However, it has also raised concerns about privacy, fake news, and the influence of algorithms on public discourse. Education and healthcare have also experienced significant changes due to digitalization. Online learning platforms have become an integral part of the education, offering flexible and accessible learning opportunities. Telemedicine has gained traction, providing remote healthcare services and improving access to medical expertise, particularly in rural areas. Digitalization has also played a vital role in shaping cultural and entertainment experiences in Europe. Streaming services, online gaming, and virtual reality have transformed the way people consume and engage with content, contributing to the evolution of cultural practices (Millard, 2017).

European governments have recognized the need to adapt to the digital era to enhance governance and public services. e-Government initiatives aim to provide citizens with efficient and transparent services through online platforms. Digitalization has streamlined administrative processes, reducing bureaucracy and enhancing the accessibility of public services. Additionally, the concept of Smart Cities has gained prominence in Europe, with urban areas leveraging digital technologies to enhance sustainability, efficiency, and the quality of life for residents. Smart transportation, waste management, and energy systems are just a few examples of how cities are incorporating digital solutions to address contemporary challenges.

Despite the numerous benefits, the digitalization of Europe is not without challenges. Concerns about data privacy, cybersecurity, and the digital divide persist. Striking a balance between technological advancement and the protection of individual rights is an ongoing challenge that policymakers grapple with. Moreover, the rapid pace of digitalization raises questions about its societal impact, including job displacement due to automation and the need for upskilling the workforce. Ethical considerations surrounding the use of artificial intelligence and algorithms also demand careful attention to ensure that technology serves humanity rather than exacerbating existing inequalities (Ježová, 2017). Digitalization in Europe is a transformative force that has reshaped economies, societies, and governance structures. The region has embraced digital technologies to drive economic growth, enhance social interactions, and improve governance. However, navigating the challenges associated with digital transformation is crucial to ensure that the benefits are inclusive and sustainable. As Europe continues its digital journey, it must strike a delicate balance between embracing innovation and addressing the ethical and social implications of a rapidly evolving digital landscape.

The EIB Digitalization Index is a composite measure, drawing on indicators related to firms' adoption of digital technology, digital infrastructure, and investments. It amalgamates firm-level data collected through the European Investment Bank Investment Survey in 2019, incorporating five key components: digital intensity, digital infrastructure, investment in software and data, investments in organizational and business process improvements, and strategic monitoring systems. The EIB Digitalization Index highlights that, on average, European firms are trailing behind their American counterparts. European companies are less likely to be fully digital, with the construction sector notably lagging in digital intensity (Paskaleva-Shapira, 2006). US firms outpace their EU counterparts in investments related to business process improvements. However, both regions perceive digital infrastructure similarly. According to this index, the best performing EU countries in terms of digitalization are:

- The Netherlands stands out as a digitalization leader, excelling in both digital intensity and digital infrastructure.
- The Czech Republic excels in investments related to software and data, as well as organizational and business process improvements.
- Finland takes the lead in implementing a formal strategic business monitoring system.

These top-performing EU countries not only outshine their European peers but also surpass the digitalization achievements of the USA.

On the other hand, this index allows us to divide the Member States of the EU in four different groups for a better understanding of the digital situation right now within the Union and choose the most representative states for this investigation.

1. **Frontrunners (Group 1):**
   (a) Denmark, Netherlands, Czech Republic, Finland
2. **Strong performers (Group 2):**
   (a) Slovenia, Sweden, Portugal, Estonia, Belgium, Luxembourg, Croatia, Slovakia, Austria

3. **Moderate adopters (Group 3):**
   (a) Hungary, Romania, Bulgaria, Germany, Spain, Malta, Cyprus, France
4. **Modest digitalization (Group 4):**
   (a) Greece, Italy, Lithuania, Poland, Ireland, Latvia

The EIB Digitalization Index provides a nuanced understanding of the digitalization landscape within the European Union. As Denmark, the Netherlands, the Czech Republic, and Finland emerge as frontrunners, it becomes clear that digitalization efforts vary significantly across EU Member States. The index not only underscores the need for targeted interventions in specific sectors but also sheds light on the areas where the EU lags behind the USA. Moving forward, this valuable tool can guide policymakers and businesses alike in crafting strategies to accelerate digital transformation and enhance Europe's competitiveness in the global digital economy (Savvas et al., 2007).

Regarding the international arena, Europe is one of the most digital societies of the planet, but it faces external threats from the implementation of different models. Two prominent players in this digital transformation are China and the USA, each carving out distinct paths influenced by their unique socio-economic and political landscapes. China stands at the forefront of global technological prowess, with rapid advancements in artificial intelligence, 5G technology, and e-commerce. Tech giants like Alibaba, Tencent, and Huawei have played pivotal roles in driving innovation and establishing a robust technological foundation. In contrast, Europe, while possessing advanced infrastructure, faces challenges in keeping pace with the speed of innovation set out by China and the USA. Nevertheless, Europe excels in specific domains such as sustainable technologies and electric vehicles. Digitalization has been a cornerstone of China's economic growth, with a thriving digital economy encompassing e-commerce, digital payments, and technology-driven services. The Chinese government actively supports digital initiatives as part of its economic development strategy (Nielsen, 2016). In Europe, the economic impact is substantial, witnessed in the growth of fintech, e-commerce, and Industry 4.0. European countries also lead in developing and implementing stringent data protection regulations, exemplified by the General Data Protection Regulation (GDPR). China's approach to e-governance involves extensive surveillance systems and digital citizen services. Cities like Shenzhen and Hangzhou exemplify China's commitment to the smart city movement, integrating technologies for urban planning, transportation, and public services. Meanwhile, Europe, especially in Scandinavia, pioneers e-governance and smart city initiatives, prioritizing sustainability, efficiency, and citizen engagement. European cities often emphasize data privacy and security in their digitalization efforts. Digitalization has profoundly reshaped Chinese society, altering communication patterns, entertainment consumption, and social interactions. Platforms like WeChat are integral to daily life. In Europe, the social impact is marked by concerns about privacy, data protection, and responsible AI. European societies exhibit caution in adopting certain technologies, emphasizing the need for ethical considerations in the digital landscape (Troitiño, 2021).

Therefore, there are two separate visions about the future, if not opponents, that could crash against each other in a hypothetical quest for supremacy or more efficient society. China and Europe take divergent approaches to regulation and data privacy. China focuses on data localization and control, resulting in the development of a distinct digital ecosystem. In contrast, Europe adopts a more assertive stance on data protection, exemplified by GDPR. European regulations empower individuals with control over their data and promote transparency in data practices, influencing global discussions on data privacy standards. The digitalization landscape in China and Europe reflects the convergence and divergence of approaches shaped by their unique contexts. China's rapid technological strides and economic focus contrast with Europe's emphasis on a balanced approach, considering ethical, social, and regulatory dimensions.

In relation with the main partner of Europe—the United States—the country stands as a global technology leader, driving advancements in artificial intelligence, 5G technology, and e-commerce. Tech giants like Apple, Google, and Amazon have played main role in pushing the boundaries of innovation and establishing a robust technological foundation. In contrast, Europe, while possessing advanced infrastructure, faces challenges in keeping pace with the rapid innovation seen in the United States. Digitalization has been a cornerstone of economic growth in the United States, with a thriving digital economy encompassing e-commerce, digital payments, and technology-driven services. Silicon Valley epitomizes the innovation hub that propels economic development. In Europe, the economic impact is substantial, witnessed in the growth of fintech, e-commerce, and Industry 4.0. The US approach to e-governance involves leveraging digital technologies for efficient government services. While not as centralized as some other countries, various cities in the USA, such as New York and San Francisco, are at the forefront of smart city initiatives, integrating technologies for urban planning, transportation, and public services. Digitalization has profoundly reshaped American society, altering communication patterns, entertainment consumption, and social interactions. Platforms like Facebook, Twitter, and Instagram are integral to daily life. In Europe, the social impact is marked by concerns about privacy, data protection, and responsible AI. European societies exhibit caution in adopting certain technologies, emphasizing the need for ethical considerations in the digital landscape (Lupu & Lazăr, 2015).

The USA and Europe take distinct approaches to regulation and data privacy. The USA generally adopts a more business-friendly approach, with a focus on fostering innovation. In contrast, Europe, particularly through GDPR, takes a more assertive stance on data protection, empowering individuals with control over their data and promoting transparency in data practices.

The digitalization landscape in the USA and Europe reflects the convergence and divergence of approaches shaped by their unique contexts. The USA's rapid technological strides and business-focused approach contrast with Europe's emphasis on a balanced approach, considering ethical, social, and regulatory dimensions. Consequently, if Europe wants to keep its social traditions, it needs to develop its own technological approach. The USA is not going to develop digital tools for social innovation in order to increase the equality in the society, because its society is not equal and does not want to be equal. The similarities in political structure, democracy, economy, and capitalism lead to a convergence, but social aspects, especially regarding welfare state policies, are a main difference, as well as protection of consumers against business whirlwind (Rek, 2010). Therefore, Europe needs to develop its own digital environment to follow its own way in the highly interconnected digital world. Obviously, individual countries of Europe cannot develop a sustainable independent digital environment because of the lack of resources to compete with giants such as China and the USA, but the union of the different particular digital strategies in a common frame, the European Union, provides the right platform to implement a European model of digital interaction.

German Strategy on Digital Transformation

Germany had been actively working on various strategies to promote digitalization and innovation. The country has launched its "Digital Agenda 2025" to guide the country's digital transformation focusing on areas such as digital infrastructure, digital innovation, and digital skills in an effort to prepare its citizens to the digital challenges and educate the workforce to the new digital market. It is important to remind the importance of Germany in economic terms inside of the European Union. Germany has the largest economy in the EU and the fourth largest in the world. Its economic strength is driven by a diverse range of industries, including manufacturing, automotive, technology, and finance. It is known for its robust export-oriented economy, and it consistently ranks among the top global exporters, and its exports play a vital role in the EU's overall trade. German goods and services enjoy high demand on a global scale. The country has a well-developed and technologically advanced industrial base being a leader in manufacturing, particularly in sectors such as automotive, machinery, chemicals, and engineering. This industrial prowess contributes significantly to the EU's overall economic output. Regarding innovation and research, it places a strong emphasis on new developments and is home to numerous world-class research institutions and companies, fostering technological advancements that benefit not only Germany but also the EU as a whole (Andraško et al., 2021). In addition, Germany is often considered a pillar of financial stability within the EU. Its strong fiscal policies and disciplined approach to economic management have helped to maintain stability within the Eurozone. Germany consistently maintains a trade surplus, exporting more goods and services than it imports, always looking for new trade possibilities and the adaptation of the existing models to the new digital frames. Consequently, the country has been a pioneer in the concept of Industry 4.0, which refers to the Fourth Industrial Revolution characterized by the integration of digital technologies into manufacturing processes. The German national government has been supporting initiatives to enhance the competitiveness of German industries through the adoption of advanced technologies like IoT (Internet of Things), artificial intelligence, and robotics.

As the driving force of the German economy, the digital priorities of Germany are mainly focusing on the creation of business fostering a culture of innovation and supporting start-ups in the digital sector. There are various funding programmes, incentives, and support structures in place to encourage research, development, and entrepreneurship in the digital space, but the results are modest comparing to other parts of the world, or other countries of Europe such as Estonia. Nevertheless, Germany invests to ensure that the workforce is equipped with the necessary digital skills, developing digital education and skills development programs. This includes initiatives in schools, universities, and vocational training (especially the last one has a huge impact as a model for the rest of the European states).

Therefore, German traditional strength in the field of economy is still a reality and the benefits of a common economic area without restrictions to the German products all over the European Union territory are a priority. Consequently, Germany has been actively engaged in the development and promotion of the Digital Single Market (DSM) within the European Union. The DSM is a strategy that aims to create a seamless and open digital environment across the EU Member States, breaking down barriers to online access, e-commerce, and digital innovation. Germany has a strong presence in e-commerce and the digital economy. German companies, particularly those in the retail and tech sectors, are active participants in cross-border online trade. Therefore, DSM facilitates a more integrated digital marketplace, allowing German businesses to expand their reach and consumers to access a wider range of goods and services. It participates in various EU-wide digital initiatives and projects aimed at harmonizing rules and standards in areas such as e-commerce, cybersecurity, and digital skills development. These collaborative efforts enhance the effectiveness of the DSM and ensure a level playing field for businesses across the EU, based on the idea that German digital companies will succeed and increase their economic muscle in free competition, providing the required scale to compete also internationally. In summary, Germany plays a significant role in advancing the Digital Single Market within the European Union by contributing to infrastructure development, supporting innovation, shaping regulatory frameworks, and actively participating in collaborative initiatives that aim to create a more integrated and dynamic digital space across the EU Member States.

French Digitalization Process

The French strategy on digital development does not differ very much from the German priorities on data protection, cybersecurity, infrastructure, education, start-ups, industry, or digital divide, creating a synergy between the two main partners of the European Union. The interconnection of both economies allows a coherent approach to the digitalization process and the implementation of a common approach in the European Union. Nevertheless, while France also prioritizes Industry 4.0, its digital strategy extends beyond manufacturing to encompass a broader range of sectors, including services, digital arts, and cultural industries. France has been actively nurturing its start-up ecosystem, particularly in the technology sector. Paris, in particular, has become a hub for start-ups and innovation. Initiatives like "La French Tech" aim to support and promote French start-ups both domestically and internationally from a nationalistic perspective far from the German global approach. Even though, there is a competition between Berlin and Paris for becoming the tech hub of Europe. Regarding education, France places a strong emphasis on digital education, integrating digital literacy into school curricula and promoting skills development for the workforce. The goal is to ensure that citizens are well-prepared for the challenges of the digital age. Germany's approach is focused on preparing the workforce for digitalization.

In addition, France counts with France's National Digital Council (Conseil National du Numérique—CNNum). It was created in 2011 as an independent advisory council to provide insights and recommendations to the French government on matters related to digital technology. Its mandate encompasses a broad spectrum, ranging from digital innovation and the digital economy to the societal implications of technological advancements. One of the primary roles of the CNNum is to advise the government on digital innovation strategies. By engaging with stakeholders from various sectors, including industry, academia, and civil society, the CNNum offers recommendations to foster innovation and support initiatives that drive technological progress. Through its reports and consultations, the council contributes valuable insights that shape policies promoting a dynamic and innovative digital landscape. It actively contributes to discussions on digital education and skills development (Dutt & Nyman-Metcalf, 2021). The council's recommendations help informing policies that integrate digital literacy into educational curricula, ensuring that individuals acquire the skills necessary to navigate and thrive in an increasingly digitalized world. Beyond economic and educational considerations, the CNNum plays a crucial role in assessing the societal impact of technology. As digital transformation accelerates, the council addresses questions related to privacy, data protection, and the ethical use of emerging technologies. By offering guidance on these critical issues, the CNNum helps strike a balance between technological innovation and the protection of individual rights and societal values, going beyond economic matters and creating a guideline for the whole European Union. In an interconnected global landscape, the CNNum plays a role not only on the national stage but also in international collaborations. By participating in dialogues with other countries and contributing to European Union initiatives, the council helps positioning France as an active and collaborative player in the global digital ecosystem. Therefore, the traditional roles of both countries with leadership in different areas still persist in the digital environment.

Netherlands' Outstanding Performance on Digital Development

Despite its impressive ranking on digital development, the digital strategy of the Netherlands does not differ much from its European partners. Briefly, the main differences are related to the population and their digital skills. The Netherlands often ranks high in terms of digital literacy and technology adoption, increasing how quickly and extensively digital technologies are embraced compared to some other European countries. Digital education is included in the national school system, as in other countries of Europe, but its results are better. Therefore, two aspects should be analysed, the working system of the digital education and the motivation for citizens to embrace new technologies. Regarding the maturity of its e-government services, the efficiency and accessibility of digital public services are higher than other European states. There are different factors influencing such a high development, first the size of the country, relatively small in the European context, facilitating the implementation of new digital policies, as in the case of Estonia. On the other hand, in economic terms the Netherlands is a giant, with a highly globalized economic system that necessitates digitalization for more efficient connections with other parts of the globe (Mulder, 2021). The start-up and innovation ecosystem in the Netherlands, particularly in cities like Amsterdam, differs from those in other European countries and focuses on interconnection.

The Netherlands plays a pivotal role in shaping digital policies and contributing to the development of the digital landscape within the EU actively participating in EU policymaking processes, contributing to discussions and decisions related to digital policies. This includes areas such as data protection, cybersecurity, digital innovation, and the regulation of emerging technologies. The Netherlands, known for its innovation-friendly environment, advocates for policies that promote digital innovation, research and development, and the growth of the digital economy within the EU. A priority for the Netherlands within the European Union is the promotion of the Digital Single Market. The Dutch perspective on issues such as e-commerce, copyright, and digital services influences the direction of these initiatives due to their expertise and its influence on European and international trade (Ramiro Troitiño, 2023b). However, the stability of the Dutch government in recent years faced disruption with the 2023 elections, potentially altering the country's priorities regarding digitalization and European integration. Nonetheless, the promotion of the Digital Single Market remains a paramount concern for the Dutch economy and is expected to persist as a leading force, regardless of political changes.

Estonia, e-Governance, and Digital Outburst

Estonia, a small Baltic state, initially gained independence after World War I but was occupied by the USSR in the aftermath, subsequently becoming a part of the Soviet Union. It successfully regained its independence in 1991. Confronted with the challenges of establishing a modern state from scratch, Estonia chose a path of innovation rather than implementing a more traditional system. The Estonian government's decision was bold, focusing on the future rather than seeking immediate solutions to address the aftermath of the complete dismantling of the Soviet governmental framework. Therefore, with the lack of traditional obstacles due to the invalidity of the Soviet system, coupled with the small size of the country and population, its northeast European location, and the visionary approach of its political leaders, Estonia emerged as a digital leader in Europe. At the core of Estonia's digital success stands the introduction of the national digital identity card. This secure digital ID enables Estonian and EU resident citizens to access a wide array of public and private services online. Furthermore, Estonia extended its digital services globally through the concept of e-residency, allowing individuals worldwide to establish and manage businesses within its digital framework. This initiative might significantly impact the European Union as a whole, because once legally resident in Estonia, as an individual or as a company, the right to access the European benefits is granted. Nevertheless, the Estonian authorities are being restrict on this issue, doble checking applications to avoid fraud, money laundering, or any other suspicious activity. Estonia's X-Road platform serves as the backbone of its e-governance infrastructure. This decentralized data exchange system facilitates secure communication between various government databases, ensuring seamless and efficient delivery of services to citizens (Cancela Outeda, 2010). Consequently, residents can conduct a range of government transactions online, from filing taxes to voting in elections. The user-friendly e-government portal, known as eesti.ee, consolidates services, making them easily accessible to citizens. Regarding digital health, the state records system is another testament to its commitment to technological advancement. Patients have control over their health data, promoting transparency and personalized healthcare solutions. Estonia's commitment to cybersecurity is rooted in its experience with a cyber-attack in 2007 which was led by Russia. The relocation of a statute of a soldier from the Red Army (a symbol of oppression for the Estonians and a symbol of liberty for Russians) triggered a campaign against the country in Russia, including a massive cyber-attack that has nearly collapsed the country for a couple of days. This event prompted significant investments in cybersecurity measures, making the State a global leader in cyber defence, a priority for the European Union.

Estonia's digital outburst has had profound implications for its society as citizens enjoy the benefits of streamlined and efficient public services, saving time and resources. It is an example for those members of the European Union with a more traditional bureaucracy and civil servant system, as France. The country has become a European leader in terms of e-governance with respect and influence within the Union in terms of digital development. Nevertheless, while Estonia's digital journey has been transformative, challenges persist. Cybersecurity threats, the need for continuous innovation, and ensuring inclusivity are ongoing concerns. Looking ahead, Estonia remains committed to maintaining its digital edge and adapting to evolving technological landscapes. In some fields like cybersecurity, the collaboration with NATO provides Estonia with more digital muscle, but also brings the country closer to the USA and the cooperation scheme, reasserting the duality of integration within the Union, but cooperation in defence. It can generate problems inside the EU as the organization really needs its own independent cybersecurity system, as it is promoted by the European Union Agency for Cybersecurity (ENISA) in order to protect its own digital facilities, such as the Single Digital Market (Mulder, 2021). In parallel, artificial intelligence is becoming a key feature in digital development demanding a substantial volume of data to fuel its algorithms. Estonia, with a population of just 1.3 million, faces challenges in generating a significant amount of data. Therefore, the sustainability of its digital development hinges on fostering integration within the European Union and gaining access to European data (Troitiño, 2008).

Estonia's digital outburst stands as a testament to the transformative power of technology when embraced with vision and determination. As a pioneer in e-governance, Estonia has not only elevated the living standards of its citizens but has also set a global example for other nations to follow. Its journey underscores the immense potential for positive change that arises when a nation leverages digital innovation for the benefit of its people. On the European level, Estonia serves as an example of digital transformation; however, its influence in the Council, the primary EU institution determining Member States' influence, is inherently limited by its size. While Estonia may not dictate the digital development of the European Union, it can wield positive influence through leading by example and contributing its expertise.

Latvia, an Example of Modest Digital Implementation

In the realm of digital innovation in the Baltic region, Estonia often takes the spotlight for its pioneering e-governance initiatives and robust digital infrastructure. Meanwhile, its neighbour Latvia has chosen a more measured approach to digitalization. Historically, both countries have been united in Livonia, with Riga as the most vibrant city of the Baltic region and Tallinn as a provincial spot. The industrialization focused on Latvia, leaving Estonia as a more agricultural part of the Baltic region in the context of the Russian Empire. Both countries became independent after WWI, occupied by the Soviet Union, and have regained the independence after the collapse of the communist regime, even collaborating peacefully with the Baltic Chain. However, the post-independence trajectories in their digital strategies diverged. Estonia embraced a bold and visionary approach early on, while Latvia, perhaps influenced by its historical, cultural, and economic context, adopted a more cautious stance. One significant factor influencing Latvia's digital landscape is its economic situation. Estonia's economy, although modest in the European context, has been more resilient and competitive. Estonia's GDP per capita has consistently been higher than Latvia's, providing Estonia with more resources to invest in digital infrastructure and initiatives. Latvia's economic challenges may have constrained its ability to allocate extensive resources to digital endeavours. Estonia's leadership demonstrated early recognition of the transformative power of technology, fostering a visionary environment for digital innovation. The commitment of Estonian leadership to digitalization, spearheaded by initiatives like the e-residency programme, set the state on an ambitious trajectory. In contrast, Latvia's leadership may have prioritized other aspects of national development, leading to a more gradual and measured approach to digital initiatives. Cultural and social factors play a role in shaping a country's approach to technology. Estonia's smaller population, characterized by a high level of digital literacy and trust in institutions, contributed to the successful adoption of digital services. In Latvia, where cultural and social dynamics differ, variations exist in the acceptance and integration of digital solutions into daily life (Hamulák, 2018). Estonia's early commitment to digitalization was accompanied by strategic investments in digital infrastructure, cybersecurity, and e-governance. Latvia, facing economic challenges and potentially different prioritization of resources, was not able to allocate comparable funds to accelerate its digital transformation.

The analysis of digital development in Estonia and Latvia provides us with an example on the impact of digital development on society. Riga, once the economic centre of the region, lags far behind Tallinn in terms of the digital economy. The initial position of Latvia was more beneficial than Estonia, with higher population, higher GDP, more connections, and more trade, but lacked the political vision of its leaders. Therefore, considering Latvia's 27th position in digital development within the European Union, as reported by the European Investment Bank in 2020, and Estonia's 9th position, excelling in certain digital aspects, it becomes evident that political vision plays a crucial role in the digitalization of the European Union. Latvia is enormously improving its digital implementation and in the world context it could be considered a digitally developed country. Nevertheless, its capacity to influence the digital development of the Union is very reduced, but it will benefit significantly from the common digital management within the EU for its internal digital development.

Conclusions

The Member States of the European Union have similar priorities in many digital fields, such as infrastructure, cybersecurity, Digital Single Market, digital education, or digital equal opportunities. It will make easier the integration, or at least the establishment of common standards in these fields. Nevertheless, the diverse environment of the Member States and their different digital development can generate tensions within the Union. The more advanced countries that necessitate additional communitarian steps are generally smaller states, possessing less capacity to influence the Union with the exception of the Netherlands. But this country had elections on 2023 and the populism, strongly reluctant of further integration in Europe, has become a leading force. Therefore, the country at the forefront of the digital integration process is, at the very least, vulnerable to the dynamics of its domestic political situation. Germany's keen interest in the Digital Single Market is likely to shape the upcoming initiatives in digitalization within the European Union, given its status as one of the most influential Member States. France will pursue some compensation; even its economy will benefit enormously from the DSM. Indeed, following the comparation of Estonia and Latvia, the European Union requires political vision, audacity, to successfully implement a digital revolution, but the role of the Council leading this transformation is doubtful because of the lack of clear leadership in digital aspects and the growing nationalism all over Europe. Hence, a traditional impediment—nationalism and populism—poses a challenge to the Council and the leadership of Member States in steering innovative societal development, particularly in digitalization. This challenge arises from the necessity for the transfer of sovereignty and the establishment of new institutions and powers within the Union. Nevertheless, the external influence of China and the USA, and the pressure to maintain some of the elements of the European way of life, is likely to compel Member States to collaborate in achieving the necessary social and economic changes.

References

Andraško, J., Hamuľák, O., & Mesarčík, M. (2021). The digital development of the European Union: data governance aspects of cooperative, connected and automated mobility. *IDP: Revista de Internet, Derecho y Politica, 34*, 1–15.

Ayata, Z., & Önay, I. (2021). *Global perspectives on legal challenges posed by ridesharing companies* (p. 281). Springer.

Cancela Outeda, C. (2010). La eurorregión Galicia-Norte de Portugal: un escenario de cooperación territorial. *Razón y Palabra, 15*(74).

Dutt, P. K., & Nyman-Metcalf, K. (2021). The legal implications of public support policies targeting research, development and innovation in the European Union. *TalTech Journal of European Studies, 11*(2), 102–129.

Hamulák, O. (2018). La carta de los derechos fundamentales de la union europea y los derechos sociales. *Estudios constitucionales, 16*(1), 167–186.

Ježová, D. (2017). Fundamental rights in the European Union—Perspective of the digital era. In *Human rights in EU external relations: Between law and politics* (pp. 79–86). Vydavateľstvo UK, Univerzita Komenského.

Lupu, D., & Lazăr, C. G. (2015). Influence of e-government on the level of corruption in some EU and non-EU states. *Procedia Economics and Finance, 20*, 365–371.

Millard, J. (2017). European strategies for e-governance to 2020 and beyond. In A. Ojo & J. Millard (Eds.), *Government 3.0—Next generation government technology infrastructure and services: Roadmaps, enabling technologies & challenges* (pp. 1–25). Springer.

Mooij, A. A. (2021). European Central Bank digital currency: The digital euro. What design of the digital euro is possible within the European Central Bank's legal framework?

Mulder, E. J. (2021). Living apart together? Discussing the different digital worlds in city government. In E. Estevez, T. A. Pardo, & H. J. Scholl (Eds.), *Smart cities and smart governance: Towards the 22nd century sustainable city* (pp. 289–302). Springer.

Nielsen, M. M. (2016). E-governance and stage models: analysis of identified models and selected Eurasian experiences in digitising citizen service delivery. *Electronic Government, an International Journal, 12*(2), 107–141.

Paskaleva-Shapira, K. (2006, May). Transitioning from e-Government to e-Governance in the knowledge society: the role of the legal framework for enabling the process in the European Union's countries. In *Proceedings of the 2006 international conference on digital government research* (pp. 181–190).

Potnis, D. D. (2010). Measuring e-Governance as an innovation in the public sector. *Government Information Quarterly, 27*(1), 41–48.

Ramiro Troitiño, D. (2023a). Mapping E-governance in the EU. In D. Ramiro Troitiño, T. Kerikmäe, & O. Hamuľák (Eds.), *Digital development of the European Union: An interdisciplinary perspective* (pp. 303–317). Springer.

Ramiro Troitiño, D. (2023b). Priorities and challenges: The digital transition in the European integration. In D. Ramiro Troitiño, T. Kerikmäe, & O. Hamuľák (Eds.), *Digital development of the European Union: An interdisciplinary perspective* (pp. 7–19). Springer.

Rashica, V. (2019). Digital diplomacy: aspects, approaches and practical use. *European Perspectives, 23.*

Rek, M. (2010). Europeanization of civil society sector in Central and Eastern Europe. *Innovative Issues and Approaches in Social Sciences, 3*(1), 160–186.

Rose, R. (2005). A global diffusion model of e-governance. *Journal of Public Policy, 25*(1), 5–27.

Savvas, I., Pimenidis, E., & Sideridis, A. (2007). A review of e-governance models in the EU. In *Proceedings of advances in computing and technology* (pp. 110–119).

Troitiño, D. R. (2008). Estonia y la Unión Europea. *RUE. Revista universitaria europea, 9*, 31–46.

Troitiño, D. R. (2021). La "Década Digital" de la Unión Europea: desarrollos e impactos sobre su ciudadanía y economía. *IDP: Revista de Internet, Derecho y Política, 34*, 1–14.

e-Identity: A Step Forward to European Digital Citizenship

David Ramiro Troitiño and Viktoria Mazur

Abstract The development of e-governance in the European Union opens new possibilities of change in so many aspects of the internal organization of the Union. This research focuses on the innovations and fields to explore in concordance with a common approach to e-governance in the European Union regarding ID card, Mobile IDs, e-Residency card, and Smart IDs. These elements will create a deeper concept of common identity among European citizens and a stronger link between the citizens and the organization of Europe. These tools together will contribute to dissemination and implementation of the concept of common e-identity among the European Union citizens, as their current status will be upgraded with the inclusions of these technological novelties on their common rights.

Introduction

Current innovations in the digital world open a new battery of opportunities for Member States to reshape their relations with its citizens. This transformative landscape extends its influence to the European Union (EU), a supranational organization characterized by profound integration and a substantial population of individuals holding EU citizenship. Unlike conventional nation-states, the European Union comprises distinct sovereign entities united by a shared citizenship, transcending the traditional emphasis on nationality. In essence, the EU represents a unique blend of diverse nations coalescing into a collective identity defined by citizenship rather than allegiance to a specific national entity. However, it is crucial to recognize that the journey toward European integration commenced in an era dominated by traditional nation-states, where nationality served as a primary identifier of Europeans and a fundamental conduit for loyalty to individual states.

D. Ramiro Troitiño (✉) · V. Mazur
Jean Monnet Chair on Digital Development of the EU, Tallinn University of Technology, Tallinn, Estonia
e-mail: david.troitino@taltech.ee; viktoria.mazur@taltech.ee

D. Ramiro Troitiño (ed.), *E-Governance in the European Union*, Contributions to Political Science, https://doi.org/10.1007/978-3-031-56045-3_5

Nationality typically refers to a person's membership or affiliation with a particular nation. It can be based on various factors, including birthplace, descent, or even the legal criteria established by a country. It is linked to an individual's cultural, ethnical, and social identity. It may not necessarily confer either legal rights or obligation, such as the right to reside in a specific country or to participate in its political life. Nevertheless, there is a widely accepted identification between nationality and citizenship when there is a national state, one nation, one state. The "nation-state" is a political entity in which the state (i.e., a defined territory with a government, a common political structure) and the nation (i.e., a group of people who share a common culture, history, language, and often, a sense of identity) largely coincide. In other words, a nation-state is a sovereign state whose citizens or residents predominantly belong to a common nation and share a common cultural and historical background. Consequently, the national state in theory includes several characteristics such as:

- Common identity: A shared national identity, which is often based on shared culture, language, history, and values. This common identity contributes to a sense of unity and cohesion within the state (i.e., nationality).
- Sovereignty: Nation-states are independent and sovereign entities with defined borders, their own governments, and the authority to make decisions within their territory without external interference (i.e., politics).
- The citizens of a nation-state: Typically belong to the same nation, and their citizenship is linked with the state. Citizenship carries with it legal rights and responsibilities, and it often reflects one's affiliation with the nation-state that has formal political structure, such as governments, legal systems, and institutions, to manage their internal and external affairs.

On the other hand, citizenship is a legal status granted by a state to an individual, typically through birthright or descent or sometimes through naturalization (i.e., a process by which a foreign national becomes a citizen). Citizenship comes with a set of legal rights and responsibilities, including the right to live and work in the country, the right to vote and participate in the country's political processes, and the obligation to obey its laws and pay taxes. It is a more specific and legally binding concept, and it is the basis for a person's legal relationship with a particular state, regardless of his nationality.

Therefore, nationality represents a cultural allegiance to a specific group, while citizenship denotes a political association with a particular state. Despite this, nations often seek to anchor their essence in the past, whether through an ethnic group, shared heroic narratives, common cultural approaches to society, or other subjective considerations lacking factual support. Nations are inherently emotional constructs, built on sentiments and feelings, serving as potent vehicles for common identification and solidarity. This emotional connection fosters a robust loyalty to the governing body, the national state. The rise of national states finds its roots in the French Revolution, even though there are previous examples as the creation of Spain, in 1479 by marriage, 1492 by conquest, and 1512 by annexation. Despite earlier instances, the main issue related to loyalty to the state remained the loyalty to the king until the French Revolution changed the previous paradigm. The instauration of the French Republic and the execution of the deposed King required a new way to reassure the loyalty of the members of the Republic, and nation was the instrument chosen by the revolutionaries, because it creates a strong link between the nationals and the state based on feelings and emotions. This connection is inherently irrational, fostering an unwavering loyalty to the nation, often transcending personal sacrifice, even to the point of laying down one's life, driven by a fervent sense of patriotism.

Nevertheless, the national states are never a perfect match within its borders in terms of nationality and citizenship. This dysfunctionality leads to internal confrontations between different national groups sharing a common state and the domination of one cultural group, nation, over the rest of the groups included in the territory of the national state. It generally means that assimilation of different cultural groups eliminates differences and increases the cohesion and loyalty to the state. In addition, the formation of national states all over Europe has meant the end of multinational states and numerous wars between nations to secure a territory for themselves, eliminating competitors. The internal conflicts rooted in nationality remain a significant source of global disputes, attributable in part to the exportation of the European model of the national state worldwide. Even within Europe, instances of national conflicts persist, exemplified by the Balkan Wars in the twentieth century and the war in Ukraine in the twenty-first century, both characterized by national confrontations and struggles for control over the state by distinct cultural groups. Nevertheless, these confrontations between national states reached its peak with the Second World War, a war between nations that had full access to the economy, army, and political instruments of the states to fight for supremacy and enlarge their national scope in terms of territory and population.

The integration and evolution toward the current European Union is a direct outcome of the historical national conflicts scattered across Europe. The architects of the integration process attempted to separate cultural aspects from the political sphere, nationality from citizenship. The logic behind this movement was not an attack on the national identity but was based on the idea that nations without access/domination to economy and politics cannot attack each other violently. The fathers of Europe, such as Jean Omer Marie Gabriel Monnet or Altiero Spinelli, envisioned a new societal paradigm where nationality would no longer be the prevailing framework or conduit for the loyalty of society's members to the state. Instead, they advocated for a shared citizenship as the unifying force. The construction of a joint Europe with many nationalities and one single citizenship, different cultural entities and one common sovereignty, and a sole management for common issues all over the members of the organization was the long-term target.

Consequently, the integration of the EU was not founded on the creation of a European nation, a shared cultural identity achieved through harmonizing cultural aspects among existing nations, as was previously done with the different existing cultural groups integrated in a common nation by the national state eliminating differences. The European Union, in contrast, does not seek to erase existing nations.

Instead, its objective is to create a division between emotions/feelings and politics, a separation between the notions of nation and citizenship.

The humble genesis of the European integration, with the European Coal and Steel Community in the 1950s already included a roadmap for the creation of a common sovereignty (common citizenship) from basic steps, to gradually be enlarged aiming for full integration in a long process of evolution based mainly on neofunctionalism, intergovernmentalism, and federalist premises. It is a transformative process, shifting the people's emotional loyalty from the individual state to a more reasoned allegiance to the Union. Evidently, the integration of Europe depends on the development of the concept of common citizenship, European Union citizenship, combined with a voluntary transfer of loyalty of the Europeans from the national level to the European level. Indeed, it is a complex process with countless obstacles facing irrationality (i.e., feelings) with a common evolution in a political frame including all the Europeans regardless of their common cultural identity. A powerful citizenship is required to consolidate the integration in Europe and foster deeper integration, and digital citizenship can play a crucial role in this process because it eliminates previous limitations, as distance or physical location. It offers a flexible approach to cultivate a shared political and social identity among Europeans, distinct from a cultural identity.

The Member States of the European Union deviate from the conventional model of purely national states. Traditionally, these states are multinational entities where one nation holds supremacy over others (Rek, 2010). This diversity is evident from the northern reaches, where Finland incorporates the Sami national group within a predominantly Finnish and Swedish population, to the southern expanse of Spain, encompassing various nationalities within its own borders. The diversity extends eastward, exemplified by countries like Romania with a significant Hungarian minority and Ukrainians, and to the west with the UK entailing England, Wales, Scotland, and Northern Ireland in a common British identity. Europe is a diverse area with numerous nations and limited states. The historical diversity of European nations has been further enriched by contemporary emigration trends, facilitated by the increased mobility of populations since the establishment of the free movement of people within the Union. This diversity has been triggered in the last few years specially by the migration from outside of Europe from different parts of the planet. Those migrants belong to highly differentiated cultural groups, diverse nations, making difficult their integration in a national state and reducing the internal cohesion of the European states based on national identity, based on common cultural aspects. Consequently, it is changing the internal composition of States, generating tensions in their internal cohesion. Therefore, the growing importance of migration in Europe reduces the traditional role of national states as instruments for the management of public common affairs and generates rigidities within the states.

Nations in Europe, viewed as a political framework for organizing collective affairs, have faced challenges as their historical quests for supremacy resulted in devastating conflicts that reverberated globally through several wars. Though, it negatively influences politics, as the conflict in Ukraine has shown, and the internal composition has been changed due to demographic issues and migrations.

Citizenship, the way chosen by implementing a common management in Europe regardless of nationality, solves these problems, but alternatively reduces the identification of the people with the political institutions due to lack of feelings or emotions in the new boundaries. Digital identity can partially solve some of the issues related to the creation of a common citizenship in Europe, a common political identity increasing the loyalty of the citizens, but cannot address completely the issue of emotions or irrational loyalty to the political structure.

Digital Identity

Digital identity refers to the online representation of an individual, organization, or entity in the digital realm. It comprises digital information and associated attributes, incorporating personal, professional, or organizational data. Employed for diverse purposes, digital identities play roles in authentication, authorization, access control, and facilitating online interactions. In general, digital identities are formed by the following elements:

1. Identity information: A digital identity typically includes personal information, such as a person's name, email address, phone number, username, or any other data that uniquely identifies them in the digital space.
2. Authentication: Digital identities are used for authentication processes, where individuals prove their identity to gain access to digital accounts, systems, or services. Common methods of authentication include passwords, biometrics (i.e., fingerprint or facial recognition), two-factor authentication (2FA), and more.
3. Authorization: After authentication, digital identities are used to determine what actions or resources an individual or entity is authorized to access or perform within a digital system or platform. Authorization defines permissions and access levels.
4. Privacy and consent: Managing digital identities also involves considerations of privacy and consent. Individuals should have control over what personal information they share and who they share it with. Concepts like "self-sovereign identity" promote user-centric control over the personal data.
5. Single sign-on (SSO): SSO systems allow individuals to use a single set of digital identity credentials (e.g., a username and password) to access multiple services or platforms. This system simplifies the login process and improves the user experience, by making it more customer friendly.
6. Digital footprint: As individuals interact with online services and platforms, their digital identity leaves a trail of data and activities, creating a digital footprint. This can include browsing history, social media posts, online purchases, and more.
7. Identity verification: Digital identities can also be used for identity verification processes, such as Know Your Customer (KYC) checks for financial services,

age verification for age-restricted content, or background checks for employment purposes.
8. Identity theft and security: Protecting digital identities from theft and unauthorized access is crucial. Cybersecurity measures, such as strong encryption, secure storage of user data, and regular password changes, are used to safeguard digital identities.
9. Digital identity ecosystem: The digital identity landscape includes various stakeholders, including individuals, businesses, government agencies, and technology providers. The concept of a trusted digital identity ecosystem aims to establish secure and interoperable systems for digital identity management.
10. Legal and regulatory considerations: Governments and regulatory bodies often establish rules and standards for digital identity management to protect individuals' rights and ensure data security.

Digital identity plays a significant role in the modern digital age, shaping the way individuals engage with online services, conduct business, and safeguard their personal information. Its influence extends to privacy, security, and the broader digital economy, transcending national boundaries.

Digital Identity and European Union

The importance of digital identity within the European Union is growing and facilitating a more direct connection between the Union and its citizens without the need for intermediation by the Member States. The EU has been actively working on various initiatives related to digital identity in order to enhance online trust, security, and convenience for its citizens, reinforcing its direct link with the citizens. The initiatives include a *European Digital Identity Framework* aiming to provide a secure and interoperable solution for digital identity across EU Member States. The framework is designed in a way as to allow EU citizens to access public and private services online with a single digital identity, reducing the need for multiple usernames and passwords. It is a basic step coordinating the Member States policies in this regard, rather than a proper integration creating a common system. It is based on the formation of common standards that will allow integration in the future, the establishment of a common frame facilitating future common implementation. Hence, establishing minimum common standards is crucial for building trust, minimizing barriers, guaranteeing safety and security, and facilitating cooperation across diverse domains. These standards play a vital role in maintaining consistency, compatibility, and interoperability.

Additionally, the EU has established the Electronic Identification, Authentication, and Trust Services (eIDAS) Regulation, which provides a legal framework for electronic identification and trust services for electronic transactions. eIDAS is designed to ensure that digital identities and electronic signatures are recognized and accepted across EU member states. With eIDAS, the EU has set a solid legal framework for secure one-click access to online services. This ensures increased security and convenience for various activities like tax declarations, university enrollment, remote banking, cross-border business setup, online payments, and bidding on tenders. The eIDAS regulation serves several purposes aimed at fostering trust, security, and interoperability in electronic transactions within the European Union. The key purposes of eIDAS are:

- Facilitating cross-border electronic transactions: eIDAS is designed to simplify and facilitate electronic transactions within the EU Member States. By providing a standardized framework for electronic identification and trust services, it reduces barriers to cross-border business and promotes the seamless provision of online services.
- Enhancing security: The regulation establishes a legal framework for electronic signatures, seals, time stamps, and other trust services. This framework ensures that these electronic methods are secure and reliable, fostering confidence in electronic transactions and communications.
- Promoting electronic identification (eID): eIDAS encourages the use of electronic identification by providing a legal basis for eIDs. Individuals can use their eIDs to access online services, and Member States are required to establish and maintain national eID schemes that comply with the Regulation.
- Legal equivalence of electronic documents: eIDAS establishes the legal equivalence of electronic documents with their paper counterparts. This recognition contributes to the wider acceptance and adoption of electronic documents in various legal contexts.
- Standardizing electronic signatures: The regulation defines three types of electronic signatures—simple, advanced, and qualified. This standardization provides clarity on the legal status and level of assurance associated with each type of signature, making it easier for businesses and individuals to use electronic signatures confidently.
- Regulating trust service providers: eIDAS sets out rules for trust service providers, including certification service providers issuing qualified certificates for electronic signatures and seals. These providers must adhere to specific security and operational requirements to ensure the reliability of their services.
- Promoting the Digital Single Market: By addressing legal and technical barriers to cross-border electronic transactions, eIDAS contributes to the development of the Digital Single Market within the EU. This market aims to create a unified online space where businesses and consumers can engage in digital activities seamlessly across Member States.

To sum up, eIDAS represents a thorough regulatory framework designed to establish a unified and secure landscape for electronic transactions within the EU. Its goal is to cultivate trust and facilitate the expansion of the digital economy. Remaining updated on policy changes, technological progress, and dialogues within the European Union and related international forums is crucial to comprehend the potential evolution of eIDAS and similar regulations in the future. Regulations in the digital identity domain are poised to adjust to the dynamic nature of technology and the evolving needs of societies and economies.

Another important initiative from the European Union aimed at enhancing the influence of the e-identity is the European Digital Identity Wallet. The European Commission is actively involved in developing measures that will empower EU citizens to securely store and manage their digital identity documents and credentials. This wallet is intended to be a user-centric solution, putting individuals in control of their personal data. Key features and aspects of the European Digital Identity Wallet include a Single Digital Identity, as the wallet is designed to allow individuals to manage and use their digital identity for various online services, such as accessing government services, banking, and other e-commerce platforms. Moreover, interoperability holds significant importance, given that one of the key objectives is to ensure seamless compatibility across EU Member States (Rashica, 2019). This means that the digital identity issued by one country should be recognized and accepted in other Member States, reducing the need for multiple identity credentials. This European initiative underscores a user-centric approach, prioritizing the empowerment of individuals to have control over their digital identity. Users/citizens are expected to have the ability to manage and share their identity information securely and with consent. Obviously, ensuring the security and privacy of personal data is a crucial aspect of the European Digital Identity Wallet. The aim is to implement robust security measures to protect user information and comply with data protection regulations. The European General Data Protection Regulation (GDPR) plays a significant role in ensuring that personal data is handled in accordance with strict privacy standards. It is a comprehensive and influential regulation that governs the processing of personal data within the European Union. It came into effect on May 25, 2018, and it applies not only to organizations based in the EU but also to those outside the EU that process the personal data of EU residents. The GDPR applies to the processing of personal data in the context of the activities of an establishment within the EU, regardless of whether the processing takes place in the EU or not. It also applies to organizations outside the EU that offer goods or services to, or monitor the behavior of, individuals in the EU. This not only strengthens the protection of EU citizens but also extends the influence of the European model in the international arena, as it is applicable to all companies situated outside the Union that handle data from Europeans. Therefore, it can lead, via soft power, to the implementation of similar measures all over the planet by free will of the companies who are trying to avoid duplicity in their working systems. However, it is not clear if soft power will work in such a sensitive field, as data is basic for the development of artificial intelligence (AI) and market initiatives, partitivities with such a relevance that provides data with a high value.

Nevertheless, the GDPR establishes several fundamental principles for the processing of personal data, including lawfulness, fairness, transparency, purpose limitation, data minimization, accuracy, storage limitation, integrity, and confidentiality. The regulation places a strong emphasis on obtaining valid consent for processing personal data. Data subjects (individuals to whom the data relates) have enhanced rights, including the right to access, rectification, erasure (right to be forgotten), data portability, and the right to object to processing. Moreover, the GDPR influences the internal composition of private companies operating in the European market, as certain organizations are required to appoint a Data Protection Officer who oversees GDPR compliance. This requirement is particularly important for organizations that process large amounts of sensitive data or engage in systematic monitoring of individuals on a large scale. In addition, organizations are required to notify the relevant supervisory authority of a personal data breach within 72 h of becoming aware of it, unless the breach is unlikely to result in a risk to the rights and freedoms of individuals.

As a result, GDPR promotes a proactive approach to data protection. Organizations are urged to implement measures that integrate privacy considerations throughout the entire data processing lifecycle. This includes data protection impact assessments (DPIAs) for high-risk processing activities. It also regulates the transfer of personal data outside the EU. Organizations must ensure that any international transfers are done in accordance with the regulation, which may involve the use of Standard Contractual Clauses or other mechanisms. The GDPR establishes a legal frame for defending its proper implementation, including significant fines for non-compliance, up to 20 million € or 4% of the annual global turnover of the preceding financial year, whichever is higher, for more serious violations (e.g., violations of the core principles of data processing, failure to obtain proper consent, inadequate security measures). It is important to note that these fines are the maximum limits, and the actual fines imposed are determined on a case-by-case basis. Factors such as the nature, gravity, and duration of the infringement, the categories of personal data involved, and the measures taken to mitigate the damage can influence the final amount. Penalties are imposed by the relevant supervisory authorities in each EU Member State. Organizations found in violation of GDPR may also face other corrective measures and consequences, such as warnings, reprimands, orders to comply, and temporary or definitive bans on data processing.

In accordance with the European Commission, the GDPR aims at providing individuals with greater control over their personal data while establishing a harmonized and robust framework for data protection across the EU. Its principles and requirements have influenced global discussions on data protection and privacy, and many countries have taken inspiration from the GDPR in developing or updating their own data protection laws. It is a basic instrument to form the European identity from a European model, differentiated from other giant international actors as the USA.

Nevertheless, punishment is not sufficient to guarantee a functional digital identity within the European Union, and the organization is working on encouraging the private sector to integrate digital identity solutions aligned with the broader goals of creating a Digital Single Market, fostering innovation, and improving user experiences while maintaining security and privacy (Hamulák, 2018). Therefore, the organization primary focuses on the involvement of the economic private actors involved in the Digital Single Market, because the digital identity is a basic step to create a common digital area where goods, services, and capital can flow seamlessly across borders. In addition, digital identity solutions can enhance the user experience in the private sector by streamlining processes, reducing the need for multiple credentials, and providing secure and convenient access to online services. This is particularly relevant in industries such as e-commerce, banking, and financial services. Encouraging private sector integration involves promoting interoperability and standardization of digital identity solutions. Common standards ensure that digital identities are recognized and accepted across different platforms and services, fostering a more cohesive and user-friendly digital environment.

Security transcends being solely a public concern; the heightened security of online transactions by Internet operators directly influences citizens' trust and, consequently, their active engagement in the digital economy. Through the implementation of robust authentication methods and encryption techniques, the private sector has the capacity to elevate the safeguarding of user data and foster trust with consumers. However, the integration of digital identity solutions by the private sector should be aligned with existing regulations, notably encompassing data protection laws like the GDPR. Ensuring compliance with these regulations, IT is essential to protect user privacy and maintain the legality of digital identity practices (Ježová, 2017). In essence, the integration of digital identity solutions in the private sector contributes to the broader digital transformation goals of the EU. It aligns with the principles of security, privacy, and user centricity, creating a more efficient and trustworthy digital ecosystem for both businesses and consumers. As a consequence, the EU is promoting the creation of European alternatives to the Internet giants coming from other parts of the world with legislation and public funding promoting the cooperation between different private sectors, social hubs, and public actors from a perspective based on common standards and interoperability frameworks for digital identity solutions to ensure that they work seamlessly across borders and sectors.

The European common digital frame requires cross-border recognition within the Member States to ensure that digital identities issued by one particular Member State are recognized and accepted in others. This aims at facilitating cross-border access to public and private services for EU citizens. Consequently, digital identity is a critical element of the EU's digital agenda, and the communitarian initiatives aim to simplify and secure online interactions for EU citizens while respecting their privacy rights. The goal is to create a unified and user-centric digital identity ecosystem that benefits both individuals and businesses across the European Union with a common digital ID card recognition by all the States and economic agents operating in the Digital Single Market.

Concurrently, mobile ID solutions have been integral to these endeavors. Nevertheless, the specific expectations and advancements can undergo evolution over time, emphasizing the importance of periodically updating goals and incorporating technological innovations. However, the overarching expectations and considerations concerning mobile ID within the European Union remain intertwined with interoperability. Once again, the primary objective is to interconnect all users within the European Union seamlessly. Additionally, the EU's vision for interoperable digital identity solutions reflects a commitment to enhancing cross-border accessibility, fostering a more connected and cohesive European digital landscape.

The emphasis on security and privacy underscores the Union's dedication to safeguarding individuals' data in an increasingly interconnected environment. The stringent security standards imposed on mobile ID systems not only protect personal information but also contribute to building trust among users, a vital aspect for widespread adoption. Compliance with the General Data Protection Regulation serves as a foundational element, ensuring that mobile ID solutions adhere to established privacy norms. In the pursuit of user-friendly experiences, mobile ID solutions are designed to be intuitive and convenient, empowering individuals to seamlessly engage in various online activities. This extends beyond public services, encompassing private organizations and economic agents operating within the Digital Single Market. Recognizing the diverse purposes for which mobile IDs can be employed, the EU is actively working on establishing a comprehensive legal framework. This collaborative effort involves close coordination with national authorities and legal systems, aiming to validate and foster broad acceptance of mobile IDs across the Union. The evolving nature of technology and the digital landscape necessitates ongoing efforts to adapt and refine these frameworks, ensuring they remain robust and effective in the face of emerging challenges and opportunities.

Smart ID represents a key facet of the European Union's digital citizenship initiatives, encompassing diverse forms of digital identity like smart cards, mobile IDs, and other secure digital credentials. The potential advantages are manifold, centering on efficiency and convenience. Smart IDs offer a streamlined and convenient approach to identity verification, surpassing traditional methods and facilitating seamless access to a spectrum of services, both online and offline. Notably, the adoption of Smart ID aligns with the EU's priority of increasing interoperability. This technological advancement enables citizens to utilize their digital identities effortlessly across Member States, enhancing accessibility for public services, financial transactions, and beyond. The emphasis on interoperability remains a cornerstone for the EU, promoting a more integrated and connected digital landscape. Beyond efficiency, Smart ID serves as a robust tool in the EU's efforts to combat fraud, thereby benefiting citizens (Gábriš & Hamuľák, 2021). The incorporation of advanced security features, including biometrics and cryptographic methods, elevates the security of identity verification, minimizing the risks associated with identity fraud. Furthermore, Smart ID introduces an element of user control. Citizens gain enhanced control over their personal data, enabling them to selectively share only necessary information for specific transactions. This empowerment contributes to a more privacy-conscious digital environment and underscores the EU's commitment to ensuring individuals have agency over their personal information in the digital realm.

However, the implementation of Smart IDs also introduces certain risks, echoing the ongoing emphasis on security in the digital development of the European Union. Despite the intended enhancement of security, the inherent susceptibility of any digital system to hacking and cyber threats poses potential dangers. Breaches could result in unauthorized access to sensitive personal information, raising concerns about data protection. Privacy considerations add another layer of complexity, particularly regarding the collection and utilization of biometric data in Smart IDs. Balancing the imperatives of security and privacy becomes paramount to gain public trust at the European level. Moreover, Smart IDs encounter technological challenges. Establishing and maintaining a secure and standardized Smart ID system across the EU may present technological hurdles, demanding a concerted effort to ensure uniformity and compatibility.

Successful implementation of Smart IDs holds the promise of facilitating seamless access to services across EU borders, fostering a more unified and interconnected European digital ecosystem. However, to actualize these benefits, the EU must institute a robust legal and regulatory framework governing Smart ID usage. This framework should address critical issues such as data protection, interoperability standards, and liability. Conversely, there is a potential risk that certain segments of the population may encounter difficulties in adopting or accessing Smart ID technologies, exacerbating existing digital divides. Lastly, the implementation of Smart IDs may carry economic implications, influencing sectors such as technology, security, and public services, requiring careful consideration and planning.

In the realm of e-identity, another pivotal aspect from the European perspective is the concept of e-Residency. Originating from Estonia, a European Union Member State, e-Residency represents a pioneering initiative that extends digital residency to individuals worldwide. Estonia's successful implementation of e-Residency has been examined and held up as a model for potential use across the European Union. However, it is important to note that not all aspects of Estonia's e-Residency model can be seamlessly transposed to the EU level. Estonia operates under a single legal and regulatory framework, whereas the EU encompasses diverse rules and regulations pertaining to digital identity, residency, and associated services. The engagement with authorities also differs; Estonia exhibits total synergy, while implementing e-Residency at the EU level requires collaboration with relevant government entities such as national digital agencies or ministries. Discussions on feasibility and legal requirements become imperative, emphasizing the need for a strong relationship between government entities for successful implementation. Yet, the security measures implemented in Estonia can serve as a valuable blueprint for the EU level. Robust security measures, ensuring the integrity and confidentiality of the e-Residency system, are pivotal. This involves the incorporation of secure authentication methods, encryption, and data protection practices. Leveraging the security measures developed in Estonia can contribute to establishing a secure and reliable e-Residency framework at the broader EU level.

Conclusions

The European Union grapples with the challenge of fostering a unified identity among its citizens. The inherent duality between the national and supranational levels creates weak connections between political subjects and the institutions tasked with managing shared sovereignty. It becomes imperative to strengthen the identification between citizens, the primary participants in Europe's integration process, and the organization that serves as a common umbrella for Europeans. Moreover, in the contemporary landscape, digital development is not merely an option but a necessity. It demands the creation of synergies among European states to adapt to the current, rather than future, challenges and safeguard their citizens from international threats. In this context, there is a convergence of European and national interests in developing a common e-identity. Collaborative efforts are essential as individual states can no longer effectively protect their citizens in isolation. The imperative for high-level protection necessitates a unified approach. The organization itself is keen on establishing direct links to interact with citizens without the mediation of Member States. This direct digital link is fundamental for empowering the Union against traditional threats, particularly the combination of nationalism and populism. It stands as a strategic tool to fortify the Union's resilience in the face of evolving challenges.

References

Al-Khouri, A. M., & Bachlaghem, M. (2011). Towards federated e-identity management across GCC—A solution's framework. *Global Journal of Strategies & Governance, 4*(1), 30–49.

Everett, C. (2011). E-Identity: an issue of trust. *Computer Fraud & Security, 2011*(3), 8–10.

Gábriš, T., & Hamuľák, O. (2021). Pandemics in cyberspace—Empire in search of a sovereign? *Baltic Journal of Law & Politics, 14*(1), 103–123.

Goodstadt, L. F., Connolly, R., & Bannister, F. (2015). The Hong Kong e-identity card: Examining the reasons for its success when other cards continue to struggle. *Information Systems Management, 32*(1), 72–80.

Hamulák, O. (2018). La carta de los derechos fundamentales de la union europea y los derechos sociales. *Estudios constitucionales, 16*(1), 167–186.

Ivic, S., & Troitiño, D. R. (2022). Digital sovereignty and identity in the European union: A challenge for building Europe. *European Studies, 9*(2), 80–109.

Jakisch, G. (2000, September). E-signature versus e-identity: The creation of the digital citizen. In *Proceedings 11th international workshop on database and expert systems applications* (pp. 312–316). IEEE.

Ježová, D. (2017). Fundamental rights in the European Union—Perspective of the digital era. In *Human rights in EU external relations: Between law and politics* (pp. 79–86). Vydavateľstvo UK, Univerzita Komenského.

Lepore, C., Laborde, R., Eynard, J., Kandi, M. A., Macilotti, G., Ferreira, A., & Sibilla, M. (2023). Assessing e-identity solutions according to self-sovereign identity: Application to eIDAS.

Neumann, L., & Sekanina, P. (2007). An analysis of e-identity organisational and technological solutions within a single European information space. In *Proceedings of the 7th European conference on e-government (ECEG 2007): ECEG* (p. 385). Academic Conferences Limited.

Průša, J. (2015, May). E-identity: Basic building block of e-government. In *2015 IST-Africa conference* (pp. 1–10). IEEE.

Ramiro Troitiño, D. (2022). The essence of Europe: Understanding Europe through its designers. In D. Ramiro Troitiño, R. M. de la Guardia, & G. A. Pérez Sánchez (Eds.), *The European Union and its political leaders* (pp. 1–4). Springer.

Rashica, V. (2019). Digital diplomacy: aspects, approaches and practical use. *European Perspectives, 23.*

Rek, M. (2010). Europeanization of civil society sector in Central and Eastern Europe. *Innovative Issues and Approaches in Social Sciences, 3*(1), 160–186.
Schulz, T., & Fritsch, L. (2014). Accessibility and inclusion requirements for future e-identity solutions. In *Computers helping people with special needs: 14th international conference, ICCHP 2014, Paris, France, July 9-11, 2014, proceedings, part I 14* (pp. 316–323). Springer.
Troitiño, D. R. (2022). The European Union facing the 21st century: The digital revolution. *TalTech Journal of European Studies, 12*(1), 60–78.
Troitiño, D. R., & Kerikmäe, T. (2021). Europe facing the digital challenge: obstacles and solutions. *IDP. Revista de Internet, Derecho y Política, 34*, 1–3.
Whitley, E. A. (2013). On technology neutral policies for e-identity: a critical reflection based on UK identity policy. *Journal of International Commercial Law and Technology, 8*, 134.

Digital Social Initiatives: Europe Connecting Citizens with Social Transformation

David Ramiro Troitiño and Viktoria Mazur

Abstract This study explores the intricate relationship between information and communication technologies (ICTs), civic engagement service innovation, and the challenges posed to traditional welfare systems in the European Union (EU). In the EU, civic engagement innovation is pivotal for democratic governance, demanding a delicate balance between technological advancement and democratic values. Initiatives like the European Citizens' Initiative (ECI) and the integration of digital platforms underscore the EU's commitment to shaping an inclusive and participatory European democracy, necessitating ongoing efforts to address challenges such as the digital divide and cybersecurity concerns. Shifting focus, the research comprehensively examines digital social innovation (DSI) within the context of a traditional welfare state facing significant challenges. Through inductive analysis, the study investigates the transformative impact of emerging digital technologies, particularly artificial intelligence, on reshaping welfare systems and addressing social risks. The chapter emphasizes the need for the EU to address societal challenges in the face of digitalization, safeguard its welfare system, and find common solutions aligned with European traditions and societal models.

Introduction

Civic Engagement Innovation: How It Shapes the Relationship Between State and Citizens

Civic engagement constitutes a multifaceted and diverse field of inquiry encompassing various initiatives characterized by distinctive ownership and governance structures. Additionally, the omnipresence of information and communication

D. Ramiro Troitiño (✉) · V. Mazur
Jean Monnet Chair on Digital Development of the EU, Tallinn University of Technology, Tallinn, Estonia
e-mail: david.troitino@taltech.ee; viktoria.mazur@taltech.ee

D. Ramiro Troitiño (ed.), *E-Governance in the European Union*, Contributions to Political Science, https://doi.org/10.1007/978-3-031-56045-3_6

technologies (ICTs) in social innovation for civic engagement manifests uniquely across different initiatives. These findings underscore the significance of this subject in its conceptualization and application to domains such as Smart City and e-Government. As we delve into the exploration of the classification and relative conceptualization of ICT-enabled civic engagement innovations, it becomes evident that this diversity extends both across types of initiatives and transversely in the application of technologies. These considerations carry implications for both research and policy.

Broadly, the role of ICTs in the development of civic engagement service innovation has been examined in functional terms concerning their contribution to the innovative potential embedded in the mapped initiatives. To a greater extent, two primary avenues for the integration of technologies in civic engagement innovations have been identified. Firstly, ICTs operate as operand, fostering efficacy and efficiency in service delivery and consumption. Secondly, ICTs function as operant, integral to the design of services. In the former case, technologies are utilized to modernize civic engagement services, establishing a contemporary support structure that enhances the effectiveness and efficiency of civic engagement. In instances where ICTs are fully integrated into the creation of new services or mechanisms, the technological infrastructure, typical of operand ICTs, serves as a foundation for the development of these innovations (Cancela Outeda, 2010). In essence, operand technologies often constitute the supporting ICT infrastructure upon which operant ICTs are integrated for the creation, delivery, and consumption of new services. This becomes more apparent when analyzing initiatives through the lens of service design logic.

Moreover, the reality reveals that sustained or incremental innovation provides the means for initiatives to enhance and update the organizational framework supporting service delivery. In contrast, radical or disruptive civic engagement services emerge through the integration of new and customized technologies, potentially establishing a new ecosystem where the integration of resources and delivery mechanisms may be institutionalized, creating new value for citizens and the government. Notably, ICTs need not necessarily be cutting-edge innovations to play a fundamental role in service provision. Well-evaluated and high-performing ICTs can reshape service paradigms, opening up unexpected opportunities for managing public and private assets (Mooij, 2022). For instance, the adoption of blockchain or artificial intelligence can act as a game-changer in service paradigms, introducing new collaborative social services. The former ensures transparency and accountability in public services provision, while the latter enhances interactions between citizens and service providers. Consider, for instance, the application of machine learning algorithms to linked open data in the context of opening up data, services, and decisions in the public sector through innovative ICTs. This presents opportunities for new perspectives on data storage and management, allowing non-state actors to provide state-like and complementary services.

In terms of service integration and distributed governance/ownership, there is no straightforward relationship between ownership/governance systems and the innovativeness of civic engagement initiatives. Specific governance and ownership arrangements undoubtedly impact the type of innovation and the value proposition of the initiative. Initiatives led by technology-savvy and innovation-driven social entrepreneurs or forward-looking third sector organizations are more likely to propose substantial civic engagement innovations than government agencies focused on efficiency savings. However, exceptions exist, as government agencies in highly digitalized communities may spearhead substantial reforms and deliver high-value innovative civic engagement services.

Traditional third sector organizations operating in digitally divided communities may exhibit conservatism in the ideation, development, and deployment of innovative civic engagement services. Exploring the innovation orientation of ownership and the ecosystem within which the initiative operates provides more explanatory power. Understanding the innovation push/pull forces within the ecosystem and how social policy actors convey these forces helps identifying causal relationships.

A critical point of discussion pertains to the representativeness of the sample. The work originates from the necessity to comprehend and classify various social innovation initiatives in the civic engagement domain in terms of their innovativeness and their utilization of technologies, particularly digital technologies.

The integration of ICTs into civic engagement innovation occurs through two primary routes. Firstly, technologies are employed to rationalize and enhance efficiency in civic engagement services, either through the digitization of supporting activities that were previously analog or through the digitization of existing services to improve beneficiary access. Although this may appear as a shift from the "real" to the "digital" world, it introduces new dynamics in service design and delivery, impacting the ownership/governance system and the relationship between the service provider and citizens (Cangiano et al. 2017). Reorganization and new management practices may be necessary to digitize services, reaching efficiency targets or rationalization objectives, typically achieved through procurement channels in governmental agencies or through limited-scale trials that may later scale up for third sector and private actors.

The second route involves the integration of technologies within service design, offering novel conceptual services or organizing service delivery and consumption in innovative ways. These cases often represent more efficient and effective approaches to providing value through novel technological solutions, enabling civic engagement services that would not be possible otherwise. In both cases, ICTs play a pivotal role in service delivery, with some initiatives featuring new technology as the service itself. These digital-born civic engagement innovations reshape the relationship between service providers and citizens, as the innovative approach to service provision does not adhere to an experiential blueprint, allowing for the design of the relationship through the delivery and consumption of services.

Civic engagement innovation within the context of the European Union (EU) represents a dynamic and evolving landscape that reflects the union's commitment to fostering active participation and collaboration between citizens and institutions. This essay delves into the various facets of civic engagement innovation in the EU, examining its importance, key initiatives, and the role of technology in shaping this transformative space. Civic engagement is fundamental to the EU's democratic principles, emphasizing the involvement of citizens in decision-making processes that impact their lives. Therefore, it goes beyond traditional methods, incorporating novel approaches to amplify citizen voices, enhance transparency, and strengthen the connection between individuals and the European Union (EU) institutions. In the EU context, civic engagement innovation is crucial for addressing the democratic deficit often associated with the complex structure of the union. By fostering innovative avenues for citizens to actively participate in policy formulation and implementation, the EU can bridge the perceived gap between its institutions and the diverse European populace.

The EU has actively pursued initiatives aimed at promoting civic engagement innovation, recognizing its integral role in ensuring a vibrant and participatory democracy. One noteworthy initiative is the European Citizens' Initiative (ECI), a unique tool that allows citizens to directly influence the EU legislative agenda (Wodak and Weiss, 2005). Through the ECI, citizens can propose legislation, providing a tangible mechanism for grassroots involvement. Additionally, the EU has embraced digital platforms to facilitate civic engagement. Projects like the EU's Citizens' Dialogues leverage online spaces to connect policymakers with citizens, fostering an inclusive dialogue on various issues. These initiatives underscore the EU's commitment to embracing innovation to enhance civic participation.

While civic engagement innovation in the EU presents significant opportunities, it also faces challenges, such as ensuring inclusivity and addressing the digital divide. Efforts must be made to guarantee that all citizens, regardless of their technological literacy or access, can actively participate in civic processes. Moreover, safeguarding data privacy and cybersecurity is paramount to maintaining the trust of citizens engaging through digital platforms. Striking a balance between embracing technological advancements and upholding democratic values remains an ongoing challenge for the EU.

Consequently, civic engagement innovation stands as a cornerstone of the EU's commitment to democratic governance. Through initiatives like the ECI and the integration of digital platforms, the EU is actively shaping a future where citizens play a more direct and influential role in the decision-making processes of the union (Ferreira and Pantidi, 2018). Embracing technology while addressing associated challenges is imperative to realizing a more inclusive and participatory European democracy. As civic engagement continues to evolve, the EU's dedication to innovation ensures that citizens remain at the heart of the European project.

Civic engagement innovation in the European Union is intricately interwoven with the union's social policy fabric, reflecting a commitment to inclusive governance, societal well-being, and participatory democracy. This research provides an in-depth exploration of civic engagement innovation through the lens of social policy, elucidating how the EU's policies and practices drive innovative approaches that empower citizens, address inequalities, and foster a cohesive and participatory society.

The EU's civic engagement innovation finds its roots in a robust foundation of social policies aimed at promoting equity, social inclusion, and the overall welfare of its diverse citizenry. These policies encompass education, healthcare, and social welfare, forming the bedrock upon which civic engagement initiatives are built. The EU's commitment to creating an inclusive society is evident in policies that prioritize the fundamental elements contributing to citizens' well-being, thereby laying the groundwork for active civic participation. Civic engagement innovation, propelled by social policy imperatives, takes a distinctly inclusive approach within the EU as part of the unique elements of Europe in comparison with the rest of the world. The design of initiatives prioritizes diversity and inclusivity, ensuring that marginalized and underrepresented communities actively contribute to the decision-making processes. Therefore, the European organization looks for implementation of programs that reach across socioeconomic and demographic divides, seeking to cultivate a sense of belonging and empowerment among all citizens. It has a double target, social development and protection, following the European welfare traditions, and increasing the loyalty of the citizens to a gradually more politically integrated Europe.

Social policies in the EU foster dynamic social dialogues that transcend traditional boundaries. Platforms like Citizens' Dialogues exemplify the union's commitment to facilitating meaningful interactions between citizens and policymakers. These dialogues, facilitated by social policy frameworks, become conduits for citizen expression, embodying the principles of participatory governance that underpin civic engagement innovation.

A central tenet of civic engagement innovation from a social policy perspective is the targeted effort to address societal inequalities. Recognizing that disparities in access to education, healthcare, and economic opportunities can impede civic participation, EU social policies work to dismantle these barriers. The aim is to create an environment where every citizen, regardless of background, enjoys equal opportunities for engagement, fostering a shared responsibility for societal well-being (Dutt & Nyman-Metcalf, 2021). The EU's civic engagement innovation finds its roots in a robust foundation of social policies aimed at promoting equity, social inclusion, and the overall welfare of its diverse citizenry. The EU's commitment to creating an inclusive society is evident in policies that prioritize the fundamental elements contributing to citizens' well-being, thereby laying the groundwork for active civic participation. Social policies in the EU foster dynamic social dialogues that transcend traditional boundaries. These dialogues, facilitated by social policy frameworks, become conduits for citizen expression, embodying the principles of participatory governance that underpin civic engagement innovation.

Despite the strides made, challenges persist. Balancing technological advancements with the human-centric focus of social policies remains an ongoing concern (Troitiño, 2022). The EU's social policy approach to civic engagement innovation must continually evolve to address emerging societal issues and ensure equitable redistribution of benefits. Future directions involve adapting policies to encompass issues such as the gig economy, digital literacy, and ethical technology use, maintaining a commitment to social justice.

Nevertheless. societal inequalities within the European Union present a multifaceted challenge that extends across economic, social, and demographic dimensions:

1. Economic disparities:

   Economic inequalities persist as a prominent feature within the EU. Disparities in income distribution and wealth accumulation often result in divergent living standards among Member States and regions. The North–South economic divide, exemplified by variations in GDP per capita, employment rates, and industrial development, underscores the persistent challenges in achieving economic convergence across the union.

2. Social inequalities:

   Social inequalities manifest in various forms, impacting access to essential services and opportunities. Disparities in education, healthcare, and housing contribute to differential life outcomes. Migrant communities and minority groups often face social exclusion, highlighting the intersectionality of social and cultural factors in perpetuating inequalities within European societies.

3. Gender disparities:

   Gender inequalities persist despite advancements in gender equity policies. Discrepancies in pay, underrepresentation in leadership positions, and unequal access to educational and professional avenues persist, impeding the achievement of true gender equality. Tackling these disparities demands a holistic strategy that confronts deeply rooted societal norms and fosters inclusivity.

4. Demographic disparities:

   Demographic factors, encompassing age and geographical location, play a pivotal role in generating inequalities in resource accessibility and opportunities. Regions with aging populations confront unique challenges like ensuring the sustainability of pensions and meeting healthcare demands. Conversely, younger populations may grapple with obstacles related to securing stable employment and affordable housing.

The EU has implemented various initiatives aimed at mitigating societal inequalities. Structural funds, social inclusion programs, and cohesion policies seek to address economic and regional disparities. Additionally, the European Pillar of Social Rights provides a framework for promoting fair labor practices, social protection, and equal opportunities, contributing to a more inclusive and equitable union. Despite ongoing efforts, challenges persist in achieving comprehensive equality within the EU. Economic and social policies must grapple with the complexities of a diverse union, navigating differing national priorities and cultural contexts. The path forward involves a continued commitment to policies that actively address the root causes of societal inequalities. Prioritizing education, healthcare, and social integration programs, alongside targeted economic development initiatives, can contribute to a more equitable future (Henman, 2019). Embracing diversity and fostering inclusive policies that consider the unique challenges faced by various demographics will be crucial in shaping a truly egalitarian European Union.

In conclusion, civic engagement innovation in the European Union, viewed through the prism of social policy, embodies a holistic approach to participatory democracy. The union's commitment to social inclusion, dynamic dialogues, and addressing inequalities forms the cornerstone of its civic engagement initiatives. As the EU navigates the ever-evolving landscape of civic engagement innovation, its social policy principles will remain instrumental in shaping a future where citizens actively contribute to a socially just and cohesive European democracy.

Digital Social Challenges in the European Union

This comprehensive work investigates the multifaceted concept of social innovation as defined by the European Commission and explores its applications in addressing various social risks within the context of a traditional welfare state undergoing significant challenges. The study delves into the intricate dynamics of digital social innovation (DSI) and examines the protective roles played by diverse sources, namely the market, the state, the family, and the community. Additionally, the chapter scrutinizes the transformative impact of emerging digital technologies, particularly artificial intelligence (AI), on reshaping welfare systems. Employing an inductive analysis of various DSI initiatives, the research seeks to unravel the intricate interplay between DSI, institutional discourse, and the crucial role of digital technology in safeguarding societal well-being.

Social innovation, as elucidated by the European Commission, encapsulates the development and implementation of novel ideas to address social needs, fostering new social relationships and collaborations. Therefore, an exploration of social innovation's efficacy in tackling a spectrum of social risks, ranging from rising poverty rates to environmental degradation, is required. Furthermore, it scrutinizes the challenges posed by a traditional welfare state confronted with aging populations, financial resource limitations, and evolving family structures, impacting both traditional and new user groups. The market's role in generating new job spotlights the limitations of an Internet-oriented approach primarily geared toward business and its inadequacy for comprehensive welfare policies. The state's protective mechanisms are dissected through an analysis of its values and the phases of digital integration, including procedural simplification, process automation, and the taxation of digital multinationals. The family's evolving role in fostering new modes of interaction is discussed, alongside the community's contribution to services funded by both private and public finance.

The profound impact of digitalization on individuals is very relevant to any study on social impact and of civic engagement because it encompasses aspects such as empowerment, the celebration of individualism, decreased barriers to access, immediateness, and potential divides. Recognizing the dualistic role of digitalization as an enabler or transformational agent, the discussion centers on its influence on participative and collaborative innovation, as well as its potential to reshape power structures and promote human capabilities. The challenges inherent in digital social innovation are expounded upon, including the "e-governance paradox" where states accumulate vast amounts of information yet struggle to translate it into effective policy actions. The systemic nature of welfare problems is explored, emphasizing the necessity for impact analysis at a broader level. The interaction between social innovation, policy makers, and social movements is dissected, highlighting the dual role of social innovation as either an enabler or a transformational agent. It is an issue also the readiness of social innovators in the welfare sector to embrace emerging digital technologies and AI. It underlines the reluctance of public decision-makers due to insufficient cost–benefit analysis and impact evaluation (Hsieh et al.

2011). The European Commission's AI Watch survey is referenced, showcasing the predominant focus on performance-based goals over inclusion in social protection initiatives. In relation to DSI initiatives, many commence at the local level but fade away after a short duration. Successful social innovations are often initiated by local authorities or integrated into local welfare administration with external funding. The role of Smart Cities in fostering innovation is elucidated, emphasizing the ongoing negotiations between municipalities and institutional subjects.

Future of the Digital Social Europe

Resilience, the capacity to adapt and recover from challenges, is a fundamental aspect of societal well-being. In the context of the EU, the pursuit of resilience has become a key principle guiding social policymaking. It delves into the multifaceted dimensions of resilience, the challenges faced by societies, and the policy measures adopted by the EU to address these challenges. A resilient society is one that can withstand, adapt to, and recover from various shocks and stresses, be they economic, environmental, or social. It is a society where individuals and communities have the capacity to cope with challenges, maintain a decent standard of living, and ensure social cohesion. Resilience extends beyond mere survival; it involves building systems and structures that can thrive in the face of adversity (Ayata & Önay, 2021). EU Member States face a range of challenges that necessitate a resilient approach to social policy. Economic fluctuations, demographic shifts, climate change, and global health crisis are among the complex issues that impact the well-being of European citizens. Moreover, the EU's commitment to fostering inclusivity and addressing inequalities adds an additional layer of complexity to policymaking. The EU's approach to social policy is characterized by its commitment to building resilient societies. This involves a multifaceted strategy that integrates economic, social, and environmental considerations. The European Pillar of Social Rights, adopted in 2017, exemplifies this comprehensive approach by outlining principles and rights aimed at ensuring fair and well-functioning labor markets, social protection, and equal opportunities. Consequently, EU social policies emphasize creating resilient labor markets through measures such as fair working conditions, adequate social protection, and active labor market policies. By investing in skills development and promoting decent work, the EU aims to enhance individuals' ability to adapt to changing economic landscapes. In addition, robust social protection systems are at the core of a resilient society. The EU encourages Member States to ensure access to healthcare, unemployment benefits, and pensions. This safety net not only provides a buffer against economic shocks but also contributes to social cohesion by reducing inequality and poverty. Moreover, inclusivity is a key component of resilience. The EU's emphasis on inclusive growth seeks to ensure that the benefits of economic development are shared equitably. Social policies that promote equal opportunities, combat discrimination, and address the needs of vulnerable groups contribute to the overall resilience of European societies. Finally, acknowledging the challenges posed by climate change, the EU integrates environmental sustainability into its social policies. Transitioning to a green economy, investing in renewable energy, and promoting sustainable consumption are part of a broader strategy to build societies capable of withstanding environmental pressures. In relation to international relations, recent global health crisis has highlighted the importance of preparedness and cooperation. The EU's commitment to strengthening health systems, ensuring access to healthcare, and fostering international collaboration underscores its dedication to building resilient societies in the face of health-related challenges (Hamulák, 2018). Despite significant strides, challenges remain in implementing and maintaining resilient social policies. Balancing economic growth with social and environmental concerns, addressing demographic imbalances, and adapting to unforeseen global challenges require ongoing efforts. Additionally, the EU must continuously assess and refine its policies to ensure they remain responsive to the evolving needs of its diverse Member States. Therefore, the concept of resilience lies at the heart of EU social policymaking. By adopting a holistic and inclusive approach, the EU aims to build societies capable of navigating the complexities of the modern world. The commitment to labor market resilience, social protection, inclusive growth, environmental sustainability, and global health preparedness reflects a vision of a Europe where individuals and communities can thrive in the face of challenges. As the EU continues to evolve, its dedication to building resilient societies serves as a model for effective and forward-thinking policymaking on the global stage.

DSI has emerged as a transformative force in the EU, bringing together technology, social entrepreneurship, and collaborative approaches to address societal challenges. As we celebrate the 1-year anniversary of this essay, it is essential to explore the intricate intersection of elements shaping DSI in the EU. This essay delves into the key components that converge to drive digital social innovation, examining technological advancements, collaborative networks, policy frameworks, and the role of individuals and organizations in fostering a culture of innovation. Technological innovation lies at the heart of DSI. The EU has witnessed a rapid evolution in digital technologies, including artificial intelligence, blockchain, and the Internet of Things. These advancements serve as the building blocks for innovative solutions to social issues. For instance, AI-powered algorithms can analyze vast datasets to identify patterns and trends in healthcare, education, and environmental sustainability (Kvasny, 2006). Blockchain technology ensures transparency and trust in social initiatives, particularly in areas such as supply chain management and charitable donations. The continuous evolution of these technologies provides a fertile ground for the growth of digital social innovation. DSI thrives on collaboration, bringing together diverse stakeholders, including civil society organizations, businesses, government bodies, and citizens. Collaborative networks act as catalysts, fostering the exchange of ideas and resources. Platforms like the EU DSI Atlas connect innovators across the continent, facilitating the sharing of best practices and the creation of synergies. The collaborative nature of DSI not only amplifies its impact but also creates a dynamic ecosystem where different actors contribute to the co-creation of solutions for societal challenges.

Regarding European policies, the EU recognizes the significance of DSI in addressing complex societal issues and has implemented policy frameworks to support and promote innovation. Initiatives such as the Digital Europe Program allocate funds to projects that leverage digital technologies for social good. Policymakers are working toward creating an environment that encourages experimentation and risk-taking in the pursuit of innovative solutions. Furthermore, the General Data Protection Regulation (GDPR) ensures that digital innovation is carried out ethically and with due consideration for privacy and data protection, reinforcing the ethical dimension of DSI.

The role of individuals and organizations is pivotal in driving DSI. Social entrepreneurs, activists within the European Union, and grassroots movements play a crucial role in identifying problems and developing innovative solutions. Moreover, established corporations are increasingly recognizing the importance of social responsibility and are incorporating DSI into their business models. By fostering a culture of innovation, individuals and organizations contribute to the scalability and sustainability of DSI projects, ensuring their long-term impact on society. Despite the promising trajectory of DSI in the EU, challenges persist. Issues such as digital divide, ethical concerns, and the need for standardized metrics to measure impact require continuous attention (Mulder, 2021). Additionally, as technology evolves, the regulatory framework of the Union must adapt to address emerging challenges. Looking ahead, the future of DSI in the EU appears bright. The ongoing collaboration between various stakeholders, the commitment of policymakers, and the innovative spirit of individuals and organizations position the EU at the forefront of digital social innovation. The coming years are likely to witness the amplification of DSI's impact, with the potential to transform the social landscape of the European Union.

In the area of governance of ICT, it really plays a pivotal role in shaping the future of welfare systems. The Collaborative Multi-Layer-Nested Welfare Model envisions a dynamic approach that integrates emerging technologies into the fabric of social services. Harnessing the power of artificial intelligence, big data analytics, and blockchain can lead to more efficient resource allocation, predictive policy-making, and improved service delivery. Therefore, the EU must prioritize the development and implementation of robust regulatory frameworks that balance innovation with ethical considerations. Common rules lead to common actions. Striking this delicate balance will ensure that ICT trends contribute to the democratization of welfare services rather than exacerbating existing inequalities. Additionally, fostering collaboration between public and private sectors, academia, and civil society is essential to harnessing the full potential of technology for the benefit of all EU citizens. The success of the Collaborative Multi-Layer-Nested Welfare Model hinges on the accessibility of resources to all segments of society (Ramiro Troitiño, 2022). The EU could focus on adopting strategies to eliminate existing barriers and create a more inclusive framework. The first is an approach based on forbid and the second on integration. Financial resources, educational opportunities, and healthcare services should be distributed more efficiently, fostering social cohesion and reducing disparities. To enhance accessibility, the EU should invest in infrastructure that ensures high-speed Internet connectivity across all regions. This not only facilitates the dissemination of information and services but also empowers individuals to participate in the digital economy. Moreover, targeted initiatives should be implemented to address specific needs of marginalized groups, ensuring that the benefits of the welfare model reach everyone, regardless of socioeconomic status or geographical location.

On the other hand, social innovation is a cornerstone of the Collaborative Multi-Layer-Nested Welfare Model, promoting adaptive and participatory solutions to societal challenges. Institutionalizing social innovation initiatives involves creating a supportive ecosystem that encourages experimentation, collaboration, and the scaling of successful innovations. The EU looks for the establishment of dedicated platforms for the exchange of best practices and the co-creation of innovative solutions. These platforms should involve a diverse range of stakeholders, including governments, businesses, NGOs, and local communities. Furthermore, financial incentives and regulatory frameworks should be designed to encourage businesses and organizations to prioritize social impact alongside economic gains. By fostering a culture of innovation and collaboration, the EU can ensure the continuous evolution and improvement of its welfare model.

The rapid pace of technological advancements necessitates a forward-looking approach to governing ICT trends within the EU:

1. Regulatory frameworks: A robust regulatory framework is essential to balance the dynamics of ICT with the need for consumer protection and data privacy. Policymakers must stay ahead of technological developments, crafting regulations that both encourage innovation and safeguard the rights of citizens.
2. Digital inclusion: As ICT becomes integral to daily life, addressing digital inclusion becomes a priority. Policies must bridge the digital divide, ensuring that every citizen has equitable access to technology and digital resources. This inclusivity fosters social cohesion and propels economic growth.
3. Cybersecurity measures: In tandem with technological growth, the EU must prioritize the establishment and enforcement of stringent cybersecurity measures. Collaborative efforts involving Member States, industry stakeholders, and research institutions are paramount to creating a resilient and secure digital environment.

The institutionalization of social innovation in the European Union requires innovation addressing the problems of society fostering civic participation and inclusivity. Nevertheless, as the first step there is a need to define what is social innovation; a clear and comprehensive definition of social innovation is a prerequisite for effective policymaking. This definition should encompass initiatives that tackle societal challenges, promote inclusivity, and contribute to sustainable development. After defining the frame, the initiatives, and the way to involve citizens, the innovative funding mechanisms play a pivotal role in driving experimentation and ensuring the sustainability of social innovation initiatives, including public–private partnerships, impact investment, and venture philanthropy. Diversifying funding models reduces dependence on traditional approaches and stimulates innovation in financial mechanisms. Funding helps the implementation of the project, but after measuring its success, the EU needs a common frame for evaluation and impact assessment. Rigorous evaluation and impact assessment processes are essential for determining the effectiveness of funding mechanisms (Ramiro Troitiño, 2023a). Assessing the social, economic, and environmental impact of initiatives informs future investment decisions and facilitates continuous improvement. Finally, it is important to remember that the nature of social innovation demands flexibility and a degree of risk tolerance in funding mechanisms. Embracing an environment that accepts failure as part of the learning process encourages experimentation and nurtures an ecosystem conducive to innovation.

Regarding Positive Innovation Networks, it is crucial to understand that they represent a paradigm shift from traditional innovation models by placing emphasis on positive outcomes, not only in terms of economic gains but also in terms of societal well-being. These networks serve as platforms where diverse stakeholders, including businesses, government entities, research institutions, and civil society, converge to collaboratively address societal challenges. The EU, with its rich cultural diversity and commitment to social progress, is an ideal environment for nurturing such networks. To facilitate the development and success of Positive Innovation Networks in the EU, a robust conceptual framework is vital. This framework should provide guidance on fostering effective co-creation and collaboration among diverse stakeholders, acknowledging the unique challenges and opportunities within the digital social innovation space. It requires networked flow referring to the seamless and dynamic exchange of ideas, knowledge, and resources among interconnected stakeholders. In the context of Positive Innovation Networks, creating a conducive environment for networked flow involves breaking down silos and fostering open communication channels (Stokes et al. 2017). The EU can leverage its existing collaborative platforms, such as Horizon Europe and the European Institute of Innovation and Technology (EIT), to encourage cross-disciplinary interactions and knowledge sharing. These actions required the incorporation of the concept of positive psychological capital, encompassing psychological attributes such as optimism, resilience, and self-efficacy, because it plays a pivotal role in fostering innovation. Within Positive Innovation Networks, stakeholders must possess the mindset and capabilities necessary to navigate uncertainty and embrace positive change. Initiatives such as training programs, mentorship schemes, and incentives for risk-taking can enhance the positive psychological capital of individuals and organizations involved in the innovation ecosystem. For instance, initiatives like the European Social Innovation Competition and the Digital Europe Program exemplify the EU's commitment to promoting positive innovation. These programs not only support technological advancements but also prioritize solutions that address societal challenges, thereby aligning with the ethos of Positive Innovation Networks.

On drivers of ICT-Enabled Social Innovation there are crucial aspects to be aware of in the context of the European Union:

- Technological advancements: The rapid evolution of ICT, including artificial intelligence, big data analytics, and the Internet of Things, has opened new avenues for social innovation. These technologies enable more efficient and targeted delivery of social services, enhancing the overall effectiveness of welfare programs.

- Increased connectivity: The widespread adoption of high-speed Internet and improved connectivity has facilitated the establishment of digital networks, connecting individuals, organizations, and communities across the EU. This interconnectedness is essential for the exchange of ideas, collaboration, and the development of innovative solutions to societal challenges.
- Changing demographics: The demographic landscape in the EU is evolving, with an aging population and diverse social needs. ICT-enabled social innovation provides a platform to address these challenges by tailoring services to specific demographic groups, ensuring inclusivity and responsiveness.
- Public awareness and participation: Digital platforms empower citizens to actively engage in the design and implementation of social services. Increased awareness and participation foster a sense of community, encouraging the co-creation of solutions that better align with the actual needs of the population.
- Digital divide: Despite advancements, a digital divide persists across the EU, with discrepancies in access to technology and digital literacy. This gap hampers the inclusive deployment of ICT-enabled social services, exacerbating inequalities and limiting the reach of innovative solutions.
- Data privacy and security concerns: The collection and utilization of personal data for social innovation purposes raise ethical concerns. Ensuring robust data privacy measures and cybersecurity safeguards is crucial to building public trust and sustaining the momentum of digital social innovation.
- Fragmented policy landscape: The EU comprises diverse Member States, each with its own policy framework. A fragmented policy landscape can impede the harmonized implementation of ICT-enabled social innovation initiatives, necessitating cohesive efforts to align policies and regulations.
- Resistance to change: Traditional approaches to social service delivery may face resistance from stakeholders accustomed to established practices. Overcoming this resistance requires comprehensive strategies to demonstrate the benefits and long-term positive impacts of digital social innovation.

Policies should prioritize the enhancement of societal well-being, economic growth, and sustainability through ICT-enabled social innovation (Ramiro Troitiño, 2023b). This involves fostering an environment where digital solutions contribute to social cohesion, economic development, and environmental sustainability. Governments within the EU should collaborate to develop conducive policies and regulatory frameworks that facilitate the seamless integration of digital technologies into social service provision. This includes standardizing data protection regulations and promoting interoperability.

Conclusions

Welfare system is a pillar of the European identity; it is being challenged by new realities and new models of society. Digitalization increases the speed of the challenges to society and the necessity to address them. If the European Union wants to last in the long term, the main social challenges of the European society should be solved or minimized. The path of integration has grown since the time of Jean Monnet, increasing the benefits for the European citizens and the Member States, but also has reduced the capacity of the States to address social problems. For example, the free movement of people eliminates most of the restrictions for people to seek the most convenient system within the Union; the European Market eliminates barriers to trade, but also contributes to the society via taxes, increasing the inequality and reducing the financial capacity of the States. In the international world, other social models, as the US or the Chinese, pretend to be more efficient managing the problems of the society, but neither of them respond to the European traditions nor its necessities. The digital revolution could lead to the implementation of either of these to alien social models within the Member States of the Union, but it also provides with novel instruments to implement common solutions matching European necessities and society models.

References

Ayata, Z., & Önay, I. (2021). *Global perspectives on legal challenges posed by ridesharing companies* (p. 281). Springer.

Cancela Outeda, C. (2010). La eurorregión Galicia-Norte de Portugal: un escenario de cooperación territorial. *Razón y Palabra, 15*(74).

Cangiano, S., Romano, Z., & Loglio, M. (2017). The growth of digital social innovation in Europe. An Open Design approach to support innovation for the societal good. *The Design Journal, 20*(sup1), S3546–S3559.

Dutt, P. K., & Nyman-Metcalf, K. (2021). The legal implications of public support policies targeting research, development and innovation in the European Union. *TalTech Journal of European Studies, 11*(2), 102–129.

Ferreira, J., & Pantidi, N. (2018). Going digital: Integrating digital technologies in local community initiatives. In *Digital participation through social living labs* (pp. 55–76). Chandos.

Hamulák, O. (2018). La carta de los derechos fundamentales de la union europea y los derechos sociales. *Estudios constitucionales, 16*(1), 167–186.

Henman, P. (2019). Of algorithms, apps and advice: Digital social policy and service delivery. *Journal of Asian Public Policy, 12*(1), 71–89.

Hsieh, J. P. A., Rai, A., & Keil, M. (2011). Addressing digital inequality for the socioeconomically disadvantaged through government initiatives: Forms of capital that affect ICT utilization. *Information Systems Research, 22*(2), 233–253.

Kvasny, L. (2006). Cultural (re) production of digital inequality in a US community technology initiative. *Information, Communication & Society, 9*(02), 160–181.

Mooij, A. A. (2022). The digital euro and energy considerations: Can the ECB introduce the digital euro considering the potential energy requirements? *German Law Journal, 23*(9), 1246–1265.

Mulder, E. J. (2021). Living apart together? Discussing the different digital worlds in city government. In E. Estevez, T. A. Pardo, & H. J. Scholl (Eds.), *Smart cities and smart governance: Towards the 22nd century sustainable city* (pp. 289–302). Springer.

Ramiro Troitiño, D. (2022). Immanuel Kant: The idea of progress and European integration. In D. Ramiro Troitiño, R. M. de la Guardia, & G. A. Pérez Sánchez (Eds.), *The European Union and its political leaders: Understanding the integration process* (pp. 29–38). Springer.

Ramiro Troitiño, D. (2023a). The European Commission, the Council, and the European Parliament: Differentiated theoretical frame for the digital revolution. In D. Ramiro Troitiño, T. Kerikmäe, & O. Hamuľák (Eds.), *Digital development of the European Union: An interdisciplinary perspective* (pp. 349–361). Springer.

Ramiro Troitiño, D. (2023b). Mapping E-governance in the EU. In D. Ramiro Troitiño, T. Kerikmäe, & O. Hamuľák (Eds.), *Digital development of the European Union: An interdisciplinary perspective* (pp. 303–317). Springer.

Stokes, M., Baeck, P., & Baker, T. (2017). *What next for digital social innovation? Realising the potential of people and technology to tackle social challenges*. European Commission.

Troitiño, D. R. (2022). El futuro digital de la política europea.

Wodak, R., & Weiss, G. (2005). Analyzing European Union discourses. In R. Wodak & P. Chilton (Eds.), *Discourse approaches to politics, society and culture (DAPSAC)*. John Benjamins.

Data Embassy in the European Union: The Digital Diplomacy

Viona Rashica

Abstract Digital technologies, the Internet, and social media have brought new opportunities into the lives of people around the world. Therefore, digital diplomacy is now an integral part of the foreign policy of the states, whether they are large, medium, or small, but also part of the activity of international organizations, both governmental and non-governmental. One of the main benefits of digital diplomacy, which is seen as an adequate way of combating cyber threats, is data embassy. The main purpose of this chapter is to specify the characteristics of EU digital diplomacy, as well as to explain when she applies the data embassy project. For the realization of the research, the qualitative methodology was used, based on the bibliography and credible Internet sources related to digital diplomacy, the data embassy project, and the EU. The results of the research have shown that data embassy, in addition to favoring small states, also finds a place in the EU, which is a sui generis entity. The conclusions of the chapter aim to provide information on the main characteristics of EU digital diplomacy.

Introduction

Digital diplomacy brings many benefits for international actors and that is why it has become so important, where in some cases it triumphs over traditional diplomatic traditions. However, the more advances there are in digital technologies, the more cyber threats increase. Consequently, states and international organizations must take very important steps. Data embassy is one of the main benefits of digital diplomacy, which proves to be quite useful when the level of cyber risks is very serious. Although it is estimated to be very favorable for small states, now we can say that it is also important for other states, even for a supranational political and economic union such as the European Union. This chapter aims to specify the main

V. Rashica (✉)
Faculty of Contemporary Social Sciences, South East European University (SEEU), Tetovo, North Macedonia

D. Ramiro Troitiño (ed.), *E-Governance in the European Union*, Contributions to Political Science, https://doi.org/10.1007/978-3-031-56045-3_7

characteristics of EU digital diplomacy, as well as to clarify when the EU takes the data embassy project into consideration. This chapter is divided into three separate sections. The first section mentions the characteristics of digital diplomacy, starting from the definition, goals, up to the growth of its role, as well as its benefits and risks. The second section is related to the data embassy project, clarifying what the latter is, when and how it is applied, as well as which country used it first. While the third section is the most important because it elaborates the digital diplomacy of the EU. In addition to the stated reasons why digital diplomacy was adopted by the EU, the section describes the use of websites and social media by EU institutions and leaders, the steps followed in the field of digitalization and protection against cyber threats, including data embassy. However, this chapter also mentions the impact that Brexit has had on EU digital diplomacy, which cannot be overlooked.

The Main Characteristics of Digital Diplomacy

An excellent opportunity to begin bridging the change management gap in diplomatic theory is offered by the recent spread of digital initiatives in foreign ministries, which probably can be described as nothing less than a revolution in the practice of diplomacy (Bjola & Kornprobst, 2015, p. 201). Digital diplomacy now can be considered as an inseparable part of the realization of the foreign policy of states and the activities of international organizations. It can be defined as a form of new public diplomacy,[1] which uses new information and communication technologies (ICT), the Internet, and social media as a means for strengthening diplomatic relations between international actors (Rashica, 2019b, p. 23). Digital diplomacy constitutes a unique strategy, the importance of which is growing tremendously, and which already has an undeniable impact on the fulfillment of state interests and the management of global changes with digital tools and virtual cooperation. Also, it is now a necessary tool for the success of the ambassadors' mission, communication and exchange of their messages, as well as changing the narrative and correcting wrong perceptions, but also harmful or untrue information. Through the adoption of digital diplomacy is aimed:

- Proper usage of knowledge;
- Increasing the effectiveness of public diplomacy;
- Evaluation and management of information and data;
- Facilitation of diplomatic and consular communications, as well as rapid responses in cases of crisis;

[1] The end of the Cold War in 1991 had resulted in the spread of democracy and its values in many countries and had facilitated and increased people's access to international information. Public diplomacy was directly affected by the forces of globalization and the revolution in ICT, and thus classical public diplomacy came to an end, opening the doors to the new public diplomacy.

- Keeping the Internet free and open as an effort to increase democracy and minimize autocracy;
- Penetration to external human resources;
- Policy planning (Rashica, 2019a, p. 77).

Websites serve MFAs to explain and record their national foreign policies and rebut unacceptable actions or claims by other states (Barston, 2014, p. 16), while social media has become diplomacy's significant tool, which provides a platform for unconditional communication, and has become a communicator's most powerful tool (Twiplomacy, 2017). Social media is a very important element for audience targeting and although there is a wide range of social media that international actors use, the most popular ones are: Twitter; Facebook; Instagram; YouTube; LinkedIn; and TikTok. When searching for information on digital diplomacy, confusion can be caused due to the variety of terms associated with it, which has also had an impact on discussions and policies in this field. The question is whether diplomacy should be "digital," "cyber," "technological," "virtual," etc., or should the prefixes "e," "net," "Twitter," "Facebook," "Instagram," etc. be used before it? Here we should not forget the special terms also created by some countries such as "la Diplomatie Numérique," "Public Diplomacy 2.0," "21st Century-Craft," "Open Policy," etc. However, the terms created above together with many other terms that may be created in the future can all together be termed as synonyms of digital diplomacy because they refer to the digitalization of diplomacy through the use of ICT, the Internet, and social media (Kurbalija, 2015).

From March 2020, the world as everyone knew it changed a lot. The coronavirus had the power to change people's lives, starting from the way their children are educated to the way they work and do business. Even the field of diplomacy was not spared from the impact of this virus. Diplomacy, as a profession that involves a lot of travel, physical meetings, and personal interactions had come to an abrupt halt as a result of travel restrictions, border closures, and strict stay-at-home orders that had made it impossible to carry out personal diplomatic activities. As the coronavirus spread globally, world leaders were forced to continue their work, being isolated in their homes. As it is known inseparable part of their work are meetings, especially meetings with other leaders, whether bilateral or multilateral, so they were forced to adapt to their work from home by holding these meetings in virtual form (Ramiro Troitiño, 2022). This virus disfavored political diplomacy, but it greatly favored digital diplomacy, thus making 2020 the year which in the literature of diplomacy will be known as the year of the brilliance of digital diplomacy. Before the outbreak of the coronavirus pandemic, it seemed totally impossible that political diplomacy would be replaced by digital diplomacy. A large number of diplomats and experts of diplomatic law thought that such a thing would never happen, regardless of the extraordinary growth of the role of digital diplomacy (Rashica, 2023, p. 59).

The bright side of digital diplomacy is characterized by a multitude of benefits such as: strengthening cooperation between international actors; speed of information penetration; facilitating audience targeting; low financial cost; favoring small states; the possibility of data protection through the data embassy project; and virtual participation in multilateral meetings. However, digital diplomacy has the other side of the coin, the dark side. Some of the main risks that follow from digital diplomacy are: the freedom that comes from the Internet and social media; lack of knowledge about the usage of ICT, the Internet and social media; fostering disputes and conflicts; the culture of anonymity on the Internet and social media; cyber threats; and disadvantages of virtual meetings. The formula for a successful digital diplomacy, whether for a state or an international organization, is the maximum utilization of the benefits of digital diplomacy, as well as recognizing and strengthening protection against its risks. As for the benefits of digital diplomacy, it should be noted that a very effective way to prevent cyber threats is the data embassy, which is quite useful for small states and not only.

The Data Embassy Project

Embassies have been havens for the people of countries they represent for hundreds of years, helping reduce some risks that their citizens can face when traveling and living abroad. A data embassy entails a set of servers in a host country that stores data directly belonging to and under the jurisdiction of another country. The data archives of one country stored in its data embassy in another country are inviolable and thus exempt from search, requisition, attachment, or execution. Overall the data embassy project creates the new normality where the state distributes its critical data and information systems in cooperation with other states to increase its digital continuity and security. The data embassy project is innovative from the intergovernmental relations, legal and technical perspective. With this project, for the first time in the world, the extension of Vienna Convention on Diplomatic Relations (VCDR) to host data and information systems was sought (Observatory of Public Sector Innovation, 2017). Data embassy applies the guidelines from international law, especially the VCDR, as follows:

- **Inviolability of premises:** The premises of a mission, defined as buildings or parts of buildings and the land ancillary thereto, irrespective of ownership used for the purposes of the mission are inviolable. This means that the host country cannot enter the physical data embassy without the permission of the country setting up the data embassy;
- **Inviolability of contents:** The archives and documents of the mission are also inviolable. The host state does not have the right to enter the mission or to seize the papers. All data and information systems therefore form part of the archives of the mission and cannot be searched, requisitioned, attached, or executed. Any equipment deployed by the host state also should be regarded as assets of the host state[2];

[2] Article 24 of the VCDR states that the archives and documents of the mission shall be inviolable at any time and wherever they may be. It should be mentioned that archives and documents also

- **Protection of premises:** The host state is obliged to take all appropriate steps to protect the premises of the mission against any intrusion or damage[3] (Basu, 2023).

One of the postulates of diplomatic law is that diplomatic missions are entitled to free communication, communication that is unmonitored, unobstructed, and free from surveillance or interference. Since Article 27 of the VCDR specifies that "the mission may employ all appropriate means" of communication, this should include the use of digital communication (United Nations, 1961). In communicating with the government and the other missions and consulates of the sending state, wherever situated, the mission may employ all appropriate means, including diplomatic couriers and messages in code or cipher. However, the mission may install and use a wireless transmitter only with the consent of the receiving State (Kurbalija, 2022).

Small states around the world are turning to the concept of "data embassies" because they are in need of sovereign and resilient infrastructure. They realize that keeping data localized within a single facility or a set geographical boundary could pose a security risk in the event of a crisis, such as a natural disaster or an armed conflict. A typical example is Estonia, which authorized a data embassy in 2015. Within the period from 27 April to May 2007, Estonia had cyberattacks in the public and private sector. Public institutions including the websites of the Prime Minister, the Parliament, and almost all of the country's government ministries were targeted by the attack. Private sector institutions such as banks, telecommunications operators and three of the country's six big news organizations and two of the major Estonian banks were targeted. Allegations have been circulating about the support by the Russian Federation to the attack, but always denied by the Russian government. Due to the nature of the attacks, public and private entities defended themselves by blocking the access from sources that were outside the countries, resulting in the obscuration of their websites to the rest of the world. Although disruptive, the DDoS attacks[4] did not create any physical damage and did not rise to the level of actual cyberwarfare (Cyber Law Toolkit, n.d.). The Estonian government evaluated the risks it faced as a small country highly reliant on digital services and determined that its threat model should include the shutdown of its data centers because of extensive denial-of-service attacks or a military invasion that crossed its borders (Meyer, 2022). Embassy resources are under Estonian state control, secured against cyberattacks or crisis situations with KSI Blockchain[5] technology, and are capable

include electronic ones.

[3] Article 22 (1) of the VCDR of 1961 states that the premises of the mission shall be inviolable. The agents of the receiving State may not enter them, except with the consent of the head of the mission. Inviolability of diplomatic premises also extends to computers, printers, and other digital facilities located on the mission premises.

[4] Distributed denial-of-service (DDoS) attack is a malicious attempt to disrupt the normal traffic of a targeted server, service, or network by overwhelming the target or its surrounding infrastructure with a flood of Internet traffic.

[5] KSI is a blockchain technology designed in Estonia and used globally to ensure networks, systems, and data are free of compromise, all while retaining 100% data privacy. A blockchain is a distributed public ledger, a database with a set of pre-defined rules for how the ledger is appended

of not only providing data backups, but also operating the most critical services. When we say "data embassy," we mean a data center. It is located in Luxembourg under a Tier 4 level of security,[6] the highest level for data facilities. It is not an embassy in the traditional diplomatic sense and while the founding agreement does take into account the VCDR, it is something completely new under international law. It is fully under the control of Estonia, but has the same rights as physical embassies such as immunity. Luxembourg is the first data embassy location because of the high quality technical capacity, but also because of their openness to work with this new concept. In this collaboration, Luxembourg and Estonia are pathfinders in creating a unique and innovative way to ensure digital continuity in the world. The data embassy kick-off took place in 2015 and the finalized agreement between Estonia and Luxembourg was signed in 2017 (e-Estonia, n.d.). The data embassy solution has drawn a new page in International law, and the idea also supports the free movement of data within the European Union (EU). Additionally, data embassy enables to test and implement new technological solutions for cyber security.

The state will come up to the level with its digital society where digital continuity is vital. In order to secure it from cyber and other threats, physical storage of data out of the country is viable option, particularly for a small state. The most crucial element for data embassy project is the trust between partners. The state hosting the data embassy has to be trustworthy, the trust needs to lie in between the technicians and lawyers. However, this project also has its legal challenges, mainly related to how to guarantee the confidentiality and security of critical data that is in the jurisdiction of another state. Therefore, to overcome this challenge, a bilateral agreement must be signed between the governments of the sending state and hosting state, which would determine the immunity for the data embassy. Then, there are also some technological challenges related to how to protect the integrity and confidentiality of critical data outside the sending country, redesigning information systems to work reliably in a globally distributed environment, etc., which they need new technological solutions. However, the data embassy solution should be considered by every government, especially if the country is a digitally advanced society and a small state. Solution is needed to ensure the state continuity and functionality, despite situations or emergencies which may hit local data centers. In fact, some governments are already also planning to establish their network of data embassies abroad (Observatory of Public Sector Innovation, 2017).

---

by the distributed consensus of the participants in the system. Due to its widely witnessed property, blockchain technology makes it also impossible to change the data already on the blockchain.

[6]Tier IV data center security marks the highest standard for data centers, usually used by large businesses, government organizations, and global enterprises that require constant availability. They have an uptime of 99.995%, meaning annual downtime of no more than 26.3 min/year.

Digital Diplomacy of the European Union

Based on the diplomatic point of view, the EU is a sui generis entity. On the one hand, it represents a political union of 27 states, with governing bodies, legislative bodies, as well as a foreign service that promotes its interests around the world. However, on the other hand, each EU member state has its government, legislative bodies, MFA, and embassies that promote its interests around the world. The political and economic importance of the EU, as well as its active role in world diplomacy, is undeniable. The EU is represented by 140 delegations and offices around the world, which for more than five decades have acted as the eyes and ears of the EU to the authorities and populations of the host countries (European Commission, n.d.-a). EU member states, institutions, agencies, and diplomatic missions have adopted digital diplomacy, constantly engaging on their websites and with their followers on social media in providing answers to questions and criticisms, as well as providing information on a multitude of issues, in order to achieve the main potential of digital diplomacy, building relations between nations and foreign publics. The digital diplomacy of the EU aims to ensure the impact of its global role in the digital world, protect its strategic interests, and promote its dynamic, human-centered regulatory framework for a comprehensive digital transformation.

In addition to the EU as a whole, its institutions also have specific websites, in which they show the specifics of their activities (Table 1).

Regarding social media such as Twitter, Facebook, Instagram, YouTube, and LinkedIn, the EU institutions have institutional and personal accounts. Twitter is the most used social network by leaders and diplomats of all EU member states, institutions, agencies, and diplomatic missions, while Facebook and Instagram are the main platforms for them. Although mainly composed of text, the posts on the institutional and personal accounts of the EU bodies on Twitter are also characterized by the attachment of an image or video, but also by links to websites whose images are automatically displayed in the tweet. Tweets with videos tend to garner the most interactions, followed by those with images and finally those with website links, as well as textual ones. On Facebook, posts with images include the largest number of all posts and generate the most interactions compared to other posts. After them are the posts with links to websites. But, Facebook videos represent a significant number of total interactions, and live videos result in the most likes, comments, and

Table 1 Official websites of the EU and its bodies

Institutions	Websites
European Union	https://european-union.europa.eu/index_en
European Commission	https://ec.europa.eu/info/index_en
European Parliament	https://www.europarl.europa.eu/portal/en
Council of the European Union	https://www.consilium.europa.eu/en/european-council/
The European Union's Common Foreign and Security Policy	https://eeas.europa.eu/headquarters/headquarters-homepage_en

shares. EU leaders use Facebook videos also to communicate directly with their audiences (Hamulák, 2018). Instagram is dedicated to visual communication and is mainly related to artistic images and videos, enabling followers to like and comment on such posts. The presence of EU bodies and leaders on Instagram was closely related to their goals for increasing influence and penetration among different audiences. Their Instagram videos tend to get the most interactions. Then, with the introduction of Instagram live video, the number of video posts has increased. In recent years, EU bodies have started using Instagram Stories, where users can add an unlimited number of images and videos that disappear after 24 h. Their posts on Instagram Stories are characterized by careful writing, relevant hashtags, locations, as well as tagging other users in these posts. Also, the use of YouTube by EU bodies should not be overlooked, where through their channels they broadcast speeches directly and show footage of their activities. While EU bodies and leaders are very active on Twitter, Facebook, Instagram, and YouTube, they do not stand out for much activity on LinkedIn and have been closed on TikTok. In recent years, there has been a ban on the use of TikTok in some countries around the world. This platform has been banned by government facilities in Canada, the USA, the UK, and a growing list of European countries. But, the usage of this social network has also been banned in EU institutions. On February 23, 2023, the European Commission has banned TikTok from official devices due to concerns about cyber security, namely the way user data is handled by this social network (Fung & Ziady, 2023). Shortly after the European Commission, the European Parliament also banned the use of TikTok. Given cyber security concerns, especially regarding data protection and data collection by third parties, the European Parliament in harmony with other EU institutions has decided to suspend the use of TikTok on devices corporations starting on March 20, 2023 (Xu et al., 2023) (Tables 2 and 3).

The EU promotes cooperation with the tech industry in key strategic areas and this is done in the framework of industrial dialogue on digital such as the trade and technology councils, digital partnerships, dialogues and alliances, as well as within key standardization bodies. The EU is working to ensure global tech giants operate

Table 2 Ranking of EU institutional and personal accounts on Twitter, Facebook, and Instagram by number of followers

Twitter	Facebook	Instagram
@EU_Commission	European Parliament	@europeancommission
@vonderleyen	President of the European Parliament	@ursulavonderleyen
@Europarl_EN	European Commission	@euparliament
@EP_President	/	@ep_president
@EUCouncil	Council of the European Union	@eucouncil
@eucopresident	Charles MICHEL	@charlesmichel
@eu_eeas	European External Action Service—EEAS	@eudiplomacy
@JosepBorrellF	/	/

Note: Data are from Twitter (n.d.-a–n.d.-h); Facebook (n.d.-a–n.d.-f); Instagram (n.d.-a–n.d.-g)

Table 3 Ranking of EU institutional and personal accounts on YouTube, LinkedIn, and TikTok by number of followers

YouTube	LinkedIn	TikTok
@EuropeanCommission	European Commission	/
/	Ursula von der Leyen	/
@europeanparliament	European Parliament	/
@RobertaMetsolapresidentep	Roberta Metsola	/
@eucouncil	Council of the European Union	/
@europeancouncilpresident	Charles Michel	/
@EUExternalAction	European External Action Service	/
/	/	/

Note: Data are from YouTube (n.d.-a–n.d.-f); LinkedIn (n.d.-a–n.d.-g)

on a level playing field and meet their responsibilities within and beyond the Union, and to better integrate new technologies in the overall EU security architecture. Since its opening on 1 September 2022, an EU office in San Francisco has managed to reinforce the Team Europe approach in EU's engagement with the Silicon Valley-based tech sector, by promoting EU digital narrative and EU-US regulatory alignment, while focusing on substantive technology issues of geostrategic importance such as Artificial Intelligence (AI), semiconductors, quantum, Metaverse (European External Action Service, n.d.-e).

Its joint contribution to the Global Digital Compact underlines the following priorities:

- The need to maintain an open, free, secure, and non-fragmented Internet;
- The need for the respect of human rights in the digital arena;
- Support for closing digital divides, especially on education and access to the Internet;
- The fight against information manipulation and interference, including online disinformation and hate speech;
- The need for regulation of AI, using a risk-based approach, which promotes innovation, and is based on the principles of transparency and accountability;
- The importance of protecting and promoting the digital commons;
- The need for trusted connectivity.

Because the Internet governance is at the heart of the global digital debates, the EU's objective is to safeguard and improve the current multistakeholder model of Internet governance, and avoid a fragmented Internet (European External Action Service, n.d.-b). Ensuring a human rights based approach to digital issues is a core element of the EU's digital agenda. The principles on which EU action will be based in the area of digital and human rights are included in the Declaration on European Digital Rights & Principles[7] and reflected in the Declaration for the Future of the

[7] The Declaration on Digital Rights and Principles presents the EU's commitment to a secure, safe, and sustainable digital transformation that puts people at the center, in line with EU core values

Internet.[8] The EU is actively engaging in the United Nations (UN) fora, including at the Human Rights Council, and through its bilateral diplomacy channels, such as Human Rights Dialogues, to call all States to combat internet shutdowns, arbitrary or indiscriminate digital surveillance and data privacy breaches and to protect human rights defenders online (European External Action Service, n.d.-h).

The European Commission and the EU High Representative have set out the Global Gateway, a new European strategy to boost smart, clean, and secure links in digital, energy, and transport sectors and to strengthen health, education, and research systems across the world (European External Action Service, n.d.-c). The EU is developing a comprehensive network of bilateral and regional partnerships. This includes digital partnerships with strategic partners, Global Gateway partnerships and alliances, as well as over 20 digital and cyber dialogues with partners from all over the world (European External Action Service, n.d.-a). The EU has built several bilateral digital partnerships as below:

- **The EU-US Trade and Technology Council (EU-US TTC)** has become the central pillar for transatlantic cooperation on international technology ecosystem based on shared democratic values;
- **The EU-India Trade and Technology Council** was launched to tackle key trade, technological and security challenges;
- **The EU-Japan Digital Partnership** is advancing cooperation on digital issues to foster economic growth, facilitate digital trade, and a human-centric digital transformation based on common values;
- **The EU-Republic of Korea Digital Partnership** promotes joint work on semiconductors, next generation mobile networks, quantum and high-performance computing, cybersecurity, artificial intelligence, platforms, data and skills;
- Under **the EU-Singapore Digital Partnership** both sides committed to joint work on critical areas such as semiconductors, trusted data flows and data innovation, digital trust, standards, digital trade facilitation, digital skills for workers, and the digital transformation of businesses and public services (European External Action Service, n.d.-d).

On the regional level, the EU has set up a number of initiatives to both promote regional cooperation among partners and increase the level of cooperation between the region and the EU. This includes the EU-LAC[9] Digital Alliance; the EU-ASEAN[10] Connectivity initiative; digital cooperation in the context of the Strategic Partnership with the Gulf; the Digital Agenda for Western Balkans; the Eastern Partnership's EU4DIGITAL; the New Agenda for the Mediterranean; the Joint Declaration by the EU and Indo-Pacific countries; the joint commitment to digital transformation in the

---

and fundamental rights.

[8] The Declaration for the Future of Internet is a call for a global partnership to support an open, free, interoperable, reliable, and secure Internet.

[9] Latin America and Caribbean.

[10] Association of Southeast Asian Nations.

EU-Africa Joint Vision for 2030 (European External Action Service, n.d.-f). The EU approach to the digital transition is firmly anchored in its commitment to multilateralism and the promotion of universal human rights and fundamental freedoms, the rule of law and democratic principles (Troitiño, 2023). The EU, with the full involvement of the member states, is developing tailored approaches to strengthen cooperation in and with the UN system, the G7, the G20, the Organization for Security and Co-operation in Europe (OSCE), the Organization for Economic Co-operation and Development (OECD), the World Trade Organization (WTO), the North Atlantic Treaty Organization (NATO), the Council of Europe and other multilateral fora, including multistakeholder organizations, and particularly in standardization bodies, in which coherent and harmonized European standards play an influential role (European External Action Service, n.d.-g).

Data embassies provide the capability for the EU to host data and service resources in a secure data center outside its physical territorial borders and operate those resources in times of crisis ranging from large-scale cyberattacks to military invasions. The principles maximize lawful and ethical secondary data processing of EU personal data. Data embassies do so by technically enforcing established EU data protection principles to satisfy additional requirements mandated by the Court of Justice of the European Union (CJEU). Data Embassy principles comprise: The General Data Protection Regulation (GDPR[11]) pseudonymization[12]; data minimization; unlinkable personal data; demonstrability; and responsibility (Feys, 2020). Here, it is very important to mention that the GDPR imposes restrictions on the transfer of personal data outside the EU to third countries or international organizations. Article 45 of the GDPR states: A transfer of personal data to a third country or an international organization may take place where the Commission has decided that the third country, a territory or one or more specified sectors within that third country, or the international organization in question ensures an adequate level of protection (General Data Protection Regulation, n.d.). When assessing the adequacy of the level of protection, the European Commission considers things like rule of law, respect for human rights and fundamental freedoms, existence of and effective functioning of an independent supervisory authority in the third country and the international commitments the third country or international organization has entered into (Outeda et al., 2020). In order to be more precise, in order to ensure that the level of protection in a third country or international organization is equivalent to the one guaranteed by the EU legislation, these factors should be taken into account:

[11] The General Data Protection Regulation (GDPR) is the toughest privacy and security law in the world. Though it was drafted and passed by the EU, it imposes obligations onto organizations anywhere, so long as they target or collect data related to people in the EU. The regulation was put into effect on May 25, 2018.

[12] It is critical to note that under the GDPR, pseudonymisation is defined as an outcome and not a technique. Before the GDPR, pseudonymisation was widely understood to mean replacing direct identifiers with tokens and was applied to individual fields within a data set. To achieve GDPR-compliant pseudonymisation, must protect not only direct identifiers but also indirect identifiers.

- Contenumnt principles:
  1) Concepts—basic data protection concepts and principles should exist;
  2) Grounds for lawful and fair data processing—personal data has to be processed in a lawful, fair, and legitimate manner;
  3) Purpose limitation principle—personal data is processed for a specific purpose;
  4) Data quality and proportionality—personal data should be accurate and kept up to date;
  5) Security and confidentiality principle—data is processed in such a way that ensures security of personal data;
  6) Transparency—each individual has to be informed about all the elements and stages of the processing, in a clear, easily accessible, concise, transparent, and intelligible form;
  7) Right of access, rectification, erasure, and objection;
  8) Data retention—data should be kept no longer than it is necessary;
  9) Restriction on onward transfers.
- Mechanisms:
  1) Competent Independent Supervisory Authority—one or more independent supervisory authorities tasked with monitoring, ensuring, and enforcing compliance with data protection and privacy rules in the third country should exist and has to act in a complete independence;
  2) The data protection system should ensure a high degree of accountability and awareness among data controllers and data processors.
  3) Accountability—data controllers and/or those processing personal data should be obliged to comply with the data protection rules in the third country.
  4) Provision of support and help to individuals—they should be able to pursue legal remedies, thus supervision mechanisms, allowing independent investigation of complaints and punishment for violations of privacy have to be present (European Commission, n.d.-b).

When discussing the digital diplomacy of the EU, it should be noted that from 2021 the EU faces several challenges as a result of the UK's voluntary withdrawal from the EU, otherwise known as Brexit. The UK is characterized by an extremely efficient and very attractive digital diplomacy, which is why it ranks among the first countries in the world in terms of the successful implementation of this form of diplomacy. Until the finalization of Brexit, the UK with its institutional and personal accounts topped the list of EU member states. Politicians, diplomats, institutions, and diplomatic missions of the UK with their maximum use and engagement in social media manage to penetrate every corner of the world, attracting audiences even outside the European continent, therefore, it is not by chance that their accounts in various social media are characterized by an extraordinary following. EU digital diplomacy without the UK as a member country has difficulty extending beyond the borders of Europe, and risks being insufficiently powerful in attracting audiences across the globe.

Conclusions

The more digital technologies advance and the use of the Internet and social media increases, the more the role and importance of digital diplomacy increases. With the outbreak of the coronavirus in 2020, what was never thought of happened, the triumph of digital diplomacy against traditional diplomatic practices. Therefore, although a form of public diplomacy and based on ICT, Internet, and social media, digital diplomacy is much more than those. Facilitation and speed of communication with targeted audiences is one of its main benefits of digital diplomacy, but cyber threats are its main risks. As a way of preventing damage caused by cyber threats is data embassy. The latter entails a set of servers in a host country that stores data directly belonging to and under the jurisdiction of another country. Every time this project is talked about, the agreement reached between two EU member states in 2017 is immediately appeared, Estonia and Luxembourg. Estonia is the first country in the world to establish a data embassy. The latter is a solution in a situation where a cyber-attack, natural disaster, or even war would compromise the functioning of a state, especially for countries that have a less advanced digital infrastructure. But, as a result of the lack of international legal precedent, data embassies have so far been created only by bilateral agreements. The goal of EU digital diplomacy is to secure the EU global role in the digital world, to protect its strategic interests and to promote its dynamic, human-centric regulatory framework for an inclusive digital transformation. In the field of digitalization, the EU has reached many bilateral and multilateral agreements. The websites of the EU bodies, as well as the institutional and personal accounts of the EU, are quite active in terms of audience targeting. The EU takes into consideration data embassy as one of the main benefits of digital diplomacy. The latter provides security for the EU in situations where the operation of hosted data and service resources inside physical territorial boundaries is diminished, denied, or destroyed. However, this sensitive data security issue in a third country or an international organization is realized when the European Commission is convinced that the third country, a territory or one or more specified sectors within that third country, or international organization, ensures an adequate level of their protection.

References

Barston, P. R. (2014). *Modern diplomacy* (4th ed.). Routledge.
Basu, A. (2023, July 20). How data embassies can promote data security for all. Datasphere Initiative Network. https://www.thedatasphere.org/news/how-data-embassies-promote-data-security-for-all/.
Bjola, C., & Kornprobst, M. (2015). *Understanding international diplomacy*. Routledge.
Cyber Law Toolkit. (n.d.). *Cyber attacks against Estonia (2007)*. Retrieved October 10, 2023, from https://cyberlaw.ccdcoe.org/wiki/Cyber_attacks_against_Estonia_(2007).
E-Estonia. (n.d.). e-Governance: Data Embassy. Retrieved October 10, 2023, https://e-estonia.com/solutions/e-governance/data-embassy/.
European Commission. (n.d.-a). *EU delegations*. Retrieved October 10, 2023, from https://neighbourhood-enlargement.ec.europa.eu/eu-delegations_en#:~:text=The%20EU%20is%20represented%20through,population%20in%20their%20host%20countries.
European Commission. (n.d.-b). *Data transfers to third countries*. Retrieved October 10, 2023, from https://ec.europa.eu/programmes/erasmus-plus/project-result-content/d103489e-1294-405c-8dc1-09239829d581/Module%207%20Transfers%20of%20personal%20data%20to%20third%20countries%20or%20international%20organisations.pdf.
European External Action Service. (n.d.-a). *Digital diplomacy: Bilateral engagement*. Retrieved October 10, 2023, from https://www.eeas.europa.eu/eeas/digital-diplomacy_en#55873.
European External Action Service. (n.d.-b). *Digital diplomacy: Building a reliable and human-centred future for the internet*. Retrieved October 10, 2023, from https://www.eeas.europa.eu/eeas/digital-diplomacy_en#55873.
European External Action Service. (n.d.-c). *Digital diplomacy: Building bilateral digital partnerships*. Retrieved October 10, 2023, from https://www.eeas.europa.eu/eeas/digital-diplomacy_en#55873.
European External Action Service. (n.d.-d). *Digital diplomacy: Contributing to the global digital compact*. Retrieved October 10, 2023, from https://www.eeas.europa.eu/eeas/digital-diplomacy_en#55873.
European External Action Service. (n.d.-e). *Digital diplomacy: Cooperation with tech sector*. Retrieved October 10, 2023, from https://www.eeas.europa.eu/eeas/digital-diplomacy_en#55873.
European External Action Service. (n.d.-f). *Digital Diplomacy: Enhancing Regional Cooperation*. Retrieved October 10, 2023, from https://www.eeas.europa.eu/eeas/digital-diplomacy_en#55873.
European External Action Service. (n.d.-g). *Digital diplomacy: Multilateral engagement*. Retrieved October 10, 2023, from https://www.eeas.europa.eu/eeas/digital-diplomacy_en#55873.
European External Action Service. (n.d.-h). *Digital diplomacy: Promoting the importance of human rights online*. Retrieved October 10, 2023, from https://www.eeas.europa.eu/eeas/digital-diplomacy_en#55873.
Facebook. (n.d.-a). *Charles Michel account*. Retrieved October 10, 2023, from https://www.facebook.com/CharlesMichel.
Facebook. (n.d.-b). *Council of the European Union account*. Retrieved October 10, 2023, from https://www.facebook.com/eucouncil/.
Facebook. (n.d.-c). *European Commission account*. Retrieved October 10, 2023, from https://www.facebook.com/EuropeanCommission.
Facebook. (n.d.-d). *European External Action Service account*. Retrieved October 10, 2023, from https://www.facebook.com/EuropeanExternalActionService.
Facebook. (n.d.-e). *European Parliament account*. Retrieved October 10, 2023, from https://www.facebook.com/europeanparliament.
Facebook. (n.d.-f). *Roberta Metsola account*. Retrieved October 10, 2023, from https://www.facebook.com/roberta.metsola.

Feys, M. (2020, July 26). EU data protection and data embassy principles. *LinkedIn*. https://www.linkedin.com/pulse/eu-data-protection-embassy-principles-magali-feys.

Fung, B. & Ziady, H. (2023, February 23). European Commission bans TikTok from official devices. *CNN Business*. https://edition.cnn.com/2023/02/23/tech/tiktok-ban-european-commission/index.html.

General Data Protection Regulation. (n.d.). *Transfers on the basis of an adequacy decision*. Retrieved October 10, 2023, from https://gdpr-info.eu/art-45-gdpr/#:~:text=A%20transfer%20of%20personal%20data,an%20adequate%20level%20of%20protection.

Hamulák, O. (2018). La carta de los derechos fundamentales de la union europea y los derechos sociales. *Estudios constitucionales, 16*(1), 167–186.

Instagram. (n.d.-a). *Charles Michel account*. Retrieved October 10, 2023, from https://www.instagram.com/charlesmichel/?hl=en.

Instagram. (n.d.-b). *Council of the European Union account*. Retrieved October 10, 2023, from https://www.instagram.com/eucouncil/.

Instagram. (n.d.-c). *European Commission account*. Retrieved October 10, 2023, from https://www.instagram.com/europeancommission/.

Instagram. (n.d.-d). *European External Action Service account*. Retrieved October 10, 2023, from https://www.instagram.com/eudiplomacy/.

Instagram. (n.d.-e). *European Parliament account*. Retrieved October 10, 2023, from https://www.instagram.com/europeanparliament/.

Instagram. (n.d.-f). *Roberta Metsola account*. Retrieved October 10, 2023, from https://www.instagram.com/roberta.metsola/.

Instagram. (n.d.-g). *Ursula von der Leyen account*. Retrieved October 10, 2023, from https://www.instagram.com/ursulavonderleyen/.

Kurbalija, J. (2015, April 17). Different prefixes, same meaning: cyber, digital, net, online, virtual, e-. Diplo Blog. https://www.diplomacy.edu/blog/different-prefixes-same-meaning-cyber-digital-net-online-virtual-e/.

Kurbalija, J. (2022, September 7). Diplomatic privileges and immunities in the internet era. *Diplo Blog*. https://www.diplomacy.edu/blog/diplomatic-privileges-and-immunities-internet-era/.

LinkedIn. (n.d.-a). *Charles Michel account*. Retrieved October 10, 2023, from https://be.linkedin.com/in/charles-michel-eu.

LinkedIn. (n.d.-b). *Council of the European Union account*. Retrieved October 10, 2023, from https://be.linkedin.com/company/eucouncil.

LinkedIn. (n.d.-c). *European Commission account*. Retrieved October 10, 2023, from https://be.linkedin.com/company/european-commission?trk=similar-pages.

LinkedIn. (n.d.-d). *European External Action Service account*. Retrieved October 10, 2023, from https://be.linkedin.com/company/european-external-action-service.

LinkedIn. (n.d.-e). *European Parliament account*. Retrieved October 10, 2023, from https://be.linkedin.com/company/european-parliament?trk=similar-pages.

LinkedIn. (n.d.-f). *Roberta Metsola account*. Retrieved October 10, 2023, from https://mt.linkedin.com/in/robertametsolapresidentep?trk=public_profile_browsemap-profile.

LinkedIn. (n.d.-g). *Ursula von der Leyen account*. Retrieved October 10, 2023, from https://be.linkedin.com/in/ursula-von-der-leyen?trk=public_profile_browsemap-profile.

Meyer, T. (2022, November 12). How data embassies can strengthen resiliency with sovereignty. *Google Cloud*. https://cloud.google.com/blog/products/identity-security/data-embassies-strengthening-resiliency-with-sovereignty.

Observatory of Public Sector Innovation. (2017, February 7). *Establishing the first Data Embassy in the world*. https://oecd-opsi.org/innovations/establishing-the-first-data-embassy-in-the-world/.

Outeda, C. C., González, P. L., & Troitiño, D. R. (2020). EU enlargement policy towards the Western Balkans: State actors, interests and strategies. *European Studies, 7*(1), 296–324.

Ramiro Troitiño, D. (2022). De Gaulle: The role of the member states in the European Union. In D. R. Troitiño, R. M. de la Guardia, & G. A. Pérez Sánchez (Eds.), *The European Union and its political leaders: Understanding the integration process* (pp. 195–206). Springer.

Rashica, V. (2019a). The benefits and risks of digital diplomacy. *SEEU Review, 13*(1), 77. https://sciendo.com/article/10.2478/seeur-2018-0008

Rashica, V. (2019b). Digital diplomacy: aspects, approaches and practical use. *International Scientific Journal on European Perspectives, 10* (1 (17)), 23. https://www.europeanperspectives.org/storage/24/DIGITAL-DIPLOMACY_Rashica.pdf.

Rashica, V. (2023). Is digital diplomacy triumphing over political diplomacy?. *International Scientific Journal on European Perspectives, 13*(2 (24)), 59. https://www.europeanperspectives.org/storage/197/EPs04-Oct22-Digital-Diplomacy-Rashica.pdf.

Troitiño, D. R. (2023). *Digital development of the European Union: An interdisciplinary perspective*. Springer.

Twiplomacy. (2017, May 31). Twiplomacy Study 2017. https://www.twiplomacy.com/twiplomacy-study-2017.

Twitter. (n.d.-a). *Charles Michel account*. Retrieved October 10, 2023, from https://twitter.com/eucopresident.

Twitter. (n.d.-b). *Council of the European Union account*. Retrieved October 10, 2023, from https://twitter.com/EUCouncil.

Twitter. (n.d.-c). *European Commission account*. Retrieved October 10, 2023, from https://twitter.com/EU_Commission?ref_src=twsrc%5Egoogle%7Ctwcamp%5Eserp%7Ctwgr%5Eauthor.

Twitter. (n.d.-d). *European External Action Service account*. Retrieved October 10, 2023, from https://twitter.com/eu_eeas?ref_src=twsrc%5Egoogle%7Ctwcamp%5Eserp%7Ctwgr%5Eauthor.

Twitter. (n.d.-e). *European Parliament account*. Retrieved October 10, 2023, from https://twitter.com/Europarl_EN.

Twitter. (n.d.-f). *Josep Borrell account*. Retrieved October 10, 2023, from https://twitter.com/JosepBorrellF.

Twitter. (n.d.-g). *Roberta Metsola account*. Retrieved October 10, 2023, from https://twitter.com/EP_President.

Twitter. (n.d.-h). *Ursula von der Leyen account*. Retrieved October 10, 2023, from https://twitter.com/vonderleyen.

United Nations. (1961, April 18). *Vienna Convention on Diplomatic Relations, 1961*. https://legal.un.org/ilc/texts/instruments/english/conventions/9_1_1961.pdf.

Xu, F., Brennan, E., & Frater, J. (2023, March 1). EU bans TikTok from official devices across all three government institutions. *CNN Business*. https://edition.cnn.com/2023/02/28/tech/tiktok-eu-ban-intl-hnk/index.html.

YouTube. (n.d.-a). *Charles Michel channel*. Retrieved October 10, 2023, from https://www.youtube.com/@europeancouncilpresident.

YouTube. (n.d.-b). *Council of the European Union channel*. Retrieved October 10, 2023, from https://www.youtube.com/@eucouncil.

YouTube. (n.d.-c). *European Commission channel*. Retrieved October 10, 2023, from https://www.youtube.com/@EuropeanCommission.

YouTube. (n.d.-d). *European External Action Service channel*. Retrieved October 10, 2023, from https://www.youtube.com/@EUExternalAction.

YouTube. (n.d.-e). *European Parliament channel*. Retrieved October 10, 2023, from https://www.youtube.com/@europeanparliament.

YouTube. (n.d.-f). *Roberta Metsola channel*. Retrieved October 10, 2023, from https://www.youtube.com/@RobertaMetsolapresidentep.

E-Democracy in the EU

Mateja Rek

Abstract Digital tools can offer citizens many advantages in their participation in political debates and decision-making processes in the EU. If applied wisely, they can contribute significantly to a more open, accessible, transparent and efficient system of policymaking at all levels of EU multilevel governance. In this way, digitalization can also help to reduce the democratic deficit in the EU. This chapter discusses the opportunities and benefits that digital tools can provide for democracy in the EU, focusing on formal processes of political participation as well as on more informal ways of civic engagement. It is argued that e-participation tools should be developed in a way to facilitate clear and efficient interaction between stakeholders in EU political processes. Such interaction would benefit from an ongoing two-way communication between citizens and policy makers fostering information sharing, mutual understanding, trust and motivation to participate.

Some problematic aspects and future possibilities of implementing e-participation in the EU are assessed. It is concluded that e-participation efforts must be accompanied by an effective mobilization and engagement strategy, building a culture of citizens participation and addressing digital divide, to leave no one behind.

An Introduction to the Field

Since the EU has been developing into the direction of a more integrated form of political entity, the issue of democracy and EUs' connection to its citizens has become increasingly relevant. Rapid innovations in ICT and their ever-increasing use in various areas of people's lives bring many opportunities, but also challenges, in building new communication paths and relationships between citizens and policy decision-makers. The EU has recognized the potential that digital tools have for

M. Rek (✉)
School of Advanced Social Studies, Nova Gorica, Slovenia
e-mail: mateja.rek@fuds.si

D. Ramiro Troitiño (ed.), *E-Governance in the European Union*, Contributions to Political Science, https://doi.org/10.1007/978-3-031-56045-3_8

bridging the gap between EU citizens and decision-makers at different levels of the EU's system of subsidiary decision-making. It has even named this decade a Digital decade and created a very ambitious plan to achieve Europe's digital transformation by 2030. Basic digital skills for all citizens are highlighted as a prerequisite to participate actively in the Digital Decade. By 2030, the EU's objective is to ensure that democratic life, secure e-voting and public services online will be fully accessible for everyone, including persons with disabilities, benefiting from the high-quality digital environment providing easy-to-use, efficient and personalized services and tools with high security and privacy standards (Troitiño, 2022). Such digital transformations can facilitate civic engagement and allow citizens to influence the direction and outcomes of decision-makers activities more efficiently and improve public services. E-governance can change the essence of the Union as it can allow a more efficient organization, closer to its citizens and has immense potential to deepen the integration bridging various national obstacles in EUs' interconnectedness.

Why would EU institutions want to increase the role of citizens and civic organizations that citizens form in decision-making processes? To answer this question, we need to remember the context in which the EU finds itself. The integrationist agenda pursued by European elites throughout the post-war period amounted to a multi-faceted constitutionalizing project which has been increasingly characterized by an overarching problem of political legitimacy. One can trace the impact of the emerging legitimacy discourse in several areas. In recent years, the debate on the involvement of citizens and civil society organizations largely has been oriented by this debate.

Engagement of citizens and civil society organizations and the networks they form across various levels of EUs' subsidiary system (local, national, EU level) are often perceived and cited as crucial factors that will drastically contribute to overcoming many deficits and crises that European Union is facing. Among them, there is a democratic deficit—a term that is well established both in scientific and political debates. It is related to the realization that EU institutions increasingly, through broadening of their policy scopes, directly influence the lives of the citizens of the EU, who are mainly not engaged in participation on the EU level and find it difficult for their voice to be heard on the level of the EU. Some argue that this might be related to the crisis of European identity, which again could be influenced by civic actors as it is envisaged that they could foster the creation and development of European unification through its activities in "European public space". There is also a crisis of the welfare state that civic organizations could, both as a service provider and as carriers of self-initiated action on the grassroots level, help to overcome or at least help with finding and applying the alternative approaches with win-win results for all included. Prompted in part by growing doubts about the capacity of the state to cope with its own welfare, developmental and environmental problems, analysts across the political spectrum have come to see civic organizations as strategic components of a middle way between policies that put primacy on "the market" and those that advocate greater reliance on the state (Makarovič & Rek, 2017).

Let's not forget the positive contribution that civic engagement can bring to the multilevel character of the European constitution. European decision-making depends not only on European institutions but also on the national, regional and local level. Civic organizations, which should by definition be in touch with the grassroots of society and, on the other hand, have (as a part of their advocacy function) access to decision-making bodies, are often seen as ideal actors that could significantly contribute to the fulfilment of the principle of subsidiarity. This assumption played a key role in defining the ways, in which civic organizations, that are active at the EU level, access and can influence EU policy making (Rek, 2012).

The use of interactive tools of e-participation at the European level can contribute to fostering democratic legitimacy of the EU and promote a more sustainable EU citizenship. In the present chapter we reserve the term e-participation for all forms of political participation making use of digital media, including both formally institutionalized mechanisms and informal civic engagement (Aichholzer et al., 2018). The drivers behind e-participation are digitalization, the development of digital tools that can be used for citizen involvement—social media, deliberative software, e-voting systems, etc. and the growing access to the internet.

"Digital tools could create stronger connections between European citizens and the EU decision-making process and, by doing so, might contribute to reducing the EU democratic deficit" (Aichholzer et al., 2018, p. 8). Despite the many benefits that wisely introducing digital forms of communication in policy consultations brings for civic engagement in the EU, it makes sense to consider the weakness of e-participation and e-governance to avoid pitfalls, possible negative side effects, or excessive expectations.

State of the Art

The concept of e-democracy, referring to online public engagement in the policy decision-making process is closely linked to ideas of participatory democracy and deliberation (Habermas, 1984). The basic idea of democracy is the principle that ordinary citizens should at least somewhat know and understand the activities of the government, have freedom of their own opinion, deliberation as well as possibility to have a voice in policy-making processes. Advocates of participatory democracy emphasize the intrinsic value of political participation and its contribution to social integration of liberal societies. Scientists have long debated how civic participation can contribute to the quality of public life. When people forge social connections, it supports the development of social norms and trust that bring along beneficial effects on education, children's welfare, safety, health, happiness and the quality of government. In this framework of thinking, civic engagement is related to political participation in the conventional sense, but it also more broadly refers to people's social connections with the life of their communities (Martens & Hobbs, 2015; Putnam, 1995). In modern liberal democracies, however, political participation is primarily implemented in the form of parliamentary and representative democratic systems, in which formal participation of the demos is largely concentrated on casting votes in elections. It may be however assumed that the growing complexity of the society makes voting as the central power-based form of participation somewhat less relevant, while the relevance of influence-based political participation is increasing (Makarovič & Rek, 2014). As claimed by a variety of authors, the decline in voting turnouts as a classical form of participation is not a reason for pessimism about the future of political participation as new, different forms are emerging. The contributions, for instance, by Holford et al. (2003) imply that more individualized forms of political participation are emerging, which enable different kinds of participation that are less elite-directed and more shaped by individuals' values and political skills. At the same time the shifting relationships between national and transnational in the context of globalization and digitalization may generate interest associations at various levels of civic global action as a way of creating better opportunities for a broader active political participation (see, for instance, Castells, 2015; Held, 2006, 2013; Bertuzzi, 2020; Jeroense & Spierings, 2023; Fink-Hafner & Bauman, 2023). Compared to voting, such influence-based participation mostly does not seem to be decreasing though its forms may be changing. While new political and social movements differ from the classical associations, such as political parties and trade unions, in the fact that the former are based on a different nature of representative link (Morales and Giugni, 2016), i.e. replacing the representations of particular constituencies by universalistic claims (e.g. human rights, ecology), the old and the new seem either to replace or, even more, to complement each other (Makarovič & Rek, 2014).

Digital tools and online social media can foster existing but also facilitate new paths of political engagement. An elaborate conceptual and empirical analysis by Gibson and Cantijoch (2013) underlines this multidimensional nature of e-participation: "Offline types of political engagement are re-emerging online" (Gibson & Cantijoch, 2013, p. 714), tend to include more and more social media-based political activities (e.g., posting to political blogs) and also lead to novel forms of engagement such as combined offline and online participation (Aichholzer et al., 2018).

E-democracy, as the support and enhancement of democracy, democratic institutions and democratic processes by means of digital information and communication technologies, is above all about democracy. Its main objective is the electronic support of democracy (Hacker & van Dijk, 2000; Päivärinta & Sæbø, 2006; van Dijk, 2012). E-democracy represents a wide variety of uses of ICT in support of democratic communication and includes all levels and modes of involvement of the public (individual citizens, informal groups and formal civil society organizations).

Let's list a few examples of e-democracy initiatives in the European Union (EU). The European Citizens' Initiative (ECI) was introduced in 2012 to give citizens more direct influence on EU policies. Citizens can propose initiatives on a range of issues such as climate change, animal welfare and human rights through the online platform. When a proposed initiative receives one million signatures from citizens across the EU, the European Commission must examine it and decide whether to implement it. The European Parliament's online petition system allows citizens to create and sign petitions on a range of issues that fall within the European Parliament's remit. If a petition receives more than one million signatures, the

European Parliament must deal with it and discuss the issue. On the portal "Have your say" citizens can give feedback on proposed legislation and policy initiatives. The feedback is considered when the EU institutions are formulating their policies. System called "Your Europe Advice" is part of a set of information and advice tools for citizens and businesses about their EU rights. There is also a digital system for complaints to European Ombudsman's office enabling investigation of the complaint and making recommendations for remedial action. These are just a few examples of e-democracy initiatives in the EU. There are many more initiatives at the national and local levels in different EU countries.

The scope of e-democracy reaches from more passive involvement of citizens, such as social media or online monitoring for purposes of informing oneself about development in society to more active behaviour, such as involving citizens in policy consultation, debate and co-creating policy documents (Aichholzer et al., 2018; Lindner & Aichholzer, 2020). Especially social media have a high potential to change both the traditional patterns of information flows and their production and have significantly contributed to the expansion of online discursive spaces, because they enable undemanding, fast establishment and maintenance of online social relationships, groups and networks that can easily co-create content, exchange ideas, lead discussions, advocate and organize action (Hafner Fink & Oblak Črnič, 2014; Price, 2013). They provide spaces for opinion formation beyond and independent from established institutions. Dahlgren (2013) summarizes the often-mentioned positive aspects and hopes for social media as follows: an increase of communication between citizens, cost-effectiveness, room for creative participation, opinion formation, mobilization and the potential for placing a spotlight on political issues, e.g. through "going viral" and personal gains such as empowerment. A special emphasis is placed on the value of social media for alternative politics (Lindner & Aichholzer, 2020). However, new digital communication tools are not just used for political participation by active citizens. They are also heavily utilized as effective tools of campaigning and persuasion by established political actors, institutions and groups (Aichholzer et al., 2018).

In the past decade a large and growing body of literature was produced with variety of issues, possibilities, empirical research and evaluations of existing attempts to engage citizens in digital political participation. The numerous claims that have been made about effects of new ICT on democracy have been summarized as follows:

1. ICT increases the scale and speed of providing information. This helps create more informed citizens.
2. Political participation is made easier and certain obstacles like apathy, shyness, disabilities, time, etc. can be lessened.
3. Digital communication creates new ways of organizing with subject-specific groups for discussion.
4. Internet allows new political communications to arise free from state intervention.
5. A hierarchical political system becomes more horizontal by increasing digital political participation.

6. Citizens have more voice in creating agendas for government.
7. Communication between citizens and policy makers can be more direct and not depending on mediators such as journalists, representatives and parties.
8. Politics can respond more directly to citizens' concerns as ICT and digitally mediated communication enable a kind of political marketing research.
9. ICT helps resolve problems of representative democracy such as territorial bases of constituencies, etc. (Hacker & van Dijk, 2000, p. 4; Hennen et al., 2020).

One of the key benefits of e-democracy is that it makes it easier for citizens to engage in political processes and express their opinions, regardless of their location or social status. E-democracy can also help to increase civic engagement and strengthen democratic institutions by providing citizens with greater access to relevant information. However, there are also challenges associated with e-democracy, such as the digital divide and the risk of online manipulation and misinformation. It is important to address these challenges and ensure that e-democracy initiatives are designed in a way that promotes transparency, accountability, social justice and fairness.

Most Problematic Aspects and Future Possibilities of Implementing Digital Reforms in the EU

There are significant differences in ways of political participation across European national democracies. In post-communist countries, political participation is more stratified than in the West, despite relatively similar laws on participation. Even though diversity is one of their characteristics and the acceptance of these differences an important value of living together—when it comes to the values underlying political participation, active citizenship and democracy, the citizens of member states in Eastern and Sothern Europe still lag far behind in their ability to influence decision-making processes both in their own countries and at the EU level (Makarovič & Rek, 2014).

Another significant challenge is the digital divide, which refers to the unequal access to digital technologies and skills (Botrić & Božić, 2021; Cruz-Jesus et al., 2016; Elena-Bucea et al., 2021; Friemel, 2016; Liao et al., 2022; Szeles, 2018; van Dijk, 2008). While digital technologies can provide new opportunities for economic growth and social inclusion, some people and communities lack the necessary infrastructure and skills to fully participate in the digital society. Addressing the digital divide requires a comprehensive approach that includes investments in digital infrastructure, digital skills training and policies to ensure that the benefits of digital technologies are shared more equitably.

Digital technology has become such a big factor in contemporary society that the digital literacy of citizens became the key to successfully deal with a variety of social, economic and political circumstances. Especially during the Covid-19 pandemic, the role of digitalization has increased markedly, as the use of technology has become more utilized than ever before. People's habits and routines have changed, the use of technology has increased drastically, and digitalization processes have accelerated in practically all areas of our lives. That is one of the reasons why strategy for the digital empowerment of the citizens of the EU is so high among the priorities of the European Commission. In addition to access to digital infrastructure it has become quite necessary for EU citizens to constantly learn and gain new digital skills as well as effective and safe ways of using information and communication technologies both at work and in private life, as digital technologies and possibilities they offer are changing and evolving all the time. People that are lacking the ability to effectively use digital devices and their functions, search or articulate their search needs, access information, process various elements (for example, text and tables), create, store and exchange data and, in general, navigate between various digital contents, are at risk to be "left behind" and unable to access many social, economic, or political services and opportunities (Van Laar et al., 2020).

Another challenge is the issue of data protection and privacy (Florida, 2020; Hoofnagle et al., 2019). The EU has made significant progress in this area with the introduction of the General Data Protection Regulation (GDPR). Nevertheless, with digital advancements, there is a growing need to regulate and protect individuals' data from unauthorized access and misuse. The EU has also taken steps to address the challenges of cybersecurity by adopting the EU Cybersecurity Act and creating the European Cybersecurity Competence Centre, but more needs to be done to ensure that the EU is prepared to address emerging threats.

A serious threat that has been gaining a lot of attention recently is an increased radicalization and mobilization potential of the internet (Hassan et al., 2018) as social media radically changed the way we communicate, get informed and form our opinions. Polarization and radicalization in societies can be reinforced by echo chambers. Cinelli et al. (2021) broadly define echo chambers as environments in which the opinion, political leaning, or belief of users about a topic gets reinforced due to repeated interactions with peers or sources having similar tendencies and attitudes. People favour information adhering to their beliefs and join groups formed around a shared narrative, that is, echo chambers. Echo chambers inadvertently fuel the promotion of homophile sorting, where individuals gravitate towards like-minded communities, potentially hindering diverse perspectives and dialogue. Such outcomes can be strengthened by a so-called "filter bubble", created by search algorithms that select results based on information on prior search behaviour and exclude results that disagree with the user's preferences and viewpoints. Online communities are constituted by the reproduction of bonding social capital, emotional bonds, in-group and out-group differentiations and shared behaviours, norms and values (Ross et al., 2022; Samuel-Arzan & Hayat, 2019). As the observed communication patterns focus on the reproduction of shared life views and moral beliefs, online communities tend to become homogeneous, lacking empathy for different minded individuals and groups. An additional issue is that online political debate poorly relies on facts and rational, considerate deliberation. Rather than engaging in such debate, jointly working out policy options to be forwarded to policymakers, sensationalist and emotional commenting on statements by policy makers is popular.

Such political debates can be strongly opinion-biased, have a weak presentation of facts, and often advocate radical positions. The wide range of ways in which information can be accessed via the internet and social media in particular has encouraged content providers to increasingly target information to different, politically narrow audiences, increasing the likelihood of fake news, disinformation and misinformation being spread.

Fake news, disinformation, or misinformation are not a new phenomenon. An insight into the history of propaganda (see, e.g., Barclay, 2018) and the psychology of lying (see, e.g., DePaulo, 2018) show the issue of power over the flow of information and control over the content of news, as well as deliberate manipulation, censorship and lying, while considered unethical and harmful, are nevertheless an integral part of mass communication processes. With the advent of digital media, it is becoming increasingly difficult to deal with the problem of disinformation, whether planned, manipulative or even unplanned. Especially concerning is unplanned disinformation arising from ignorance or a firm, even fundamentalist belief in certain interpretative frameworks of reality. The lack of accountability, quality accuracy assurance tools for messages disseminated via social media, blogs, sharing networks, social news, etc. leads to a manipulative use of communication infrastructures that are used to produce, disseminate and amplify disinformation on a larger scale than before, often in new ways that are not yet sufficiently grasped and understood (de Cock Buning, 2018). The most common ways to counter the spread and harmful effects of fake news and other forms of disinformation are initiatives that help to increase citizens' resilience and empower the various actors involved. Examples include initiatives to identify and document sources of disinformation, policies aimed at ensuring and enabling good quality news media and professional journalism, and investments in media and information literacy that would strengthen people's resilience. This places new demands on the literacy skills that people need to master to participate in modern communication streams. In addition to basic literacy, media literacy, which refers to the skills, knowledge and understanding that enable users of media services and products to use media effectively and safely, has become indispensable. It is the ability of individuals to use the flow, content, values and consequences of using different media messages, while interpreting them independently and critically, and participating in the creation of media messages themselves (Buckingham, 2020; Martens & Hobbs, 2015).

Fighting disinformation is a crucial issue for the EU as it can undermine democratic values, affect public trust and have serious consequences for social or political stability. It is a complex issue that requires a multi-faceted approach and the EU does play an important role in coordinating efforts to combat disinformation and promote media literacy, transparency and cooperation in Europe. EU also facilitates other digital reforms that have the potential to bring many benefits to the EU, including increased efficiency, improved public services and economic growth. The EU is investing in digital infrastructure, such as high-speed broadband networks, to improve access to digital technologies. Initiatives to support digital education to improve the digital skills of its workforce and also broader digital media literacy of its citizens could help close the skills gap and reduce the digital divide. EU is well aware of the importance of supporting digital civic engagement skills and supports a range of initiatives enabling individuals to access and engage with relevant information, network with others, engage in deliberation as well and advocate responsibly and efficiently.

Conclusions on the Impact of Digital Reforms on EU Development

Digital citizenship engagement, the use of digital technologies and platforms, can encourage citizens to connect and participate in policy decision-making processes across the subsidiary systems in the EU. They can initiate or be engaged in online consultations, social media campaigns, digital petitions and other forms of online participation that allow citizens to voice their opinions and contribute to decision-making processes. Communication using digital tools does foster transparency and accountability of policy-making processes and offer citizens more easily accessible virtual public space for their ideas, needs, opinions, feedback, complaints or disagreements, outrage and protest. Digital tools can be used to gather feedback and input from citizens on a wide range of issues, from public policy and budget priorities to municipal development and infrastructure projects.

Overall, digital citizen participation has the potential to revolutionize the way citizens interact with government and participate in the democratic process by making it more accessible, transparent and responsive to citizens' needs and interests. They are however a new form of communication that changes very quickly due to the very rapid development of diverse digital communication techniques and the many opportunities they offer. The introduction of novelties and innovations in communication and citizen engagement can be challenging for several reasons. People are often resistant to change, especially if they are used to doing things a certain way. Introducing a novelty means that they have to change their habits, and this can be difficult. When something is new, there is often a lot of uncertainty about how it will work and what the results will be. This uncertainty can make people reluctant to adopt novelty, as novelties often require resources such as time, money, open mind, new skills and expertise. If these resources are limited, it can be difficult to introduce the novelty successfully. Despite these challenges, introducing new tools to facilitate democratic efforts can also be exciting and rewarding.

Since its introduction, the digital tools used for bringing the citizens closer to policy making are being monitored and evaluated to determine their value, effectiveness, quality and ability to deliver on high expectations but also to observe shortcomings. Evaluations help to identify areas for improvement and make necessary changes to improve quality and can provide valuable information that can help make informed decisions about future planning and program design.

As far as the potential to contribute to more inclusive policymaking and bridge the gap between citizens and the EU institutions, current forms of e-participation have some shortcomings. To increase their transparency the participatory process and the contribution of its outputs to the overall decision-making process must be clear to participants from the start (Hamulák, 2018). Information on the criteria for weighting contributions and deciding whether to take them into account should be made clearer and more interesting and accessible to a broader, general public. A very large share of political participation, especially on the EU level, includes mainly experts, epistemic communities, professionals from civic organizations and interest groups. Such civic political engagement has a very professional character that does not allow for the people to take on a Europeanising function in the sense of active European citizenship (Dieker & Galan, 2014; Kohler-Koch et al., 2017; Kohler-Koch & Friedrich, 2020; Schoenefeld, 2021). It can even lead to undemocratic forms of monopoly or oligopoly, where a minority of "very interested and active knowledgeable citizens" can influence the decision-making process on behalf of the passive majority of citizens.

The EU is a diverse socio-economical and multicultural and as already noted the behaviour and values attributed to both political participation and digital literacy vary significantly between regions. The citizens of Central-East Europe and some Southern countries still lag far behind in their motivation and ability to influence decision-making processes both in their own countries and at the EU level. Europeanization in a sense of simply copying and applying mechanisms and good practices that exist in some member states (such as the Scandinavian or Central European states) does not necessarily bring progress in others. Therefore, when thinking about new mechanisms and institutions of e-participatory democracy, one should also look realistically at the cultural traits as well as political and economic context of the society to which these mechanisms are applied.

E-participation must be accompanied by an effective mobilization and engagement strategy, involving communication instruments tailored for different target groups. While the EU has made efforts to promote diversity in political participation and has taken measures to narrow the digital divide, there are still challenges. For example, women, people with disabilities, ethnic minorities and young people are underrepresented in the EU's decision-making processes (Armingeon & Schädel, 2015; Filetti & Janmaat, 2018; Hoskins & Janmaat, 2019; Stockemer & Sundström, 2019). Women, who make up more than half of the EU population, are still underrepresented in many political institutions, including the European Parliament and the European Commission. Efforts have been made to address this through measures such as quotas and gender mainstreaming, but progress has been slow compared to the speed of digital transformations. People with disabilities also face barriers to political participation, such as inaccessible polling stations, lack of political representation and discrimination. The EU has introduced legislation such as the European Accessibility Act to promote the rights of persons with disabilities and improve their access to political participation. Digitalization can significantly contribute to that goal, especially if it would be possible to grant digital access and skills adopted to special needs of people with disabilities.

Ethnic minorities, including immigrants and refugees, also face barriers to political participation due to discrimination, language barriers and lack of representation.

Efforts have been made to promote inclusion, such as the establishment of the European Network Against Racism, but more needs to be done. Finally, young people's political participation is also low and many feel disconnected from politics. The EU has introduced measures such as the European Youth Strategy and the European Solidarity Corps to engage young people and promote their participation in the EU, but more needs to be done to ensure that all voices are heard and represented in the decision-making processes that affect their lives.

References

Aichholzer, G., Rose, G., van Keulen, I., Korthagen, I., Goos, K., Hennen, L., & Lindner, R. (2018). *Prospects for e-democracy in Europe*. EPRS - European Parliamentary Research Service, Scientific Foresight Unit (STOA), European Parliament.

Armingeon, K., & Schädel, L. (2015). Social inequality in political participation: The dark sides of individualization. *West European Politics, 38*(1), 1–27.

Barclay, A. D. (2018). *Fake news, propaganda and plain old lies. How to find trustworthy information in the digital age*. Rowmand & Littlefield.

Bertuzzi, N. (2020). The individualization of political activism: A reflection on social movements and modernization, starting from the case of Italian animal advocacy. *International Journal of Sociology and Social Policy, 40*(3/4), 282–303.

Botrić, V., & Božić, L. (2021). The digital divide and E-government in European economies. *Economic Research-Ekonomska Istraživanja, 34*(1), 2935–2955.

Buckingham, D. (2020). Epilogue: Rethinking digital literacy. Media education in the age of digital capitalism. *Digital Education Review, 37*, 230–239.

Castells, M. (2015). *Networks of outrage and hope: Social movements in the internet age*. John Wiley & Sons.

Cinelli, M., De Francisci Morales, G., Galeazzi, A., Quattrociocchi, W., & Starnini, M. (2021). The echo chamber effect on social media. *Proceedings of the National Academy of Sciences, 118*(9), e2023301118.

Cruz-Jesus, F., Vicente, M. R., Bacao, F., & Oliveira, T. (2016). The education-related digital divide: An analysis for the EU-28. *Computers in Human Behaviour, 56*, 72–82.

Dahlgren, P. (2013). Do social media enhance democratic participation? The importance and difficulty of being "realistic". Policy Paper 04/2013. https://edoc.vifapol.de/opus/volltexte/2014/5550/pdf/PolicyPaper_04_2013.pdf. Accessed 20 Oct 2023

de Cock Buning, M. (2018). *A multi-dimensional approach to disinformation: Report of the independent high level group on fake news and online disinformation*. Publications Office of the European Union.

DePaulo, M. B. (2018). *The psychology of lying and detecting lies*. CreateSpace Independent Publishing Platform.

Dieker, J., & Galan, M. (2014). Creating a public sphere in cyberspace: The case of the EU. In E. G. Carayannis, D. F. J. Campbell, & M. P. Efthymiopoulos (Eds.), *Cyber development, cyber-democracy and cyber-defence: Challenges, opportunities and implications for theory, policy and practice* (pp. 231–258). Springer.

Elena-Bucea, A., Cruz-Jesus, F., Oliveira, T., & Coelho, P. S. (2021). Assessing the role of age, education, gender and income on the digital divide: Evidence for the European Union. *Information Systems Frontiers, 23*, 1007–1021.

Filetti, A., & Janmaat, J. G. (2018). Income inequality and economic downturn in Europe: A multilevel analysis of their consequences for political participation. *Acta Politica, 53*, 327–347.

Fink-Hafner, D., & Bauman, S. (2023). Interest group strategic responses to democratic backsliding. *Politics and Governance, 11*(1), 39–49.

Florida, L. (2020). The fight for digital sovereignty: What it is, and why it matters, especially for the EU. *Philosophy & Technology, 33*, 369–378.
Friemel, T. N. (2016). The digital divide has grown old: Determinants of a digital divide among seniors. *New Media & Society, 18*(2), 313–331.
Gibson, R., & Cantijoch, M. (2013). Conceptualizing and measuring participation in the age of the internet: Is online political engagement really different to offline? *The Journal of Politics, 75*(3), 701–716.
Habermas, J. (1984). *The theory of communicative action (2 volumes)*. Beacon.
Hacker, K. L., & van Dijk, J. (Eds.). (2000). *Digital democracy: Issues of theory and practice*. Sage.
Hafner Fink, M., & Oblak Črnič, T. (2014). Digital citizenship as multiple political participation? Predictors of digital political participation in Slovenia. *Teorija in praksa, 51*(6).
Hamulák, O. (2018). La carta de los derechos fundamentales de la union europea y los derechos sociales. *Estudios constitucionales, 16*(1), 167–186.
Hassan, G., et al. (2018). Exposure to extremist online content could lead to violent radicalization: A systematic review of empirical evidence. *International Journal of Developmental Science, 12*(1–2), 71–88.
Held, D. (2006). *Models of democracy*. Polity.
Held, D. (2013). *Political theory and the modern state*. John Wiley & Sons.
Hennen, L., Van Keulen, I., Korthagen, I., Aichholzer, G., Lindner, R., & Nielsen, R. Ø. (2020). *European e-democracy in practice* (p. 359). Springer Nature.
Holford, J., et al. (2003). Lifelong learning, governance and active citizenship in Europe. In *Final report of the ETGACE research project: Analysis of adult learning & design of formal, non-formal & informal educational intervention strategies. Supported by the European Commission.*
Hoofnagle, C. J., Van Der Sloot, B., & Borgesius, F. Z. (2019). The European Union general data protection regulation: What it is and what it means. *Information & Communications Technology Law, 28*(1), 65–98.
Hoskins, B., & Janmaat, J. G. (2019). *Education, democracy and inequality: Political engagement and citizenship education in Europe*. Springer.
Jeroense, T., & Spierings, N. (2023). Political participation profiles. *West European Politics, 46*(1), 1–23.
Kohler-Koch, B., & Friedrich, D. A. (2020). Business interest in the EU: Integration without supranationalism? *JCMS: Journal of Common Market Studies, 58*(2), 455–471.
Kohler-Koch, B., Kotzian, P., & Quittkat, C. (2017). The multilevel interest representation of national business associations. *West European Politics, 40*(5), 1046–1065.
Liao, S. C., Chou, T. C., & Huang, C. H. (2022). Revisiting the development trajectory of the digital divide: A main path analysis approach. *Technological Forecasting and Social Change, 179*, 121607.
Lindner, R., & Aichholzer, G. (2020). E-democracy: Conceptual foundations and recent trends. *European e-Democracy in Practice*, 11–45.
Makarovič, M., & Rek, M. (2014). Power and influence-based political participation in European democracies. *Sociológia, 46*(6).
Makarovič, M., & Rek, M. (2017). Experts and the macro level decision-making in the information society. In B. Rončević & M. Tomšič (Eds.), *Information society and its manifestations: Economy, politics, culture*. PL Academic Research.
Martens, H., & Hobbs, R. (2015). How media literacy supports civic engagement in a digital age. *Atlantic Journal of Communication, 23*(2), 120–137.
Morales, L., & Giugni, M. (Eds.). (2016). Social capital, political participation and migration in Europe: Making multicultural democracy work?. Springer.
Päivärinta, T., & Sæbø, Ø. (2006). Models of e-democracy. *Communications of the Association for Information Systems, 17*(1), 37.
Price, E. (2013). Social media and democracy. *Australian Journal of Political Science, 48*(4), 519–527.

Putnam, R. D. (1995). Bowling alone: America's declining social capital. *Journal of Democracy, 6*(1), 65–78.
Rek, M. (2012). Civic experts: The case of the EU. *Research in Social Change, 4*(1), 37–61.
Ross A., Robertson, C., Fletcher, R., & Nielsen, R. (2022). Echo chambers, filter bubbles, and polarisation: A literature review. Reuters Institute and University of Oxford. https://ora.ox.ac.uk/objects/uuid:6e357e97-7b16-450a-a827-a92c93729a08/download_file?safe_filename=Arguedas_et_al_2022_echo_chambers_filter.pdf&file_format=pdf&type_of_work=Report. Accessed 17 Oct 2023.
Samuel-Arzan, T., & Hayat, T. (2019). Online news recommendations credibility: The tie is mightier than the source. *Comunicar, 60*, 71–80.
Schoenefeld, J. J. (2021). Interest groups, NGOs or civil society organizations? The framing of non-state actors in the EU. *Voluntas: International Journal of Voluntary and Nonprofit Organizations, 32*(3), 585–596.
Stockemer, D., & Sundström, A. (2019). Young deputies in the European Parliament: A starkly underrepresented age group. *Acta Politica, 54*, 124–144.
Szeles, M. R. (2018). New insights from a multilevel approach to the regional digital divide in the European Union. *Telecommunications Policy, 42*(6), 452–463.
Troitiño, D. R. (2022). The European Union facing the 21st century: The digital revolution. *TalTech Journal of European Studies, 12*(1), 60–78.
van Dijk, J. A. G. M. (2008). *The digital divide in Europe. The handbook of internet politics.* Routledge.
van Dijk, J. A. G. M. (2012). Digital democracy: Vision and reality. In I. Snellen, M. Thaens, & W. van de Donk (Eds.), *Public administration in the information age: Revisited* (pp. 49–61). IOS-Press.
Van Laar, E., Van Deursen, A. J., Van Dijk, J. A., & de Haan, J. (2020). Determinants of 21st-century skills and 21st-century digital skills for workers: A systematic literature review. *SAGE Open, 10*(1), 2158244019900176.

General Data Protection Regulation: Current Challenges and Future Directions

Matúš Mesarčík and Ondrej Hamuľák

Abstract The paper provides a comprehensive analysis of the General Data Protection Regulation (GDPR), with a focus on transparency, fairness, and security in the processing of personal data. The authors examine the provisions of the GDPR, emphasizing the importance of lawful and transparent processing, purpose limitation, data accuracy, and security measures. They also explore the rights of data subjects, including access, rectification, erasure, and data portability, which enhance individual control over personal data. Cross-border data transfers require compliance with GDPR, necessitating adequate safeguards or reliance on specified exceptions. The authors highlight the pivotal role of supervisory authorities in enforcing GDPR, conducting inspections, initiating proceedings, and imposing fines for non-compliance. Private enforcement mechanisms also empower non-profit organizations. Looking ahead, the authors discuss how GDPR can be adapted to emerging technologies such as artificial intelligence and IoT. They also propose amendments to harmonize enforcement practices across EU member states, which will strengthen data protection mechanisms in the face of technological advancements.

The paper was prepared within the implementation of the project no. 20-27227S "The Advent, Pitfalls and Limits of Digital Sovereignty of the European Union" funded by the Czech Science Foundation (GAČR).

M. Mesarčík (✉)
Faculty of Law, Comenius University, Bratislava, Slovakia
e-mail: matus.mesarcik@uniba.sk

O. Hamuľák
Faculty of Law, Palacký University, Olomouc, Czech Republic
e-mail: ondrej.hamulak@upol.cz

D. Ramiro Troitiño (ed.), *E-Governance in the European Union*, Contributions to Political Science, https://doi.org/10.1007/978-3-031-56045-3_9

Introduction

The processing of the personal data of individuals represents the everyday reality of the majority of the population. Individuals use smart devices and applications to foster efficiency in their lives or to improve their health. Our payments are made via mobile phones, and we spend our time on social media targeting us with personalized content and advertisements based on our online behaviour and predictions (Carrière-Swallow & Haksar, 2019). Such everyday reality triggers questions of respect for the right to privacy and the right to data protection, both being relative fundamental rights in the European Union (EU). As a separate fundamental human right, the right to privacy can be found both in the European Convention for the Protection of Human Rights and Fundamental Freedoms (Article 8) and in the Charter of Fundamental Rights of the European Union (CFR) (Article 7). In its case law, the European Court of Human Rights (ECtHR) has long placed the issues of personal data processing within the context of Article 8 of the Convention, even though the protection of personal data is not explicitly provided for therein (Kokott & Sobotta, 2013).

In EU law the situation is different as the Charter of Fundamental Rights of the European Union explicitly enshrines the right to personal data protection in its Article 8 (CFR, Article 8).[1] It is neither the aim nor the ambition of this chapter to analyse the relationship between the right to privacy and the right to personal data protection. However, if we want to summarize research in this area, we may emphasize three main approaches. The first stream of opinion reflects the idea that the right to privacy and the right to the protection of personal data are complementary rights that protect human dignity (van der Sloot, 2017). The second interpretation promotes the view that the right to the protection of personal data has evolved and derived from the right to privacy in light of technological developments, in particular the Internet (Eskens, 2020). The third group of commentators distinguishes the right to privacy and the right to protection of personal data, where the latter is defined widely and protects more assets, including privacy (Lynskey, 2016).

At EU level, the General Data Protection Regulation (GDPR)[2] offers a technology-neutral regulation aimed at creating the free movement of personal data

---

[1] Article 8 of the Charter of Fundamental Rights of the European Union (CFR) reads:

1. Everyone has the right to the protection of personal data concerning him or her.
2. Such data must be processed fairly for specified purposes and based on the consent of the person concerned or some other legitimate basis laid down by law. Everyone has the right of access to data that has been collected concerning him or her, and the right to have it rectified.
3. Compliance with these rules shall be subject to control by an independent authority.

[2] Regulation (EU) 2016/679 of the European Parliament and of the Council of 27 April 2016 on the protection of natural persons with regard to the processing of personal data and on the free movement of such data, and repealing Directive 95/46/EC (General Data Protection Regulation). OJ L 119, 4.5.2016, p. 1–88 (hereinafter—GDPR).

within the EU and the EEA (GDPR, Article 1 [3]) and creating unified rules for the processing of personal data in all Member States (GDPR, Article 1 [1]). The GDPR has been in force since 25 May 2018 and represents a general, complex, and comprehensive piece of data protection regulation influencing data protection laws in third countries. The interpretation of GDPR is reserved to the European Data Protection Board (EDPB), successor of Article 29 Data Protection Working Party and national data protection authorities.

However, the law is not without flaws and application challenges. According to the Article 97 GDPR the European Commission shall evaluate and review the regulation in question every 4 years, beginning with May 2020. Until now, one report has been conducted. The report shows certain challenges and future directions for the EU data protection law.

This chapter proceeds as follows. In section one the analysis of the scope of GDPR is presented. The second section focuses on the principles of processing of personal data. The third section analyses the rights of data subjects as foreseen by GDPR. The fourth section provides an overview of cross-border transfers to third countries followed by an outline of the oversight of the regulation in the fifth section. Section six presents future directions of EU data protection laws considering new technologies and new data laws being adopted. The chapter is not only a brief analysis of the current legal framework but also highlights issues in practices and the Commission's insights from the report and points out future directions.

Scope

Before we delve into specific requirements for processing personal data according to the GDPR, we must discuss the territorial, material, and personal scope of the regulation.

The GDPR regulates the *territorial scope* under Article 3 of the GDPR. From the provisions in question, we can derive two territorial GDPR regimes, namely (1) the intra-territorial scope of the GDPR (GDPR, Article 3 [1]) and (2) the extra-territorial scope of the GDPR (GDPR, Article 3 [2], Article 3 [3]).

The intra-territorial scope of the GDPR is reflected in Article 3(1) of the GDPR, which provides that this Regulation shall apply to the processing of personal data in the course of the activities of an establishment of a controller or processor in the Union, regardless of whether the processing is carried out in the Union or not (GDPR, Article 3 [1]). For the GDPR to apply within the meaning of that Article, the processing of personal data must be in the course of the activities of an establishment in the European Union. The term "establishment" tends to be interpreted quite broadly, and most often may refer to a subsidiary or an exclusive business representation. In the light of the case law, the term "activity of an establishment" is also interpreted broadly to include even minimal activity of the establishment in one of the Member States of the European Union (Bradford et al., 2020). The GDPR also applies in certain circumstances where the entity does not have a physical establishment within the European Union (extra-territorial scope) (Gstrein & Zwitter, 2021). Article 3(2) of the GDPR provides that the GDPR applies to the processing of personal data of data subjects located in the Union by a controller or processor not established in the Union, where the processing activity relates to (1) the offering of goods or services to those data subjects in the Union, regardless of whether the data subject is required to make a payment, or (2) the monitoring of their behaviour with regard to their behaviour within the EU. This means that if a foreign company offers goods and services to data subjects in the EU or monitors their behaviour, the GDPR applies to that company (GDPR, Article 3 [2]). However, the GDPR does not define when an offer of goods and services is made. For the interpretation of this concept, it is necessary to consult the case law of the CJEU, which states that an offer of goods and services to persons in the EU is made if, for example, a website offers the import of goods into an EU country, is in the language of an EU Member State, can be paid in the currency of EU Member States or the website contains references from EU residents (Court of Justice of the European Union, 2010). The company may track the behaviour of residents, for example utilizing behavioural advertising or the processing of IP addresses or cookies. Another type of extra-territorial application of the GDPR is where the processing of personal data is carried out by a controller who is not established in the EU, but where, based on public international law, the law of a Member State applies. Typically, this will be the case for the processing of personal data in embassies and consulates.

Organizations processing personal data fall under the provisions of the EU data protection law represented by GDPR. It is of the essence to establish to whom and under what circumstances data protection laws apply considering *the personal scope* of the GDPR.

Historically, requirements of compliance with data protection laws apply to controllers and processors processing personal data about data subjects. Controllers are entities that solely or jointly with others determine purposes and means of the processing of personal data (GDPR, Article 4 [7]) and are primal carriers of responsibility for compliance with data protection rules (Van Alsenoy, 2012). The entity is classified as a controller when five elements are fulfilled (European Data Protection Board, 2020).[3] Firstly, the controller shall have a determinative influence (or control) (European Data Protection Board, 2020, pp. 10–11) over the data processing and this control may stem from explicit legal competence, implicit legal competence, or factual influence (European Data Protection Board, 2020, pp. 10–12). Secondly, the controller shall exercise the determinative influence over purposes and means of processing. In other words, the controller is the entity specifying the "why" and "how" of processing operations (European Data Protection Board, 2020, pp. 13–15). Thirdly, the influence shall be exercised by one or more entities classifying as controllers. The institute of joint controllers has emerged during the interpretation of *"jointly"* out of the definition of the controller in Directive 95/46/EC

[3] EUROPEAN DATA PROTECTION BOARD (2020). Guidelines 07/2020 on the concepts of controller and processor in the GDPR. Version 1.0. Adopted on 02 September 2020.

(European Data Protection Board, 2020, pp. 12–13) and joint controllers are now explicitly provisioned in the GDPR. It shall be noted that the interpretation of the notion of joint controllers is still part of the academic debate and practice. The relationship of joint controllers shall be based on the factual circumstances (European Data Protection Board, 2020, p. 17). It is detrimental to analyse if joint participation in determining the means of purposes has been involved in the processing operations. The joint participation may take the form of joint decisions or converging decisions (European Data Protection Board, 2020, pp. 18–19). The fourth condition relates to the status of the controller as the controller may be a natural or legal person, public authority, agency, or other body. The definition is thus not reserved for organizations but a natural person processing personal data may qualify as a controller as well (European Data Protection Board, 2020, p. 10). The fifth condition represents the fact that control shall be exercised over the *processing of personal data* (European Data Protection Board, 2020, pp. 15–16).

On the other hand, processors process personal data on behalf of controllers (GDPR, Article 4 [8]). Two basic building blocks are part of the definition of the processor. Firstly, it must be a separate entity from the controller (European Data Protection Board, 2020, p. 24). Secondly, the processing operations by the processor shall be conducted on behalf of the controller (European Data Protection Board, 2020, pp. 24–25). This relationship is best described as a form of delegation where a controller determining the purposes and means of processing outsources processing operations to another entity—the processor. In light of technological development, the notions of controllers and processors are blurring as micro-analysis of responsibilities and processing operations is required to correctly establish the relationship (Veale et al., 2018). This is one of the biggest challenges of current data protection law in the EU. Furthermore, GDPR compliance is also applicable to SMEs. As the Commission emphasizes, compliance with GDPR for SMEs may be particularly challenging as many high-risk operations may take place within their activities.[4]

GDPR further includes the definition of other actors of data processing—recipients, third parties, and data subjects. Data subjects are persons whose personal data are processed (GDPR, Article 4 [1]). The recipient is defined broadly as any "natural or legal person, public authority, agency or another body, to which the personal data are disclosed, whether a third party or not" (GDPR, Article 4 [9]). Public authorities accessing data due to their public tasks are excluded from the definition. Lastly, third parties represent "means a natural or legal person, public authority, agency or body other than the data subject, controller, processor and persons who, under the direct authority of the controller or processor, are authorised to process personal data" (GDPR, Article 4 [10]).

[4] COMMUNICATION FROM THE COMMISSION TO THE EUROPEAN PARLIAMENT AND THE COUNCIL. Data protection as a pillar of citizens' empowerment and the EU's approach to the digital transition—2 years of application of the General Data Protection Regulation. {SWD(2020) 115 final}. Brussels, 24.6.2020. COM(2020) 264 final.

The material scope of the GDPR is regulated in Article 2(1) GDPR: "This Regulation shall apply to the processing of personal data carried out wholly or partly by automated means and to processing by means other than automated means of personal data which form part of an information system or are intended to form part of an information system" (GDPR, Article 2 [1]). The article in question regulates the positive material scope of the GDPR. According to the wording of the article in question, the GDPR applies to the processing of personal data which is carried out (1) by automated means, (2) by partly automated means or (3) manually, where the personal data form part of an information system. Thus, the basic concepts for determining positive subject matter jurisdiction are the processing of personal data and the notion of personal data itself. The processing of personal data is defined in Article 4(1) of the GDPR by a demonstrative enumeration of processing operations that can be subsumed under the definition of processing of personal data (GDPR, Article 4 [1]).

However, the central concept of the GDPR is the definition of personal data. Personal data "is any information relating to an identified or identifiable natural person" (GDPR, Article 4 [1]). An identifiable natural person can be identified, directly or indirectly, in particular by reference to an identifier such as a name, an identification number, location data, an online identifier, or by reference to one or more factors specific to the physical, physiological, genetic, mental, economic, cultural, or social identity of that natural person (Ramiro Troitiño, 2023). The concept of identifiability is further interpreted by Recital 26 of the GDPR, which states: "To determine whether a natural person is identifiable, account should be taken of all means which are reasonably likely to be used by the controller or any other person, for example by specific choice, to identify the natural person, directly or indirectly. To determine whether the means are reasonably likely to be used to identify a natural person, account should be taken of all objective factors such as the cost and time required for identification, taking into account the technology available at the time of processing as well as technological developments" (GDPR, Recital 26). This recital represents the so-called reasonable likelihood test, which answers whether a particular data subject is identifiable. This test was also addressed by the CJEU in *Patrick Breyer v the Federal Republic of Germany* (Court of Justice of the European Union, 2016). This decision thus means that if there are legally permissible means of identifying an individual, this will be personal data. For example, the university has what are known as university personal numbers of students (a numerical series of characters). This constitutes personal data for the university about a particular student, as the university has other identifiers that it can associate with this information and identify the person concerned. Another illustration is if a cyber-attack occurs on a public authority's website and the authority only has the IP address of the attacker.

Article 2(2) of the GDPR regulates the negative scope of the Regulation (GDPR, Article 2 [2]). This means situations where the GDPR does not apply. These are primarily situations to which European Union law does not apply, national security and intelligence issues or issues falling within the scope of the Law Enforcement Directive. A particularly interesting issue is the exemption from the scope, which applies where the processing of personal data is carried out by an individual in the context of a purely personal or domestic activity. However, the GDPR does not define which situations are specifically at issue, but the case law of the CJEU does point in a certain direction (Chen et al., 2020). Processing in the context of a purely personal or domestic activity will not be the case if personal data is published on the internet (Court of Justice of the European Union, 2003) or if a public street is monitored by a CCTV system placed over the door of a house (Court of Justice of the European Union, 2014). For example, if a person takes notes of meetings in his or her diary, this will indeed be the processing of personal data, but solely in the context of personal activity and the GDPR will not apply (Hamuľák et al., 2020).

Certain elements of processing of a personal data according to the GDPR was left to EU member states discretion.[5] This is the case of so-called opening clauses, e.g. in case of the age of valid digital consent of minors or more precise specification of legal grounds of public interest and legal obligation. "As a result, there is still a degree of fragmentation which is notably due to the extensive use of facultative specification clauses".[6]

Principles of Processing Personal Data and Selected Requirements

Article 5 of GDPR provisions basic principles of processing personal data (GDPR, Article 5). The principle of lawfulness, transparency, and fairness is provisioned in Article 5(1)(a) GDPR stating that personal data shall be "processed lawfully, fairly and in a transparent manner in relation to the data subject". The principle in practice means that all processing operations shall be based on an appropriate legal ground(s) (GDPR, Article 6) and processing operations as such shall comply with the law. The requirements of fairness and transparency are also included in the principle.

Transparency of processing operations is ensured by Articles 12–14 GDPR. Article 12 of GDPR states requirements of informing data subjects about processing their personal data especially that the information provided shall be provided "in a concise, transparent, intelligible and easily accessible form, using clear and plain language, in particular for any information addressed specifically to a child". (GDPR, Article 12). Articles 13 and 14 provide a framework for what information ought to be provided to the data subject if collected directly (GDPR, Article 13) or indirectly (GDPR, Article 14) from the data subject. Information includes purposes and legal grounds of processing, categories of data, recipients, and cross-border transfers providing the data subject with essentials of "what", "how", "why", "when", and "with whom".

[5] Ibid.

[6] Ibid.

The quantity of data is one of the most troubled relationships in terms of data protection and new technologies. Article 5(1)(b) of the GDPR specifies the purpose limitation principle stating that personal data shall be "collected for specified, explicit and legitimate purposes and not further processed in a manner that is incompatible with those purposes". (GDPR, Article 5[1][b]). It means that the controller shall before commencing processing operations determine "why" personal data are processed (the purpose). Furthermore, GDPR provides exceptions for processing for research and scientific purposes (GDPR, Article 5 [1] [b]). Another principle is the principle of accuracy in Article 5 (1) (c) (GDPR, Article 5 [1] [c]). Personal data shall be accurate and, where necessary, kept up to date. This principle shall be assessed together with the principle of purpose limitation. In other words, where accuracy is crucial for achieving the purposes, more emphasis and efforts shall be made towards ensuring the accuracy of data. Security of personal data processing is provisioned in Article 5 (1) (f) GDPR as well as an in-general security clause in Article 32 GDPR: "Taking into account the state of the art, the costs of implementation and the nature, scope, context, and purposes of processing, as well as the risk of varying likelihood and severity for the rights and freedoms of natural persons, the controller, and the processor, shall implement appropriate technical and organizational measures to ensure a level of security appropriate to the risk" and providing a non-exhaustive list of suitable security measures (GDPR, Article 5 [1] [f], Article 32).

The proactive and pre-emptive obligations of controllers are explicitly stated in the principle of accountability. "The controller shall be responsible for, and be able to demonstrate compliance with paragraph 1 [principles of processing]". (GDPR, Article 5 [2]). This principle reflects the need for high engagement with data protection law and requires a proactive approach instead of formal compliance and documentary obligations.[7] The pertinent principle materializes in several general (GDPR, Article 24) and specific obligations in the GDPR, including the requirement for designation of Data Protection Officer (GDPR, Articles 37–39), data protection by design and by default (GDPR, Article 25) or conducting Data Protection Impact Assessments (DPIA) (GDPR, Article 35). These obligations provide specific mechanisms for showing accountability and compliance with data protection law (Alhadeff et al., 2012).

According to Article 35(1) GDPR "where a type of processing, in particular, using new technologies, and taking into account the nature, scope, context, and purposes of the processing, is likely to result in a high risk to the rights and freedoms of natural persons, the controller shall, before the processing, assess the impact of the envisaged processing operations on the protection of personal data. A single assessment may address a set of similar processing operations that present similar high risks". (GDPR, Article 35 [1]). Using this instrument controllers of

[7] Article 29 Data Protection Working Party, "Opinion 3/2010 on the principle of accountability", adopted on 13 July 2010. 00062/10/EN WP 173. See also Alhadeff, J. et al. (2012). The accountability principle in data protection regulation: origin, development, and future directions. In D. Guagnin, L. Hempel, C. Ilten a.o. (eds.), *Managing Privacy through Accountability*, 2012, Palgrave Macmillan, 49–82.

personal data before commencing the processing operation analyses the risks of processing by focusing on the rights and freedoms of the data subject including the assessment of necessity and proportionality. DPIA is mandatory in scenarios foreseen by Article 35(3) GDPR, namely in cases of (i) "a systematic and extensive evaluation of personal aspects relating to natural persons which are based on automated processing, including profiling, and on which decisions are based that produce legal effects concerning the natural person or similarly significantly affect the natural person; (ii) processing of special categories of data referred to in Article 9(1) on a large scale, or processing of personal data relating to criminal convictions and offenses referred to in Article 10; or (iii) a systematic monitoring of a publicly accessible area on a large scale". Notions of legal effects, publicly accessible areas, or large scale are interpreted by the guidelines provided by the WP29.[8]

Rights of Data Subjects

Under the GDPR, the data subject has several individual rights against the personal data controller. The controller is obliged to enable and facilitate the exercise of these rights (GDPR, Article 12). However, it should be noted that many of these rights of the data subject are subject to specific conditions and are also subject to exceptions, where the controller may refuse to grant a request to exercise the data subject's right. These rights are therefore not absolute.

The Commission emphasizes that GDPR fulfils the aim of empowering individuals to control their data.[9] The most fundamental right of the data subject is the right to information, which is mirrored in the information obligation of the controller. This right is also naturally subject to certain exceptions, which are subject to review by the controller. Articles 13 and 14 of GDPR contain lists of information to be provided to data subjects together with specific exceptions when this right does not apply (GDPR, Article 13, Article 14).

The right to information is followed by the right of access under Article 15 of the GDPR, with the basic difference between the right to information and the right of access being that, in the case of information, the controller provides general, generic information about an indefinite number of data subjects, whereas, in the case of the right of access, the controller is obliged to indicate to the data subject precisely what data about him or her he or she processes. This right includes the right to obtain

[8] Article 29 Data Protection Working Party, "Guidelines on Data Protection Impact Assessment (DPIA) and determining whether the processing is "likely to result in a high risk" for the purposes of Regulation 2016/679" Adopted on 4 April 2017. As last Revised and Adopted on 4 October 2017, WP 248 rev.01.

[9] COMMUNICATION FROM THE COMMISSION TO THE EUROPEAN PARLIAMENT AND THE COUNCIL. Data protection as a pillar of citizens' empowerment and the EU's approach to the digital transition—2 years of application of the General Data Protection Regulation. {SWD(2020) 115 final}. Brussels, 24.6.2020. COM(2020) 264 final.

confirmation from the controller as to whether personal data relating to the data subject are being processed and, if so, the right to obtain access to those personal data or a copy of the personal data processed (GDPR, Article 15).

Data subjects also have a right to rectification, under which the data subject has the right to have inaccurate personal data concerning him or her rectified by the controller without undue delay. Having regard to the purposes of the processing, the data subject shall have the right to have incomplete personal data completed, including by providing a supplementary declaration. This right comprises two sub-rights, namely the right to rectification of inaccurate personal data and the right to completion of incomplete personal data (GDPR, Article 16).

Article 17 of the GDPR governs the right to erasure (GDPR, Article 17). Under this provision, the data subject has the right to obtain from the controller the erasure of personal data concerning him or her without undue delay, whereby the controller is obliged to erase the personal data without undue delay if one of the grounds set out in Article 17(1) of the GDPR is fulfilled (GDPR, Article 17 [1]). Thus, the controller shall first examine whether there is a legitimate reason for erasure. Where the controller has disclosed personal data and the data subject has successfully invoked the right to erasure, he or she shall, taking into account the technology available and the cost of implementing the measures, take reasonable steps, including technical measures, to inform the controllers processing the personal data that the data subject has requested them to erase all references to those personal data or a copy or replica thereof (GDPR, Article 17 [2]). At the same time, none of the exemptions under Article 17(3) GDPR shall apply (GDPR, Article 17 [3]). For example, if the data that the data subject requests to be erased would be necessary to pursue legal claims in court during the limitation period, the controller does not have to erase the data in question even if there is a legitimate reason to do so.

Another of the data subject's rights is the right to restriction of processing under Article 18 of the GDPR (GDPR, Article 18). The meaning of this right is that if at least one of the grounds under Article 18(1) GDPR is met, the controller is obliged to restrict the processing of personal data to storage only and thus cannot carry out further processing operations such as transmission or analysis (GDPR, Article 18 [1]). An exception to this is where the controller processes the data only with the data subject's consent or for the establishment, exercise, or defence of legal claims or the protection of the rights of another natural or legal person, or reasons of substantial public interest of the EU or a member state (GDPR, Article 18).

A new feature of the data protection regulation is the right to data portability under Article 20 of the GDPR. The practical meaning of this right is user convenience when changing digital service providers. Thus, if a user wants to change social networks, he or she can ask Facebook to “transfer” his or her data to Twitter, where the user can start working comfortably. However, this right can only be exercised under fairly strict conditions. The first is that it must be personal data processed based on consent or the performance of a contract. The second condition is that the processing is carried out by automated means. Moreover, the right to data portability only applies to directly provided data, which in practice means that it does not apply to derivative data, which constitute the intellectual property of the controller. For example, specific profiles or predictions from user activity will not be subject to the right of portability. If such a transfer is made, this data transfer must be made in a structured, commonly used, and machine-readable format (GDPR, Article 20). The Commission highlights the positive effect of the right but concerns remain about the full usability of the right.[10]

The data subject also has the right to object under Article 21 of the GDPR. This right shall apply if the personal data are processed based on a public interest or a legitimate interest, in which case the controller must be able to demonstrate the overriding of such interest over the rights, freedoms, and interests of the data subject. If a controller fails to meet this burden, the processing of personal data must cease. In situations where the data subject objects to processing for direct marketing purposes, the personal data may no longer be processed for such purposes (GDPR, Article 21).

Additionally, GDPR provides the data subject with the right not to be subject to a decision based solely on automated processing, including profiling, which produces legal effects concerning him or her or similarly significantly affects him or her (GDPR, Article 22). In regulation-prescribed cases the data subject has the right to human intervention, contest the decision, or express his/her point of view (GDPR, Article 22 [3]). The interpretation of Article 22 and related terms is provided by the European Data Protection Board in its guidelines (European Data Protection Board, 2020).

Cross-Border Transfer of Personal Data to Third Countries

In today's globalized world, it is essential to carry out cross-border transfers of personal data. Whether we are talking about transfers between EU or European Economic Area (EEA) countries or outside these two groupings to third countries, the provision of digital services depends on cross-border transfers (Wagner, 2018).

The GDPR introduces a four-step test for cross-border transfers, which is based on an analysis of the country to which the controller wishes to transfer personal data and its legal framework. The basic rule is that free movement between EU and EEC member states is guaranteed. If the country is outside these two groupings, the controller must choose the appropriate legal basis.

The first option is that the European Commission has adopted an adequacy decision for the third country (Hamulák, 2018). This is a rather lengthy process that involves a comprehensive assessment of the third country's legal system with regard to international obligations, the legal framework for the protection of personal data, or the existence of a supervisory authority. Subsequently, in case of a positive outcome, the decision is published in the Official Journal of the EU and is reviewable by the CJEU. The well-known saga of Schrems cases reflects issues connected to

[10] Ibid.

the adequacy decisions related to the EU-US relationships (Stehlík & Vardanyan, 2020).

In the absence of an adequacy decision for a third country and where the controller wishes to transfer personal data from the EU to that country, adequate safeguards are available to the controller under Article 46 of the GDPR. The most commonly used adequate safeguards are the so-called Standard Contractual Clauses (SCCs), which are contractual documents, approved by the European Commission or a supervisory authority, that contain the specific wording of a contract for the transfer of personal data, and which controllers may not interfere with in such a way as to reduce the level of protection (Juliussen et al., 2023). However, considering the Schrems II decision, it should be noted that a controller in the EU is obliged to examine the level of protection of personal data in a third country before initiating a cross-border transfer (Troitiño, 2022). Other appropriate safeguards are, for example, the use of Binding Corporate Rules for groups of undertakings, a legally binding and enforceable instrument between public authorities or public bodies, a code of conduct, or a certification mechanism (Hallinan et al., 2021).

If the controller cannot rely on either of the reasonable safeguards, he or she may make use of one of the exceptions in Article 49 of the GDPR. However, this is the last option available to the controller and several of the exemptions are tied to the requirement of occasional transfers and thus cannot be used regularly. Article 49 of the GDPR includes explicit consent, the performance of a contract, the conclusion of a contract, an important reason of public interest, the exercise of legal claims, vital interests of data subjects, and transfers from registers as legal grounds for cross-border transfers. As a special case, Article 49 of the GDPR also provides for a compelling legitimate interest of the controller (GDPR, Article 49).

In this respect, it may be noted that supervisory authorities in Member States have the power to prohibit cross-border transfers to a specific third country. This can be illustrated by the example of the Irish supervisory authority, which prohibited Facebook from transferring personal data between the EU and the USA following the Schrems II decision.[11]

Oversight

Compliance with data protection regulations is supervised by independent supervisory authorities in each EU country. These supervisory authorities have several functions and tasks. Perhaps the most important is the supervision of compliance with the rules on personal data protection. In this respect, inspections in the field of personal data protection and the conduct of administrative proceedings may be highlighted. It should be noted that the employees of supervisory authorities have

[11] Techcrunch (2020). https://techcrunch.com/2020/09/09/facebook-told-it-may-have-to-suspend-eu-data-transfers-after-schrems-ii-ruling/.

quite broad powers when carrying out checks and may, for example, enter premises where personal data are processed, check the security of information systems, or request various documents from controllers (Troitiño et al., 2020). At the same time, the supervisory authorities may directly order the controller to refrain from processing personal data, modify its processes, or punish the controller in other ways such as imposing an administrative fine. If a breach is found, the supervisory authority is entitled to initiate administrative proceedings, whether based on an inspection or other complaint, which may also result in the imposition of an administrative fine.

Other activities of the supervisory authorities include providing public consultation or guidance and issuing methodological material in relation to the interpretation of legal norms.

Perhaps the most attention in the context of the adoption of the GDPR has been paid to sanctions, which are higher than under the previous legislation. The GDPR provides for two levels of administrative fines, with the defining criterion being which instrument the controller or processor has infringed (Rosen, 2012). In the case of a minor breach of the GDPR, the controller faces an administrative fine of up to EUR 10000000 or, in the case of an undertaking, up to 2% of the total worldwide annual turnover for the preceding financial year, whichever is the higher. However, if the controller infringes any of the principles on the processing of personal data or the right of the data subject, the controller shall be liable to an administrative fine of up to EUR 20000000 or, in the case of an undertaking, up to 4% of the total annual worldwide turnover for the preceding financial year, whichever is higher. The Commission's report concerning oversight highlights that not every EU member state allocates sufficient resources for the effective functioning of data protection authorities.[12] Similarly, the imposition of administrative fines is subject to criticism, as some data protection authorities impose higher fines than others.

A specific dimension of enforcement is the so-called private enforcement in data protection. Article 80 of the GDPR regulates the representation of data subjects by non-profit bodies, organizations, or associations established by the law of a Member State, the objectives of which, according to their statutes, are in the public interest and which are active in the field of the protection of the rights and freedoms of data subjects regarding the protection of their data (GDPR, Article 80). Such associations may lodge a complaint on behalf of the data subject or represent them in administrative or judicial proceedings in the field of personal data protection, as well as assert a right to compensation.

[12] COMMUNICATION FROM THE COMMISSION TO THE EUROPEAN PARLIAMENT AND THE COUNCIL. Data protection as a pillar of citizens' empowerment and the EU's approach to the digital transition—2 years of application of the General Data Protection Regulation. {SWD(2020) 115 final}. Brussels, 24.6.2020. COM(2020) 264 final.

Future Directions

Although GDPR is drafted as a technologically neutral regulation, certain cases of innovative and new technologies require more guidance and specific attention. The same conclusion was held by the Commission in the evaluation report: "Future challenges lie ahead in clarifying how to apply the proven principles to specific technologies such as artificial intelligence, blockchain, Internet of Things or facial recognition which require a monitoring on a continuous basis".[13] This is especially correct nowadays when rules are being applied towards artificial intelligence (AI) in phases of training models and deployment. French Data Protection Authority (CNIL) recently issued comprehensive guidelines on the application of GDPR concerning training AI models with personal data.[14] The guidelines in question explain how to apply GDPR to the processing of personal data in terms of scope, definition of purposes, classification of stakeholders involved in processing personal data, selection of correct legal grounds, conducting DPIA, and implementation of data protection by design choices.[15] Such guidelines shall be deliberated also on the level of the EU to provide legal certainty for AI developers. In the phase of deployment (but not limited to), certain provisions in the proposal for the EU Artificial Intelligence Act (AIA)[16] governs data protection aspects. The data management requirements are contained in Section 10 of the AIA, which establishes quality requirements for training, validation, and test data sets (AIA, Article 10 [1]). These data must be sufficiently relevant, representative, error-free, and complete (AIA, Article 10 [3]). At the same time, procedures must be in place for these datasets for data collection, assessment of suitability and availability, or review for potential bias (AIA, Article 10 [2]). Training, validation, and test datasets shall, where required by the intended purpose, take into account features or elements that are specific to the particular geographic, behavioural, or functional conditions in which the high-risk AI system is to be used (AIA, Article 10 [4]). The above requirements apply not only to AI systems that need to be trained but to high-risk AI systems in general (AIA, Article 10 [6]).

Concerning future directions, the EU shall carefully assess the symbiosis of proposed and adopted data policies in general (Vardanyan & Kocharyan, 2022). Namely, the EU adopted the Data Governance Act (DGA)[17] complementing public

---

[13] Ibid.

[14] CNIL. Artificial intelligence: the CNIL opens a consultation on the creation of datasets for AI., https://www.cnil.fr/en/artificial-intelligence-cnil-opens-consultation-creation-datasets-ai.

[15] Ibid.

[16] Proposal for a regulation of the European parliament and of the council laying down harmonized rules on artificial intelligence (artificial intelligence act) and amending certain union legislative acts. COM/ 2021/206 final (hereinafter—AIA).

[17] The Regulation (EU) 2022/868 on European data governance and amending Regulation (EU) 2018/1724 (Data Governance Act) (DGA).

sector information regulation and proposed Data Act[18] governing Internet of Things, B2B, and B2C data sharing issues. In case of sharing or processing of personal data, GDPR as general law shall remain applicable in these cases. That would require a careful approach from controllers and processors.

Finally, the Commission is aware of the different severity of enforcement of GDPR in the EU member states. Taking into consideration these aspects and the aim of the unification, the EU introduced a proposal for GDPR procedural rules for data protection authorities.[19] The proposal harmonizes the requirements for a cross-border complaint to be admissible and removes any obstacles imposed by data protection authorities by different rules. In cases where their complaints are partly or wholly rejected, it lays down the mutual right of complainants to be heard. It lays down rules to ensure that they are properly involved in the investigation of complaints. The proposal provides the parties under investigation with the right to be heard at key stages in the procedure, including during dispute resolution by the EDPB, and clarifies the content of the administrative file and the parties' rights of access to the file. The proposal provides for the early provision by data protection authorities of their views on an investigation, and they will be able to benefit from all available cooperation tools under the GDPR including mutual assistance (European Commission, 2023).

References

Alhadeff, J., Van Alsenoy, B., & Dumortier, J. (2012). The accountability principle in data protection regulation: Origin, development, and future directions. In D. Guagnin, L. Hempel, & C. Ilten (Eds.), *Managing privacy through accountability* (pp. 49–82). Palgrave Macmillan.

Article 29 Data Protection Working Party, "Opinion 3/2010 on the principle of accountability," adopted on 13 July 2010. 00062/10/EN WP 173.

Article 29 Data Protection Working Party, "Guidelines on Data Protection Impact Assessment (DPIA) and determining whether the processing is "likely to result in a high risk" for the purposes of Regulation 2016/679" Adopted on 4 April 2017. As last Revised and Adopted on 4 October 2017, WP 248 rev.01.

Bradford, L. R., Aboy, M., & Liddell, K. (2020). International transfers of health data between the EU and USA: A sector-specific approach for the USA to ensure an 'adequate' level of protection. *Journal of Law and the Biosciences, 7*, 1–33. https://doi.org/10.1093/jlb/lsaa055

Carrière-Swallow, Y., & Haksar, V. (2019). The economics and implications of data: An integrated perspective. In *IMF departmental papers/policy papers 2019/013*. International Monetary Fund.

Chen, J., Edwards, L., Urquhart, L., & McAuley, D. (2020). Who is responsible for data processing in smart homes? Reconsidering joint controllership and the household exemption. *International Data Privacy Law, 10*(4), 279–293. https://doi.org/10.1093/idpl/ipaa011

[18] Proposal for a REGULATION OF THE EUROPEAN PARLIAMENT AND OF THE COUNCIL on harmonized rules on fair access to and use of data (Data Act). COM/ 2022/68 final.

[19] Proposal for a REGULATION OF THE EUROPEAN PARLIAMENT AND OF THE COUNCIL laying down additional procedural rules relating to the enforcement of Regulation (EU) 2016/679. COM/ 2023/348 final.

COMMUNICATION FROM THE COMMISSION TO THE EUROPEAN PARLIAMENT AND THE COUNCIL. Data protection as a pillar of citizens' empowerment and the EU's approach to the digital transition - two years of application of the General Data Protection Regulation. {SWD(2020) 115 final}. Brussels, 24.6.2020. COM(2020) 264 final.

Eskens, S. (2020). The personal information sphere: An integral approach to privacy and related information and communication rights. *Journal of the Association for Information Science & Technology, Association for Information Science & Technology, 71*(9), 1116–1128. https://doi.org/10.1002/asi.24354

European Commission. (2023). Data protection: Commission adopts new rules to ensure stronger enforcement of the GDPR in cross-border cases. From: https://ec.europa.eu/commission/presscorner/detail/en/ip_23_3609

EUROPEAN DATA PROTECTION BOARD. (2020). Guidelines 07/2020 on the concepts of controller and processor in the GDPR. Version 1.0. Adopted on 02 September 2020.

Gstrein, O. J., & Zwitter, A. J. (2021). Extraterritorial application of the GDPR: Promoting European values or power? *Internet Policy Review, 10*(3). https://doi.org/10.14763/2021.3.1576

Hallinan, D., Bernier, A., Cambon-Thomsen, A., et al. (2021). International transfers of personal data for health research following Schrems II: A problem in need of a solution. *European Journal of Human Genetics, 29*, 1502–1509. https://doi.org/10.1038/s41431-021-00893-y

Hamulák, O. (2018). La carta de los derechos fundamentales de la union europea y los derechos sociales. *Estudios constitucionales, 16*(1), 167–186.

Hamulak, O., Kocharyan, H., & Kerikmäe, T. (2020). The contemporary issues of post-mortem personal data protection in the EU after GDPR entering into force. *Czech Yearbook of Public and Private International Law, 11*, 225–238. https://rozkotova.cld.bz/CYIL-vol-11-2020/224/

Judgment of the Court, 6 November 2003, C-101/01 – Lindqvist.

Judgment of the Court (Grand Chamber), 7 December 2010, C-585/08 – Pammer a Hotel Alpenhof.

Judgment of the Court (Fourth Chamber), 11 December 2014, C-212/13 – Ryneš.

Judgment of the Court (Second Chamber), 19 October 2016, C-582/14 – Patrick Breyer v Bundesrepublik Deutschland.

Juliussen, B. A., Kozyri, E., Johansen, D., & Rui, J. P. (2023). The third country problem under the GDPR: Enhancing protection of data transfers with technology. *International Data Privacy Law, 13*(3), 225–243. https://doi.org/10.1093/idpl/ipad013

Kokott, J., & Sobotta, C. (2013). The distinction between privacy and data protection in the jurisprudence of the CJEU and the ECtHR. *International Data Privacy Law, 3*(4), 222–228. https://doi.org/10.1093/idpl/ipt017

Lynskey, O. (2016). *The foundations of EU data protection law*. Oxford University Press.

Proposal for a REGULATION OF THE EUROPEAN PARLIAMENT AND OF THE COUNCIL on harmonized rules on fair access to and use of data (Data Act). COM/2022/68 final.

Proposal for a REGULATION OF THE EUROPEAN PARLIAMENT AND OF THE COUNCIL laying down additional procedural rules relating to the enforcement of Regulation (EU) 2016/679. COM/2023/348 final.

Proposal for a regulation of the European parliament and of the council laying down harmonized rules on artificial intelligence (artificial intelligence act) and amending certain union legislative acts. COM/2021/206 final (AIA).

Ramiro Troitiño, D. (2023). EU elections and internet voting (i-voting). In *Digital development of the European Union: An interdisciplinary perspective* (pp. 319–333). Springer International Publishing.

Regulation (EU) 2016/679 of the European Parliament and of the Council of 27 April 2016 on the protection of natural persons with regard to the processing of personal data and on the free movement of such data, and repealing Directive 95/46/EC (General Data Protection Regulation). OJ L 119, 4.5.2016, p. 1–88 (GDPR).

Rosen, J. (2012). The right to be forgotten. *Stanford Law Review Online, 64*, 88–92. https://review.law.stanford.edu/wp-content/uploads/sites/3/2012/02/64-SLRO-88.pdf

Sloot, B. V. (2017). *Privacy as virtue: Moving beyond the individual in the age of big data* (p. 230). Intersentia. https://www.larcier-intersentia.com/en/privacy-virtue-9781780685052.html

Stehlík, V., & Vardanyan, L. (2020). Schrems II: Will it really increase the level of privacy protection against mass surveillance? *Bratislava Law Review, 4*(2), 111–128. https://doi.org/10.46282/blr.2020.4.2.215

Techcrunch. (2020). https://techcrunch.com/2020/09/09/facebook-told-it-may-have-to-suspend-eu-data-transfers-after-schrems-ii-ruling/

The Regulation (EU) 2022/868 on European data governance and amending Regulation (EU) 2018/1724 (Data Governance Act) (DGA).

Troitiño, D. R. (2022). El futuro digital de la política europea.

Troitiño, D. R., Kerikmae, T., Barbosa, P. A. R., & Shumilo, O. S. (2020). El libro blanco sobre inteligencia artificial: análisis y comentarios sobre mercado, valores y cooperación europea. In *Inteligencia artificial: de la discrepancia regional a las reglas universales: integración de percepciones políticas, económicas y legales* (pp. 303–318). Thomson Reuters Aranzadi.

Van Alsenoy, B. (2012). Allocating responsibility among controllers, processors, and "everything in between": The definition of actors and roles in directive 95/46/EC. *Computer Law and Security Review, 28*, 25.

Vardanyan, L., & Kocharyan, H. (2022). The GDPR and the DGA proposal: Are they in controversial relationship? *European Studies, 9*(1), 91–109. https://doi.org/10.2478/eustu-2022-0004

Veale, M., Binns, R., & Ausloos, J. (2018). When data protection by design and data subject rights clash. *International Data Privacy Law, 8*(2), 105–123. https://doi.org/10.1093/idpl/ipy002

Wagner, J. (2018). The transfer of personal data to third countries under the GDPR: When does a recipient country provide an adequate level of protection? *International Data Privacy Law, 8*(4), 318–337. https://doi.org/10.1093/idpl/ipy008

European Union E-Governance: E-Governance Tools for the Correct Implementation of Digital Single Market

Daniela Jezova

Abstract The article deals with different aspect of Digital Single Market as one of the priorities of European Union. Article includes the comparison of internal market and the digital single market. The consumer protection and the New Deal including the geo-blocking issues are covered in this article. Article continues with the e-governance and artificial intelligence topic and covers also Single Digital Gateway and electronic identification.

Introduction

Digitalization is the key aspect and milestone of this century. Since the computers were firstly introduced to our society, the world started to change in every aspect. The ways of life have significantly changed through the emergence of information and technology. The Internet that allowed the most accessible "transport" media for informational exchange enabled the globalization to evolve (Bauman, 2000). Digitalization brings together people from various countries into one place building one team committed to a common goal and purpose creating an international and multicultural environment (Dávidekova, 2017, pp. 46–52). In digital world parallel to real world is created by virtual reality and other technologies. The virtual reality technology represents interactive virtual environment with the most possible resemblance to physical reality. In the information age there is a greater parallel that can be drawn between the networks in which firms are embedded and the networks in which territorial areas are engaged (Alcácer et al., 2016, pp. 499–512). The changes that have taken place in the way markets function, the facilitation and the rapidity of communications and the new modes of governance that extend outside the national borders have steered a vivid discussion on globalization and its implications for the state (Ladi, 2006) (Ježová, 2018).

D. Jezova (✉)
Bratislava, Slovakia
e-mail: jezova@lawyer.com

D. Ramiro Troitiño (ed.), *E-Governance in the European Union*, Contributions to Political Science, https://doi.org/10.1007/978-3-031-56045-3_10

Digital technologies and in particular the internet is transforming our world and the European Commission wants to make the EU's single market fit for the digital age—moving from 28 national digital markets to a single one. The idea of digital single market was created as after the digitalization got the significant impact in the world and relates to the single market four freedoms. The Digital Single Market strategy was adopted on 6 May 2015 and is one of the European Commission's 10 political priorities. The creation of a Digital Single Market introduced by the Strategy Europe 2020 (Europe, 2020, 2010) (following Lisbon strategy) to expand Single market to the digital world. The Digital Single Market strategy specified three policy pillars: (1) Improving access to digital goods and services; (2) An environment where digital networks and services can prosper; (3) Digital as a driver for growth. A Digital Single Market is one in which the free movement of goods, persons, services and capital is ensured and where individuals and businesses can seamlessly access and exercise online activities under conditions of fair competition, and a high level of consumer and personal data protection, irrespective of their nationality or place of residence (Commission, 2015).

Together with the digitalization a necessity to use the information technology in public service arose, known as e-governance. Using information technology in public governance increases the efficiency of the service, connects public officials and citizens in more convenient way, increases transparency and is more time and financial efficient. Technologies can be named as essential instrument in the transformation of governments and their way of operation, structures and transparency. Indeed, modern or good governance is not just about delivering services. This notion includes democratic and cooperative policy formulation, citizen and civil society involvement, transparent and participative implementation of policies, as well as continuous independent evaluation of their results, and accountability of public decision makers to improve policy making in the future (Coleman & Gøtze, 2001; EIPA, 2003).

There are challenges for the digital single market on different fields: political, legal and technical (Mergel et al., 2018). The digital single market provides a radical, disruptive, experience for the otherwise rather path-dependent civil service (Mazzini, 2019, p. 101). From changing the workforce through digital service teams (Clarke, 2017), the way these teams work by changing from waterfall to agile collaboration methods (Dupont, 2019, pp. 1–5) or ensuring in-house expertise with the correct mindset (Efrat & Geraghty, 2017, p. 390)—while difficult on a national level—seems almost impossible in a context like the European Union (Schmidt & Krimmer, 2022, pp. 59–80).

Up until now, EU citizens and businesses have often faced barriers when using online tools and services. These barriers mean that consumers have restricted access to some goods and services, businesses cannot reap all benefits from digitization and governments and citizens cannot fully benefit from this digital transformation. The Digital Single Market opens new opportunities, as it removes key differences between online and offline worlds, breaking down the barriers to cross-border online activity. Increase of usage of artificial intelligence influenced the evolution of e-governance tools on national and European level. Artificial Intelligence and

Internet could improve the efficiency and effectiveness of public services. In response to fast digital technology development, smart, innovative governance has been imagined as an evolution of e-government to invent ways for the government to achieve better citizen participation, transparency and connectivity (Gil-Garcia et al., 2016, p. 524). The advent of smart governments is inextricably tied to using smart (AI) systems that depend on massive amounts of data, which is frequently accessible via Internet of Thinks (Al-Besher & Kumar, 2022).

When talking about the e-government tool and barriers removal we need to mention also the single digital gateway to provide access to information, to procedures and to assistance and problem-solving services (Regulation 2018/1724). Full applicability of the regulation will help to improve and increase the efficiency of the e-Government services and EU citizens can identify and authenticate themselves simply, safely and with sufficient confidence.

Internal Market vs. Digital Single Market

The EU Internal Market as a territory of free movement of goods, services, capital and person is still developing and can be considered as a gradual process, which is characterized by its complexity (Arnold & Wörgötter, 2011). Four freedoms are essential part of our daily lives and have become an integral part of the EU citizen's daily life and the EU economy. Negative integration consists, in the EU, of the powerful mechanisms of free movement (of goods, services, capital, labour and, now also, codified technology as in patents or other IPRs), backed up by both central and decentralized implementation and enforcement. Positive integration is about appropriate and proportionate EU regulation and/or common policies as well as common EU institutions, yielding the proper functioning of the single market (Pelkmans, 2019). In the Digital Single Market the four freedoms are used without barriers hindering the use of digital technologies and online services (Ručinská & Fečko, 2017). One cannot exist without another.

Barriers can be understood as physical barriers, technical barriers, fiscal barriers, social and cultural barriers, etc. In Internal market we have already identified almost all barriers and removed them. In Digital Market we are still in the process. The barriers can be understood as insufficient internet access, geo-blocking, level of digital skills, funds for technical equipment, etc. (Marcut, 2017). The widening function of the Digital Single Market is widening the Single Market by reaching more and more citizens and users of the four freedoms. This means expansion of economics. In case of the Single Market, we must discuss competition policy, aiming to provide businesses with level playing field and consumers with a wide range of options. In the case of the Digital Single Market, deepening can refer to a more enhanced relation between the digital spaces and the citizens-users, which stems from the constant state of innovation characteristic to the digital space as well as from the improvement of users' digital skills (Marcut, 2017, p. 100).

Digital Single Market and Online Barriers for Consumers

Once buying online the barriers for free movement in digital world include different prices (price discrimination) and conditions based on location of the customer. Geo-blocking is a discriminatory practice that prevents online EU customers from accessing and purchasing products or services from a website based in another member state. To remove this barrier, the EU is putting in place a geo-blocking regulation (Regulation 2018/302). Banning the geo-blocking practices is necessary for removal of online barriers.

In e-commerce within EU connected with online purchases the protection of consumer in online environment is important for the creation of digital single market. The so-called "New Deal for Consumers" is a name for package of significant changes in EU legislation adopted by directive in EU (Directive 2019(2161). The aim is to adapt the EU consumer protection to digital single market and digital environment, to provide better guarantees for EU consumers rights, strengthen the public and private enforcement of these rules, ensure that authorities have sufficient power to impose sanctions and ensure effective enforcement of consumer protection. The New Deal is amending four already existing Directives—Directive for unfair terms in consumer contracts (Directive 93/13/EEC), consumer protection in the indication of the prices of product offered to consumers (Directive 98/6/EC), unfair business to consumer commercial practices (Directive 2005/29/EC) and consumer rights directive (Directive 2011/83/EC). The system of fines and penalties was moreover inspired by GDPR system, where the directive gives power to national authorities to impose penalties in a coordinated manner working cross-border out of their jurisdiction in connection with authorities of other member state to identify and penalize infringement across several EU member states. The maximum fine is up to 4% of the trader's annual turnover in the member state(s) where the breach occurred, or €2 million in cases where information on turnover is not available. The New Deal also contains a directive on representative actions for the protection of the collective interest of consumers (Directive 2020/1828) which enables the protection of the consumers collective interests in the EU via the legal actions brought by representative entities (qualified entities). Injunctive measures and redress measures can be sought before national courts and authorities. Importance in the creation of digital single market and removing barrier in online purchases play cross-border parcel delivery services, which is covered by EU regulation (Regulation 2018/644), giving basic ground for barrier removal, mostly with transparency principle in that area.

For safer online shopping and safer free movement of good in digital environment the European Online Dispute Resolution (ODR) platform was established by EU regulation (Regulation 524/2013). ODR is elaborated later as far it has interconnection with artificial intelligence.

Digital Markets Act (Regulation 2022/1925) and Digital Services Act (Regulation 2022/2065) are creating unified rules for digital platforms which are far above one state jurisdiction, having dominant position and significant advantages influence.

The DSA could herald a new period for digital platforms and indirectly for users worldwide due to another perpetuation of the "Brussels effect" (Bradford, 2012, 2020). According to Bradford, the EU developed a strong regulatory power at a global scale through its legal institutions and standards. Indeed, the EU aims for high standards in the Digital Single Market and could potentially develop what lawmakers consider a gold standard for platform regulation—beyond the EU's borders (Heldt & Hennemann, 2021).

E-Governance and Artificial Intelligence

Artificial intelligence can be described as the ability of a non-natural entity to make choices by an evaluative process (Turner, 2019, p. 7). Artificial intelligence as a concept used to describe computer systems that can learn from their own experiences and solve complex problems in different situations—abilities we previously thought were unique to mankind. And it is data that fuels these systems, enabling them to learn and become intelligent (Russel & Norvig, 1995, p. 31). Artificial Intelligence can be defined as software (and possibly also hardware) systems designed by humans that, given a complex goal, act in the physical or digital dimension by perceiving their environment through data acquisition, interpreting the collected structured or unstructured data, reasoning on the knowledge, or processing the information, derived from this data, and deciding the best action to take to achieve the given goal (Ethics Guidelines, Commission, 2019). Based on the ethics guidelines trustworthy artificial intelligence has three components, which should be met throughout the system's entire life cycle: (1) it should be lawful, complying with all applicable laws and regulations; (2) it should be ethical, ensuring adherence to ethical principles and values; and (3) it should be robust, both from a technical and social perspective, since, even with good intentions, artificial intelligence systems can cause unintentional harm.

The European AI strategy is recognizing the development of technologies including EU, aims to have large AI development in EU, to boost the European economy and to serve European citizens (Troitiño, 2022). European Commission proposes a three-step approach in the form of increasing public and private investment in artificial intelligence, preparing for socio-economic changes and creating an ethical and legal framework. EU provides four ethical principles for AI: (1) respect for human autonomy; (2) prevention of harm; (3) justice; (4) explain ability and defines seven requirements for AI: Human factor and oversight, technical resilience and security, privacy and data governance, transparency, diversity, non-discrimination and fairness, social and environmental well-being and responsibility (ethics guidelines, Commision, 2019). European Commission started to prepare for the first legislation piece by issueing the Communication Artificial Intelligence for Europe (Commission, 2018).

The AI Communication states the principle that large-scale use of AI-enabled tools in business-to-consumer transactions needs to be fair, transparent and compliant with consumer legislation. Commission underlines the need that consumers receive clear information on the use, features and properties of AI-enabled products, that individuals can control the data generated by using such products and that they know whether they are communicating with a machine or another human. It is further suggested that when interacting with an automated system, users are informed on how to reach a human and how to ensure that a system's decision can be checked or corrected (Mazzini, 2019, pp. 266, 267).

Commission proposed a new piece of EU legislation a Regulation on artificial intelligence (Commission, 2021). The proposal differentiates four different levels of risk while using AI specified: unacceptable risk, high risk, limited risk and minimal risk. The regulation is considered as the world's first comprehensive AI law. The aim is to have safe and transparent AI supervised by humans. AI is powered by data usage of which is already governed by GDPR, considered as the base stone of the digital single market creation. In the regulation these are proposed to be defined prohibited AI practices such as biometric identification system in public places, emotion recognition systems, predictive policy systems, etc. (European Parliament, 2023).

Current technical options in legal sector have come much further than just electronic managements or CRM systems. They offer fully automated systems, algorithm, that can handle minor legal cases independently, such as drafting easy contract and giving advice on flight compensation cases. The structure and form of artificial intelligence consisting of bits moving through the Internet could undermine certain assumptions that gave rise to traditional model of jurisdiction (Woodrow, 2018, p. 30). Another body of law which will be challenges using artificial intelligence relates to the issue of authenticating artificial intelligence when used for evidentiary purposes in court proceedings (p. 32). The questions whether the lawyers' professions can be substituted by AI in future are discussed also by legal theory (Laitinen et al., 2020). There is an opinion that this is a welcome disruption in the legal profession and one that will not bring about employment but rather a redefinition of job description (Dervanović, 2018, p. 227). AI systems will need human supervision and human lawyers will be the ones helping the development of these systems using their skills, expertise and understanding of legal concept (Henket, 2003, p. 128). Practical usage of AI might be in different areas of law such as competition law or providing due diligence (Buyers, 2018). The usage of AI in legal risk assessment is increasing interest in the adoption of risk management methods borrowed from other disciplines that can be effectively adapted for use in the legal domain (Compagnicci, 2020, p. 269). Currently legal assessment systems are managed reactively instead of proactively before damage or loss occurs (Compagnicci, 2020, p. 269). Raising issues about the time of contract consultation when contracting with a machine and signing the contract—the primary legal focus is on use of a security procedure—particularly digital signatures and on procedures for verifying that a message is that of specified person or detecting error in the content of the message (Davey, 2019, pp. 331–364). The common issues for law and AI and its governance can be divided into four different groups that shed light on how legal perceptions and rules have evolved, or are currently under strain, because of the rapid in AI-based technology. A first group is AI triggered systematic changes to regulations, institutions and the legal academy. A second group is the risk of fragmentation that may follow the context-dependent approach of current legal regulation, both national and international levels. The third group includes several different ways in which legislators and policymakers address the challenges of AI through methods of legal experimentation (Japan, UK, US) and the fourth group is the examination models of legal regulation and governance for AI (Barfield & Pagallo, 2020, pp. 180–184).

The legal technology of AI might be used in online dispute resolution governing by EU regulation (Regulation 524/2013). Expanding access to justice through ODR involves three major shifts in the dispute resolution practices. These are the shifts from a physical, face-to face setting to a virtual one, the shift from human intervention and decision making to software supported processes and the shift from an emphasis on the value of confidentiality to an emphasis on collecting, using and reusing data in order to prevent disputes (Katsh & Rabinovich Einy, 2017, pp. 46, 47). European Online Dispute Resolution (ODR) combined the technologies and the alternative dispute resolution mechanism and seeks out-of-court resolution of disputes initiated by EU consumers or traders. ODR is a platform created by European Union as "a single point of entry to consumers and traders seeking to resolve disputes out-of-court which have arisen from online transactions". The ODR platform provides general information regarding the out-of-court resolution, allows consumers and traders to submit complaints by filling in an electronic complaint form, transmits complaints to an ADR entity competent to deal with the dispute concerned (Hamulák, 2018). The ODR platform offers, free of charge, an electronic case management tool. ODR idea is not new, was already applied by several platforms such as eBay. ODR is based on the principles of transparency, voluntariness and fairness of treatment. The outcome of ADR proceedings has no binding force, and different solutions might be adopted in national law (Mania, 2015, pp. 76–86). Concurrently to the rise of ODR the use of artificial intelligence (AI) systems in dispute resolution has grown significantly. AI can be utilized in a plethora of ways (Carneiro et al., 2014, p. 212). For example, AI can act as a mediator or provide a quantitative breakdown in assets (Alessa, 2022). Artificial intelligence-driven software is limited to binary logic, which is written in binary code. Advanced forms such as learning systems can transform new data into decisions without significant human interaction. Other responsive systems can even dynamically modify the previous patterns (Wischmeyer, 2018, p. 3). However, algorithms lack common sense and soft decision factors such as intuition, value judgement or holistic thinking. Machines cannot think, nor can they answer deep philosophical questions (Grupp, 2020, p. 664).

The role of AI in ODR is identified by Carneiro et al. (2014) as usage of supportive AIsystems. For example, systems which allow the more effective management of ODR cases or support users by dealing with complex calculations and algorithms on their behalf (Alessa, 2022). Others like Orr and Rule (2018) would be willing to have a fully automated ODR system. Authors Rifkin (2010) and Katsh et al. (2001) seek to describe the role of AI in ODR as a phenomenon that shapes the nature of the discourse—as a so-called "fourth party" negotiator. Arguably, there exist two primary ways in which AI technology is currently being employed in the field: either in a support capacity or a substitutive one (Alessa, 2022). When AI is used in a support role, the third party uses it as a tool to accomplish their goal. When used in a substitutive capacity, the AI begins to take on the essential functions traditionally associated with the third party altogether, for example by coming to decisions or making inquiries of the first and second parties. This is not to say that it is necessary for a system to entirely replace a third-party negotiator (Alessa, 2022).

Single Digital Gateway and Electronic Identification

The single digital gateway provides online access to information, administrative procedures and assistance services that EU citizens and businesses may need in another member states. EU Digital Single Gateway Regulation (Regulation 2018/1724) provides three phases—(1) Access to the information about the procedures (from 12 December 2020) (2) Services provided online (from 12. December 2023) (3) Access to the assistance services (from 12. December 2023).

The Gateway is accessible through the Your Europe portal. From the portal after choosing the area the user is redirected to the websites of other EU member states which are relevant for the issue. The areas are such as starting a business and closing, study, registering a car, etc. The aim is to remove obstacles for citizens of member states with living and doing business in any other EU member state.

The Regulation should promote and facilitate the streamlining of governance arrangements for the services covered by the gateway (recital 72). The objective of the Regulation is to ensure that users who operate in other Member States have online access to comprehensive, reliable, accessible and understandable Union and national information on rights, rules and obligations, to online procedures that are fully transactional cross-border and to assistance and problem-solving services (recital 73). Once-only principle is specified in recital 44: The "once-only" principle provides the basis for the creation and use of a fully operational, safe and secure technical system for the automated cross-border exchange of evidence between the actors involved in the procedure, where this is explicitly requested by citizens and businesses (see also Art. 14.7). Where the exchange of evidence includes personal data, the request should be considered to be explicit if it contains a freely given, specific, informed and unambiguous indication of the individual's wish to have the relevant personal data exchanged, either by statement or by affirmative action. Article 14.8 contains a purpose limitation principle.

The only evidence that must be made available for exchange within the scope of the SDGR are those which are already issued "in an electronic format that allows automated exchange". If such evidence are available, they must also be made available in the same format (Troitiño & Kerikmäe, 2021). This raises a key issue: when exactly can evidence be considered to be "in an electronic format that allows automated exchange"? More specifically, does this description imply that the evidence must be formatted in a semantically meaningful way. Or from the opposite perspective: does it imply that unstructured evidence, such as a graphic image (a bitmap,

JPEG or PDF scan without a semantic structure), should not be considered to be evidence falling within the scope of Article 14? Author Graux (2021) concludes that, if such documents are the available and relevant evidence in the issuing country, it seems that they satisfy the requirements of the SDGR, even though they are arguably a practice that's subject to significant improvement.

Research of Estonia University in the area of Practical usage of the Digital Single Gateway Regulation in the field of study in another member states shows that the level of digitalization of each member states has a significant importance and makes different impact of the regulation in each member state (Bhattarai et al., 2019).

In digital administration and e-government digital identification plays a significant role. The Commission in the Communication 2030 Digital Compass (Commission, 2021a) introduced the vision for 2023 in digital economy and society. Digital citizenship is mentioned in the communication, where citizens should first have access to affordable, secure and high-quality connectivity, be able to learn basic digital skills—which should become a right for all. The four cardinal points are: (1) A digitally skilled population and highly skilled digital professionals, (2) Secure and performant sustainable digital infrastructures, (3) Digital transformation of businesses (4) Digitalization of public services. There are goals set to reach until 2030 such as key public services should be available online, citizens shall have access to electronic medical records; citizens shall have access to secure electronic identification meaning that they are recognized throughout the Union, enabling them to have full control over identity transactions and shared personal data.

The Electronic Identification, Authentication and Trust Services (eIDAS) Regulation (Regulation, 2014) sets the basis for cross-border electronic identification, authentication and website certification and aims to create a predictable regulatory environment. The eIDAS lays down the conditions under which Member States recognize electronic identification means of natural and legal persons falling under a notified electronic identification scheme of another Member State; lays down rules for trust services, in particular for electronic transactions; and establishes a legal framework for electronic signatures, electronic seals, electronic time stamps, electronic documents, electronic registered delivery services and certificate services for website authentication. The face-to-face presence for identification is not necessary.

Conclusion

The process of creation of the Digital Single Market could be compared to the times when the Single Market was created. We all know that has changed our lives forever. Digital Single Market has the ability to do so. There are still many barriers to remove in the digital world, many electronic infrastructures to build, and many steps to take to live in free movement electronic and online EU. Usage of AI in the digital world is another legal and human challenge which has the ability to boost the evolution at breakneck speed. Usage of ODR and expanding the experience to classic justice systems might facilitate the access to justice in positive way. Ethic guidance and human supervision and ability to change and interact are essential in the AI usage. Education plays significant role, too.

The European integration is strengthened by the Digital Single Market creation, and we could say the member states share more power with the EU. To feel safe in digital environment the data shall be safely processed which is regulated by GDPR, that can be named as the basic stone of the digital single market. This article was not focused on discussion of GDPR but we always need to mention that once discussing and elaborating the digital space. Protecting the personal data which is a fuel of the digital space is essential and necessary to evolve further, so is the safety of the digital space. The Digital Single Market will require continuous evaluation due to the progress in digital technologies, where new technologies, practices, software, hardware are constantly created and improved. A creation of specialized committees or working groups supported by experts in different areas of Digital Single Market might be helpful to constantly evolve the DSM with actual digital trends.

References

Al-Besher, A., & Kumar, K. (2022). Use of artificial intelligence to enhance e-government services. *Measurement: Sensors, 24*, 100484. https://doi.org/10.1016/j.measen.2022.100484

Alcácer, J., Cantwell, J., & Piscitello, L. (2016). Internationalization in the information age: A new era for places, firms, and international business networks? *Journal of International Business Studies, Palgrave Macmillan Journals, 47*, 499–512.

Alessa, H. (2022). The role of artificial intelligence in online dispute resolution: A brief and critical overview. *Information & Communications Technology Law, 31*(3) Special Issue: Technology and Regulation: Which is the Tail and which is the Dog? 319–342. https://doi.org/10.1080/13600834.2022.2088060

Arnold, J. M., & Wörgötter, A. (2011). Structural reforms and the benefits of the enlarged EU internal market: Still much to be gained. *Applied Economics Letters, 18*(13), 1231–1235.

Barfield, W., & Pagallo, U. (2020). *Advanced introduction to law and artificial intelligence* (pp. 180–184). Elgar.

Bauman, Z. (2000). *Globalizácia—Dôsledky pre ľudstvo* (1st ed., p. 124). Kallingram.

Bhattarai, R., Pappel, I., Vainsalu, H., Yahia, S. B., & Draheim, D. (2019). The impact of the single digital gateway regulation from the citizens' perspective. *Procedia Computer Science, 164*, 159–167. https://doi.org/10.1016/j.procs.2019.12.168

Bradford, A. (2012). The Brussels effect. *Northwestern University Law Review, 107*(1), 1–67. https://doi.org/10.1093/oso/9780190088583.003.0003. crossref: Heldt, A. (2022) EU digital services act : The white hope of intermediary regulation. *Digital Platform Regulation*. Palgrave Global Media Policy and Business. https://doi.org/10.1007/978-3-030-95220-4_4

Bradford, A. (2020). *The Brussels effect: How the European Union rules the world*. Oxford University Press. crossref: Heldt, A. (2022) EU digital services act: The white hope of intermediary regulation. *Digital Platform Regulation*. Palgrave Global Media Policy and Business. https://doi.org/10.1007/978-3-030-95220-4_4

Buyers, J. (2018). Artificial intelligence. In *The practical legal issues*. Law Brief Publishing.

Carneiro, D., Novais, P., Andrade, F., Zeleznikow, J., & Neves, J. (2014). Online dispute resolution: An artificial intelligence perspective. *Artificial Intelligence Review, 41*, 211–212. https://doi.org/10.1007/s10462-011-9305-z

Clarke, A. (2017, July 12). Digital government units: Origins, orthodoxy and critical considerations for public management theory and practice. *Orthodoxy and Critical Considerations for Public Management Theory and Practice*. https://doi.org/10.2139/ssrn.3001188.

Coleman, S., & Gøtze, J. (2001). Bowling together: Online public engagement in policy deliberation. http://bowlingtogether.net

Commission. (2015). Communication from the Commission to the European parliament, the Council, the European economic and social committee and the Committee of the regions: A Digital Single Market Strategy for Europe, (COM(2015) 192), p. 3.

Commission. (2018). Communication from the Commission to the European Parliament, the European Council, the Council, the European Economic and Social Committee and the Committee of the Regions Artificial Intelligence for Europe COM/2018/237 final.

Commission. (2019, April 2019). *Ethics guidelines for trustworthy AI*. High-Level Expert Group on Artificial Intelligence. Available https://digital-strategy.ec.europa.eu/en/library/ethics-guidelines-trustworthy-ai

Commission. (2021) Proposal for a Regulation of the European Parliament and of the Council Laying Down Harmonised Rules on Artificial Intelligence (Artificial Intelligence Act) and Amending Certain Union Legislative Acts Com/2021/206 Final.

Commission. (2021a). Communication from the Commission to the European Parliament, the European Council, the Council, the European Economic and Social Committee and the Committee of the Regions 2030 Digital Compass: the European way for the Digital Decade COM/2021/118 final.

Compagnicci, C. M. (2020). *Perspectives in law, business and innovation, big data, databases and "ownership" rights in the cloud* (p. 269). Springer.

Davey, F. (2019). Making contracts online: Old wine in smart bottles? In *Law, policy and the internet* (pp. 331–364). Hart.

Dávidekova, G. (2017). Case study: Impacts of globalization on socio-economic domain of employees in the area of Czech and Slovak Republic. *AD ALTA: Journal of Interdisciplinary Research, 2*, 46–52.

Dervanović, D. (2018). Inhuman lawyer: Developing artificial intelligence in the legal profession. In *Robotics, AI and the future of law* (p. 227). Springer.

Directive (EU) 2005/29/EC of the European Parliament and of the Council of 11 May 2005 concerning unfair business-to-consumer commercial practices in the internal market and amending Council Directive 84/450/EEC, Directives 97/7/EC, 98/27/EC and 2002/65/EC of the European Parliament and of the Council and Regulation (EC) No 2006/2004 of the European Parliament and of the Council ('Unfair Commercial Practices Directive').

Directive (EU) 2011/83/EU of the European Parliament and of the Council of 25 October 2011 on consumer rights, amending Council Directive 93/13/EEC and Directive 1999/44/EC of the European Parliament and of the Council and repealing Council Directive 85/577/EEC and Directive 97/7/EC of the European Parliament and of the Council.

Directive (EU) 2019/2161 of the European Parliament and of the Council of 27 November 2019 amending Council Directive 93/13/EEC and Directives 98/6/EC, 2005/29/EC and 2011/83/EU of the European Parliament and of the Council as regards the better enforcement and modernisation of Union consumer protection rules.

Directive (EU) 2020/1828 of the European Parliament and of the Council of 25 November 2020 on representative actions for the protection of the collective interests of consumers and repealing Directive 2009/22/EC.

Directive (EU) 93/13/EEC of 5 April 1993 on unfair terms in consumer contracts.

Directive (EU) 98/6/EC of the European Parliament and of the Council of 16 February 1998 on consumer protection in the indication of the prices of products offered to consumers.

Dupont, L. (2019). Agile innovation: Creating value in uncertain environments. *Journal of Innovation Economics Management, 28*, 1–5. https://doi.org/10.3917/jie.028.0001

Efrat, Z., & Geraghty, K. (2017). Interview: Digital transformation requires a different mindset. *Governance Directions, 69*(7), 390–391. https://doi.org/10.3316/informit.993620269074709

EIPA (European Institute of Public Administration). (2003). *e-Government in Europe*. The State of Affairs. http://www.eipa.nl
Europe 2020 - A strategy for securing of a smart, sustainable and inclusive growth (COM (2010) 2020).
European Parliament. (2023). Amendments adopted by the European Parliament on 14 June 2023 on the proposal for a regulation of the European Parliament and of the Council on laying down harmonised rules on artificial intelligence (Artificial Intelligence Act) and amending certain Union legislative acts (COM(2021)0206—C9–0146/2021–2021/0106(COD)).
Gil-Garcia, J. R., Zhang, J., & Puron-Cid, G. (2016). Conceptualizing smartness in government: An integrative and multi-dimensional view. *Government Information Quarterly, 33*(3), 524–534.
Graux, H. (2021). The single digital gateway regulation as an enabler and constraint of once-only in Europe. In *The once-only principle* (pp. 83–103) Available https://link.springer.com/chapter/10.1007/978-3-030-79851-2_5
Grupp, M. (2020). Legal Tech—Impulse fur Streitbeilegung und Rechtsdienstleistung. In *Anwaltsblatt* (p. 664) Crossref: Buchholtz, G: Artificial Intelligence and Legal Tech: Challenges to the Rule of Law, *Regulating Artificial Intelligence*, 2020, Springer, p. 183.
Hamulák, O. (2018). La carta de los derechos fundamentales de la union europea y los derechos sociales. *Estudios constitucionales, 16*(1), 167–186.
Heldt, A., & Hennemann, M. (2021, July 15). *Die Goldenen Zwanziger Jahre der Technikregulierung [The golden twenties of tech regulation]*. Tagesspiegel Background Digitalisierung & KI. https://background.tagesspiegel.de/digitalisierung/die-goldenen-zwanziger-jahre-der-technikregulierung. Crossref: Heldt, A. (2022). EU Digital Services Act: The White Hope of Intermediary Regulation. *Digital Platform Regulation*. Palgrave Global Media Policy and Business. https://doi.org/10.1007/978-3-030-95220-4_4
Henket, M. (2003). Great expectations: AI and law as an issue for legal semiotics. *International Journal for the Semiotics of Law, 16*(2), 128. https://doi.org/10.1023/A:1022849231673. Crossref: Dervanović, D.: Inhuman Lawyer: Developing Artificial Intelligence in the Legal Profession, In: *Robotics, AI and the Future of Law*, 2018, Springer, p. 227. https://europa.eu/youreurope/index_en.htm
Ježová, D. (2018). GDPR—Result of globalization? In *Globalization and its socio-economic consequences: Proceedings* (pp. 167–174). Žilinská univerzita.
Katsh, E., Katsh, M., & Rifkin, J. (2001). *Resolving conflicts in cyberspace* (p. 17). Jossey-Bass.
Katsh, E., & Rabinovich Einy, O. (2017). *Digital justice—Technology and the internet of disputes* (pp. 46–47). Oxford University Press.
Ladi, S. (2006). Globalization and Europeanization: Analysing change. Available https://www.ibei.org/globalization-and-europeanization-analysing-change_20692.pdf. Accessed 12 Mar 2023.
Laitinen, E., Troitiño, D. R., & Kerikmäe, T. (2020). European Union and Great Britain: After Brexit, who wins the break-up? In *The EU in the 21st century: Challenges and opportunities for the European integration process* (pp. 103–116).
Mania, K. (2015). Online dispute resolution: The future of justice. *International Comparative Jurisprudence, 1*(1), 76–86.
Marcut, M. (2017). *Crystalizing the EU digital policy—An exploration into the digital single market* (pp. 85–104). Springer.
Mazzini, G. (2019). The approach of the European Commission on artificial intelligence. *Digital Revolution—New Challenges for Law*, 266–267.
Mergel, I., Edelmann, N., & Haug, N. (2018). Defining digital transformation: Results from expert interviews. *Government Information Quarterly, 36*(4), 101385. https://doi.org/10.1016/j.giq.2019.06.002
Orr, D., & Rule, C. (2018). Artificial intelligence and the future of online dispute resolution. *Santa Clara High Technology Law Journal, 10*.
Pelkmans, J. (2019). The Single market remains the decisive power of the EU. CEPS policy priorities for 2019–2024. https://www.ceps.eu/wp-content/uploads/2019/10/The-single-market-remains-the-decisive-power-of-the-EU.pdf. Accessed 8 Oct 2023.

Regulation (EU) 2018/1724 of the European Parliament and of the Council of 2 October 2018 establishing a single digital gateway to provide access to information, to procedures and to assistance and problem-solving services and amending Regulation (EU) No 1024/2012.
Regulation (EU) 2018/302 of the European Parliament and of the Council of 28 February 2018 on addressing unjustified geo-blocking and other forms of discrimination based on customers' nationality, place of residence or place of establishment within the internal market and amending Regulations (EC) No 2006/2004 and (EU) 2017/2394 and Directive 2009/22/EC.
Regulation (EU) 2018/644 of the European Parliament and of the Council of 18 April 2018 on cross-border parcel delivery services.
Regulation (EU) 2022/1925 of the European Parliament and of the Council of 14 September 2022 on contestable and fair markets in the digital sector and amending Directives (EU) 2019/1937 and (EU) 2020/1828 (Digital Markets Act).
Regulation (EU) 2022/2065 of the European Parliament and of the Council of 19 October 2022 on a Single Market for Digital Services and amending Directive 2000/31/EC (Digital Services Act).
Regulation (EU) No 524/2013 of the European Parliament and of the Council of 21 May 2013 on online dispute resolution for consumer disputes and amending Regulation (EC) No 2006/2004 and Directive 2009/22/EC (Regulation on consumer ODR).
Regulation (EU) No 910/2014 of the European Parliament and of the Council of 23 July 2014 on electronic identification and trust services for electronic transactions in the internal market and repealing Directive 1999/93/EC (The Electronic Identification, Authentication and Trust Services (eIDAS) Regulation).
Rifkin, J. (2010). Online dispute resolution: Theory and practice of the fourth party. *Conflict Resolution Quarterly, 19*, 117.
Ručinská, S., & Fečko, M. (2017) European Union digital single market—Get connected or still a vision from the Slovak Republic perspective?. pp. 19, 20. https://doi.org/10.24989/ocg.v325.2.
Russel, S. J., & Norvig, P. (1995). *Artificial intelligence: A modern approach* (pp. 31–35). Prentice Hall.
Schmidt, C., & Krimmer, R. (2022). How to implement the European digital single market: Identifying the catalyst for digital transformation. *Journal of European Integration, 44*(1), 59–80. https://doi.org/10.1080/07036337.2021.2011267
Troitiño, D. R. (2022). La estrategia de las instituciones de la Unión Europea ante el reto de digitalización. *Revista CIDOB d'Afers Internacionals*, 17–40.
Troitiño, D. R., & Kerikmäe, T. (2021). Europe facing the digital challenge: Obstacles and solutions. *IDP Revista de Internet, Derecho y Política, 34*, 1–3.
Turner, J. (2019). *Robot rules, regulating artificial intelligence* (p. 16). Palgrave Macmillan.
Wischmeyer, T. (2018). Regulierung intelligenter Systeme. *Archive des offentlichen Rechts*, 3–13. Crossref: in Buchholtz, G. (2020). Artificial Intelligence and Legal Tech: Challenges to the Rule of Law. In: Regulating Artificial Intelligence, Springer, p. 183.
Woodrow, B. (2018). Towards a law of artificial intelligence. In *Law of artificial intelligence* (pp. 30–32). Elgar.

Digital Competition Law Issues and Interrelated Aspects of Law

Pawan Kumar Dutt

Abstract The legislative package comprising of the Digital Markets Act was adopted by the European Union along with the Digital Services Act in July 2022. This was partly in response to the rise of star technology firms in recent years and the need for competition law to address wider socio-economic interests such as redistribution of wealth, protection of labour and ensuring fairness. This chapter is an indepth analysis of the Digital Markets Act and relevant case laws and their influence on the European Digital Single Market. The author's analysis of traditional competition law reveals that it is inadequate when dealing with the challenges of the digital market. Effective eGovernance necessitates a competent legislative framework which allows for meaningful digital economic development and hence the role of a fair and contestable Digital Single Market is essential for eGovernance. The author's research shows that competition law alone cannot answer all the above challenges and hence, a holistic view of the various legal elements is required so as to meet the digital market challenges of today and the future. For this purpose, the author has examined the confluence of several legal areas, namely intellectual property laws, competition law in the digital environment, human rights law, ethics, morality, public ordre, consumer protection and the necessity for EU wide integration when it comes to digital services. Key words: competition, consumer protection, Digital Markets Act, eGovernance, ethics, digital single market, human rights, intellectual property.

Introduction

Neoliberal economics notwithstanding, competition law and the enforcement thereof are back in focus due to efforts by various governments to restore trust in markets (especially high technology markets) which have been recently affected by

P. K. Dutt (✉)
Law School, Tallinn University of Technology, Tallinn, Estonia
e-mail: pawan.dutt@taltech.ee

D. Ramiro Troitiño (ed.), *E-Governance in the European Union*, Contributions to Political Science, https://doi.org/10.1007/978-3-031-56045-3_11

several high-profile cases, public dissatisfaction with growing economic imbalances in the digital world and the realisation that perhaps competition law entails diverse faces and roles within society.[1]

However, competition by itself is not a panacea, if the consumer is unable to make well-informed and active choices while buying a product that is most suitable for her. For this, she must ideally rely on the four aspects as outlined by Amelia Fletcher (namely, engage the market, access relevant information, assess that information and subsequently act on it).[2] The reality, though, can be quite different since the consumer very often has not only limited information but also limited abilities to process the same. Add to that everyday phenomena such as search and switching costs, cognitive limitations, behavioural biases, decisions constrained by imperfect information, incoherent rankings, procrastination and failure in selecting preferred options, etc. and one can see how the abovementioned aspects are not easily performable functions for consumers. Such poor choices made by consumers in turn affect market outcomes.[3]

The meteoric rise of star technology firms (also known as GAFAM[4]) has brought forth the question of whether the role of competition law should be enlarged to cover wider socio-economic interests such as redistribution of wealth, protection of labour and ensuring fairness.[5]

In July 2022, a legislative package comprising the Digital Markets Act[6] (DMA) was adopted along with the Digital Services Act[7] (DSA). This package has the following twin goals, namely promotion of fundamental rights (in the context of digital services) and promotion of technological innovativeness within the European Single Market (by means of common rules which would be applicable to all digital service providers, within and outside the European Union (EU)).[8] In a way, this could be seen as an admission that the retailers of the e-commerce sector differ significantly, both in novelty and complexity, from retailers of the traditional brick-and-mortar sector.[9]

But the question arises as to what are the relevant borders of the DMA and how will it influence the European Digital Single Market? The author analyses whether traditional competition law is compatible with the challenges of the digital markets and what needs to change. Since effective eGovernance requires a competent legislative framework which allows for meaningful digital economic development, then the role of a fair and contestable Digital Single Market is essential for eGovernance.

---

[1] Stylianou and Iacovides (2022), p. 620.

[2] Fletcher (2021), p. 256.

[3] Crawford et al. (2021), pp. 109–110.

[4] Acronym for Google, Amazon, Facebook, Apple and Microsoft.

[5] Stylianou and Iacovides (2022), p. 621.

[6] Regulation (EU) 2022/1925.

[7] Regulation (EU) 2022/2065.

[8] Cauffman and Goanta (2021), p. 758.

[9] OECD Handbook (2022), p. 33.

But can competition law alone answer all these challenges, or do we need a holistic view of the various legal elements which comprise the digital market challenges of today and the future?

Competition Law Designed for Traditional Markets

Arising out of neo-classical price theory, one can see that traditionally competition law has concerned itself with the goals of ensuring efficiency (both at the allocative and productive levels), lower prices and higher outputs. This is designed to benefit consumers (which in the EU include both direct and indirect users and also competitors of the supplier in markets which are downstream) and to perpetuate competition in the market.[10]

The enforcement of competition law offers competitive pricing to consumers, provides opportunities to the poor and promotes social mobility, by limiting profit margins of business enterprises and transferring wealth from producers to consumers.[11]

The pre-existing measures to prevent unfair competition are Articles 101 and 102 of the Treaty on the Functioning of the European Union (TFEU).[12] Article 101 has the primary object of targeting restrictive practices between two or more undertakings, while Article 102 is directed at the conduct of one undertaking (which is powerful and dominant and abuses its market power, although dominance by itself is not against the law). Dominance is assessed based on variables such as the product market, geographical market, temporal factors, vertical integration, economies of scale, advantages in technological terms and rapid changes in the market.[13] EU competition law upholds fairness, targets unfair pricing and addresses wider policy matters such as protection of social and consumer interests.[14]

Various judgements have described dominance as being a position of economic strength, whereby an undertaking feels empowered enough to behave independently of the market competition, its own customers and general consumers, thereby preventing effective competition within the relevant market.[15]

A distinction is drawn between abusive conduct and aggressive competitiveness, since the ultimate goal of these legal provisions is consumer protection, rather than protection of business competitors.[16] It should be noted that the TFEU specifically

---

[10] Darr (2021), p. 1.

[11] Ezrachi et al. (2023), p. 55.

[12] Whish (2003), p. 427.

[13] Nyman-Metcalf et al. (2014), p. 7.

[14] Ezrachi et al. (2023), p. 53.

[15] Some such cases are United Brands and United Brands Continental v Commission, C-27/76, ECLI:EU:C:1978:22; Hoffmann-La Roche v Commission, Case C-85/76, ECLI:EU:C:1979:36; and Microsoft v Commission, Case T-201/04 ECLI:EU:T:2007:289.

[16] Nyman-Metcalf et al. (2014).

states that there should be a high level of consumer protection within the union and consumer protection requirements are essential while union policies are defined and interpreted.[17]

Challenges of Digital Markets

Over the last decade, there have been substantial developments within the sphere of digital markets. While this phenomenon has greatly benefited consumers in general, the risk of high levels of concentrations in the markets has also increased.[18] In the context of digital markets it can be seen that anti-competitive mergers, competitors entering into illicit agreements among themselves and vertical restraints have the potential to be as harmful as in traditional markets. Digital markets contain features which can amplify the above harms thanks to the rise of peculiarly novel forms of misconduct.[19]

In the twenty-first century, the challenges for competition law are increasingly driven by the role played by major internet platforms in enabling customers to acquire information, communicate within social groups and spend/earn their economic capital. However, such digital dominance can potentially diminish consumer choices, undermine privacy and cause general harm at economic, social and political levels. This goes beyond the interests of consumers and sometimes the only solution appears to be to divest platforms of their assets and break them into smaller business units.[20]

It is noteworthy that two main areas of concern for competition authorities with respect to digital markets are dynamic competition and the misuse of data.[21] Interestingly enough, data is the most essential element of the digital market as it serves several key roles, including working as an asset which enhances competitiveness, serving as a potential entry barrier for newcomers and adding a high degree of quality to everyday technical and business functions. For example, data has enabled new business models centred around personal pricing strategies.[22]

Managing online consumer data (which is constantly being accumulated) in the hands of large online platforms is especially problematic, since such data is often collected either for the purposes of monetisation or to attract a consumer's attention. Which is why there is a strong need for regulation by enabling online privacy features to be simplified and standardised, while allowing consumers to set default

---

[17] Articles 12 and 169, TFEU.

[18] Fabiana et al. (2021), p. 88.

[19] OECD Handbook (2022), p. 3.

[20] Kuenzler (2022), p. 253.

[21] OECD Handbook (2022), p. 4.

[22] OECD Handbook (2022), p. 18.

limits on the amount and type of personal data which can be collected online.[23] This can also help to tackle the dangers of discrimination against vulnerable consumers through the misuse of collected data by means of algorithms or direct targeting.[24]

Data portability and interoperability play an essential role in the promotion of competition among and within digital platforms. Data portability promotes competition in two ways: by reducing costs related with user switching and reducing friction for users who want to try newer services. This can alleviate movement barriers and prove helpful for new entrants in the digital markets. Interoperability works at the system level, by enabling communication between different systems, thereby allowing multi-homing (using multiple competing platforms at the same time[25]) and increased market contestability.[26]

In highly concentrated markets (such as the digital market), consumers are often unable to choose between different options of alternative values. This results in loyal consumers being locked in an unequal relationship with certain providers due to lack of productive rivalry and the product design choices (such as tying, refusal-to-deal practices, etc.) of the leading digital actors can directly entrap a consumer's influence.[27]

Digital markets are characterised by certain key aspects, namely multi-sided markets (gathering together different consumer groups within a platform), powerful network effects (enabling growth of the value of the product to mirror user growth in numbers), outsized economies of scale and scope, a business method which relies upon collection and usage of substantial amounts of user data, and a business revenue model whereby zero (or low) priced products are offered in lieu of consumer data (collected by the digital market player to be used for advertisement purposes or to leverage customer relationships). These practices go hand-in-hand with other notable features such as high switching costs for users (who have invested time, effort and money in creating social media profiles or reputations, and now risk losing it all by switching to a competitor). Digital markets also readily embrace disruptive innovations which can reduce costs while side-stepping regulatory frameworks which limit incumbency-led competition. In the case of a digital ecosystem, cross-market consolidation of power and anti-competitive results can also be achieved by misusing bundling and tying strategies, and through the coercive use of Intellectual Property Rights (IPR).[28]

Thus, the ever-present risk is that a vertically integrated "gatekeeper" styled digital platform can streamline different levels of the supply chain within itself, thereby facilitating business transactions for other downstream business users while simultaneously competing with the very same business users by means of preferential

[23] Crawford et al. (2021), p. 135.

[24] Crawford et al. (2021), p. 138.

[25] OECD Handbook (2022), p. 10.

[26] OECD Handbook (2022), p. 54.

[27] Kuenzler (2022), p. 257.

[28] OECD Handbook (2022), pp. 13, 14.

offering of its own goods and services (on advantageous terms) to common end users. In effect, it performs the dual role of an intermediary as well as a provider of complementary services. While vertical integration is economically efficient (as it eliminates double marginalisation, lowers transaction costs and enables the raising of volumes), it also enables the platform to attain a certain size whereby it could be tempted to close access to its competitors and capture most of the platform's rents.[29]

At the same time, statistics related to concentrations or revenue shares can be very misleading indicators about market power (and dominance) and do not always reveal the correct picture about the intensities of competition in digital markets.[30]

It should be noted that standard competition rules are often unable to address the challenges posed by digital markets.[31] Market analyses of digital markets by competition authorities, based on standard methodologies such as the SSNIP test (the small but significant non-transitory increase in price test) are usually ineffective, while the hypothetical monopolist test may still be valid. The analysis by competition authorities needs to adapt to the new ground realities of rapidly changing competitive digital landscapes, geographically borderless dimensions of the digital markets and the unique issue of non-price competitions within the envelope of network effects and multi-sided platform markets.[32] Other forms of misconduct, such as algorithmic collusion (namely, algorithms by design and/or algorithmic interdependent pricing which can act without human intervention), are more innocuous and create a grey zone between pro-competitive conduct (by enabling optimisation of the enterprises' business activities and processes thereby enhancing competitiveness; fostering innovation and enabling efficiencies which are directed towards consumer welfare by offering dynamic pricing, transparent markets, etc.) and anti-competitive conduct (by allowing algorithmic explicit collusion enabled pricing to be a tool for price-fixing and cartelisation; algorithmic tacit collusion which allows prices to be fixed autonomously without human intervention or reciprocal interactions, etc.), while being difficult for competition authorities to satisfactorily analyse.[33]

The market power of various digital platforms can be gauged from the following factors: business models based on strong returns to scale, the existence of substantial network effects among incumbents and the high degree of data dependency which exists for a predominant number of online service providers. The abovementioned factors enable established digital players to exercise extraordinary control (and dominance) over smaller digital players, thanks to the massive accumulation of data.[34]

---

[29] Knapstad (2023), pp. 9, 10.

[30] OECD Handbook (2022), p. 17.

[31] Fabiana et al. (2021), p. 88.

[32] OECD Handbook (2022), pp. 28–29.

[33] Caforio (2023), pp. 9, 15–18.

[34] Fabiana et al. (2021), p. 89.

We can see that many legal doctrines, developed for a different era, have had to be broadened in unimaginable ways due to the rise of the internet. This was necessitated by the fact that while the legislature was too slow to respond to the increasing challenges of the digital world, the judiciary had no option but to use the very doctrines which were developed for an analogue world of the brick-and-mortar economy and modify them to cope with the era of digitisation brought in by internet giants such as Google, eBay, Facebook and others. This can especially be seen in the case of the doctrine of competition law dealing with the concept of tying and bundling, which was originally developed for instances when sales of more than one product were combined, often to the detriment of the consumer.[35] This doctrine has now been expanded in an ingenious manner, to cover instances where software was integrated into an operating system[36] and where a company's own services were displayed in a prioritised manner within the ranking system of a search engine owned and operated by the said company.[37]

Establishing a theory of harm in the case of tying and bundling in digital markets is easy because the marginal revenue therein is very much higher than marginal costs and digital goods are considered to be non-rivalrous in nature (being simultaneously consumable by several customers). Digital goods are also infinitely expansible in nature as their quantity can be vastly expanded in arbitrary terms with almost zero costs. Other risk factors include network effects, the temptation to prolong temporary monopolies (which run the risk of being readily toppled by upstarts utilising superior technologies) through the coercive use of high market entry barriers, and the fact that software can be conveniently bundled. All the above make the anti-competitive practice of tying and bundling a particularly effective way to decrease incentives for innovation, deter market entry and cement pre-existing dominance.[38]

Overlap of Different Legal Aspects

Some scholars claim that a quantitative analysis of over 4000 various sources (including case laws, opinions, decisions, speeches, etc.) reveals that the main goals of EU competition law encompass efficiency, welfare of consumers, freedoms (economic and commercial freedoms, freedom to compete, etc.), safeguarding of the market structure, fairness, integration of the EU's single market and ensuring the competition processes.[39]

---

[35] Holzweber (2018), pp. 342–3.

[36] Case T-201/04 Microsoft 2014.

[37] Commission decision AT.39740 Google Search (Shopping) (C(2017) 444, 27 June, 2017).

[38] Holzweber (2018), pp. 351–3.

[39] Stylianou and Iacovides (2022), p. 632.

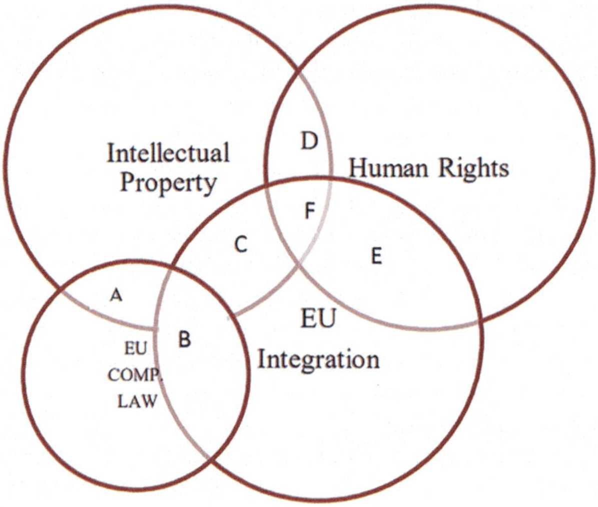

Fig. 1 The overlap of different legal aspects related to digital competition law. A: TTBER (Commission Regulation (EU) No 316/2014 of 21 March 2014 on the application of Article 101(3) of the Treaty on the Functioning of the European Union to categories of technology transfer agreements); B: DMA (Regulation (EU) 2022/1925 on contestable and fair markets in the digital sector and amending Directives (EU) 2019/1937 and (EU) 2020/1828 (Digital Markets Act)) and DSA (Regulation (EU) 2022/2065 on a Single Market For Digital Services and amending Directive 2000/31/EC (Digital Services Act)); C: TFEU (Treaty on the Functioning of the European Union) IPR Article 118 (Article 118 TFEU, wherein European IPR are to be created in the context of the establishment and functioning of the internal market); D: Ethics, Morality, Public Ordre; E: ECHR (European Convention on Human Rights, Rome, 1950) and the Lisbon Treaty of 2009 whereby the EU acceded to the ECHR; F: Consumer protection

A careful analysis of the various relevant (and topical cases) in this regard reveals four distinct streams, namely the confluence of IP laws, EU competition law in the digital environment, human rights law and the necessity for EU wide integration when it comes to digital services. The overlapping regions cover specific legal aspects and regulations, as outlined in Fig. 1.

The Overarch of Human Rights

Recital 109 of the DMA states that it respects the fundamental rights recognised by the Charter of Fundamental Rights of the EU[40] and especially the freedom to conduct a business, right to an effective remedy and a fair trial, and the right against double jeopardy.

However, some authors claim that competition laws cover even human rights, as outlined below. When competition law deals with rights, the neoliberal conception thereof covers the rights to liberty, equality, security and property, which are distinct from the view of economists belonging to the Chicago School (who tend to have a more economic approach). Distributive justice or human rights are often seen as being incompatible with competition law, although some scholars assert that the right to health (thereby regulating the pharmaceutical industry and its "misuse" of patent monopolies) or the right to food (thereby regulating the "misuse" of power by larger multinational corporations who exploit small suppliers of food products and consumers who are vulnerable to price shocks) are integral aspects of competition law. Similarly, while the right to property forms the foundations for competition law, it should be noted that in the digital economy, the right to privacy (being a core principle of the EU) is paramount along with sustainable and balanced growth. Thus, it is challenging for competition law to retain its core values of promoting openness, competition and prevention of abuse of economic power by dominant undertakings, to the detriment of the human rights of consumers.[41]

Some other relevant rights, besides the prevention of arbitrary or disproportionate exercise of power by the EU Commission, include rights to a fair hearing (including within a reasonable time), good administration, equal treatment (when it comes to assessment of fines and other penalties), presumption of innocence; compatibility of the search-and-seizure powers enjoyed by competition law authorities to the right to privacy, inviolability of home, legal professional privilege (including prohibition of a "fishing expedition") and of course the right to be heard in merger control cases.[42]

Similarly, when it comes to the standard of proof requirements for proceedings to impose "harsh" pecuniary penalties under competition law, it must be noted that under human rights law the determination of criminal charges (leading up to the imposition of fines upon dominant enterprises which misuse their market power) gives rise to protections, particularly concerning the presumption of innocence.[43]

A sub-corollary is consumer protection[44] especially since competition and consumer protection go hand-in-hand towards facilitating good outcomes for

---

40 2000/C 364/01.

41 Darr (2021), pp. 3, 4, 8 and 9.

42 Andreangeli (2017), pp. 524, 528, 529 and 536

43 Yeung and Yeung (2021), p. 353.

44 Crawford et al. (2021).

consumers.[45] For example, in a decision upheld by the UK Advertising Standards Authority, Amazon was found to be guilty of misleading consumers into subscribing for its Amazon Prime service in two ways—by misusing its market power (which raised antitrust issues) and by using dubious marketing methods (which raised consumer protection issues).[46]

It is especially important to take note of consumer protection issues for online markets by keeping large online platforms in mind because they serve as critical gatekeepers (with the unique potential to alter market functions) and have access to large swathes of consumer data (which they can effectively mine to garner information about relevant behaviour patterns by using machine learning algorithms). Further, the large online platforms enjoy a huge asymmetry in terms of power balance vis-à-vis consumers and there exists a real and present danger that they could enhance their own market power significantly in case of weak consumer protection.[47]

Third-party business users who offer their goods/services on large gatekeeper platforms can sometimes misuse consumer trust by indulging in illegal sales practices or by blatantly violating consumer protection laws. In order to prevent such breaches, it is essential that large gatekeeper platforms should be held to be more responsible.[48]

The Confluence of Intellectual Property and Competition

The intersection between intellectual property (IP) law and competition law, originally seen as conflict-prone has now considerably softened, so much so that both are now perceived as being complementary to each other.[49] Although IP law grants exclusive exploitation rights, it is nonetheless subject to Article 101 TFEU, even though both streams of law share the same objectives of promotion of consumer welfare and allocation of resources efficiently.[50]

Venegas analyses various case laws and states that IPRs create an *incentive effect*, while any limitations on IPR holders (for example, through the use of competition law restrictions against monopolistic behaviour of dominant enterprises) create a *discouragement effect*. He states that in the context of digital markets, the courts have held that the forcible licensing of IPR (especially digital IP) on the basis of FRAND[51] licensing terms or through compulsory licensing can only be allowed

45 Crawford et al. (2021), p. 108.

46 ASA ruling G19-1021643 (2019) as mentioned in Crawford et al. (2021), p. 112.

47 Crawford et al. (2021), pp. 116–117.

48 Crawford et al. (2021), p. 141.

49 Nyman-Metcalf et al. (2014).

50 Zevgolis (2018), p. 31.

51 FRAND—fair, reasonable and non-discriminatory.

if: the licence is indispensable to compete on a downstream market; refusal to licence prevents the appearance of a new product; refusal to licence risks the elimination of effective competition on the downstream market; and the dominant undertaking is unable to justify its refusal to licence.[52]

This is especially relevant for Standard Essential Patents (SEP) where two case laws, namely Motorola[53] and Samsung[54] stand out, because the Commission had held that SEP rights should be limited due to competition concerns regarding standard process patents. Further, in Huawei/ZTE,[55] the Court of Justice of the EU (CJEU) confirmed the Commission's approach towards SEPs, albeit in a narrow manner (namely, that SEPs are different from usual patents and if a company agrees to a licence on FRAND terms then no injunctions should be granted by the court).[56]

The Need for EU Wide Integration

Vosskuhle states that one definite success story of Europe in recent times has been the development of a fully functional European legal community which provides cohesiveness and stability, despite the presence of multiple member states, each of which very often has its separate and diverse interests. In the Costa v Enel[57] judgement, the European Court of Justice had held that Union law should receive precedence over national law. It is no wonder that for the European idea to be realised, the key is to have Rule of Law in EU legal provisions.[58]

EU integration is dominated by two perspectives—intergovernmentalism (which states that member states dominate the system) and neo-functionalism (where domestic societal groups form an association with supranational actors as they push the integration process forward).[59]

Several authors have stressed that European integration is synonymous with the internal market and this is one of the main goals of competition law in the EU.[60] The emphasis on market integration within the EU, as outlined in Consten and Grundig[61] in the 1960s, predates most other EU competition case laws. There, the court held that the single market imperative was central to all applications of competition law, and that neither exclusive distribution agreements nor trademark licence agreements

---

[52] Venegas (2023), pp. 39, 40–42, 47.

[53] Case AT.39985 Motorola—Enforcement of GPRS standard essential patents (2014).

[54] Case AT.39939 Samsung—Enforcement of UMTS standard essential patents (2014).

[55] Case C-170/2013 of CJEU, Huawei Technologies Co. Ltd. v. ZTE Deutschland GmbH.

[56] Zevgolis (2018), pp. 34, 36.

[57] Flaminio Costa v ENEL (1964) Case 6/64.

[58] Vosskuhle (2017), pp. 146, 149 and 164.

[59] Selck et al. (2007), p. 189.

[60] Stylianou and Iacovides (2022), p. 629.

[61] Joined Cases 56/64 and 58/64, Consten and Grundig.

could be allowed to divide the market along national lines, notwithstanding any claims of efficiency enhancements.[62] Thus, the promotion of EU wide market integration trumped every other consideration, be it IP related or otherwise.[63]

EU Competition Law (Especially in the Digital Environment)

A perusal of some relevant cases, which touch upon the dynamics of assorted digital economic disputes, showcases the new and complex dynamics which are displayed by the e-commerce enterprises. As the brief analyses shows, the e-commerce sector has its own peculiarities and challenges, which makes the role of competition law authorities even more complicated. This is especially so because it is not possible to rely on traditional competition law approaches when dealing with the digital arena.

Interestingly, the DMA attempts to address many of the concerns raised in the case laws. The DMA focuses on gatekeepers who provide core platform services within the digital sector and seeks to work for the benefit of business users (established in the EU) and end users (established or located in the EU) by providing fair market conditions.[64] Gatekeepers are designated on the basis of their entrenched and durable positions (whether actual or foreseeable), significant impact and importance of their core platform service.[65] Articles 5 and 6 prescribe obligations for gatekeepers which regulate, inter alia, the processing, combining and cross-use of personal data; activities of business users and end users; online advertising services; easy installation/un-installation of software applications (including those of third parties); easy switching between the various software applications; the enablement of effective interoperability and the ensuring of effective portability of data. The gatekeeper is also expected to apply FRAND terms while providing access to data to business users. Article 30 provides for fines upon errant gatekeepers up to 10% of their total worldwide turnover and which can go up to 20% in case of repeat offences.

There is also the added threat of structural remedies under Article 18, although the efficiency of such a harsh remedy would be difficult to justify and it also carries the challenge of identification of suitable parts deemed worth divesting. Such a controversial remedy is very rare in the EU context, although the breakup of Standard Oil by the US antitrust authorities can serve as an example. It would nonetheless be limited by the principles of proportionality, necessity and effectiveness.[66]

---

[62] Bacharis (2021), pp. 553, 555.

[63] Nyman-Metcalf et al. (2014), p. 10.

[64] Art. 1 DMA. The provisions of the DMA are without prejudice to Articles 101 and 102 of the TFEU.

[65] Art. 3 DMA. It also outlines certain presumptions based upon criteria such as annual union turnover or number of users.

[66] Knapstad (2023), pp. 1, 3.

The DMA is a novel piece of legislation and it is influenced by both pre-existing scholarly work in the field of competition law and relevant case laws. New theories of harm and novel approaches towards the designing of digital markets have been incorporated therein. Further, the competencies are centralised, thereby strengthening the hands of the Commission.[67]

The relevant case laws which shaped the DMA are outlined as follows[68]:

Case law	Pertinent notes
L'Oréal SA vs eBay[a]	This was one of the earlier cases where liability of an online-marketplace operator was examined in the context of Directives 2000/31/EC[b] and 2004/48/EC.[c] In this case goods intended (by the proprietor of the trademarks) for sale in third states were offered for sale on an online marketplace in the EU and their packaging was removed. It was held that the operator would be liable if it should have shown diligence and awareness regarding unlawful offers for sale, and if on becoming aware it had failed to act expeditiously in accordance with Article 14(1)(b) of Directive 2000/31. Further, it was held that IP injunctions should not be used to create barriers to legitimate trade.
Tom Kabinet[d]	With regard to the virtual market for second hand e-books, the concept of exhaustion of copyright has been turned over its head by holding that dematerialised digital copies are not prone to deterioration, unlike ordinary printed books. By including this interpretation of the concept of communication to the public within the scope of Article 3(1) of Directive 2001/29/EC,[e] the concept of digital exhaustion has been introduced. This will have an adverse effect on the vital intersection of IP and Competition law in the context of exhaustion.
Coty vs Amazon[f]	Here, the e-commerce platform (Amazon) was not merely a warehouse-keeper (storing goods on behalf of a third party with a view to dispatching the goods when sold in an online marketplace) but was instead playing an active role on behalf of the third party by promoting the infringing goods on its website (Amazon Marketplace) and through advertisements on Google. However, Article 9(2)(b) of Council Regulation No. 207/2009[g] and Article 9(3)(b) of Regulation 2017/1001[h] in the context of hosting under Directive 2000/31/EC[i] were interpreted as meaning that a person who unknowingly stores goods (which infringe trademarks of another) on behalf of a third party must be regarded as not stocking those goods, if that was not his aim. It should be noted that in this case, shipping services were provided by an external service provider.

[67] Hoffmann et al. (2023), pp. 1, 2.

[68] See also Crémer et al. (2022), where many of the cases listed in this table have been sourced from.

Case law	Pertinent notes
Louboutin vs Amazon[j]	Conversely, in this case the court held that when an operator of an online sales website incorporates an online marketplace and publishes advertisements of third party sellers, then the views of a well-informed and reasonably observant user become relevant, in order to determine "use" in terms of Article 9(2) of Regulation 2017/1001. If such a user establishes a link between the services of that operator and the infringing trademark, then there is a risk that such a user will form the impression that the operator by itself is marketing the goods bearing the infringing trademark. Relevant factors as far as the conduct of the operator are concerned include usage of a uniform method of presenting the published offers, displaying advertisements equally (i.e., both its own and those of third party sellers), allowing the placement of its own logo in all the advertisements, and offering marketing as well as additional services (such as storage and shipping) to third party sellers.
Meta/Facebook (Germany)[k]	No processing, cross-using or fusion of personal data—without express consent of the user. Since there is an imbalance of power between the data subject and the controller (in this case the social media operator), the need for consent should be free, specific and withdrawal of such consent should not be detrimental to the user. This is similar to obligations for gatekeeper under Article 5(2) of the DMA.
Booking.com (France)[l]	The hotel booking platform cannot force price parity clauses or parity obligations onto hotels. Further, the hotels can apply lower rates on competing web platforms and can also offer lower rates to customers who benefit from loyalty programs. This is similar to obligations for gatekeepers under Article 5(3) of the DMA.
Amazon E-book Most Favoured Nation[m]	Amazon is vertically integrated being active upstream as a publisher and downstream as an e-book retailer. Amazon's various most favoured nation (MFN) clauses and Parity Clauses (Business Model Parity Clause, Selection Parity Clause, Agency Price Parity Clause, Promotion Parity Clause, Discount Pool Provision, Wholesale Price Parity Clause, Agency Commission Parity Clause) and price-related Notification Provisions were held to be abusive under Article 102 TFEU due to Amazon's dominance in the relevant markets for English and German language e-books. The above clauses discouraged (or were likely to discourage) new companies and start-ups from entering the market, hindered (or were likely to hinder) alternative e-books business models from emerging and reduced (or were likely to reduce) incentives to support/invest in new and innovative business models for e-book suppliers. This is similar to obligations for gatekeepers under Article 5(3) of the DMA.
Amazon (Germany)[n]	Amazon.de was accused of several abusive malpractices, including lack of transparency in its business terms, exclusive jurisdiction of the court in Luxembourg which resulted in additional expenses for European sellers, extensive liability and obligation to indemnify Amazon against third-party claims, surprising termination and blocking of sellers' accounts causing loss of turnover, parity requirements, disadvantageous consequences due to negative seller ratings (unlike transactions by Amazon Retail which were non-rated) and strict regulation by Amazon of any public statements/contact with authorities by the sellers. Amazon was forced to amend its general terms of business for sellers on its marketplaces. This is similar to obligations for gatekeepers under Article 5(6) of the DMA.

Case law	Pertinent notes
Microsoft (tying)[o]	Microsoft was charged under Article 102 (TFEU) with illegally tying its web browser Internet Explorer to its separate product, namely the dominant Windows operating system. This tying prevented rival web browsers from competing on merits and resulted in foreclosing of competition, thereby reinforcing Microsoft's very strong position in the client personal computer operating system market. Microsoft had to make commitments enabling original equipment manufacturers and end users to turn Internet Explorer off and on, and to freely choose whichever competing web browser(s) to install, in a fair and unbiased manner, without any fear of retaliation. This is similar to obligations for gatekeepers under Articles 5(8) and 6(3) of the DMA.
Google Android[p]	Google was held liable under Article 102 (TFEU) with regard to its smart mobile operating system (Android) and mobile apps. Google abused its dominant position and tied its two distinct products—Google Search app and the Play Store—with each other. The portfolio-based revenue share payments were also conditional upon the pre-installation of no competing general search service on any device. The Commission found that these acts were unjustified and were capable of restricting competition. This is similar to obligations for gatekeepers under Articles 5(8) and 6(3) of the DMA.
Apple App Store, 2020[q]	The Commission has opened an investigation under Articles 101 and 102 (TFEU) regarding Apple's rules for app developers on the distribution of apps via the App Store. iPhone users can only download non-web-based apps via the App Store. Of concern is the mandatory use of Apple's in-app purchase system (IAP) for distributing paid digital content, for which Apple charges 30% commission on all subscription fees. Further, developers are restricted from informing their users about alternative (and cheaper) purchasing possibilities outside the apps. The IAP obligation also ensures that Apple controls the customers of its competitors, who subscribe in the app. This "dis-intermediates" Apple's competitors from their own customer's data, to the advantage of Apple. This is similar to obligations for gatekeepers under Articles 5(5) and 6(4) of the DMA.
Apple App Store rules for music streaming providers[r]	The Commission has taken the view that Apple may be abusing its dominant position and distorting competition in the music streaming market by setting strict App Store rules which disadvantage competing music streaming services. Apple serves as a gatekeeper to iPhone users via the App Store and these users are usually very loyal to Apple (and do not switch easily). Apple insists upon mandatory use of the IAP system for the distribution of paid content and charges high commission fees for each transaction in the App Store for rivals. Further, Apple forbids the rivals from informing their customers about alternative (and possibly cheaper) subscription options through anti-steering provisions. In view of the above, Articles 101 and 102 (TFEU) may be violated. This is similar to obligations for gatekeepers under Articles 5(4), 5(5) and 6(4) of the DMA.

Case law	Pertinent notes
Google and the online advertising technology sector[s]	The Commission is investigating whether Google has violated Articles 101 and 102 (TFEU) by favouring its own online display advertising technology services and is distorting competition in the market. Since many publishers rely on online display advertising in order to offer free online content to their customers, the collected user data is very important for monetising their online services through targeted advertising. Google has imposed obligations to use its Display and Video 360 and/or Google Ads service to purchase online advertisements on YouTube. Further, Google favours its own services and restricts access to data regarding user identity/behaviour by third parties such as advertisers, publishers or competitors under the guise of data protection laws (while allowing its own advertising intermediation services access to the above data). Google also prohibits third parties from placing cookies on Google Chrome and prevents the advertising identifier from being available to third parties on smart phones which use Android, when the user opts out of personalised advertising services. This is similar to obligations for gatekeepers under Articles 5(8) and 6(8) of the DMA.
Apple (Netherlands)[t]	Apple imposed conditions on dating app providers for controlling the sale of digital content such as boosts, superlikes, etc. In effect, customers of the dating apps could make payments only through Apple by using special IAP software, to the exclusion of all other payment options. It was held that the above strict provisions turned the users of the dating apps into customers of Apple. Further, Apple did not share customer data with the dating apps, which resulted in "dis-intermediation" due to the inability of the dating apps to conduct personal security checks of their customers or to provide them services such as billing, cancellations, refunds, etc. These business practices of Apple were found to harm the interests of customers. This is similar to obligations for gatekeepers under Articles 5(5) and 6(4) of the DMA.
Facebook Marketplace[u]	The Commission has opened an investigation into the business practices of Facebook with reference to its Marketplace, especially since Facebook has over 3 billion users. When advertising companies (which are competitors of Facebook) also use its services with regard to online classified advertisements, it is probable that valuable data regarding user preferences is generated. This data can be misused by Facebook to indulge in unfair competition against its rivals, thereby distorting competition. In view of the above, Articles 101 and 102 (TFEU) may be violated. This is similar to obligations for gatekeepers under Article 6(2) of the DMA.

Case law	Pertinent notes
Amazon-Buy Box and Marketplace[v]	The Commission concluded that Amazon had been abusing its dominance, in violation of Article 102 (TFEU), by accessing non-public data from third-party sellers on its marketplace. Amazon Retail was identifying products of third-party sellers which are due to be launched, their sale periods, prices and terms, inventories, etc. from the above data. Amazon could also identify the suppliers of the third party sellers. All these data collecting activities enabled Amazon to favour its own retail offers. Further, it was held that Amazon misused its Buy Box and loyalty programs so as to favour itself and disadvantage third-party competitors through unequal conditions and criteria. Subsequently, Amazon agreed to remedy its malpractices by removing all forms of discrimination from the conditions and criteria of its Buy Box program offers. It agreed to display the offers of competitors next to its own Featured Offers and not to misuse third party data for its own logistics operations. This is similar to obligations for gatekeepers under Article 6(2) of the DMA.
Google Android[w]	Google forced original equipment manufacturers (OEMs) to pre-install Google Search and Google Chrome in the devices sold by them. If they did not do so, then they could not get the licence to use Google Play Store. Further, OEMs could only sell devices (containing pre-installed Google apps) which ran versions of Android which were pre-approved by Google. Google shared some percent of its advertising revenue (under its revenue share agreements) only with those OEMs and mobile network operators who agreed not to pre-install any competing search apps in the devices sold by them. The Commission held that by using the above product bundles, exclusivity payments and anti-fragmentation obligations, Google was misusing its Android operating system and abusing its dominant position in violation of Article 102 (TFEU). This is similar to obligations for gatekeepers under Article 6(3) of the DMA.
Google Search (Shopping)[x]	The Commission held that Google was dominant in the markets for online general search services and online comparison shopping services and it abused its dominance (under Article 102 TFEU) by positioning its own general results pages of its own comparison shopping service in a favourable position/display, when compared to its competitors. Google also misused a specific "Panda" algorithm to demote the comparison shopping services of its rivals. Google also displayed its own services in a rich, graphical format within a box which appeared in a highly visible place. This resulted in increased online traffic to Google's own comparison shopping service, to the detriment of its rivals' comparison shopping services. This is similar to obligations for gatekeepers under Article 6(5) of the DMA.
Apple Pay[y]	The Commission has opened an investigation into Apple's mobile payment solution named Apple Pay. The issue is that Apple has abused its dominance to force the integration of its Apple Pay in merchant apps and websites. Apple Pay is the only mobile payment solution that is permitted to access its proprietary Near Field Communication (NFC) "tap and go" technology which is embedded on iOS mobile devices, for the purposes of store payments. Access to Apple Pay has also been restricted on iOS mobile devices, when it comes to specific products of its rivals, through the use of anti-interoperability measures. In view of the above, Articles 101 and 102 (TFEU) may be violated. This is similar to obligations for gatekeepers under Article 6(7) of the DMA.

Case law	Pertinent notes
Google (France)[z]	The French Autorité de la concurrence held that Google had abused its dominant position while negotiating with press agencies and publishers in France. Google had imposed unfair settlement conditions and had refused to negotiate and pay for the display of protected press content (under copyright and related rights). Google was also held to have adopted discriminatory practices by forcing zero remuneration on all publishers and press agencies, thereby (without any objective justification) treating in an identical manner, economic stakeholders in different situations. Google was required to open negotiations in good faith, so as to formulate financial proposals for the display of protected content on its services. Google's failure to comply with the above resulted in a further antitrust investigation in France, on the basis of which Google offered commitments to remedy its past behaviour, negotiate in good faith, facilitate a transparent evaluation and submit before an independent monitoring trustee approved by the Autorité. This is similar to obligations for gatekeepers under Article 6(12) of the DMA to apply FRAND general conditions of access.

[a]Case C-324/09

[b]Directive 2000/31/EC on certain legal aspects of information society services, in particular electronic commerce, in the Internal Market ('Directive on electronic commerce')

[c]Directive 2004/48/EC on the enforcement of intellectual property rights

[d]Case C-263/18

[e]Directive 2001/29/EC on the harmonisation of certain aspects of copyright and related rights in the information society

[f]Case C-567/18

[g]Council Regulation (EC) No. 207/2009 on the Community trade mark

[h]Regulation (EU) 2017/1001 on the European Union trade mark

[i]Directive on electronic commerce

[j]Joined Cases C-148/21 and C-184/21

[k]Case C-252/21, opinion of Advocate General Rantos (20th September, 2022)

[l]Autorité de la concurrence, 21st April, 2015, 15-D-06

[m]Case AT.40153

[n]Bundeskartellamt B2–88/18

[o]Case COMP/C-3/39.530

[p]Case AT.40099

[q]EC Press release 16 June, 2020

[r]EC Press release 30 April, 2021

[s]EC Press release 22 June, 2021

[t]Authority Court of Rotterdam ROT 21/4781 and ROT 21/4782

[u]EC Press release 4 June, 2021

[v]Cases AT.40703 Amazon-Buy Box and AT.40462 Amazon Marketplace

[w]Case T-604/18

[x]Case T-612/17 for annulment of Commission decision (Case AT.39740)

[y]EC Press release 16 June, 2020

[z]Autorité de la concurrence, 21st June, 2022, 22-D-13

Conclusion

Thus, we can see that the DMA (being the latest EU law designed to regulate the Digital Single Market) is largely reliant upon self-enforcement, but it is at the same time subject to the push and pull of various other legal aspects. Recital 107 of the DMA outlines its objective in a very broad sense and covers contestability, fairness, promotion of innovation, high quality services at fair and competitive prices and more choices for end users in the digital sector. As discussed, above, in order to attain these objectives, the DMA encompasses the intersection of EU competition law, IP law, human rights law and need for EU wide integration, giving rise to an interesting mix of priorities (and limitations) for the commission. The DMA regulates the obligations of gatekeepers and carries the threat of fines and/or structural reorganisation.

Knapstad opines that *ex ante* interventions by regulatory authorities have positive qualities as these can tackle structural problems in a better manner vis-à-vis *ex post* competition law rules. But are gatekeepers in the digital sector really comparable to network industries (for example in the energy sector) where parts of networks have been divested as a means of resolving abuse of dominance? And more importantly, do digital gatekeepers provide basic needs (which stand in the same category as electricity, transport, etc.) in order to justify their commonality with network industries?[69]

Another criticism is that such harmonised legal obligations at the Union level carry the risk of conflict with other European laws. Under the DMA, the Commission alone can designate gatekeepers and list core platform services. Decentralised private enforcement,[70] while encouraged by the DMA, could be subdued because the Commission is now more powerful than national competition law authorities of the member states. While focusing exclusively on the gatekeepers, the DMA's centralisation approach could potentially end up privileging the very same gatekeepers. This may arise when national competition laws of the member states (which aim to alleviate competitiveness and fairness for all enterprises in the digital market) are blocked from applying to gatekeepers, while they may still continue to apply to competing non-gatekeepers, thereby putting the latter in a rather disadvantageous position.[71]

[69] Knapstad, 2023, p. 6, 10, 11.

[70] As recommended in Case C-453/99, Courage v Crehan.

[71] Hoffmann et al. (2023).

As time progresses and the relevant caselaw develops, more criticisms of the DMA are bound to emerge. This is normal and to be expected. Sooner than later the DMA will need specific rules defining its borders, so as to enable not only a fair and contestable Digital Single Market but also an effective eGovernance system so that Europe truly becomes *fit for the digital age*. Hopefully, this work can help to identify the wider legal aspects at play here and the manner in which they influence not only each other but also our evolving understanding of the intricacies of the digital market.

List of Cases

Motorola - Enforcement of GPRS standard essential patents (2014), Case AT.39985.

Samsung - Enforcement of UMTS standard essential patents (2014), Case AT.39939.

Huawei Technologies Co. Ltd. v. ZTE Deutschland GmbH, Case C-170/2013 of CJEU.

United Brands and United Brands Continental v Commission, C-27/76, ECLI:EU:C:1978:22.

Hoffmann-La Roche v Commission, Case C-85/76, ECLI:EU:C:1979:36.

Microsoft v Commission, Case T-201/04 ECLI:EU:T:2007:289.

Commission decision AT.39740 Google Search (Shopping) (C(2017) 444, 27 June, 2017).

Flaminio Costa v ENEL (1964) Case 6/64.

Joined Cases 56/64 and 58/64, Consten and Grundig.

Case C-324/09 L'Oréal SA and Others v eBay International AG and Others.

Case C-263/18 Nederlands Uitgeversverbond and Groep Algemene Uitgevers v Tom Kabinet Internet BV and Others.

Case C-567/18 Coty Germany GmbH v Amazon Services Europe Sàrl and Others.

Joined Cases C-148/21 and C-184/21 Louboutin/Amazon.

Case C-252/21, Meta Platforms Inc., formerly Facebook Inc., Meta Platforms Ireland Limited, formerly Facebook Ireland Ltd., Facebook Deutschland GmbH v Bundeskartellamt, intervener:

Verbraucherzentrale Bundesverband e.V. opinion of Advocate General Rantos (20th September, 2022).

Autorité de la concurrence, 21st April, 2015, 15-D-06 Booking.com B.V., Booking.com France SAS et Booking.com Customer Service France SAS.

Case AT.40153 Amazon E-book MFNs and related matters.

Bundeskartellamt B2–88/18 Amazon.

Case COMP/C-3/39.530 Microsoft (tying).

Case AT.40099 Google Android.

Authority Court of Rotterdam ROT 21/4781 and ROT 21/4782 Apple.

Cases AT.40703 Amazon-Buy Box and AT.40462 Amazon Marketplace.

Case T-604/18 Google and Alphabet v Commission (Google Android).

Case T-612/17 for annulment of Commission decision (Case AT.39740) Google, Alphabet, Inc. and others v. European Commission.
Autorité de la concurrence, 21st June, 2022, 22-D-13 Google.
Case C-453/99, Courage v Crehan.
ASA ruling G19–1021643 (2019) Amazon Europe Core Sarl.

Legal Texts

Commission Regulation (EU) No 316/2014 of 21 March 2014 on the application of Article 101(3) of the Treaty on the Functioning of the European Union to categories of technology transfer agreements.
Regulation (EU) 2022/1925 on contestable and fair markets in the digital sector and amending Directives (EU) 2019/1937 and (EU) 2020/1828 (Digital Markets Act).
Regulation (EU) 2022/2065 on a Single Market For Digital Services and amending Directive 2000/31/EC (Digital Services Act).
Treaty on the Functioning of the European Union.
European Convention on Human Rights, Rome, 1950.
Directive 2000/31/EC on certain legal aspects of information society services, in particular electronic commerce, in the Internal Market ('Directive on electronic commerce').
DIRECTIVE 2004/48/EC on the enforcement of intellectual property rights.
Directive 2001/29/EC on the harmonisation of certain aspects of copyright and related rights in the information society.
Regulation (EC) No. 207/2009 on the Community trade mark.
Regulation (EU) 2017/1001 on the European Union trade mark.
The Charter of Fundamental Rights of the EU (2000/C 364/01).

References

Andreangeli, A. (2017). Competition law and fundamental rights. *Journal of European Competition Law & Practice, 8*(8), 524–538.
Bacharis, G. (2021). 'Consten and Grundig' and the inception of an EU competition law. *European Papers, 6*(1), 553–566. https://hdl.handle.net/1814/71898, pp. 553, 555
Caforio, V. (2023). Algorithmic tacit collusion: A regulatory approach. *Competition Law Review, 15*(9), –30.
Cauffman, C., & Goanta, C. (2021). A new order: The digital services act and consumer protection. *European Journal of Risk Regulation, 12*(4), 758–774.
Crawford, G., Crémer, J., Dinielli, D., Fletcher, A., Heidhues, P., Luca, M., Salz, T., Schnitzer, M., Morton, F., Seim, K., & Sinkinson, M. (2021). Consumer protection for online markets and large digital platforms. In *Policy discussion paper 1*. Tobin Centre for Economic Policy, Yale University.

Crémer, J., Heidhues, P., Dinielli, D., Kimmelman, G., Monti, G,. Podszun, R., Schnitzer, M., Scott Morton, F. M., & de Streel, A. (2022). Enforcing the digital markets act: Institutional choices, compliance, and antitrust. Available at SSRN: https://ssrn.com/abstract=4314848

Darr, A. (2021, August 5). Competition law and human rights: A complex relationship. Wirtschaft und Wettbewerb 2021, Available at SSRN: https://ssrn.com/abstract=3915662

EC Press release 16 June, 2020. https://ec.europa.eu/commission/presscorner/detail/en/ip_20_1075, https://ec.europa.eu/commission/presscorner/detail/en/ip_20_1073

EC Press release 22 June, 2021. https://ec.europa.eu/commission/presscorner/detail/en/ip_21_3143

EC Press release 30 April, 2021. https://ec.europa.eu/commission/presscorner/detail/en/ip_21_2061

EC Press release 4 June, 2021. https://ec.europa.eu/commission/presscorner/detail/en/ip_21_2848

Ezrachi, A., Zac, A., & Decker, C. (2023). The effects of competition law on inequality—An incidental by-product or a path for societal change? *Journal of Antitrust Enforcement, 11*(1), 51–73.

Fabiana, D. P., Tatjana, G., Gabriele, V., & Riccardo, I. (2021). 'I see something you don't see'. A computational analysis of the digital services act and the digital markets act. *Stanford Computational Antitrust, 6*.

Fletcher, A. (2021). Disclosure as a tool for enhancing consumer engagement and competition. *Behavioural Public Policy, 5*(2), 252–278.

Hoffmann, J., Herrmann, L., & Kestler, L. (2023). Gatekeeper's potential privilege—The need to limit DMA centralization. *Journal of Antitrust Enforcement, 00*, 1–22.

Holzweber, S. (2018). Tying and bundling in the digital era. *European Competition Journal, 14*(2–3), 342–366.

Knapstad, T. (2023). Breakups of digital gatekeepers under the digital markets act: Three strikes and you're out? *Journal of European Competition Law & Practice, 14*(7), 394–409.

Kuenzler, A. (2022). Competition law as a catalyst for collective market governance: Gauging the discursive benefits of intensified administrative action. *Yearbook of European Law, 41*, 252–278.

Nyman-Metcalf, K., Dutt, P. K., & Chochia, A. (2014). The freedom to conduct business and the right to property: The EU technology transfer block exemption regulation and the relationship between intellectual property and competition law. In T. Kerikmäe (Ed.), *Protecting human rights in the EU: Controversies and challenges of the charter of fundamental rights* (pp. 37–70). Springer Verlag.

OECD. (2022). OECD handbook on competition policy in the digital age. https://www.oecd.org/daf/competition-policy-in-the-digital-age/

Selck, T. J., Rhinard, M., & Häge, F. M. (2007). The evolution of European legal integration. *European Journal of Law and Economics, 24*, 187–200.

Stylianou, K., & Iacovides, M. (2022). The goals of EU competition law: A comprehensive empirical investigation. *Legal Studies, 42*(4), 620–648.

Venegas, V. B. (2023). Intellectual property rights, enforcement costs and EU competition law. *Journal of Antitrust Enforcement, 11*(Supplement_1), i37–i56.

Vosskuhle, A. (2017). «European integration through law» - The contribution of the federal constitutional court. *European Journal of Sociology, 58*(1), 145–168. Law in action, at pp. 146, 149 and 164.

Whish, R. (2003). *Competition law* (5th ed.). Lexis Nexis Butterworths.

Yeung, J., & Yeung, A. (2021). The neglected nexus between competition law and human rights: Standard of proof for pecuniary penalties. *Legal Studies, 41*(2), 336–354.

Zevgolis, N. E. (2018). The interaction between intellectual property law and competition law in the EU: Necessity of convergent interpretation with the principles established by the relevant case law. In A. Bharadwaj, V. Devaiah, & I. Gupta (Eds.), *Multi-dimensional approaches towards new technology*. Springer. https://doi.org/10.1007/978-981-13-1232-8_2

European Union Contracts in Digital Environments

Zeynep Ayata

Abstract One of the most important aims of the Digital Single Market Strategy is to ensure better access to digital services for consumers as traditional contract and consumer law may be inadequate or insufficient in providing protection. When products are faulty, consumers are often uncertain about their rights. Many businesses also hesitate to offer their products to consumers abroad, because of differences in national contract laws. The European Union Commission has initiated many legislative measures to satisfy changing needs of business and consumers in digital spaces. In 2015 the European Commission proposed two directives on contracts for the supply of digital content and digital services and on contracts for the sale of goods. The European Parliament and the Council adopted these Directives on 20 May 2019. Following their publication in the Official Journal, Member States had until 1 July 2021 to transpose them in their national law. The directives harmonise key consumer contract law rules across the EU. The directives aim to ensure a high level of consumer protection and increase legal certainty for both consumers and traders in millions of everyday transactions concerning goods, smart goods, digital content and digital services. This chapter explores the challenges triggered by digitalisation in terms of consumer contracts and examines the solutions proposed in European Union policy and law, focusing in particular on measures provided by the two recent directives.

The digital revolution has irreversibly transformed purchasing and selling arrangements. On a global scale, e-commerce may not be the predominant method of sale, but it certainly is the growing one and may perhaps be gradually replacing brick-and-mortar sales in developed countries. Businesses increasingly turn to digital tools and mediums to provide goods and services to benefit from lower costs and wider consumer reach. During the COVID-19 pandemic online purchasing established itself as the primary instrument for accessing even basic needs of households

Z. Ayata (✉)
Istanbul, Turkey

D. Ramiro Troitiño (ed.), *E-Governance in the European Union*, Contributions to Political Science, https://doi.org/10.1007/978-3-031-56045-3_12

across the world. This period has also shown the extent to which consumer habits and behaviour have responded to digitalisation. It has also become clear in the last few years that not only large online platforms, but also small and medium enterprises increasingly opt for online sales to connect with a greater set of consumers. Digitalisation is not only a deep and irreversible transformation, but also a rapid one. Yet, legal rules are still not fully equipped and adapted to the digital transformation. Rules that have been designed for traditional, in other words offline purchasing arrangements, often do not provide necessary and sufficient protection or remedies for consumers. This problem is aggravated by the fact that information asymmetry is deeper in digital environments as not only consumers but, under certain circumstances, sellers also have access to less information. The European Union (EU) was one of the first jurisdictions to see that existing contract law may not provide adequate protection for traders and consumers. E-commerce and its challenges were recognised as one of the most important pillars of the Digital Single Market (DSM) Strategy adopted in 2015. The goals set in the DSM Strategy clearly showed that the E-commerce Directive dating back to 2010 was not sufficient to meet the needs of rapidly changing digital contracts. Thus, the Commission soon came to realise the shortcomings of the Directive and the necessity of new rules governing contracts in digital environment. In light of the aims of set by the DSM Strategy two new directives, namely the Directive 2019/770 on Contracts for the supply of digital content and digital services (Digital Content Directive—DCD) and the Directive 2019/771 on Contracts for the sale of goods (Sales of Goods Directive—SGD) were adopted in 2019. Both directives have entered into force in 2019 and the time limit to transpose them for all Member States has expired on July first, 2021 (with a 6-month period of *vacatio legis* date of entry into force of the transposition is January first, 2022). Although the EU did not opt for full harmonisation, these new rules have been interpreted as a step towards a common private law of the digital economy in the EU (Staudenmayer, 2020). Indeed, they are designed to provide better, higher and more adapted protection for consumers in digital contracts across the EU. This chapter will firstly define the relevant challenges for contract law in digital environments. Secondly, EU's general policy and past regulatory framework for e-commerce will be examined. The final section will focus on the relatively new legislative acts on digital contracts and discuss their implications.

E-Commerce: Opportunities and Challenges

The OECD defines e-commerce as "the sale or purchase of goods or services, conducted over computer networks by methods specifically designed for the purpose of receiving or replacing orders" (OECD, 2019). Today, e-commerce encompasses widespread trade activities through the use of digital interfaces, bringing significant advantages to both consumers and businesses. It is at the core of the developing and widening data economy. Use of digital tools in daily transactions depends on the level of economic and technological development of each country; however, almost all states see the potential benefits of the digital economy.

Three crucial dimensions of e-commerce identified by the OECD must be underlined in order to understand its impact on trade (OECD, 2019). Firstly, digitalisation allows companies to widen the scope of products and services they offer. Businesses that sell their goods and services electronically also provide services such as logistics, insurance, remote assistance, etc. Secondly, digitalisation allows sellers to reach customers on a much larger geographical scale. This expansion creates further value chains and increases efficiency at a global scale. Finally, digitalisation increases the speed of trade and allows for many services to be provided fast and efficiently.

These advantages can also be specified. As digital content is accessible on an almost global scale, sellers are not only more visible but also more reachable and this effect may diminish advertisement costs. Visibility may be increased through the seller's own website or through a digital marketplace. Closely linked to this advantage is the removal of geographical limitations. If there are no barriers to trade, as in the example of the EU internal market, sellers can easily provide products and services to consumers in other countries. From a consumer's point of view, e-commerce offers the advantage of purchasing at any time, from anywhere. Unlike brick-and-mortar shopping digital mediums do not have opening hours. Furthermore, in many countries large platforms deliver within a day. Consumers therefore can enjoy more flexibility and better time management.

Most importantly, e-commerce lowers production and transaction costs. Digital tools allow for sellers to operate faster and more efficiently and therefore reduce transaction costs. This is perhaps the most cited advantage of digitalisation, and it holds not only for e-commerce sales but any service that is provided digitally. However, in the context of e-commerce digitalisation also reduces production costs. Online sales do not require display of products in physical spaces. The sellers can therefore economise on rent, storage, shop design, etc. Reduction of transaction and production costs increases income and economic efficiency.

However, e-commerce also has significant shortcomings and problems. First of all, not all products can be sold online to distant geographies. The most obvious example of goods that may not always be provided online is of course fresh foods and beverages. This finding implies that not all sellers are able to sell online. The OECD states that small and business enterprises are the most affected by these limitations but also explains how technological or business model innovation may help use this potential (OECD, 2019).

Secondly, sellers may find that long distance sales cause more risk and higher cross-border sales costs because of delivery terms. Large platforms are vertically integrated and often employ their own logistics infrastructure including delivery services. Smaller sellers may not be able to provide delivery services of high quality and fall behind in the competition. On the other hand, sellers that choose to work with large marketplace platforms to compensate their lack of infrastructure may have to incur costs for services provided by the platform.

There may also be geo-blocking issues. Geo-blocking occurs when the provider refuses to sell to buyers placed outside the country of origin or buyers located in certain countries. There are several ways in which the provider may geographically restrict selling. The most straightforward example is when the seller refuses to deliver to certain locations. Another example is when the provider prevents access to the website when the buyer is connected from another country. The seller may also require payment with a credit card issued by the country of origin. Geo-blocking deprives the consumer from benefits such as price comparison, wider choice of products, etc.

Finally, and perhaps most importantly, lack of uniform rules or minimum standards may have a deterring effect on both supply and demand side. The trader may have difficulty in gaining full knowledge of applicable rules for cross-border sales. This problem may be exacerbated by language barriers and differences in legal terms and institutions. As a matter of fact, the seller may have to seek legal advice from local practitioners. Also, there may be additional bureaucratic procedures such as getting permits or licences. If the rules entail different or additional product requirements, the seller may alter the product or may exit the market. Thus, differences in applicable norms may lead to significant increases in both transaction and production costs.

On the other hand, divergence of rules may also weaken the trust of the consumer in online sales. Digital markets are marked with higher information asymmetry. Understanding how platforms operate requires some level of digital literacy and awareness. Furthermore, consumers are often constrained by privacy terms. They may not always have full knowledge of their rights and how to invoke them. These concerns may be aggravated by the applicability of different (foreign) norms to their contracts. Uniformity of rules may help overcome these problems to a certain extent.

It is often suggested that digital spaces should not be over regulated or regulated at all as regulation hampers flexibility and increases transaction costs. Self-regulation is often advanced in this context, arguing that digital service providers should be allowed to develop mechanisms that eliminate and monitor market failures (Parker et al., 2016). The review system used by all large platforms is a good example of such self-monitoring and punishment mechanism. Presumably, users can leave negative reviews when a product is not satisfactory or defective and an accumulation of such reviews could force the supplier to improve their service or to exit the market. Reviews are indeed an effective monitoring system, but they are not flawless. In the case of marketplaces, it is often the large platform that controls reviews and small and medium business that use the platform (business to business—B2B—relationships) may not always have access to all the information and data that is collected (recent EU legislation such as the Digital Markets Act and the Digital Services Act imposes certain obligations on large platforms to provide access to data to remedy this problem). Furthermore, online service providers may sometimes not have sufficient incentive to allow all negative reviews. Most importantly, leaving and reading reviews would require a certain level of digital literacy and awareness on the demand side. However, as stated before, consumers face higher information asymmetry in digital spaces and may not always have the necessary confidence, knowledge and skills to use this mechanism. Moreover, they may have privacy concerns when leaving comments if they do not trust the platform. Review systems may thus prove to be an important tool for self-regulation, but they may not be sufficient to mitigate all problems faced by consumers.

On the other hand, there are several measures that policy makers can adopt to increase consumer trust in e-commerce. Some policies may involve educational measures for enablement and awareness raising such as public programs for increasing digital literacy, improving technologies accessible to consumers to better screen e-commerce tools, etc. However, most policies require regulatory measures. Especially in the context of cross-border trade cooperation between various authorities and achieving a certain level of uniformity of rules would be an important step for incentivising online purchases. Stricter rules may be necessary for eliminating unfair trading terms such as providing misleading information, deceptive advertisement, etc. (Mariniello, 2022).

Development of EU Policy

The EU internal market, based on free movement principles, has been the cornerstone of EU integration and has played an important role in establishing EU sovereignty in certain policy fields. For more than a decade, EU policy makers have tried to achieve a similar integration and area of sovereignty in digital environments. The EU has not only seen digital transformation as an important opportunity for economic growth, but has also tried to develop a holistic strategy encompassing all areas of digitalisation, to establish itself as a pioneer in regulatory frameworks (Manganelli & Nicita, 2022). To this end, it has announced its DSM Strategy in 2015. However, prior to the Strategy, the EU already had taken important steps in the field of e-commerce with the Directive 2000/31 on certain legal aspects of information society services, in particular electronic commerce (Directive 2000). In order to better examine current legislative efforts and rules, it is necessary to briefly look at the framework provided by this Directive.

Directive 2000, aiming to remove obstacles to cross-border online sales in the EU, applied both to business to consumer (B2C) and B2B contracts. The main general exception to the scope of the directive was media services (then covered by the audio-visual media service directive 2010/13). The directive tried to achieve a technology-neutral regulatory environment to pave the way for economic growth while giving consumers important protections applied to all online services (Slakoper & Tot, 2022). Notably, the directive imposed transparency and information requirements for online service providers in order to build consumer trust in selling arrangements. Another important element of the directive was rules regarding online intermediaries, which are currently the most significant actors in online sales. The Directive introduced the concept of control for the liability (article 12) of Intermediary Service Providers (ISPs). Accordingly, ISPs may be held liable if they have some control over the content and information provided. They are, however, not liable if the activities they carry are mere conduit, caching or hosting. It should be borne in mind that at the time Directive 2000 was adopted large intermediary and marketplace platforms had not grown and were not dominating the market. Currently the services provided by these platforms are blurred as it is difficult for traders and consumers to distinguish between mere service and actual sale of products. As digital markets change rapidly, many of the rules established by Directive 2000 have become insufficient and the Commission saw the need to revise them with the inception of the DSM strategy.

The DSM strategy intends to establish a coherent set of rules for all policy areas of digitalisation in the EU. Five years after the Commission's digital agenda, it reiterates the EU's determination in defining long-term goals for the digital economy. The strategy identifies three pillars: "better access for consumers and businesses to digital goods and services across Europe", "creating the right to conditions and a level playing field for digital networks and innovative services to flourish" and "maximising the growth potential of the digital economy". Cross-border e-commerce falls under the first pillar along with rules regarding geo-blocking, copyright law and parcel delivery.

In 2015 as part of the DSM strategy the EU Commission launched a sector inquiry into e-commerce in order to identify key trends in the market and policy implications. The inquiry targeted two areas: consumer goods and online content. The final report was published in 2017 (EU Commission, 2017). According to the report, in terms of online of goods e-commerce provides many benefits for consumers as it increases price transparency. Buyers thus have an opportunity to "instantaneously" obtain and compare prices online. This benefit may result in higher competition between suppliers not only for price but also for quality of services. However, as the report indicates it may also lead to price collusion since suppliers are increasingly more capable of tracking their competitors' prices and achieving coordination through use of algorithms.

In the same year as the DSM, the Commission also published the impact assessment report on proposals for directives on contracts for the supply of digital content and on online sales of goods (EU Commission, 2015). It is clear from this report that the Commission aims to ensure the growth of e-commerce as it "still has a significant untapped potential" (EU Commission, 2015). Also, according to the report, significant barriers to the supply of digital content hamper the achievement of DSM Strategy. It should be noted that the report focuses almost entirely on B2C contracts. There are two main reasons for this limitation of scope. Firstly, freedom of contract should be the prevailing principle when it comes to contracts concluded between businesses. Secondly, stakeholders that have responded to the public consultation have mostly considered that specific contract rules that apply to B2B do not necessarily or clearly create a hindrance. In other terms, there was not significant demand for regulation of digital B2B contracts.

Thus, the report displays the challenges that are encountered in the formation and execution of B2C digital contracts. One significant impediment for cross-border sales of goods and digital content in the case of EU internal market is obviously differences in Member States rules governing contracts. This problem is partly due to the fact that the EU has chosen to proceed with directives in this field, leaving Member States some discretion in choosing adequate tools for implementation. For example, in terms of notification duty by the consumer for defects which falls within the scope of Directive 2000 there were important disparities between Member States. Furthermore, the report states that majority of Member States do not yet have specific national rules on digital content and these transactions are often subject to traditional national laws which are not within the competence of the EU. National legislative efforts emerging at the time of the consultation period also differed significantly in substance and as it is stated in the report would therefore not create more legal certainty for online transactions.

According to the report EU legislators must tackle two main problems in future legislative efforts: "differences in consumer contract law rules hinder traders from selling digital content online cross-border" and "consumers are not confident when buying digital content and goods online cross-border" (EU Commission, 2015). For the former the Commission draws attention to the increase of transaction and production costs that may deter businesses from cross-border sales. For the latter the Commission underlines the importance of legal certainty and of choice and price competition. Furthermore, costs related to legal disparities would impose more burden on small and medium businesses, rather than large platforms, keeping them from expanding their business. Finally, the report explains why B2C contracts require regulation at the EU level given that consumers need clear and precise protective rules and rights especially in the context of digital content. The overall conclusion is thus that the EU must act and establish harmonised rules to realise the full growth potential of e-commerce.

The Commission then considers several options to achieve its objectives and argues that the most adequate option for EU's digital policy is "setting up targeted, fully harmonised rules for the supply of digital content and (...) online sales of goods" (EU Commission, 2015). This choice is justified by the fact that businesses and consumer associations have supported fully harmonised rules for supply of digital content and have moreover warned about the difficulties that would arise if there were disparities between rules applicable to online sales of goods and to supply of digital content. Consumer representatives have also clearly indicated that harmonised rules should provide high-level protection. Fully harmonised rules would also serve better the overarching goals of the DSM Strategy as it would lead to further consistency with other policy areas such as regulation and liability of platforms.

Recent Legislation on Digital Contracts

In light of the findings stated above, the Commission initiated a proposal for two directives on the sales of goods and supply of digital content which were adopted in 2019. Though the Commission did not opt for using regulations which evidently would have provided complete harmonisation, consumer protection provided in the directives is said to be of maximum harmonisation (unlike the Directive 2000 which had allowed significant discretion to Member States). Member States may not restrict the scope of the directives but may extend it for material regimes concerned. Thus, from a general point of view within their scope of application the directives should enhance legal certainty for cross-border sales of goods and digital content as intended by the DSM strategy. The time limit for transposing the directives has expired at the end of 2021.

It should be noted in 2019 the EU has also adopted the Directive 2019/2161 on better enforcement and modernisation of consumer protection rules. Although it does not directly target online sales the Directive has some provisions which should enhance consumer enablement in e-commerce. The Directive requires sellers to disclose several information such as the party responsible for shipping and delivery of the product, the factors that determine the ranking system of products, conditions for returning the product, etc. which should allow the consumer to better assess risks entailed in their transactions. Traders also must provide information on personalised pricing and price discrimination based on the use of personal data and profiling. Under the directive, consumers also benefit from improved access to compensation, for example, if they are victims of unfair commercial practices. Under such circumstances consumers can claim compensation from national consumer protection authorities of their country of residence even if the purchase is cross-border. These provisions related to online and/or cross-border sales of Directive 2019/2161 will complement the Directives on Digital Contracts and enhance consumer trust and transparency of transactions (Mak, 2020).

The Directive 2019/2161 and the Directives on Digital Contracts are examples of increasing harmonisation at EU level of consumer and contract law, especially in digital context, signalling that the EU is "coming closer to comprehensive regulation of consumer contracts" (Carvalho, 2019). The DCD can be considered as the first piece of legislation to regulate supply of digital content. Although the two directives are similar in terms of their scope and requirements, there are differences in terms of how much discretion they leave to the Member States. This section explores in detail the scope of the directives, its requirements for conformity, liabilities foreseen for the seller and remedies provided under the directives.

Scope

Both Directives adopt the same definition of the consumer: "any natural person who, in relation to contracts covered by this Directive, is acting for purposes which are outside that person's trade, business, craft or profession". Member States may extend this protection by granting other persons the status of consumer, but they may not restrict it. In order to understand how the concept of consumer was interpreted and implemented in EU law prior to these directives one must look at the case of dual-purpose contracts. Previous legislation, such as the Directive 2011/83 on consumer rights, provided that dual-purpose contracts would be qualified according to the predominant use criterion. Thus, it was EU law that determined how the contract would be qualified and if the person's professional link to the contract was marginal, he/she would be qualified as a consumer and would benefit from the protection. However, the current directives adopt a different regime, giving authority to national rules to decide whether the person is a consumer. This is clearly a step back from the overall purpose of harmonising consumer protection but would only concern a limited number of cases.

The scope of the SGD on the sale of goods is more straightforward as it gives a definition of a sales contract. According to article 2(1) a sales contract is "any contract under which the seller transfers or undertakes to transfer ownership of goods to a consumer, and the consumer pays or undertakes to pay the price thereof". In line with previously applicable legislation, SGD thus covers contracts for goods that have been or will be manufactured. The SGD also applies to contracts regarding goods with digital elements. This would be the case where a digital service or content is "incorporated" into sales contract for the provision of a good, irrespective of whether the digital content or service is provided by the same party or a third party.

The DCD on the supply of digital content does not provide a clear definition of contracts which fall within its scope. This policy choice is understandable as contracts for the supply of digital content may be qualified differently under different jurisdictions. It does, however, define digital service as "a service that allows the consumer to create, process, store or access data in digital form or a service that allows the sharing of any other interaction with data in digital form uploaded or created by the consumer or other users of that service". The directive thus adopts a broad definition of digital service in order to prevent national rules from limiting the scope of application.

A very important point in the DCD, qualified as ground-breaking by Staudenmayer, is the adaptation of the notion of payment to digital economy (Staudenmayer, 2020). To that end, it accepts that a service may be not only paid with money but also with access to data. It therefore recognises data as de facto currency of digital transactions. This is a very significant step forward and displays how well the Commission has grasped the functioning of digital markets. Thus, a consumer may only enter personal data in return for the provision of a digital service, and the transaction may appear to be free for lack of payment in money, but the DCD will accept that there has been a payment, and a contract for the provision digital content has been formed. Article 3 (2) provides an exception for this rule. If the trader processes the accessed personal data for the sole purpose of supplying digital content or to comply with legal requirements, the provision of personal data by the consumer will not be regarded as payment. Member States are also granted discretion on determining whether provision of personal data has met the requirements, and a valid contract has been formed, which is a continuation of the effort not to interfere too much with national contract law (Sein & Spindler, 2019a). This exception aside, the fact that access to data constitutes payment has crucial implications for digital economy actors who often grow through processing and compiling of personal data and profiling.

A prominent point of discussion has been the implementation and complementarity of these Directives with the General Data Protection Regulation (GDPR) especially regarding the provisions of DCD on access and use of personal data. The European Data Protection Supervisor has also raised certain concerns in its Opinion 4/2017 on the use of notion of consideration in the DCD. The focal point of this criticism is the comparison of data with money. Accordingly, consumers lack awareness when giving access to data, which is not the case with money. Furthermore, under GDPR a user has more freedom in withdrawing consent than the consumer whose counter-performance is money. However, the reality of digital markets is undeniably transactions where users do not have to pay in money, which is crucial where the supply of a digital service or content is concerned. Qualified as zero-price markets in EU competition law, these data collectors make profits through providing services on one side of the platform while charging professional users on the other (Rochet & Tirole, 2003). This is the most common business model in digital platforms. It is therefore necessary to account for contracts where the consumer would only be providing data in return of a digital service or content. Otherwise, the DCD would have insufficient and limited impact now and in the future.

Requirements for Conformity

The Directives have predominantly established objective criteria for conformity in the sense that the criteria to be fulfilled are statutory. However, both directives also provide subjective criteria to be determined according to the contract. Therefore, the regime of these directives establishes a distinction between objective and subjective criteria. Apart from this novelty there are no significant changes to requirements found in past legislations. It should be noted that requirements for conformity are within the scope of maximum harmonisation and thus Member States will not be able to restrict them.

As it was in prior legislation, both directives establish the objective conformity criterion requiring the product to be fit for purpose. In other terms, the product has to correspond to what would be normally expected from products of same use or purpose. The DCD does not deviate from this requirement in terms of digital content. Public statements made in previous chain of transactions will be used to determine normal expectation for digital content. Comments, rankings, complaints visible on the link or previews and trial versions especially would constitute such public statements. It should be noted that the latter, i.e. samples provided by the seller would be part of subjective criteria whereas consumer expectations are part of objective criteria. The seller would not be liable for the statements made by previous buyers or other third parties only under conditions specified by the Directives and not by national law of Member States.

An important objective criterion established by the Directives is durability (or continuity). This criterion is a novelty introduced under the influence of sustainability goals of the EU. Recital 32 of the SGD provides that "than ensuring longer durability of goods is important for achieving more sustainable consumption patterns and a circular economy". However, the general approach of the directive is to give priority to sector-specific rules to determine reasonable expectations for the durability of the good. Thus, the SGD does not establish a general criterion for assessing durability of goods and prefers to commit to EU sectoral norms. Member States are also allowed to foresee longer periods of liability of the seller than what is established by EU rules.

Requirements for updates are also noteworthy and of course highly relevant for digital services and content and goods with digital elements. The Directives follow the general approach of reasonable expectation in this context as well. The seller thus has an obligation to update within the period which the consumer may reasonably expect given the type and purpose of the product with digital elements, digital services or digital content. The nature and circumstances of the contract shall also be considered when assessing reasonable expectation. There is no general obligation to update for the consumer but not doing so may exonerate the seller from liability. Indeed, when the trader has informed the consumer of the availability of an update and the consequences of non-installation, the trader will not be held liable if lack of conformity is due to lack of update by the consumer.

Subjective criteria in both Directives relate to features of the product or digital content. Among these criteria are description, quality and quantity. Significant novel elements are requirements on interoperability, functionality and compatibility. These requirements are specific to digital products but have been extended in the SGD to products with digital elements. Accordingly, consumers may reasonably expect products to fulfil their functions with usual hard/software (compatibility) or alternative hard/software (interoperability). While interoperability is strictly a subjective criterion, in order to avoid product regulation, compatibility is qualified as both objective and subjective (Sein & Spindler, 2019b). Pre-contractual obligation duties also entail a compatibility requirement.

Liabilities of the Seller and Remedies

As a general rule the trader will be liable for a 2-year period for any lack of conformity which exists at the time of delivery of the good. The general rule applies to goods with a digital element under the SGD and to one or a series of individual act of supply under the DCD. If the supply of digital content is on a continuous basis, the digital service must be in conformity as long as the contract remains in force. However, when the consumer no longer has access to the content, conformity will become irrelevant. The goods, digital service or content which does not conform should be brought to conformity free of charge and within a reasonably time period.

In case of lack of conformity, the consumer has a right to a set of remedies. The SGD establishes the concept of "bringing into conformity" instead or repair or replacement used in prior legislation. It is the trader who will determine how this goal will be achieved, which shows the legislator's effort to ensure proportionality of remedies. As such, the consumer cannot claim the remedy of bringing into conformity if the costs would be disproportionately high for the trader under the DCD and the seller can refuse bringing into conformity for the same reason under the SGD. However, this discretion of the trader is bound to restrict protection of the consumer. Accordingly, the consumer may request a price reduction in case of lack of conformity despite an attempt to bring into conformity, lack of attempt to bring the goods or digital content into conformity, serious lack of conformity, explicit or implicit declaration of the trader that the good will not be brought into conformity. The consumer would not have to pay for the normal use "in accordance with the nature and the purpose" (Recital 57 of SGD) of a good prior to its replacement.

E-commerce offers many benefits rooted in the flexibility and pace of online transactions. However, digital spaces create challenges such as deeper information asymmetry, less transparency and lack of awareness of users. Providing adequate protection for consumers in online transactions is a significant concern for policy makers. The EU has adopted several measures to increase consumer trust in online commerce. The DCD and the SGD are part of this effort. They display the increasing trend of harmonisation of consumer and contract law and of regulation of digital spaces in the EU. Although they will certainly contribute to achieving uniform protection of consumers across the internal market, it is unclear whether they will maximise consumers' ease and trust in e-commerce. The DCD brings certain novel elements attune to the reality of digital markets such as payment with access to data. Concerns of bringing prejudice to the GDPR aside, this approach is consistent with other EU policies (such the DMA and the DSA) scrutinising large platforms and their business models. Impact of EU's sustainability goals can also be seen in both directives through the criterion of durability of goods for conformity. Both directives also entail conformity criteria regarding updates, compatibility and interoperability which are necessary elements of legislation well adapted to digital transactions. However, novelties pertinent to digitalisation are limited. Many of the requirements and remedies provided in the directives are reflections of the attempt to harmonise contract and consumer law at the EU level. In the coming years, the Directives may in fact pave the way for a unified regime on lack of conformity in all Member States. However, there are significant shortcomings in terms of consumer protection and empowerment, especially in terms of remedies and may also lead Member States to recede to a limited and minimal level of consumer protection. This would be an undesirable outcome in digital spaces where users are faced with greater challenges and should benefit from clear and strong rights and increased protection.

References

Carvalho, J. M. (2019). Sales of goods and supply of digital content and digital services—Overview of Directives 2019/770 and 2019/771. *Journal of European Consumer and Market Law, 2019*(5), 194–200.

EU Commission. (2015). Impact Assessment accompanying the document proposals for directives of the European Parliament and of the Council (1) on certain aspects concerning contracts for the supply of digital content and (2) on certain aspects concerning contracts for the online and other distance sale of goods. https://eur-lex.europa.eu/legal-content/EN/TXT/?uri=SWD%3A2015%3A274%3AREV1

EU Commission. (2017). Sector inquiry into e-commerce. https://competition-policy.ec.europa.eu/sectors/ict/sector-inquiry-e-commerce_en

Mak, V. (2020). Challenges of digitalisation for consumer contracts. *Annuario Di Diritto Comparato E Di Studi Legislativi, 11*, 63–64.

Manganelli, A., & Nicita, A. (2022). *Regulating digital markets: The European approach.* Palgrave Macmillan.

Mariniello, M. (2022). *Digital economic policy: The economics of digital markets from a European Union perspective.* Oxford University Press.

OECD. (2019). *Unpacking e-commerce: Business models, trends and policies.* OECD Publishing. https://www.oecd-ilibrary.org/sites/23561431-en/index.html?itemId=/content/publication/23561431-en

Parker, G. G., Van Alstyne, M. W., & Choudary, S. P. (2016). *Platform revolution: Now networked markets are transforming the economy and how to make them work for you.* Norton.

Rochet, J.-D., & Tirole, J. (2003). Platform competition in two-sided markets. *Journal of the European Economic Association, 1*(4), 990–1029.

Sein, K., & Spindler, G. (2019a). The new directive on contracts for supply of digital content and digital services—Scope of application and trader's obligation to supply—Part 1. *European Review of Contract Law, 15*(4), 365–391.

Sein, K., & Spindler, G. (2019b). The new directive on contracts for supply of digital content and digital services—Conformity criteria, remedies and modifications—Part 2. *European Review of Contract Law, 15*(4), 365–391.

Slakoper, Z., & Tot, I. (2022). Contract and tort law in the digital ager. In Z. Slakoper & I. Tot (Eds.), *Digital technologies and the law of obligations* (pp. 1–23). Routledge.

Staudenmayer, D. (2020). The directives on digital contracts: First steps towards the private law of the digital economy. *European Review of Private Law, 2*, 219–250.

European Education Area and Digital Education Action Plan (2021–2027): One More Step Towards the Europeanisation of Education Policy

Celso Cancela Outeda

Abstract The advances and transformations in the field of digital education experienced by the EU cannot be explained solely by technological changes or the COVID-19 crisis. For several decades, other factors such as economic globalisation, xenophobia, terrorism, European identity, etc. have stimulated the adoption of European measures. Today, education is presented as an autonomous and strategic sector in the EU. We are already witnessing the configuration of the European Education Area, which opens the door to a European dimension for education, going beyond the national and the economic towards the adoption of a common, global and integral perspective based on shared values. Moreover, the Digital Education Action Plan (2021–2027) is also a recent EU policy initiative. Its objective is to support the adaptation of the education and training systems of the Member States to the digital age. It is inspired by a common vision of high-quality, inclusive and accessible digital education. Such initiatives, based on the establishment of common standards (standardisation), ultimately promote the Europeanisation of education.

Introduction

The sudden and abrupt crisis triggered by Covid-19 in the early 2020s precipitated the use of digital communication systems. Both public and private organisations initiated or intensified the use of a range of apps and platforms to perform their tasks and functions and deliver basic public services. This meant that certain traditional socialisation spaces were replaced by a dense network of apps. It has also

This chapter is part of the research activities of the Jean Monnet Chair European Institutions and Citizens: Adapting the EU to the Digitalisation Challenges (EICAEUD).

C. C. Outeda (✉)
Political Science and Administration, Vigo University, Pontevedra, Spain
e-mail: ccancela@uvigo.gal

D. Ramiro Troitiño (ed.), *E-Governance in the European Union*, Contributions to Political Science, https://doi.org/10.1007/978-3-031-56045-3_13

accelerated the digital transformation of Public Administration in most countries and has increased the social digital divide. Education, healthcare and welfare sectors, along with political actions, were involved in improving the digital competences of citizenship to allow and enhance citizens' interactions with these online public services. Therefore, training in digital competences is one of the main challenges of the knowledge society (Morte-Nadal & Esteban-Navarro, 2022).

In fact, this was linked to the implementation of e-government, which involves the use of ICT in internal government processes (portals, social networks, virtual communities and so on) and in the delivery of products and services by public administrations to citizens in order to improve efficiency and effectiveness (Ramiro, 2023). E-government allows citizens and organisations to carry out their interactions with the government faster and cheaper and more easily. The European Commission (EC) is taking concrete actions to develop digital public services (digitalisation). Effective e-government can provide a wide variety of benefits: more efficiency and massive savings for governments and businesses, increased transparency and greater participation of citizens in political life (Centeno et al., 2005). E-government is becoming mandatory in many countries. Consequently, citizens are forced to interact with the government using these applications. The implementation of electronic government in a democratic system requires the digital inclusion of citizens. Therefore, training and education in ICT to guarantee access and use of public services is a key factor.

Furthermore, the advance of the digital economy, which is associated with digital platforms and algorithms, has an impact beyond the economic sphere, reaching society as a whole (Jiménez & Rendueles, 2020). The knowledge society generates new needs (social cohesion, active citizenship, personal fulfilment, etc.) that can be met through education and training. In the context of a knowledge-based economy, education and training also support recovery, growth and employment by favouring the emergence of a highly qualified, versatile and adaptable citizenry in a highly competitive geopolitical context. Indeed, neither education nor training is exempt from these profound transformations. In particular, the professional skills and qualifications needed to access and perform jobs in a digitised economy require new skills and capabilities. In addition to increasingly rapid economic and technological change, other factors such as the lengthening of people's average working lives mean that they will need to update their skills and qualifications more frequently. This requires citizens that have a certain level of digital skills.

As a result of these changes, since the beginning of the twenty-first century, the EU has been highly active in education policy from a European perspective. In practice, it provides constant support for the transformation and modernisation of the education systems of its member states in accordance with the principle of subsidiarity (Alexiadou, 2007; Pépin, 2007). Initially, education initiatives were clearly linked to economic and social policy; they were oriented towards the achievement of goals connected to economic growth, full employment or social cohesion. Today, however, they present 'a greater autonomy in the European strategic framework, becoming a fundamental tool for the promotion of European identity, the consolidation of an EU citizenship, and giving rise to some remarkable initiatives for their positive impact on the life chances of European citizens' (Gago & Alzina, 2022). As a result of these developments, a Council Resolution states that 'education and training have a vital role to play when it comes to shaping the future of Europe, at a time when it is imperative that its society and economy become more cohesive, inclusive, digital, sustainable, green and resilient, and for citizens to find personal fulfilment and well-being, to be prepared to adapt and perform on a changing labour market and to engage in active and responsible citizenship'.[1]

The EU has moved towards adopting a European perspective on education which inspires and stimulates cooperation between member states (public administrations, private actors, etc.) as shown by the European Education Area (EEA). Recent educational initiatives continue other actions in the current context and help to define a coherent and global strategy. In particular, support for digitalisation acts as a driver for further integration (Ivic & Ramiro, 2022). Building on the Digital Education Action Plan 2018–2020, the European Commission formally adopted the new Digital Education Action Plan 2021–2027. On the same day, it also published the Communication on the European Education Area (EEA) by 2025, as well as the Communication on the European Research Area (ERA).[2] Together with others adopted previously, these initiatives and documents reveal an intensification of European intervention in the field of education that is based on a shared European approach (values). These official documents on education are evidence of the transformation and relevance acquired by this public policy at the European level. Thus, the demands arising from digital education drive a gradual Europeanisation of this policy. These initiatives and documents reveal an intensification in European intervention in the field of education based on a shared European approach (values and objectives). They are also evidence of the transformation and relevance acquired by this public policy at European level. The demands arising from digital education are now driving a European education policy that is gradually leading towards the Europeanisation of this field.

This chapter is structured around four main sections. The first outlines the notion of Europeanisation which will guide this study. The second examines the evolution of education policy in the EU framework. The third looks at the European Education Area and the Digital Education Action Plan 2021–2027. Finally, the fourth section contains a series of reflections on the impact of these initiatives on the Europeanisation of education.

[1] Council Resolution on a strategic framework for European cooperation in education and training towards the European Education Area and beyond (2021–2030) (2021/C 66/01).

[2] Communication from the Commission to the European Parliament, the Council, the European Economic and Social Committee and the Committee of the Regions on achieving the European Education Area by 2025, COM(2020) 625 final.

Communication from the Commission to the European Parliament, the Council, the European Economic and Social Committee and the Committee of the Regions A new ERA for Research and Innovation, COM(2020) 628 final.

What Does 'Europeanisation' Mean?

The term 'Europeanisation' has no single definition.[3] From a theoretical perspective, Europeanisation has different profiles or meanings (Börzel & Risse, 2006). This concept has been used as an analytical tool in the political science field (Börzel & Risse, 2006; Closa, 2001) to highlight a series of transformations, formal and informal, intentional and unintentional, superficial and profound, that affect institutions, political actors, the political process and sectoral policies at the state level as a consequence of the impact of the European integration process.

Accordingly, Dosenrode states that (2020), 'it refers to the mutual influence of the EU and its member states, to interactions within and between member states driven by the EU, and to the effect of the EU on EU applicant states. Thereby, it affects domestic politics, policy, and polity and therefore is relevant for citizens and businesses'. In a similar sense, Börzel and Risse (2006) consider that 'Europeanisation would refer to the "domestic impact of Europe"—the various ways in which institutions, processes and policies emanating from the European level influence policies, politics, and polities at the domestic level (be it member or non-member states)'. This domestic impact can take several forms: direct (adjustment or adaptation to measures established by the EU), indirect (emulation of direct adaptation by certain states), transversal (the EU establishes frameworks, with little institutional intervention, that allow for the exchange of good practices and experiences between member states) and horizontal (response of one state to measures adopted by another member state) (Carlson et al., 2018).

The impact of the EU—Europeanisation—is felt in many different areas. As Morata (2013) pointed out, it affects public opinion, political actors (political parties), political and administrative institutions (state, regional, local) and public policies (agriculture, environment, energy, telecommunications, interior and justice, etc.).

Basically, it is assumed here that it gives rise to a certain convergence between the systems involved in the integration process, although this is a debatable issue (Börzel & Risse, 2006; Morata, 2007). However, Europeanisation is not a mechanism or automatism that, once activated, triggers a series of inevitable effects or consequences. In this sense, Closa points out that 'the effects of EU integration are conditioned by the myriad of characteristics that make up the political system of each member state: its political culture (conflictive or consensual), the type of relations between civil society and state institutions (corporatist, statist, pluralist), its territorial structure (federal, autonomous, regional or centralised), its political history, its so-called economic constitution, etc.' (Closa, 2001).

Precisely, Börzel and Risse (2006) write that 'some member states have undergone deeper policy changes than others. While this may vary across issue areas, the Southern European latecomers (Spain, Greece, Portugal) have been generally more

[3] In 1994, Robert Ladrech used and defined the term "Europeanisation" for analysing the effect of the European Community on its member states. See, Dosenrode (2020).

affected'. Therefore, in the face of European measures or initiatives, one cannot expect an identical response or behaviour at the state level. This approach is interesting when predicting European initiatives such as the Lisbon Agenda or the Europe 2020 Strategy.[4] In the following, we will analyse the path taken by the EU in the field of education.

Education and European Integration: From Unconcern to Europeanisation

Two decades ago, Ponce (2003) wrote that 'our time is witnessing a radical revision of education in terms of its dimension and, with it, its function. Proof of this is, for example, to consider that permanent education, continuing education, lifelong learning, or any of the other similar denominations, is indicating from the outset that education is not circumscribed to a particular field. These dimensions will be taken into consideration in order to be able to plan the various educational plans and programmes in the European Union and will therefore be starting points for understanding the emerging criteria for establishing a European education policy'. The EU has indeed felt the impact of these changes. Today, they are joined by those resulting from the knowledge society and economy and digitalisation, which have pushed the EU to weave an education policy on the basis of programmes and initiatives based on common priorities and objectives. Let us briefly review its most important steps.

The Treaty establishing the European Economic Community (ECT, 1957) included in Article 128 a mere reference to vocational training.[5] The achievement of a certain harmonisation in this educational sector was a condition for the promotion of the free movement of workers which, in the end, turned out to be a key aspect in the progressive development of the common market, the promotion of employment and economic development.[6] However, in its first years, specific community actions

[4] For example, in reference to Spain, the Agenda aimed at structural reforms and economic liberalisation, but was hardly taken into consideration by Spanish governments for economic reasons (strength of the Spanish economy based on the construction sector) and political reasons after 2005 (fear of electoral costs). In short, "the spirit of Lisbon" did not permeate the economic and social actors it was aimed at (Morata, 2013).

[5] Generally speaking, Article 3(q) of the Treaty stated that 'in order to achieve the objectives set out in Article 2, action by the Community shall involve, in accordance with the conditions and at the pace provided for in this Treaty: [...] (q) a contribution to education and training of good quality and to the development of the cultures of the Member States'.

[6] Council Decision of 2 April 1963 laying down general principles for implementing a common vocational training policy (63/266/EEC). Available at https://eur-lex.europa.eu/legal-content/EN/TXT/HTML/?uri=CELEX:31963D0266 (last access 25 de October 2023).

in the field of education were scarce and secondary (Matarranz et al., 2020).[7] Thus, Etxeberría (1996) referred to a 'period of disregard for educational issues'.

From this starting point, it is possible to establish a set of phases that show the progression of EU education policy (Matarranz et al., 2020; Valle, 2004). The first stage runs from 1957 to 1976. It was precisely the Resolution of the Ministers of Education of 16 November 1971, aimed at promoting cooperation in the field of education, which was a milestone. From then on, the intellectual (general principles of vocational training of 1963, the Spinelli Report of 1972 and the Janne Report of 1973) and institutional infrastructures took shape. At the height of the 1973 oil crisis, the Council of Ministers adopted the second resolution on cooperation in the education sector.[8] 1974 also saw the creation of the 'Education Committee' (a body responsible for monitoring cooperation and preparing regular meetings of education ministers) and, the following year, the European Centre for the Development of Vocational Education and Training (CEDEFOP). This phase was marked by the negative impact of the oil crisis on employment and the consequent need to adapt training to the demands of the labour market ('post-industrial' or third industrial revolution). At that time, vocational training and the qualification and specialisation of the workforce were conceived as basic elements for recovering economic growth (Arriazu, 2011). However, educational and cultural concerns were also gaining ground on the European agenda as member states became aware of the importance of creating a European identity and establishing a cultural and ideological foundation for the economic process. In particular, after the events of May '68, the need to incorporate young people into the European project led to a rethinking of positions and the attribution of greater relevance to 'spiritual values' (Etxeberría, 1996; Pérez, 2020).

In 1976, the First Action Programme for Education was launched,[9] which enabled the start of a second phase up to 1992 to be established. Now, the priorities were based on the anticipation of the establishment of the single market in 1993. Specifically, the priority objectives of the Programme were summarised as follows: cultural and vocational training in the Member States, improvement of the correspondence of education systems in Europe, systematisation of statistics, cooperation in the field of higher education, preservation of equal opportunities and integration of the European dimension in education (Arriazu, 2011). In this period, sectoral programmes were activated in specific areas (PETRA, EUROTECNET,

---

[7] As Pépin (2007) says, the Council of Europe was then the locus of European cultural and educational cooperation, and remained so until the early 1970s, when the developing European Community began to open up to education issues.

[8] Resolution of the Ministers of Education, meeting within the Council, of 6 June 1974 on cooperation in the field of education, OJ C 98, 20. 8. 1974. Available at https://eur-lex.europa.eu/legal-content/EN/TXT/?uri=CELEX:41974X0820 (last access 25 October 2023).

[9] Resolution of the Council and of the Ministers of Education, meeting within the Council, of 9 February 1976 comprising an action programme in the field of education, OJ C 38, 19.2.1976. Available at https://eur-lex.europa.eu/legal-content/EN/TXT/HTML/?uri=CELEX:41976X0219 (last access 20 October 2023).

DELTA, ERASMUS, TEMPUS, LINGUA, HELIOS, FORCE, etc.) (Matarranz et al., 2020). In addition, various bodies, committees, expert working groups and instruments linked to the education sector were established, which boosted the educational institutional framework; for example, this was the case of the European University Institute in Florence (1976) or the European Community Educational Documentation and Information Network (EURYDICE). Standardisation then took its first steps in the field of education.

In the mid-1980s, the first major reform of the founding treaties was adopted in the form of the Single European Act. In reference to education, Egido wrote that 'in this new Treaty, concrete references to education still do not explicitly appear. However, some of the policies cited as priorities are closely related to educational aspects. In the context of these policies, education and training are central to the completion of an internal market, the development of a technological Europe and the strengthening of economic and social cohesion. The isolated actions that had been undertaken up to that point were expanded and strengthened, and seven lines of action in Community education policy were implemented, mainly through the Action Programmes. The mechanism of the Action Programmes is used because no general rules can be established' (Egido, 2015). In reality, a debate took place about the inclusion in the competences of the European Communities of areas such as culture, education, health or European citizenship, which, in the end, remained in the sphere of cooperation between state governments.

The third phase began in 1992 and lasted until 2000. During this period, integrated global programmes were promoted, seeking to coordinate the previous sectoral education programmes. These initiatives aimed at harmonisation, coherence and optimisation of the resources involved in the various European education programmes (Etxeberría, 1996). Their main priority was the harmonisation of the education system in higher education, against the background of political integration, social Europe or European citizenship. Thus, programmes emerged in three main areas: (1) education (Socrates I¸ Programme 1995, oriented to all education except vocational training, integrating actions such as Erasmus, Lingua and Comenius programmes), (2) vocational training (Leonardo da Vinci Programme, 1995, was linked to vocational training and hosted actions such as Petra) and (3) culture (Youth Programme).

These transformations were eventually reflected in the founding Treaties (Ponce, 2003). Thus, the Maastricht Treaty (1992) recognised education as an EU competence. This enabled the continuity of previous educational actions and laid the legal foundations for the development of the European dimension of education. In particular, Article 3 TEEC provided that Community action would involve '(...) a contribution to quality education and training and to the development of the cultures of the Member States'. The former Title III of the TEC on social policy was converted into Title VIII under the title 'Social, Education, Vocational Training and Youth Policy'. In addition, it added Chap. 3 consisting of Articles 126 and 127 TEC. The first stipulated that 'the Community shall contribute to the development of quality education by encouraging cooperation between States and, if necessary, by supporting and supplementing their action, while fully respecting the responsibility of the

Member States for the content of teaching and the organisation of education systems and their cultural and linguistic diversity'. Article 126(2) TEEC provided for Community action to develop the European dimension in education, to encourage mobility of students and teachers and cooperation between educational establishments, to develop exchanges of information and experience, etc. Article 127 TEEC specifically referred to the Community development of a vocational training policy (adaptation to industrial change, improvement of initial and continuing vocational training, exchange of information and experience, etc.) which should reinforce and supplement the action taken by the Member States, while fully respecting their responsibilities as regards its content and organisation.

Policy changes were accompanied by the development of strategic documents.[10] The European Commission published the Green Paper on the European Dimension of Education (1993),[11] the direct precedent of the White Paper on education and training—Teaching and Learning—Towards the Learning Society (1995).[12] This document listed a series of challenges connected with the advancement of the information society, globalisation, technology and science and proposed certain measures to be taken at European level. In this way, the initiative passed to the European Commission, which gradually displaced the intergovernmental initiative. Moreover, as Pépin (2007) points out, 'Community cooperation on education [moved] into high gear. With a specific article on education [...], the legal conflicts that prevailed during the second half of the 1980s in the adoption of the various programmes no longer exist and relations between the Member States and the European Commission are calmer'. In political terms, the inclusion 'of an education policy in the EU treaties entails an effort to consolidate the Europeanist project and the feeling of belonging to it on the part of European citizens' (Gago & Alzina, 2022).

The Treaty of Amsterdam hardly changed this sphere; it only minimally affected Article 127.4 TEC and converted Articles 126 and 127 into Articles 149 and 150 TEC, respectively. However, in 1998, in the La Sorbonne Declaration,[13] the education ministers of Germany, France, the United Kingdom and Italy declared themselves in favour of deepening the cultural and educational dimension of the EU,

---

[10] Growth, Competitiveness, Employment the Challenges and Ways forward into the twenty-first century White Paper. With a view to the development of a single market, economic growth and full employment, this document devotes specific attention to education in several of its sections: "Committing to education and training: Knowing and knowing how, throughout life" and "Adapting education and vocational training systems". Available at https://op.europa.eu/en/publication-detail/-/publication/4e6ecfb6-471e-4108-9c7d-90cb1c3096af/language-en (last access 28 October 2023).

[11] Available at https://op.europa.eu/en/publication-detail/-/publication/ca1f0e1a-7e3c-4093-ac92-b5ffd0c38082 (last access 17 October 2023).

[12] Available at https://op.europa.eu/en/publication-detail/-/publication/d0a8aa7a-5311-4eee-904c-98fa541108d8/language-en (last access11 October 2023).

[13] Joint declaration on harmonisation of the architecture of the European higher education system by the four Ministers in charge for France, Germany, Italy and the United Kingdom, Paris, the Sorbonne, May 25 1998. Available at https://www.ehea.info/media.ehea.info/file/1998_Sorbonne/61/2/1998_Sorbonne_Declaration_English_552612.pdf (last access 10 October 2023).

going beyond the historical economic, monetary and financial objectives. It was primarily aimed at promoting mobility and cooperation at the university level. In 1999, based on the previous Declaration, the well-known Bologna Declaration[14] was formulated, which was the first step towards the configuration of a European Higher Education Area.[15] Basically, it was based on a system of credits valid at European level (ECTS) and semesters (comparability and compatibility of education systems) and on the objective of favouring mobility and the elimination of obstacles to the exchange of students, teachers, technical and administrative staff of universities and research centres. In short, it was an intergovernmental impulse that intensified and strengthened European activity in the field of university education.

The fourth stage runs from 2000 to 2010 (Matarranz et al. refer to the stage of strategic plans 2000–2020 with two sub-stages). It constituted a transition phase towards a European education policy and the European Education Area (Lawn, 2011). The main objective was the conversion of the EU into a competitive and dynamic knowledge-based economy with education as a fundamental pillar for its achievement. Precisely at the beginning of 2000, the European Council held in the Portuguese capital adopted the so-called Lisbon Strategy (Fredriksson, 2003). Accordingly, this institution 'explicitly referred to education as a key policy field in which the OMC [Open Method of Coordination] should be applied. This was part of the Lisbon Council's intention to weave together the social and the economic aspects of European integration. Education, with its dual functions in constructing national identities and preparing young people for the labour market, was seen as "core" in achieving the ambitious Lisbon goal of making Europe not only the most competitive, but also the most socially cohesive area of the world' (Alexiadou, 2007). According to the Strategy, by the end of the decade, the EU was to 'become the most competitive and dynamic knowledge-based economy in the world, capable of sustainable economic growth with more and better jobs and greater social cohesion'. This was arrived at after noting that the EU was facing 'enormous change as a result of globalisation and the imperatives of a new knowledge-based economy'. It also pointed out that these changes required not only 'a radical transformation of the European economy', but also 'an ambitious programme of modernisation of social welfare and education systems'. In this respect, Pépin (2007) comments, on the one hand, that 'this is the first time that the European Council has so clearly indicated the way forward in an area which, until then, had been rather on the periphery of the Union's economic and social policies' and, on the other hand, that this Strategy signifies progress towards a competitive and dynamic educational area destined to become a reference system (Fredriksson, 2003).

The Stockholm European Council (2001) again turned its attention to education. In particular, it considered it necessary to raise the general level of education in the

[14] Joint declaration of the European Ministers of Education Bologna, 19 June 1999. Available at https://www.ehea.info/media.ehea.info/file/Ministerial_conferences/02/8/1999_Bologna_Declaration_English_553028.pdf (last access 25 October 2023).

[15] In the field of vocational training, mention should be made of the Copenhagen Process (2002) which seeks to stimulate cooperation and convergence at European level.

Member States and, in particular, digital and information technology skills in order to boost the European economy, as well as the training of scientific and technical personnel. It therefore decided to increase investment in 'education, training and lifelong learning' to raise the EU's employment rate. Along these lines, three strategic objectives were adopted to be achieved by the end of 2010: quality mix, accessibility and openness of education and training systems to the world. The following year, the Barcelona European Council approved a work programme entitled 'Education & Training 2010' (E&T 2010) (2002). Based on the coordination of state education policies with the support of the EU, the aim was to make Europe's education and training systems 'a world quality reference by 2010'. From then on, education became central to the European agenda. The European Council recognised the role of education and training systems in the economic and social strategy and the future of the EU. In addition to the numerous documents on education, action programmes and long-term working strategies were formulated (Erasmus+ as an umbrella programme for Socrates and Leonardo; E&T 2010 as a working strategy that builds on the Lisbon Strategy).

In 2001, the Treaty of Nice further reformed European education policy. In particular, it was placed in Title XI under the heading 'Social, education and youth policy'. The central provisions then became Articles 149 TEC (education) and 150 TEC (vocational training) in Chap. 3 'Education, vocational training and youth'. However, their content remained unchanged. Almost at the same time, the Charter of Fundamental Rights of the European Union (2000) was proclaimed, Article 14.1 of which states that 'everyone has the right to education and to have access to vocational and continuing training'.[16]

Later on, the Lisbon Treaty (2007), in its Title XII 'Education, Vocational Training, Youth, and Sport', included two articles in the Treaty on the Functioning of the European Union (Articles 165 and 166). Additionally, it added Article 9 of the Treaty on the Functioning of the European Union (which forms the so-called horizontal social clause) in which it mentions education. Literally, it states that 'in defining and implementing its policies and actions, the Union shall take into account the requirements related to promoting a high level of employment, ensuring adequate social protection, combating social exclusion, and achieving a high level of education, training, and human health protection'. This legal framework is complemented by Article 6 of the Treaty on the Functioning of the European Union in which education is among the areas where 'the Union shall have competence to carry out actions in order to support, coordinate, or supplement the action of the Member States. The areas for such actions shall be, in pursuing its European objectives: [...] (e) education, vocational training, youth, and sport; [...].'

Finally, a fifth stage can be outlined, spanning from 2010 to 2023. During this period, the objective is to establish a Common Educational Policy based on the common points of ongoing programmes and strategies. From a strategic perspective, it also aims to restore Europe as a global economic and political power, based

[16] See also Article 16 of the Draft Treaty Establishing a Constitution for Europe, 2003.

on the transition from information to knowledge through reflection (Arenas, 2017). In 2010, a new 'Education and Training 2020' (E&T 2020) Strategy was approved, emphasising education as an instrument for progress towards a smart, sustainable and inclusive society.[17] In this phase, one of the major initiatives in the higher education sector was activated: the Erasmus+ programme (2014).[18] In terms of standardisation, it is worth noting that both strategies contain strategic objectives, specific goals and several dozen indicators that enable their evaluation and comparison (Fredriksson, 2003).

The role of European institutions has been on the rise. In 2012, the European Commission presented the communication 'A New Concept of Education: Investing in Skills for Better Socioeconomic Outcomes', also known as the 'Rethinking Education' initiative. Among its priorities is the enhancement of the provision of cross-cutting skills that increase employability, entrepreneurial initiative, digital skills and languages. In 2016, the EU launched the New Skills Agenda for Europe, with its main priority being the improvement of educational systems as a condition for promoting quality employment. At the same time, the European Commission published the communication 'Enhancing and Modernising Education', which underscores the strategic nature of investment in education, its contribution to cohesion and social inclusion objectives and advocates for the modernisation of European educational systems and increased access to education.[19]

In 2017, on the occasion of the European Council in Gothenburg (proclaiming the European Pillar of Social Rights, which includes the right to education), the communication 'Strengthening European Identity through Education and Culture' was made public.[20] It outlined several educational objectives to be achieved by

[17] Communication from the Commission Europe 2020 A Strategy for Smart, Sustainable and Inclusive Growth, COM(2010) 2020. Also adopted were the Conclusions of the Council and of the Representatives of the Governments of the Member States, meeting within the Council, on the priorities for enhanced European cooperation in vocational education and training for the period 2011–2020. 2010/C 324/02. Available at https://eur-lex.europa.eu/legal-content/EN/TXT/HTML/?uri=CELEX:42010Y1201(01)]. (last access 15 October 2023).

[18] This programme unified the initiatives of Erasmus Mundus (which has been used by the European Commission for international cooperation and mobility since 2004) with Erasmus, Tempus, and Jean Monnet, as well as initiatives in school education like the Comenius project, and for adult education, like Grundtvig.

[19] 'Quality education for all is fundamental for social cohesion and for an open society. Quality education is much more than an economic investment. It is essential for personal, social, and professional development, as well as lifelong employability. It is one of the most effective means of addressing socioeconomic inequalities and promoting social inclusion. To achieve these goals, educational systems must be accessible and provide equal opportunities for everyone, regardless of their background, and deliver high-quality outcomes'. Communication from the Commission to the European Parliament, the Council, the European Economic and Social Committee and the Committee of the Regions Improving and Modernising Education COM/2016/0941 final. Available at https://eur-lex.europa.eu/legal-content/EN/TXT/HTML/?uri=CELEX:52016DC0941 (last access 5 October 2023).

[20] Communication from the Commission to the European Parliament, the Council, the European Economic and Social Committee and the Committee of the Regions. Strengthening European

2025, while connecting them to the promotion of the European identity necessary for the consolidation of European citizenship. It also presented the vision of a European Education Area and announced a Digital Education Action Plan. In 2018, the Digital Education Plan was approved to facilitate the transition to new digital models.[21] In the same year, several recommendations were developed concerning the assurance of skills for lifelong learning, the automatic mutual recognition of qualifications and learning titles abroad, and the education of youth in a European dimension of teaching, promoting education about Europe and emphasising the importance of learning and adopting common values (Carlson et al., 2018).

In 2019, the Council published the Council Resolution on the further development of the European Education Area to support future-oriented education and training systems.[22] In mid-2019, the European Council adopted the Strategic Agenda for 2019–2024. It mentions education, stating that 'we must increase investment in people's training and education, place greater emphasis on fostering entrepreneurship and innovation, and intensify efforts in the field of research, particularly by addressing the fragmentation of research, development and innovation at the European level'. Thus, education is recognised as a key element in achieving its top priorities.

From a legal perspective, Article 165 of the Treaty on the Functioning of the European Union (TFEU) states that the EU contributes to the development of quality education through the promotion and encouragement of cooperation among its Member States and through support for and complementation of their actions. Therefore, national authorities are responsible for organising their education and training systems and the content of teaching programmes (Hamulák, 2018). This aligns with the principle of subsidiarity, where the primary responsibility for education and training policies lies with the Member States, while the EU plays a supportive role. However, in practice, as evidenced by the previous overview, European institutions (the European Commission, Council, European Council and European Parliament) have increasingly assumed a more prominent role in education matters during the early decades of the twenty-first century. As Matarranz et al. (2020) point out, documents produced by European institutions on education have grown progressively and exponentially (particularly, there has been a 'documentary explosion' since 1992). After analysing EU education documentation and distinguishing between binding and non-binding documents, these authors note that 'non-binding

Identity through Education and Culture The European Commission's contribution to the Leaders' meeting in Gothenburg, 17 November 2017 COM/2017/0673 final. Available at https://eur-lex.europa.eu/legal-content/EN/TXT/?uri=CELEX:52017DC0673 (last access 7 October 2023).

[21] Communication from the Commission to the European Parliament, the Council, the European Economic and Social Committee and the Committee of the Regions on the Digital Education Action Plan 17.1.2018. COM(2018) 22 final. Available at https://eur-lex.europa.eu/legal-content/EN/TXT/HTML/?uri=CELEX:52018DC0022 (last access 9 October 2023).

[22] Council Resolution on further developing the European Education Area to support future-oriented education and training systems (2019/C 389/01). Available at https://eur-lex.europa.eu/legal-content/EN/TXT/HTML/?uri=CELEX:32019G1118(01) (last access 30 September 2023).

documents "constitute the largest volume of documents issued by the EU". This confirms the hypothesis that EU education policy is primarily a form of "soft policy"'. They continue to comment that 'it is, however, important to highlight that these non-binding documents, often referred to as "soft laws" or "soft power", generally undergo a process of participation, consensus, and decision-making, resulting from a dialogue among different stakeholders. This process provides them with a certain degree of legitimacy. Therefore, non-binding policy also has a certain power of influence on the education systems of member countries' (Matarranz et al., 2020).

In this sense, as Lawn (2006) indicates, 'the EU uses law and regulation as a key part of its governing armoury, but in addition, it appears to emphasize the use of soft power as its preferred governing mode; that is, it mobilizes governance by nurturing support and meaning from subjects. It has developed particular governing devices (networking, seminars, reviews, expert groups, etc.) in education for this purpose'. In addition, he points out that 'European education policy has been driven by European policy objectives, derived from the Lisbon and post-Lisbon methods of coordination. This has pushed on with standards and data production to construct and govern Europe. [...] Assembling and governing this policy space in education is happening simultaneously. It is being assembled in the contemporary European way, by constructing it as a performance area, and governing it by indicators, benchmarks and comparison. […]. The effect of drawing in or recreating the area of European education is that the main standardization process—the production of benchmarks and indicator data—has begun to reshape it at all levels as the EU has created its own centres of calculation' (Lawn, 2011).

The European Education Area and the Digital Education Action Plan 2019–2027: Advancing Educational Europeanisation

In its communication 'Strengthening European Identity through Education and Culture' (2017), the European Commission presented a vision for the creation of a European Education Area (EEA).[23] In short, this document aimed at the establishment of 'a Europe where learning, studying, and researching are not hindered by borders. A continent where temporarily living in another Member State for studying, learning, or working has become the norm, and where speaking two languages, in addition to one's mother tongue, is the standard. A continent where people

[23] Communication from the Commission to the European Parliament, the Council, the European Economic and Social Committee and the Committee of the Regions Strengthening European Identity through Education and Culture. The European Commission's contribution to the Leaders' meeting in Gothenburg, 17 November 2017. COM/2017/673 final. See https://eur-lex.europa.eu/legal-content/EN/TXT/HTML/?uri=CELEX:52017DC0673 (last access 23 de April 2023).

strongly feel their European identity, the cultural heritage of Europe, and its diversity'.[24]

Its objective is the creation of a genuine European common learning space founded on trust, mutual recognition, cooperation and the exchange of best practices, mobility and growth. The need to adopt a common vision or approach and provide joint responses to common challenges (population aging, a lack of skilled workers, global competition, early childhood education, etc.) serves as inspiration for the EEA.[25] This shared vision is reflected in the anticipation of various aspects such as: (1) Improving the quality and equity in education and training; (2) Enhancing the status of teaching professions and offering high-quality initial education and professional development opportunities to all teachers, trainers and school administrators; (3) Promoting a high-performance European digital education ecosystem and enhancing digital skills and capabilities of citizens for the digital transition; (4) Strengthening sustainability-related competences (environmental education); (5) Enhancing international cooperation ('European Education Area in the world').

Its implementation involves actions by Member States and the European Commission, such as: promoting mobility for learning purposes in general, removing obstacles to the recognition of qualifications at all levels of education; modernising curricula; encouraging language learning; establishing top-tier European universities capable of working together transnationally; enhancing and promoting lifelong learning; fostering innovation in education in the digital age; preserving cultural heritage and promoting a sense of European identity and culture (Carlson et al., 2018; Kushnir, 2022). Unlike previous educational initiatives, the current ones are aimed at various educational levels (early childhood education, primary, secondary, higher education, vocational training, adult learning) and all educational institutions, education professionals and students as a whole. In essence, the EEA implies a comprehensive and shared European approach that requires the intensification of cooperation. In this sense, Kushnir (2022) writes 'specifically, the EEA, inspired by the crises, has been a driver for a common European identity, the European economy, the EU as a socially-just society and the EU as a continent of progress'.

In this context, the Digital Education Action Plan (2021–2027) is a key element in achieving the European Education Area by 2025. Naturally, as it was designed to tackle digital transformation, it also contributes to the goals of the European Skills Agenda, the Action Plan of the European Pillar of Social Rights, and the 'Digital

[24] Communication from the Commission to the European Parliament, the Council, the European Economic and Social Committee and the Committee of the Regions on achieving the European Education Area by 2025 COM/2020/625 final. Available at https://eur-lex.europa.eu/legal-content/EN/TXT/HTML/?uri=CELEX:52020DC0625 (last access 25 September 2023).

[25] Council Resolution on a strategic framework for European cooperation in education and training towards the European Education Area and beyond (2021–2030) 2021/C 66/01. Available at https://op.europa.eu/en/publication-detail/-/publication/b004d247-77d4-11eb-9ac9-01aa75ed71a1 (last access 23 September 2023).

Compass 2030: the European approach for the digital decade'. As mentioned, in the spring of 2020, the pandemic suddenly required the widespread and intensive use of digital tools and resources for the continuity of educational activities. In fact, by that time, the EU already had the Digital Education Action Plan 2018–2020 in place to address the challenges and opportunities arising from digital education. The pandemic experience further drove the EU to support the sustainable and effective adaptation of Member States' education and training systems to the digital age.

At present, the Digital Education Action Plan 2021–27 provides a strategic approach and strives to act proactively in strengthening cooperation at the European level. To achieve its objectives, it establishes two priority areas: promoting the development of a high-performance digital educational ecosystem and enhancing digital skills and capabilities for digital transformation. Both entail the deployment of digital technologies and the dissemination of skills and competencies. It outlines priorities and actions where the EU can add value. Specifically, the Plan states that the EU 'offers a long-term strategic vision of high-quality, inclusive, and accessible European digital education; addresses the challenges and opportunities posed by the COVID-19 pandemic, which has led to an unprecedented use of technology for education and training; seeks greater EU-level cooperation in digital education and underscores the importance of working together in all sectors to bring education into the digital age; and presents opportunities, including improving the quality and quantity of digital technology-related teaching, promoting the digitization of teaching methods and pedagogies, and providing the necessary infrastructure for inclusive remote learning'.

The implementation of specific actions derived from the Digital Education Action Plan 2021–2027 involves a certain standardisation, which, when combined with the EEA (common values and European identity), contributes to the promotion of the Europeanisation of education at the European level. In fact, considering its two priorities (Priority 1: Fostering the development of a high performing digital education ecosystem and Priority 2: Enhancing digital skills and competences for the digital transformation), it is possible to note specific actions such as setting up the European Digital Education Hub to promote a stronger coordination and cooperation in this field,[26] launching an online self-assessment tool for teachers, SELFIE for Teachers, Common guidelines for teachers and educational staff to foster digital literacy, and tackling disinformation through education and training or updated European Digital Competence Framework to include AI and data-related skills and support the development of AI learning resources for education and training.

[26] Among its objectives: monitor the implementation of the Action Plan and the development of digital education in Europe, including through results from EU-supported projects; share best practices by contributing to research experimentation and the systematic collection and analysis of empirical evidence, in part through peer learning; support cross-sector collaboration and new models for the seamless exchange of digital learning content addressing issues, such as interoperability, quality assurance, environmental sustainability, accessibility and inclusion and EU common standards for digital education.

Precisely, Decuypere (2016) indicates that 'education governance is increasingly affected by and effectuated through digital means'. In reference to the dissemination of educational data through websites, this author writes 'in sum, websites are greatly assistive in composing a European educational policy space, distributing and popularizing both hard as well as soft evidence, and more specifically conveying some sense about what 'European education' could and/or should be, now as well as in the future. In that sense, these websites equally actively contribute to the Europeanisation of education: by putting European countries side by side, for instance, some sense of 'Europe' as well as a sense of 'European education' are at once presupposed and actively being enacted (as is similarly regularly done with singular countries' (Decuypere, 2016).

In sum, Lawn says that 'standardizing processes in Europeanization are closely connected to a soft governance approach: that is governing uses a persuasive and attracting power which draws actors in, across a range of levels, places and spaces, to community engagement at micro and meso scales'. He also points out that 'the production and use of standards creates an apparently "loose" form of governing in which "professional and organizational knowledge-practices are reinvented in increasingly formalized, universalized and standardized ways" [...]. A new governing architecture of public and private actors and sites is building European education through arrays of interlocking standards. Governing by standardizing excludes politics and relies on experts while offering workable solutions to governing and being governed in Europe' (Lawn, 2011).

Conclusions

Since the beginning of the twenty-first century (Lisbon Strategy), the EU has experienced a significant acceleration in the field of education. The European Commission, the European Council and the Council of the Union have gained significant prominence, resulting in a marked drive towards the Europeanisation of education, primarily of a cross-cutting nature. The EEA and the Digital Education Action Plan 2021–2027 represent another step in that direction, following the logic of standardisation.

Lacaita et al. point out that '[…], today we can speak of a real European education space, built by different social actors: political decision-makers, technocrats, lobbies, academics, private agencies, associations. […]. The Europeanisation of education systems is a recent development. Theoretically, education should be the responsibility of member states: education in European countries has always been a national affair, functional to the consolidation of the identity and culture of a community. Each educational system has had its own history, linked to the evolution of its policy, geography, traditions, language and society. As it happens, however, although education formally remains a national competence, since the Maastricht Treaty of 1992, a new 'orthodoxy', based on the comparison of education systems, has been gradually introduced into the educational policies of the whole continent' (Lacaita et al., 2018).

Furthermore, the EU has undergone a gradual shift in educational discourse, although its practical implications have begun to be felt in recent decades. Since the mid-1970s, the development of European awareness became one of the pillars on which to build the future of economic and social Europe. Starting in 1988, educational objectives and measures aimed to foster this European awareness among students and engage citizens in the European integration project (Pérez, 2020). Following the 2008 crisis and its aftershocks in 2011, and in accordance with the European Council's conclusions of December 2017, education is seen as a key element in building inclusive and cohesive societies and maintaining European competitiveness. For the first time, education and training occupy a central position on the European political agenda. Prior to that, at the Social Summit in Gothenburg (2017), the European Pillar of Social Rights established the right to inclusive and quality education and training, as well as lifelong learning for all as the first principle. It also recognised the right to timely and personalised support to improve employment prospects or self-employment, including training and professional development, as the fourth principle. It further acknowledged the right of children to high-quality education and care and the right of children from disadvantaged backgrounds to specific measures to enhance equal opportunities, as the eleventh principle.

State systems are called upon to play a leading role in the modernisation and transformation of education and training. For this, the support of a strong European framework (EEA) that promotes European cooperation in education and training is crucial. Based on common objectives, this framework should drive the improvement of education and training systems in the Member States. They must harmonise their education systems with the support of the EU. Today, education is no longer a mechanism for national differentiation and consolidation in line with global economic trends and the expansion of digitalisation, not to mention geopolitical implications (Europe's global attractiveness in education).

Education and training policy are at the heart of knowledge creation and transmission and are an essential factor in the innovative potential of any society. For this reason, it is a key element, in synergy with other policies such as employment, research and innovation, business, information society, the internal market, etc. Human resources are the EU's most valuable asset, and it is widely recognised that investment in this area is a determining factor for growth and productivity, on a par with investment in capital or equipment. Furthermore, education policy has a positive impact on employment, healthcare, social inclusion and active citizenship. Today, education and training enjoy greater autonomy compared to other sectoral policies (employment, economy, etc.).

In summary, the European dimension of education has gradually taken shape (Europeanisation). Gone are the initial references almost exclusively to language learning; today, the topics (digital skills, exchange of best practices, recognition of qualifications, etc.) and educational levels are much broader, representing this wide range of initiatives. In this way, the EU has achieved a comprehensive orientation of

European education that aims to provide a global and coherent response to certain challenges (international competition, etc.). There is a reference point for the development of programmes and initiatives that respond to a clear educational course of action. The adoption of a comprehensive approach is motivated by external factors (international economic competition, talent acquisition) and internal factors (driving digitalisation, efficient management of economic resources, avoiding disconnections, overlaps, double actions and overall inefficiency). Europeanisation also extends to research and technological development, where the EU also funds research projects in the field of education through programs like Horizon 2020 to promote innovation and improvement in European education systems.

In addition to programmes that promote the exchange of knowledge and best practices among Member States (Erasmus+), the EU establishes standards and guidelines in specific areas of education, such as the quality of higher education, vocational training, recognition of qualifications and degrees, comparability of educational systems, inclusive education and the promotion of digital skills. These standards influence state education policies. In general, political Europeanisation in the field of education involves greater integration and collaboration among EU Member States to address common challenges and promote excellence in education. However, it is essential to emphasise that education remains largely the responsibility of the Member States, and the EU acts as a facilitator and promoter of cooperation in this area. Along this line, in March 2024, the European Commission adopted a package of proposals in the field of higher education to create a European degree through transnational cooperation. In addition to providing skills to graduates, it also seeks to reinforce the common European identity and generate a sense of European belonging and strengthen common academic values.[27]

References

Alexiadou, N. (2007). The Europeanisation of education policy: Researching changing governance and 'new' modes of coordination. *Research in Comparative and International Education, 2*(2), 102–116. https://doi.org/10.2304/rcie.2007.2.2.102

Arenas, S. (2017). Evolución de la política europea de Formación Profesional desde los principios de 1963. *Journal of Supranational Policies of Education*. Available at https://revistas.uam.es/jospoe/article/view/8090

Arriazu, R. (2011). Metamorfosis de la política educativa en Europa: de los Programas Sectoriales al Espacio Europeo de Educación [Superior Metamorphosis of the educational policy in Europe: from Sectorial Programs to the European Higher Education Area]. *Tejuelo, 12*, 80–99.

Börzel, T., & Risse, T. (2006). Europeanization: The domestic impact of European Union politics. In K. E. Jørgensen, M. A. Pollack, & B. Rosamond (Eds.), *Handbook of European Union politics*. SAGE Publications. https://doi.org/10.4135/9781848607903

[27] See, "Commission presents a blueprint for a European degreel". Available at https://education.ec.europa.eu/news/commission-presents-a-blueprint-for-a-european-degree (last access 4 April 2024).

Carlson, S., Eigmüller, M., & Lueg, K. (2018). Education, Europeanization and Europe's social integration. An introduction. *Innovation: The European Journal of Social Science Research, 31*(4), 395–405. https://doi.org/10.1080/13511610.2018.1550388

Centeno, C., van Bavel, R., & Burgelman, J. C. (2005). A prospective view of e-government in the European Union. *The Electronic Journal of e-Government, 3*(2), 59–66.

Closa, C. (2001). Introducción. In C. Closa (Ed.), *La europeización del sistema político español*. Istmo.

Decuypere, M. (2016). Diagrams of Europeanization: European education governance in the digital age. *Journal of Education Policy, 31*(6), 851–872. https://doi.org/10.1080/02680939.2016.1212099

Dosenrode, S. (2020). Europeanization, Oxford research encyclopedia of politics. https://doi.org/10.1093/acrefore/9780190228637.013.1477.

Egido, I. (2015). Política educativa de la Unión Europea: principales etapas de desarrollo. *Tendencias Pedagógicas, 2*, 19–29. Available at https://revistas.uam.es/tendenciaspedagogicas/article/view/tp1996.2.ART002

Etxeberría, F. (1996). Política educativa de la Unión Europea: evolución reciente y perspectivas de futuro. *Revista Española de Pedagogía, 204*, 231–247.

Fredriksson, U. (2003). Changes of education policies within the European Union in the light of globalisation. *European Educational Research Journal, 2*(4), 522–546.

Gago, C., & Alzina, V. (2022) Política de educación y formación profesional en la Unión Europea, https://www.comunidad.madrid/sites/default/files/2022_politicas-ue_educacion_formacion_3.pdf. Accessed 15 Oct 2023.

Hamulák, O. (2018). La carta de los derechos fundamentales de la union europea y los derechos sociales. *Estudios constitucionales, 16*(1), 167–186.

Ivic, S., & Ramiro, D. (2022). Digital sovereignty and identity in the European Union: A challenge for building Europe. European studies–The review of European law. *Economics and Politics, 9*, 80–109. https://doi.org/10.2478/eustu-2022-0015

Jiménez, A., & Rendueles, C. (2020). Capitalismo digital: Fragilidad social, explotación y solucionismo tecnológico. *Teknokultura. Revista de Cultura Digital y Movimientos Sociales, 17*(2), 95–101.

Kushnir, I. (2022). The role of the European education area in European Union integration in times of crises. *European Review, 30*(3), 301–321. https://doi.org/10.1017/S1062798721000016

Lacaita, F., Latempa, R., & Pietrandrea, P. (2018). *The 'Europeanization' of schooling: What is a European education?* Open Democracy. Available at https://www.opendemocracy.net/en/can-europe-make-it/europeanization-of-schooling/. Accessed 28 Oct 2023

Lawn, M. (2006). Soft governance and the learning spaces of Europe. *Comparative European Politics, 4*, 272–288. https://doi.org/10.1057/palgrave.cep.6110081

Lawn, M. (2011). Standardizing the European education policy space. *European Educational Research Journal, 10*, 259–272. https://doi.org/10.2304/eerj.2011.10.2.259

Matarranz, M., Valle, J. M., & Manso, J. (2020). Después del 2020… Hacia un Espacio Europeo de Educación en 2025. *Revista Española De Educación Comparada, 36*, 98–128. https://doi.org/10.5944/reec.36.2020.27040

Morata, F. (2007). Introducción: el proceso de europeización y España. In F. Morata & G. Mateo (Eds.), *España en Europa-Europa en España 1986–2006*. Fundació CIDOB.

Morata, F. (2013). Spain: Modernization through Europeanization. In S. Bulmer & C. Lesquene (Eds.), *The member states of the European Union*. OUP.

Morte-Nadal, T., & Esteban-Navarro, M. A. (2022). Digital competences for improving digital inclusion in e-government services: A mixed-methods systematic review protocol. *International Journal of Qualitative Methods, 21*, 1–9. https://doi.org/10.1177/16094069211070935

Pépin, L. (2007). La educación en el proceso de construcción europea. Un ejemplo único de aplicación del principio de subsidiariedad. *Revista de Educación., 343*, 601–620.

Pérez, G. Á. (2020). The European Union crossroads: Current situation and future challenges. In G. A. Pérez Sánchez, D. Ramiro Troitiño, T. Kerikmae, & R. M. de la Guardia (Eds.), *The*

EU in the 21st century: Challenges and opportunities for the European integration process (pp. 11–26). https://doi.org/10.1007/978-3-030-38399-2_2

Ponce, E. (2003). La Unión Europea y la política educativa. *Revista de Derecho de la Unión Europea, 4*, 153–172.

Ramiro, D. (2023). Mapping e-governance in the EU. In *Digital development of the European Union. An interdisciplinary perspective* (pp. 303–317). Springer.

Valle, J. M. (2004). La política educativa de la Unión Europea. Fundamentos, evolución histórica y propuesta de un modelo para su análisis crítico. *Revista Española de Educación Comparada, 10*, 17–59.

Transparency of Political Party Financing Through Blockchain: Designing a Blockchain System to Generate Transparency for EU Finances

Annelieke A. M. Mooij

Abstract Recent corruption scandals have led to a call for increased transparency in political party financing. This chapter discusses the possibility of organizing political party financing through a blockchain. A blockchain design can increase the transparency of political party financing and increase enforcement against illegal donations. Through a permissioned blockchain the possibility to make donations to political parties can be limited to EU eligible voters. The system could automatically limit the donations a person is allowed to make and publish the necessary data when high donations are made. Furthermore a blockchain system would increase transparency before elections, thereby allowing voters to hold their parties accountable. The blockchain, however, should be limited to registering donations and not become the platform for political discussions. Therefore this chapter recommends that any decisions are made off-chain and through public debate.

Introduction

Democracies consists of a plurality of political parties. The democratic building block of the European Union is the election of its parliament. During these elections political parties are chosen to represent the people. To promote their message and get elected parties conduct political campaigns to convince potential voters. To aid with the conducting of campaigns the European Union Parties can generate funds from different sources. Such sources can include their electorate or party members but also donations from businesses and foreign entities. The latter two raise the question whether it should be legal to donate large sums to political parties. Large donations from rich entities may distort the political process by buying influence (Stiglitz, 2013). Most developed democracies, including the EU, have therefore

A. A. M. Mooij (✉)
Public Law and Governance, Tilburg University, Tilburg, Netherlands
e-mail: a.m.mooij@tilburguniversity.edu

D. Ramiro Troitiño (ed.), *E-Governance in the European Union*, Contributions to Political Science, https://doi.org/10.1007/978-3-031-56045-3_14

introduced legislation on political funding and transparency. Despite the current legislation on party financing, recent corruption scandals have led to calls for reform.

Bribery and corruption have led to the recent arrest of several prominent EU Members of the European Parliament and staff (Renderson, 2022). The wide-spread nature of the corruption has led to the questioning of the current legislation concerning the financing of political parties. One of these calls is for increased transparency (European Parliament, 2022). Transparency is a fundamental building block for the electorate to exercise electoral accountability. Transparency into party financing allows the electorate to adjust their voting behavior accordingly (Trapman, 2022). The current legal focus, however, may prove insufficient. The focus of the legislator is through a system of self-reporting of the political parties. And whilst the statement is verified by an accountant, it primarily relies on the honesty of a political party. In the period preceding the elections this reliance is stronger as the parties have to report donations every month without accountment statement. Considering this reliance on self-reporting and the current corruption scandals, avenues to increase transparency are needed. A blockchain can provide real-time transparency into the financial contributions made to the political parties. It can furthermore provide a ledger system that is independent of authorities and cannot be easily altered. It has thus been suggested as a revolution to political transparency (Tapscott & Tapscott, 2018).

This article therefore explores the blockchain design best suited to create transparency in party financing. In order to explore this design this article will use the blockchain design policy choices as formulated by Tan et al. (2022). Their research has formulated three different levels of design choices for implementing a blockchain to execute public policy. These three layers, Micro, Meso, and Macro will be used to design a blockchain for party finance. However, before analyzing the specific design needs for the party finance blockchain Sect. 2 of this article will briefly assess how blockchains are currently applied within public policy. The current applications provide a basis for the party finance blockchain.

Blockchains in Public Policy

The following paragraphs will provide a brief overview of the current use of blockchains within public policies. These examples will be used to extrapolate a framework for the successful implementation of a blockchain. Blockchains are considered a potentially revolutionary tool to promote transparency within the public process (Tapscott & Tapscott, 2018). In particular blockchains can promote transparent information sharing through a public ledger (Bonsón & Bednárová, 2019). The public ledger can promote transparency among the larger public, the immutability of the ledger can create trust whilst remaining efficient. Some researchers therefore consider replacing the bureaucratic system with a blockchain (Jun, 2018). It will take some time before human-dependent systems will be replaced with technology. Nevertheless there are some experiments with replacing (parts of) centralized systems with a blockchain. The following paragraphs will provide a brief overview of governments experimenting with a blockchain (though their government refers to it as distributed ledger technology (DLT)). The first example of a country investigating the possibilities of blockchain is that of the United Kingdom. The second and third example that will be discussed is Georgia and Sweden as they have experimented with implementing a blockchain.

The first example of countries analyzing the potential applications of the blockchain is the United Kingdom (UK Government Chief Scientific Adviser, 2016). Their analysis focusses on various aspects of using blockchain for its security and transparency. One of the applications considered is to use blockchain to secure the operation of vital infrastructure such as bridges. The reasoning behind this application lies with security. Decentralized ledgers are not stored through a single server but rather through a network of nodes. If a single node is hacked, this does not compromise the integrity of the system. Therefore increasing the difficulty for potential hackers to take control over the entire system (UK Government Chief Scientific Adviser, 2016). The U.K. is furthermore investigating the opportunity to reduce fraud in welfare and increase accessibility of aid systems (UK Government Chief Scientific Adviser, 2016). The report considers fraud reduction through digital identification via DLT. This would reduce costs and increase accessibility of those un- or underbanked. The use of a blockchain can increase transparency and reduce fraud. In theory a virtual currency can be used to provide financial services to underbanked people. Nevertheless the UK's report is vague and it is difficult to extrapolate the government's vision upon the system. The fourth and fifth application the UK is investigating is to promote start-ups organize licensing and registration and for paying VAT (UK Government Chief Scientific Adviser, 2016). These applications are theoretically possible but these are also poorly described in the report. The exact vision is therefore unclear. These visions may become clearer if the UK leaves the experimentation phase. Nevertheless the UK provides some interesting guidelines on government strategy concerns. In order to determine whether blockchain is a potentially useful tool, the UK asks three questions. The first is whether multiple entities are needed to write data. The second is whether there is a lack of trust between the entities. Last whether there is a central authority to write the data on behalf of the entities (UK National Cyber Security Centre, 2021). These guiding questions are interesting questions when considering whether a blockchain can be successful in solving a policy issue. Whilst the report from 2016 is promising, the UK has not replaced centralized systems with a blockchain. More advanced is the experiment with land registry via DLT conducted in Georgia and Sweden.

Landownership depends upon the accuracy of a registry. The lack of a trustworthy registry of land titles has a serious impact upon the economy. A government should protect property rights in order to improve economic growth (Gwartney et al., 2006). If ownership rights are guaranteed by strong institutional frameworks, a country can expect more investment (Heilbron & Whyte, 2019). In response several countries have experimented with the use of blockchain technology to introduce a trustworthy land registry. In theory a blockchain can provide a secure land register (Krishnapriya & Greeshma, 2020). The Georgian land registry authority

NAPR therefore decided to experiment with the introduction of a blockchain in 2016. The use of a blockchain aimed to improve transparency and eliminate red tape and data corruption (Lazuashvili et al., 2019). The challenge when implementing a blockchain for land registries is the file storage. Public blockchains cannot (yet) store large amounts of data (Graglia & Mellon, 2018). Georgia therefore opted for a hybrid blockchain model. Whereby a private blockchain recorded the data and generated hashes and the hashes were stored upon the public blockchain (Shang & Price, 2019). The process initially seemed a success by significantly reducing the costs and time it took to register land (Saari et al., 2022). Unfortunately in the case of Georgia the blockchain was not fully integrated into the system. The difference is described as the difference between registration and recording (Proskurovska & Dörry, 2022). Recording is the storing of the information as was done in Georgia. Registration is a fully integrated process whereby the entire transaction is automatically connected to the blockchain. Using the blockchain for registration can strengthen the process of validating the titles (Proskurovska & Dörry, 2022). The Georgian use of the blockchain as a storage facility, without integration into the process of documentation left the system vulnerable to data corruption before storage (Lazuashvili et al., 2019). Sweden, on the other hand, has designed a system that integrates the front-end digital interface with the blockchain storage (McMurren et al., 2018). In the case of Sweden the integration came forth from the desire to increase efficiency in housing data. This efficiency was required after a tightening of the Swedish legislation on lending (Proskurovska & Dörry, 2022). The experiment in Sweden demonstrated a proof-of-concept for land registry through a blockchain. Unfortunately whilst the technology was well integrated, the Swedish law did not recognize electronic signatures (Saari et al., 2022).

The case of Georgia and Sweden therefore demonstrate that it is important to assess the legal and political environment. In Sweden the legal environment was not able to allow digital purchasing of real-estate. Whilst the blockchain could provide the necessary efficiency and transparency the law blocked effective use. In Georgia the corrupt environment could benefit from the use of a blockchain. Unfortunately the blockchain was not integrated into the whole system, thus allowing corrupt information to enter the blockchain. These two examples therefore demonstrate two important criteria: integration into and of the environment. With regard to integration into the environment the UK example defines three questions that should be considered. The next paragraphs will discuss the UK pre-integration questions with regard to European political party financing in depth.

Blockchain Suitability

These paragraphs will concretely design and evaluate a blockchain-based design for political parties. This section will be structured along the three governance questions as formulated in the research by the United Kingdom. This section furthermore discusses the legal requirements of the EU political financial obligations that should be reflected within the blockchain.

Legislative Restrictions to Party Funding

A blockchain to improve transparency into the European political party financing requires the recording of income and outgoing in accordance with the legislative requirements. The legal requirements have been codified within Regulation EU 1141/2014 on the statute and funding of the European political parties and European political foundations (OJ L 317, 4 November 2014). The funding requirements can be divided into three different categories.

The first category is that of the income that parties are (allowed to) receive. The first category is the subsidy provided by the EU budget. Second, the parties are allowed to receive funding through memberships and donations. There are, however, several restrictions regarding the amount and origin of this category. The parties are not allowed to receive more than 40% of their budget through membership fees (article 20(8) Regulation EU 1141/2014) and per donor per year there is a restriction of €18.000 (art. 20(1)). Donations, furthermore, cannot be received anonymously (art. 20(5)(a)) or from the budget of European Fractions (art. 20(5)). The fourth important restriction is that of donations by third-country parties. Parties are not allowed to receive donations from third-country governments or governmental corporate vehicles (art. 20(5)(c)). Such restrictions are also in place for donations from private entities or people from third-countries who are not eligible to vote at the European Parliament (art. 20(5)(d)). The blockchain would therefore have to be able to recognize such contributions and take appropriate action. Such action can be; to prevent the donation from coming through, automatic return of the payment or report the transaction to the Authority. The difficulty within recognition of who makes the donation lies in particular with the risk of anonymous donations through shell corporations and cryptocurrencies.

The introduction of virtual currency has created a new risk to funding transparency. Cryptocurrency can be transferred through different wallets. These wallets consist of two different categories: the first is the so-called custodian wallet. These wallets store both the public and private key of their customers. This category of wallets is included in the EU Directive on the prevention of money laundering and financing of terrorism (Directive EU 2018/849). Those using this wallet are therefore identifiable through the provider. If donations are made through such wallets, they are pseudonymous but not fully anonymous. The second category of wallets are the non-custodian wallets. These are wallets that only store the public key and not the private key of their owners. These type of wallets are not included under the supervisory framework (arts. 8 & 9, Directive EU 2018/843). These wallets can be created anonymously and with relative ease. Whilst it is possible to recover the identity of the owner through digital forensics (Koerhuis et al., 2020), this process is difficult. Cryptocurrency thereby creates a risk to transparent party financing and thus a risk to the democratic legitimacy (Goossens, 2021). One example where cryptocurrencies were used was that of the USA. During the US elections in 2016 a party was financed from Russia through virtual currency (Burcher, 2019). Part of the problem was the limited regulatory obligations concerning cryptocurrency donations (Burcher, 2019). Therefore anonymous donations through cryptocurrency are a real risk. Similar to virtual wallets anonymous payments arrive through shell corporations. Through the shell corporations a smokescreen can be created between the donor and his identity (Trapman, 2022). The use of shell corporations is, however, a little bit more difficult than the use of virtual wallets. In particular because a donor that does not keep control of the donation through the chain of companies, risks losing it. Without influence on all the corporations in between, the donor risks that one of the chains does not forward the money. The donor therefore must have some level of control upon the entire chain. To ensure the donor cannot provide an anonymous donation the ultimate beneficial owner should be traceable. To reduce the risk of money laundering the EU has created the Ultimate Beneficial Owner registry (UBO) (art. 3(6) Directive 2015/849). To prevent anonymous donations or the use of shell corporations, the information from the UBO could be automatically incorporated into the donation system.

The second category of financial duties are the reporting duties. The parties are obliged to provide the Authority for European Political Parties and European Political Foundations (Authority) with a donor list. This list includes the total amount of donors for the financial year, their names and donations. The exception to this rule are donations not exceeding €1500 made by natural persons. Donations made between €1500 and €3000 are not published unless consent is given by natural person making the donation (art. 32(1)(e)). Additionally any single donation exceeding €12.000 has to be reported to the Authority immediately (art. 20(4)). In the 6 months preceding the elections, the reporting duty increases. During this period parties have to report once a week to the Authority. The reporting of donations to the Authority is important with regard to the prevention of illicit donations. Reporting on its own without publication, however, does not provide direct insight into the donations made in the run-up of an election. However, these donations close to an election enable the voters to hold their party accountable. The donations from private entities may reveal to a voter where the parties' interests lie (*Kamerstukken II* 2020–21, 35,657,3). The information should be published in order for potential voters to hold the parties accountable during the elections.

The third category of restriction is that of the action to take after funds are provided through unlawful origins. If a party receives a donation that falls outside the previously mentioned donation limits, the party is required to return the donation (art. 20(6)(a) Regulation EU 1141/2014). If it cannot be returned, the party is required to forward the donation to the general budget of the EU (art. 20(6)(b)). Theoretically the inability to keep donations is sufficient to prevent parties from seeking to obtain such donations. The BREXIT-campaign, however, suggests that an automatic prevention mechanism is necessary. The problem with the current legislation is the ex-post enforcement. The disadvantage of which was clearly visible in the BREXIT referendum. During the referendum a cap was in place on how much could be spent on campaigns. After the referendum it was discovered that the Leave campaign spent roughly 2.7 million pound extra through the sister party BeLeave (Coates, 2016; Vote Leave broke spending limits in Brexit referendum, activist claims, 2018). The problem was that the referendum had taken place. Whilst the cap violation constituted a violation of the UK electoral law, the referendum outcome was not affected. Similarly if parties do not report or do not payback the illegal donations, post-election enforcement may be ineffective. It would therefore be more effective if violations could be prevented.

A resulting blockchain system should be able to accommodate the previously mentioned legal requirements. Additionally in order to consider introducing the blockchain system, it would have to be able to improve certain facets. The next section will therefore discuss whether the blockchain system has the potential to improve the current system of self-reporting.

Blockchain: Preliminary Questions

This section will analyze whether a blockchain meets the pre-implementation requirements as formulated by the UK whitepaper. The first question that the UK whitepaper asks is whether there are multiple parties that need to be able to write data (UK National Cyber Security Centre, 2021). The legislative requirements assign roles to various institutions. The political parties are required to self-report and have the financial audit conducted by an accountant. In addition the Authority and European Anti-Fraud Office (OLAF) have been assigned supervisory roles. The involvement of these various parties fulfills the first criterion of the UK report.

The second question, according to the UK, is whether there is a lack of trust between the entities. The lack of trust between the entities can also be considered as true. The financial statements generated by the parties should be verified by an accountant. This obligation in itself is a statement of distrust. Furthermore the current corruption affair has demonstrated that to a certain degree the level of distrust is not unfounded. Another important relationship to keep in mind is that of the trust between the political parties and their electorate. A reason for introducing the blockchain is to improve trust and transparency. Various democracies around the globe currently suffer from trust issues. Less than half the population in 2021 trusts the European Union (European Commission, 2021). The lack of trust from its citizens decreases the legitimacy of the EU. It is therefore worthwhile to improve the trust from its citizens. The second criterion of lack of trust is thereby fulfilled.

The third question is whether there is a central authority who could write the data on behalf of the entities. There is no central authority that has primary access to the data when it is generated. Donations arrive either through different bank accounts or in cash. This means that the different banks should function as the centralized authority. The commercial banks are a (public) authority that can function as a centralized authority. Nor does it seem to make practical sense for bank representatives to come together to write a donation list. Alternatively, the donations could arrive through the Authority (Troitiño, 2022), whereby the donations are sent to a bank account of the Authority and then forwarded by the authority. This system, however, would place the Authority into a difficult and potentially political debate, in particular when mistakes are considered to have been made. Furthermore, it would entail a massive task for the Authority to process all the incoming donations. An automated blockchain system would thus be preferable. This would not require a review process of the Authority. The blockchain system could furthermore be examined by all parties as to avoid politicalization of a single responsible institution. The next paragraphs will therefore continue by examining what choices should be made with regard to the blockchain design.

Designing the System

Micro-Level

The first set of questions raised by Tan et al. are those at micro-level. The micro-level questions examine the infrastructure, application, and interoperability choices. The first choice is that of infrastructure. The infrastructure question refers to whether the blockchain used will be permissioned or permissionless and public or private (Tan et al., 2022). The choice between those systems will come with trade-offs.

Participation

The first trade-off is that of participation. A public blockchain entails that everyone without exception can participate on the blockchain. This would allow an easy access for those wishing to make a donation to a political party. The disadvantage is that the ex-ante check of the permissibility of the donation will be impossible. It is possible to check donations ex-post through analyzation of the transactions. But this would be no different than that of analyzing the bank statements of the political parties. Therefore it would not be a real improvement upon the previous system. The permissioned blockchain, however, would be able to limit the participants and donations ex-ante. One way to create such a system would be to have a single authority in charge of connecting the population to the blockchain. The system could function a little like that of the Estonian e-voting (Ehin et al., 2022), except by offering donations instead of votes, whereby people can connect to the system through their European Digital Identities (e-ID). Through the e-ID the person can provide the Authority with the donation and the intended party, through a two-step verification system. This would allow for an ex-ante check of the permissibility of the donor to make a donation and to keep a record of the donation(s) made. The record could be used to prevent avoiding the threshold of publishing donor information by making various small donations. The Authority could function as a clearing house between the donations made in euros and the blockchains cryptocurrency used for registering party funding and vice versa. The initial block offering would look like Fig. 1.

Initially a public blockchain therefore seems less ideal compared to that of a permissioned blockchain. The main advantage with a public blockchain, however, is its instant transparency.

Privacy and Transparency

The information on a public blockchain can be read by everyone without permission. A permissioned blockchain, on the other hand, requires permission to be read. The trade-off between these two designs is primarily between privacy and transparency. As stated in the previous section a motivation for introducing the system is to ensure transparency of political party finance. A public blockchain has a major advantage that it is transparent (Niranjanamurthy et al., 2019). Considering the importance of transparency a public blockchain would be preferable. This would allow each member of the public to directly access who the parties are funded by. The disadvantage, however, is that of privacy. Because the public can directly access all the data this includes privacy sensitive data. If data is wrongfully published, it can be removed but this is a difficult process (Ølnes et al., 2017). There are two possible solutions to this trade-off. The first is to opt for a private blockchain only accessible to the government and publish the data per x amount of time. This option allows for a privacy check before the data is published. It, however, requires a body to be responsible for publishing and checking the data. This would include additional labor for the body that is selected. Furthermore, if the primary data is only accessible to government institutions, it may not inspire public confidence (Ivic & Troitiño, 2022). The second solution is to prevent sensitive information from being published. Whilst this solution is the most favorable it is difficult to achieve and requires a strong clarity on what data must be published.

The legislator introduces the duty donor identification when the donation reaches the threshold of €3000. The €3000 is a clear line that will not cause much debate.

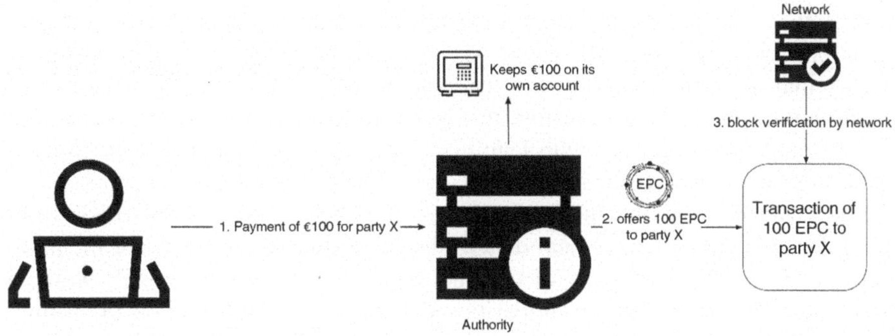

Fig. 1 Blockchain offering

The question is what data should be published. Without such guidance it is likely the publication is not in line with the general data protection regulation. Furthermore, the publication of such data is not per se permitted either. As was the case in the public availability of the information of the UBO registry. In its recent judgment on the UBO registry the Court of Justice of the European Union (CJEU) has limited the extent to which the information can be published (UBO Registry, 2022).

The CJEU has examined to what extent publicly publishing the details of the UBO was a violation of their privacy. The case concerned the UBO published by Luxembourg which was accessible by any member of the public. The CJEU examined if the public access to the UBO was a violation of privacy under article 8 European Convention Human Rights (ECHR) and 7 Charter of Fundamental Rights EU (further: EU Charter). The case concerned a UBO whose personal information had been published (Ramiro Troitiño, 2023). The UBO had asked the Luxembourg authorities to seal the information, as he faced risk of blackmail and kidnapping. The authorities had refused to consider the availability of his information as a disproportionate risk. The CJEU was therefore asked to consider whether the public availability of such information was a violation of privacy. The CJEU considered that the publication of the data in such a manner can be accessed by an unlimited amount of persons (paraf. 42). Persons who may not per se have a legitimate interest in accessing that information. In addition the CJEU considers that once published the information can be consulted, stored, and further disseminated. This, the CJEU considers, creates a system whereby it becomes near impossible for data subjects to defend themselves (paraf. 43). On the other hand, the CJEU considers that publishing the information contributes to greater scrutiny of civil society. It furthermore promotes the integrity of the financial system by preventing money laundering and the financing of terrorism (paraf. 56). The CJEU, however, also notes that in this case it concerned the information of private people. The principle of transparency increases in importance when it concerns public funds and/or institutional transparency (paraf. 61). The CJEU then considers that to prevent money laundering it is beneficial for the public to have access to this information (paraf. 67). The publication nevertheless must be strictly necessary. This includes precise rules on what data is published and what the safeguards are for the individual subjects (paraf. 65). Furthermore the provision of this data to the larger public is unnecessary according to the CJEU. The authorities supervising money laundering should have access to the information. Access to the larger public, however, creates a large intrusion of privacy that does not off-set against the benefits (paraf. 85). The CJEU bases this conclusion on the legislative history that primarily entailed the information would only be published to parties with legitimate interests. The definition of legitimate interests would, however, be too difficult, hence the publication to the public.

The UBO registry and the political party blockchain carry similarities. Both entail the publication of personal data to the larger public. Furthermore the party financing is a special category of personal data, as it reveals someone's political preferences. Based upon these similarities it is easy to conclude that the publishing of the donor's data to the general public would be unlawful. There are, however, some differences between the two. The donor's private information is prima facie, not of a public institution. However considering that it concerns the financing of the political parties, it is also data concerning public institutions. By whom political parties are financed is also a question of the financing of public institutions. When two businesses interact, the risk of damage to a third-party is limited. It is therefore only within the interest of the contracting parties to verify who the UBO of their contracting partner is. This is different when a party is financed by a certain person or company, as a potential voter might be damaged by this relationship (*Kamerstukken II* 2020–21, 35,657,3). The data therefore does not only lie within the private domain but also within the public. Publishing the data therefore does not seem unlawful perse. Nevertheless publication upon a blockchain still entails that the data is permanently present. One possibility would be to encrypt the blockchain and use a different cryptographic key each year. If information of a certain year is considered to be irrelevant due to the passing of time, the key could be removed from the public. Similarly if information was wrongfully placed upon the blockchain, the key could be withheld until the information is removed. Another limitation to the access of the information could be obtained through e-ID. Whereby only the citizens who are eligible to vote in the EU elections can read the blockchain. Thus limiting the initial access of the information to those with an interest in the knowledge of party funding. To ensure privacy can be upheld the best choice is therefore a permissioned, rather than a public blockchain (Krishnamoorthi et al., 2021). A public blockchain, however, has more participants and is therefore generally considered more secure. The question thus becomes whether a permissioned blockchain is sufficiently safe.

Security

The first design question is to reduce reliance on the integrity of the parties. A blockchain that is private can be altered by a single moderator. This does not improve trust and makes the system reliant on the moderator. A permissioned system with multiple users who can verify and add data therefore seems more appropriate. The different political parties can function as nodes who can offer information (namely payment requests) and verify the information offered by others. The parties can thus check each other. Such a system would require a sufficient level of parties participating to ensure that there is no collusion. The number of political parties participating in the elections is over 100. This would mean that in order to change the system the number of parties colluding would need to be high. Depending on the type of blockchain the number of parties needed for successful collusion would vary between 30 and 51+. It is unlikely that such a collusion would take place unnoticed. A permissioned blockchain would thereby not rely on the integrity of the parties themselves but on the integrity of a large number of parties (see Fig. 2). The difficulty with a permissioned blockchain, however, is the throughput.

Permissioned blockchains are generally based upon the Byzantine Fault Tolerance (BFT) consensus mechanism. This mechanism is considered slow; with transaction times being up to 24% slower than with NFS protocols (Castro & Liskov,

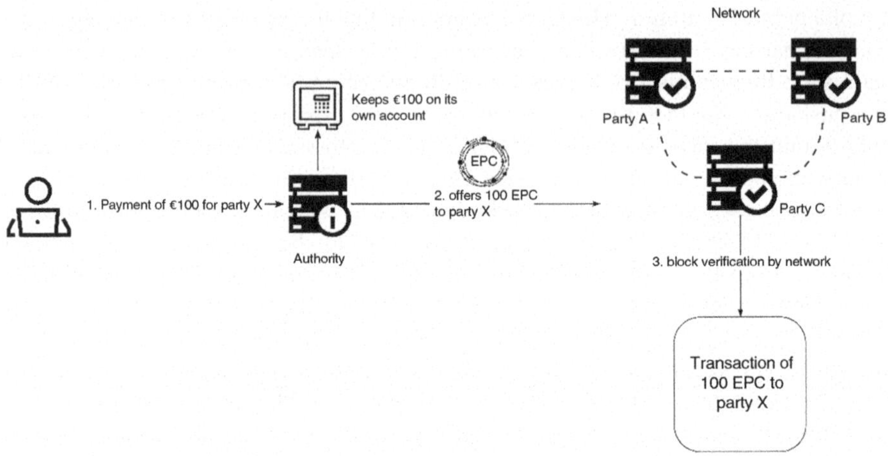

Fig. 2 Blockchain verification

2002). For a system that needs to handle donations to parties from potentially the entire EU voting population, a low throughput is not an optimal choice. Though the BFT was considerably slower in the early 2000s, the technology has improved. Using resilientDB Rahnama et al. created a BFT-based blockchain with high throughput. Unfortunately their research examined the non-monetary possibilities of a blockchain (Rahnama et al., 2020). Gupta et al. examined the resilientDB design in a more general manner. Their research indicates that a well-designed BFT system could reach up to 175 k per second (Gupta et al., 2020). This type of throughput is sufficient for a political financial system. Other types of permissioned blockchains rather than BFT are also an option to create instant transactions (Min et al., 2016). It therefore seems that the necessary throughput of a permissioned blockchain can be achieved.

With regard to the micro-level decision making, the blockchain would have to be permissioned. Whereby the various political parties are nodes that can initiate and verify transactions, whereby the Authority functions as a clearinghouse between donors and the political parties. Thus providing ex-ante verification of transactions. Furthermore whilst it would be beneficial to transparency to allow the larger public to read the information, this should be limited to eligible voters.

Meso-Level

The design questions with regard to the Meso-level are threefold. The first is the decision-making mechanism. The second is the incentive mechanism, the incentive is not relevant to this chapter. In a blockchain that depends on attracting miners from the larger public, the blockchain needs to provide an incentive to attract miners. In the case of a government run blockchain system, the costs of running the blockchain are carried by the government. A private incentive is therefore not necessary. The third design question at meso-level is what kind of consensus mechanism should be used.

Starting with the first question regarding the decision-making process. This process regards when or how changes to the rules of the system should be made and implemented. There are two different mechanisms. The first is an on-chain governance. This type of governance is where changes are implemented through the different nodes. They engage in direct discussion and vote on implementing changes. Once a majority is reached, the underlying code is directly changed (Tan et al., 2022). In off-chain governance, on the other hand, the changes to the protocol are generated from outside the blockchain (Tan et al., 2022). On-chain governance is faster and is generally considered more transparent (Dursun & Üstündag, 2021). The on-chain decision making can be stored and is therefore auditable by the larger public (Dursun & Üstündag, 2021). Nevertheless the question is whether this would fit a system as currently required.

It is most likely that the rules considering political funding and what information of donors should be published will change. It is inherent in legal systems that they change over time. Changes come through the legislative process. This process includes political parties and therefore prima facie, an on-chain governance would be ideal. The protocol could be discussed and voted on by the different parties on chain. Any change would be logged thus increasing transparency. Nevertheless this option is far from ideal. The voting protocol would have to be adapted according to election results. It is furthermore questionable whether it is democratically desirable to have discussions removed from the legislative house to blockchains. In addition changes in legislation, whilst primarily through the legislator, may also rise from a judicial verdict. Using an on-chain governance structure is therefore far from ideal. The off-chain governance structure, on the other hand, is considered slow due to its centralization and less transparent. The transparency of decision making takes place outside the system and hence is considered less audible (Dursun & Üstündag, 2021). Changes in the legislative structure of political party financing, however, take place through public debate or through judicial decisions. The debates, votes, and judicial decisions are open to the larger public. The scrutiny of decision making thus takes place through transparency within the legislative process. Furthermore, in order to implement decisions through off-chain management often requires a "hard-fork." The hard-fork is one whereby the participants on the blockchain have to manually accept the changes that are made and update their blockchain system. This type of fork is generally considered a disruption to the efficiency of the blockchain (Dursun & Üstündag, 2021). A soft fork, on the other hand, allows the participants to continue using the blockchain under the new rules without noticing. A hard-fork, whilst inefficient, would prevent changes being made to the system without the knowledge and consent of the parties (Hamulák, 2018). Thereby providing an additional check upon the system to prevent unknown changes. The use of off-chain management therefore seems to be more efficient than on-chain management. The next question is then what type of consensus mechanism should be chosen.

As discussed in the third section of this chapter, the system must increase transparency without relying on the integrity of the parties. If each party in the system could individually add or change transactions, the system would not be trustworthy. Therefore a consensus mechanism must be applied to the blockchain. This mechanism is what allows the parties to collaborate without trusting each other. The first option would be to have each member agree with the transaction. This option, however, is not viable. If a single node is compromised or offline, the blockchain would fail to function. In such a system a single political party's refusal to comply could prevent the system from working. This would be highly impractical and dangerous. Therefore a form of consensus that does not require all nodes yet provides integrity should be introduced. There are roughly two systems that are used to reach consensus on blockchains. The first is a Proof-of-X (PoX) algorithm which relies on proof from the node of a certain effort (work) or monetary stake. These algorithms are generally used on public blockchains (Li et al., 2021). Private blockchains more often use a RAFT consensus (Li et al., 2021).

A RAFT consensus mechanism operates with three forms of nodes: leaders, candidates and followers. The process starts by the election of a leader by the followers. The leader is in charge of adding information to the blockchain. When the leader fails, the followers choose a new leader from the candidates. The new leader is then responsible for adding information. A follower may become candidate when it has not received information from the leader over a certain period of time (Verma et al., 2022). This system could theoretically be applied to the party financing blockchain as it does not rely on all nodes. If a political party is inactive due to power or internet disruption, the RAFT can still function. It can function as long as half the nodes are operating (Gorniak & Kudin, 2020). Nevertheless the latency of a RAFT consensus mechanism is generally considered relatively low (Verma et al., 2022). There are proposals to increase the efficiency of the RAFT consensus but these are in early stages (Zhang et al., 2017). More problematic is that the RAFT consensus can tolerate up to half of the nodes offline but not corrupt nodes (Tian et al., 2021). Therefore if a political party wishes to disrupt the system it does not require the collaboration of other nodes. This type of risk is contrary to the aims of the system which is to improve trust. It is unlikely the system is trustworthy if a single party can tamper with it. To prevent tampering researchers have suggested adding a Byzantine Fault Tolerance layer to the RAFT system (Tian et al., 2021).

The Byzantine consensus is a generic term for adaptations on consensus via "Byzantine Fault Tolerance" (BFT). This system works by a majority voting and is secure as long as the compromised nodes do not exceed 1/3 of the total nodes (Li et al., 2021). Whilst 1/3 is lower than half it is unlikely that more than 1/3 of the political parties is colluding to corrupt the system. As in practice this would mean that at least 30 parties would have to secretly collude. Furthermore a BFT requires less computational power than RAFT (Li et al., 2021). It would therefore be more implementable as a system.

Decision Making at Macro-Level

Tan et al. describe the decision making at macro-level to concern the decision making, accountability, and implementation of the overall system (Tan et al., 2022). The background to these decisions is described by Tan et al. as the implementation of norms deriving from constitutional, cultural, historical, and legal context (Tan et al., 2022). The case of Sweden, discussed in Sect. 2, demonstrates the importance of adjustment of the legal system to the blockchain system and vice versa. It is therefore important to evaluate the blockchain finance system to the constitutional and legal norms present in the system. The importance of this discussion is present within the first question of Tan et al.

The first question that Tan et al. ask is that of the organization of governance. This question relates to whom may take decisions about the blockchain network (Tan et al., 2022). Their article recommends that a permissioned blockchain is best governed by a centralized structure (Tan et al., 2022). Meaning that the governance of the blockchain for party financing is best awarded to a single institution. Whilst this idea is theoretically sound, the practice is more difficult. A constitutional debate surrounds the question of who should monitor the expenses. A purely managerial perspective considers that the institution with the best information and overview should be in charge of monitoring. Considering this perspective the Authority would be the best option, as this Authority has the most information of what party is participating in the elections. There is, however, the constitutional question of neutrality. The Authority is an a-political body, assigning it this task could compromise its neutrality (Broeksteeg & Gijssenbergh, 2022). A similar debate is held in the Netherlands whereby the Council of State therefore recommends a new body to be created specifically for this task (De Afdeling advisering van de Raad van State, 2023). It considers that adding this task to the electoral committee could compromise its authority as a neutral institution (De Afdeling advisering van de Raad van State, 2023). It is likely that the new committee would face similar issues as the electoral committee. It would be left with little authority if it makes a politically unpopular decision. The Dutch Council of State therefore advises this task to be assigned to the Minister of Interior affairs (further: Minister). The Minister is advised by the committee on party financing with regard to its discretionary powers (*Kamerstukken II* 2020–21, 35,657,3). The reasoning is that the Minister can be held accountable by the parliament (Broeksteeg & Gijssenbergh, 2022; Trapman, 2020). Nevertheless the Minister is part of a political party which can lead to the appearance of politically motivated decision making. A centralized governance structure, which is the advice of Tan et al., is not favorable to this system. The centralized system would clash with constitutional norms and may result in distrust in the system. A decentralized system whereby multiple institutions are involved seems preferable. The next question at macro-level is that of governance accountability and control.

The governance accountability concerns whether rules are binding and whether they are applied strictly (Tan et al., 2022). The governance control level raises the question to what extent changes to the system and decisions are made by humans or are automated (Tan et al., 2022). There are different reasons why certain systems could be chosen. For example, automated decision making can reduce energy cost (Tan et al., 2022)s. It is, however, important to remember that this system is designed to be transposed into an existing legal framework. The legal framework currently in place is one whereby there is a strict legal framework. It is not optional for parties to comply with the regulation. Hence the question of whether the regulation should be binding or voluntary must comply with the legal framework existing outside the blockchain. A similar reasoning should be used for the question of human or automated decision making. In theory oracles connected to the blockchain can provide knowledge of legislative changes. Thus providing semi-autonomous decision making (Tan et al., 2022). This would require a connection between the legislator and the courts and the blockchain system. The connection would have to be able to send information to the blockchain. The blockchain would then have to use natural language processing to transpose the law into code. Whilst theoretically possible, it is unlikely that with the current state of technology such a system would function without flaws. Human decision making would therefore be a safer option than automated decision making.

Furthermore, law is defined by ambiguous natural language. Machine learning is improving and adapting to use natural law in its coding (Hassan & Filippi, 2017). Nevertheless, this system is far from perfect. Automation without human control would therefore pose a serious risk to the correct transcribing of law into code. In addition, when adding oracles to the system, they constitute another element. These elements may malfunction or even get corrupted (Al-Breiki et al., 2020). Hence the oracles must be properly secured, which poses another challenge. Therefore, instead of opting for an automated design it seems prudent to leave the decision making to the government and courts. The results should then be manually altered into the system.

Conclusion

This chapter introduced a blockchain to increase transparency of political party financing. It researched the possibility of introducing such a system based upon EU legislation. The chapter started in Sect. 2 by analyzing the different applications of blockchains within public policy. It considered three different countries, namely the United Kingdom, Georgia, and Sweden. These countries demonstrate the importance of integrating the blockchain system into the environment. Using these case studies as example Sect. 3 of this chapter concludes that a blockchain system could provide increased transparency into the party financing, as it would take away the need to primarily rely on the integrity of the individual political parties. Furthermore, a blockchain system can provide a direct overview of the incoming donations. This increases the ability for voters to hold their political parties accountable for their financial resources. Section 4 then continued by analyzing the specificalities for the blockchain.

This chapter concludes that a permissioned blockchain is more appropriate than a public blockchain. This conclusion is based upon privacy aspects, as a permissioned blockchain can be limited to eligible EU voters. Furthermore with a permissioned blockchain the nodes that verify transactions can be limited to the participating political parties. This provides security against a foreign interference with the system. To increase throughput a BFT consensus mechanism can be used. BFT has a relatively high throughput but lower level of nodes needed to collude. Nevertheless, collusion would still require around 30+ parties. It is highly unlikely that such a number would collude unnoticed. The final technical aspect is that of making changes to the blockchain. Changes will be required if legislation is altered or if judicial decisions require changes. These changes can be discussed and voted on either through the blockchain or off the blockchain. Whilst transparency is theoretically increased through on-chain voting, this chapter considers off-chain voting more appropriate. The deliberation of legislative change should be conducted through the plenary debates rather than through blockchains. Furthermore automatically implementing judicial verdicts creates technical risks that are largely unnecessary.

This chapter therefore concludes that it is possible to increase transparency and voter accountability through a permissioned blockchain system.

References

Al-Breiki, H., Rehman, M. H., Salah, K., & Svetinovic, D. (2020). Trustworthy blockchain oracles: Review, comparison, and open research challenges. *IEEE Access, 8*, 85675–85685.

Bonsón, E., & Bednárová, M. (2019). Blockchain and its implications for accounting and auditing. *Meditari Accountancy Research, 27*, 725–740.

Broeksteeg, J., & Gijssenbergh, J. (2022). De evalutatiewet Wfpp: Tussenstation of voorlopig eindstation. *Tijdschrift voor Constitutioneel Recht*, 202.

Burcher, C. U. (2019). Cryptocurrencies and political finance. *International IDEA Discussion Paper*, 1–34.

Castro, M., & Liskov, B. (2002). Practical byzantine fault tolerance and proactive recovery. *ACM Transactions on Computer Systems, 20*, 398–461.

Coates. (2016, February 17). Brexit group's plot to break campaign spending limit. *The Times*.

De Afdeling advisering van de Raad van State. (2023). *Voorlichting RvS onderzoek buitenlandse financiering van politieke partijen*. NJB.

Dursun, T., & Üstündag, B. B. (2021). A novel framework for policy based on-chain governance of blockchain networks. *Information Processing & Management, 58*, 1–25.

Ehin, P., Solvak, M., Willemson, J., & Vinkel, P. (2022). Internet voting in Estonia 2005-2009: Evidence from eleven elections. *Government Information Quarterly, 39*, 101718.

European Commission. (2021, April 23). *Eurobarometer: Trust in the European Union has increased since last summer.* Retrieved from https://ec.europa.eu/commission/presscorner/detail/en/ip_21_1867

European Parliament. (2022, December 15). *Corruption scandal: MEPs insist on reforms for transparency and accountability*. European Parliament.

Goossens, J. (2021). Blockchain and democracy: Challenges and opportunities of blockchain and smart contracts for democracy in the distributed, algorithmic state. In O. Pollicino & G. D. Gregorio (Eds.), *Blockchain and public law. Global challenges in the era of decentralisation* (pp. 79–80). Edward Elgar.

Gorniak, K. S., & Kudin, A. (2020). Aspects of blockchain reliability considering its consensus algorithms. *Theoretical and Applied Cybersecurity, 2*, 5–9.

Graglia, J. M., & Mellon, C. (2018). Blockchain and property in 2018: At the end of the beginning. *Innovations: Technology, Governance, Globalization, 12*, 90–116.

Gupta, S., Rahnama, S., & Sadohi, M. (2020). Permissioned blockchain through the looking glass: Architectural and imlementation lessons learned. In *International conference on distributed computing systems* (pp. 754–764). IEEE.

Gwartney, J. D., Holcombe, R. G., & Lawson, R. A. (2006). Institutions and the impact of investment on growth. *Kyklos, 59*, 255–273.

Hamulák, O. (2018). La carta de los derechos fundamentales de la union europea y los derechos sociales. *Estudios constitucionales, 16*(1), 167–186.

Hassan, S., & Filippi, P. D. (2017). The expansion of algorithmic governance: From code is law to law is code. *Artificial Intelligence and Robotics in the City, 17*, 88–90.

Heilbron, A., & Whyte, R. (2019). *Institutions for investment: Establishing a high-performing institutional framework for foreign direct investment*. World Bank.

Ivic, S., & Troitiño, D. R. (2022). Digital sovereignty and identity in the European union: A challenge for building Europe. *European Studies, 9*(2), 80–109.

Jun, M. S. (2018). Blockchain government - A next form of infrastructure for the twenty-first century. *Journal of Open Innovation: Technology, Market, and Complexity, 4*(1), 7.

Koerhuis, W., Kechadi, T., & Le-Khac, N.-A. (2020). Forensic analysis of privacy-oriented cryptocurrencies. *Forensic Science International: Digital Investigation, 33*, 1–11.

Krishnamoorthi, P., Shahid, S., & Boydell, O. (2021). Preserving privacy in private blockchain networks. In *International conference on blockchain* (pp. 118–128). Springer.

Krishnapriya, S., & Greeshma, S. (2020). Securing land registration using blockchain. *Procedia Computer Science, 171*, 1708–1715.

Lazuashvili, N., Norta, A., & Draheim, D. (2019). Integration of blockchain technology into a land registration system for immutable traceability: A case study of Georgia. In C. D. Ciccio, R. Gabryelczyk, L. García-Bañuelos, T. Hernaus, R. Hull, M. I. Stemberger, & M. Staples (Eds.), *Business process management. Blockchain and Central and Eastern Europe forum* (pp. 225–248). Springer.

Li, Y., Qiao, L., & Lv, Z. (2021). An optimized Byzantine Fault Tolerance alogrithm for consortium blockchain. *Peer-to-Peer Networking and Applications, 14*, 2826–2839.

McMurren, J., Young, A., & Verhulst, S. (2018). *Addressing transaction costs through blockchain and identity in Swedish land transfers*. GovLab.

Min, X., Li, Q., Liu, L., & Cui, L. (2016). A permissioned blockchain framework for supporting instant transaction and dynamic block size. In *ISPA* (pp. 90–96). IEEE.

Niranjanamurthy, M., Nithya, B. N., & Jagannatha, S. (2019). Analysis of blockchain technology: Pros, cons and SWOT. *Cluster Computing, 22*, 14743–14757.

Ølnes, S., Ubacht, J., & Janssen, M. (2017). Blockchain in government: Benefits and implications of distributed ledger technology for information sharing. *Government Information Quarterly, 34*, 355–364.

Proskurovska, A., & Dörry, S. (2022). The blockchain challenge for Sweden's housing and mortgage markets. *Economy and Space, 54*, 1569–1585.

Rahnama, S., Gupta, S., Qaday, T., Hellings, J., & Sadohi, M. (2020). *Scalable, resilient, and configurable permissioned blockchain fabric*. U.S. Department of Energy.

Ramiro Troitiño, D. (2023). Mapping e-governance in the EU. In *Digital development of the European Union: An interdisciplinary perspective* (pp. 303–317). Springer International Publishing.

Renderson, J. (2022, December 14). Who's who in the Qatar corruption scandal? *Politico*.

Saari, A., Vimpari, J., & Junnila, S. (2022). Blockchain in real estate: Recent developments and empirical applications. *Land Use Policy, 121*, 1–11.
Shang, Q., & Price, A. (2019). A blockchain based land titling project in the republic of Georgia: Rebuilding public trust and lessons for future pilot projects. *Innovations: Technology, Governance, Globalization, 12*, 72–78.
Stiglitz, J. E. (2013). *The price of inequality*. Penguin Books.
Tan, E., Mahula, S., & Crompvoets, J. (2022). Blockchain governance in the public sector: A conceptual framework for public management. *Government Information Quarterly, 39*, 101625.
Tapscott, D., & Tapscott, A. (2018). *Blockchain revolution*. Penguin Books.
Tian, S., Liu, Y., Zhang, Y., & Zhao, Y. (2021). A byzantine fault-tolerant raft algorithm. In *15th international conference on ubiquitous information management and communication* (pp. 1–5). IEEE Xplore. https://doi.org/10.1109/IMCOM51814.2021.9377376
Trapman, L. (2020). Regulering van microtargeting volgens de Staatscommissie parlementair stelsel: een verkenning. *Tijdschrift voor Constitutioneel Recht, 2*, 12.
Trapman, L. (2022). *Follow the money 2.0. De herziening van de Wet financiering politieke partijen* (pp. 23–24). Ars Aequi.
Troitiño, D. R. (2022). La estrategia de las instituciones de la Unión Europea ante el reto de digitalización. *Revista CIDOB d'Afers Internacionals*, 17–40.
UBO Registry, Joined Cases C-37/20 & C-601/20 (Court of Justice of the European Union November 22, 2022).
UK Government Chief Scientific Adviser. (2016). *Distributed ledger technology: Beyond block chain*. Government Office for Science.
UK National Cyber Security Centre. (2021). *Distributed ledger technology. The nature and applications of distributed ledger technology*. UK National Cyber Security Centre.
Verma, S., Yadav, D., & Chandra, G. (2022). Introduction of formal methods in blockchain. *IEEE Access, 10*, 66611–66624.
Vote Leave broke spending limits in Brexit referendum, activist claims. (2018, March 25). *BBC*.
Zhang, Y., Han, B., Zhang, Z.-L., & Gopalakrishnan, V. (2017). *Network-assisted raft consensus algorithm* (pp. 94–96). Association for Computing Machinery.

Europeanization the Digital Way: Trans-European IT Systems—The Case of EESSI

Evert-Jan Mulder

Abstract This article explores the role of Information Technology (IT) in the Europeanization process, focusing on Trans-European IT systems. Despite the growing significance of IT in national policy implementation across Europe, the use of IT in the European Union (EU) remains relatively unexplored. Trans-European IT projects, such as the Electronic Exchange Social Security Information (EESSI), exemplify a unique form of Europeanization. This study delves into the complexities of the EESSI-case, shedding light on the challenges and outcomes of implementing a cross-border IT system with extensive functionalities. As a result, the analysis suggests that the Commission's perspective leaned toward perceiving EESSI primarily as an IT solution to enforce EU policy, potentially overshadowing its original purpose as a tool for facilitating necessary and useful data exchange aligned with domestic business practices at the Member State level.

Introduction

Surprisingly quite little literature on Europeanization is to be found on the contribution of Information Technology (IT). Where IT has become a major important element in policy implementation by national governments all around Europe, the way IT is used in the European Union (EU) to facilitate policy implementation is rather a black box. Nonetheless, also at the EU-level substantial and complex IT projects are executed. Some of these IT systems are somehow visible to the public, e.g., the Schengen Information System that is used in border-control shows its face when people enter or leave European airports. Others stay under "the radar," especially those systems that facilitate information exchange between the different Member States and do not involve interaction with European citizens. These so-called

E.-J. Mulder (✉)
Consultancy, Red Plume, Afferden, Netherlands
e-mail: ejmulder@redplume.nl

D. Ramiro Troitiño (ed.), *E-Governance in the European Union*, Contributions to Political Science, https://doi.org/10.1007/978-3-031-56045-3_15

Trans-European IT systems[1] connect the back-offices of national governments in the EU and are in use for several purposes, like carrying out custom procedures, processing traffic fines, or validating driver's licenses.

Trans-European IT projects[2] can be seen as a way of Europeanization (Featherstone, 2003; Radaelli, 2003): the idea embraced at the EU level to develop an IT system facilitating data exchange between Member States for specific policy purposes, which comes to life through an IT project that is organized at the EU level and executed with full participation of the Member States, based upon an EU-driven design, technology, and strategy. In the end, the project must lead to implementation and use of the IT systems by the Member States and (hopefully) prove to suit its purpose.[3]

The Europeanization by Trans-European IT systems has some specific characteristics, as we would like to demonstrate here further:

- First, Europeanization stresses the importance of change, since it involves the domestic assimilation of EU policy and politics. This change has special significance in the light of IT, since the system designed and developed at the EU level should be in alignment with the "business" in the Member States. This is one of the important lessons of Information Management (IM) research of the last decades, encapsulated under the term "Business and IT alignment" (Henderson & Venkatraman, 1993). The "business" is a part of the domestic way of doing things, performed by numerous national or subnational institutions that have to implement and use the Trans-European IT system. The adoption of the system should be in alignment with the way of working of the Member States and more specifically the processes, organization, planning and IT frameworks of the institutions involved.
- Second, Europeanization involves different actors (organizations or individuals) participating in or influenced by the EU policy process. When it comes to organizations, the reference to the concept of Multi-Level Governance (MLG) is important. This concept refers to the networked governance relations between supranational, national, and subnational governments, and other non-state actors (Bache, 2012; Peters & Pierre, 2001). The MLG concept is useful in the context

[1] We use this term because it is also used by the Commission. However, an even better term in our understanding would be EU trans-border IT systems. Source: https://joinup.ec.europa.eu/sites/default/files/inline-files/EU35%20TES%20Trans-European%20Systems%20Study.pdf.

[2] In our definition the IT-system is about the designed technology artifacts and all the procedures for use, maintenance, etc. The IT project is about realizing and implementing the system, according to goals and a plan. Source: https://wikidiff.com/project/system.

[3] In the definition of Radaelli (2003, p. 30) "processes of (a) construction (b) diffusion and (c) institutionalization of formal and informal rules, procedures, policy paradigms, styles, 'ways of doing things' and shared beliefs and norms which are first defined and consolidated in the making of EU public policy and politics and then incorporated in the logic of domestic discourse, identities, political structures and public policies."

of Trans-European IT systems, since not only the European Commission[4] and national ministries are involved in these projects, but also other government and non-government actors, like IT providers. Often overlooked but of special importance regarding IT systems are executive government agencies. Since the early 1990s, with the introduction of managerialism in public sector, reforms have been taking place in public sector administration (Pollitt et al., 2007). One particular kind of reform included the restructuring of bureaucracies, resulting in the establishment of autonomous agencies. Due to their executive mission, these agencies are by definition IT intensive organizations. They are highly dependent on the use of IT in their operation and invest heavily in measures to guarantee continuity.

- Third, Europeanization is a two-way process: Member States upload their preferences to Brussels and then download them from different policy menus. When it comes to an IT system, the whole process of uploading business requirements and downloading an IT system has to meet specific conventions in terms of governance, strategy, and methodology. A Trans-European IT system demands at the EU level a business logic that fits all the organizations that have to connect to the system. Downloading, or implementing a Trans-European IT system for those organizations is most often not a stand-alone event but it requires an integration with back-office systems, adjustment of processes and instructions, and sometimes even organizational restructuring.
- Fourth, Europeanization can lead to different outcomes at the national level. Best case it leads to absorption or even transformation at the national level, worst case to inertia or retrenchment. With implementing IT, individual Member States with a critical attitude toward the system in the end are more or less forced to implement the system after the majority of other Member States have done this. Otherwise, they "disconnect" or "isolate" themselves from this part of the EU. So, inertia toward an IT system, in the long run, is not sustainable. This is all the more interesting, since the system has to be implemented by both digitally advanced and less-advanced countries. The latter often express hardly any opposition against the introduction of the system, since they usually gain by its new functionality or operate from a green field situation. The group of advanced countries have to integrate the new system in their existing IT architectures, experiencing all kind of problems, and often see the new system as less-advanced, according to their own standards.
- Fifth, Europeanization by a cross-border IT system is more than only EU-anization. It is not only about uploading business logic preferences and downloading the EU system, but it is also about new connections between Member States and their organizations. Because of the digital exchange of information,

[4] A Trans-European IT system does not necessarily be coordinated and managed by the Commission. There are also examples of Trans-European IT systems set up and managed by the Member States. An example is EUCARIS, the European CAR and driving license Information System. Source: https://joinup.ec.europa.eu/collection/egovernment/document/eucaris-european-car-and-driving-licence-information-system-eucaris-0.

the organizations involved need to have a cross-border understanding of how to interpret the system, what should be done in case of failures or exceptions, etc. This way the digital connection is often followed by and embedded in new physical or other connections between Member States.

In perceiving Trans-European IT Systems as a—special—way of Europeanization, we would like to discuss the case of EESSI: Electronic Exchange Social Security Information. EESSI is considered a complex Trans-European IT system, since it covers a wide range of functionalities, using technology partially managed by the Commission, partially by the Member States (Hamulák, 2018). In addition, the implementation of EESSI was not a walk in the park since the system went live 7 years later than originally planned and has been subject to a lot of criticism, especially from the side of more digitally advanced Member States. Although the EESSI-case is quite unique in its sort, it offers a rich starting point for reflection.

This case study is based on information gathered as participant in the EESSI-project. As national EESSI-program coordinator for the Netherlands, we engaged in meetings and discussion both at the EU and the Dutch national level during the period of 2018–2022. Our information is based on direct observations, EESSI-project documentation and conversations held with other participants in the project, including (former) representatives of the European Commission, other Member States, and the Dutch government. The writing of this chapter is to be considered as a reflection-on-action (Schön, 1983).[5]

From our position as a practitioner operating from a national perspective, it will not be a surprise that we take a bottom-up perspective in our reflection on EESSI. In doing so, we will reflect on both the strategy and the structure of the project.[6]

In the remainder of this chapter we present the EESSI-case study, our reflections, and some conclusions to the end.

[5] During this period, a log book was kept with notes and reflections on the program.

[6] With "strategy" we refer to the determination of long-term goals and objectives, the adoption of courses of action and associated allocation of resources required to achieve goals. With "structure"" we refer to the design of authorities and responsibilities, the way tasks are performed and information flows between actors involved. Source: https://www.researchgate.net/publication/313444758_THE_CONNECTION_BETWEEN_STRATEGY_AND_STRUCTURE/link/589b017392851c8bb68443e1/download.

EESSI

General

The free movement of persons is a fundamental right in Europe. Citizens of the EU and the European Free Trade Association (EFTA) countries can travel freely within the EU/EFTA area, take up employment, and establish residence in other Member States.

EESSI is legally mandated by the European Commission (EC), based on two regulations: Article 78(1) of Regulation (EC) 883/2004 provides that "Member States shall progressively use new technologies for the exchange, access and processing of the data required to apply this Regulation and the Implementing Regulation. The European Commission shall lend its support to activities of common interest as soon as the Member States have established such data-processing services. Furthermore, under Article 4 of Regulation (EC) 987/2009, the transmission of data between the institutions or the liaison bodies shall be carried out by electronic means, while the Administrative Commission (*the steering committee with representatives from the Member States—author—)* shall lay down the detailed arrangements for the exchange of documents and structured electronic documents" (EDPS, 2023).

The innocent reader may conclude from this legal mandate that the Member States were in the EESSI driver seat and that the Commission had a more or less facilitating and supporting role. As we will discuss later, nothing could be further from the truth. In practice it turned out the Commission held both hands firmly around the steering wheel, and the Member States had to follow the route that was outlined by the Commission.

The EESSI-system was designed to facilitate the electronic exchange of social security data between EU/EFTA countries,[7] enabling faster and more efficient processing of citizens' applications for benefits, pensions, and allowances. Other advantages include more accurate data exchange between national authorities and the secure handling of personal data. Additionally, EESSI is intended to serve as a foundation for improved statistical information on the implementation of social schemes across Europe (ILO, 2010).

The EESSI-system has a wide scope in functionality, since it covers all areas of social security coordination, such as accidents at work and occupational disease benefits, family benefits, pension benefits, recovery of benefits and contributions, sickness and healthcare benefits, unemployment benefits, etc. In terms of use, EESSI also has a wide scope since the system has to be implemented across 32 different countries,[8] involving a total of 10,000–15,000 institutions[9] and

[7] In this chapter all the countries participating in EESSI will be referred to as "Member States".

[8] Although the Brexit, the UK keeps participating in EESSI.

[9] These 10,000–15,000 institutions participate in the EESSI data exchange. A number of approximately 5000–6000 institutions are actually connected to the EESSI infrastructure, including vari-

100,000–200,000 clerks, who are the actual users of the system. EESSI is not accessible for EU citizens. It is purely designed for back-office data exchange.

Architecture

In terms of technology, EESSI comprises international (EU) and national (Member States) components. This mixture of central and decentral components working together needs to enable flawless and secure data exchange among all connected institutions.

The high-level IT architecture of EESSI can be outlined as follows (ELRC Conference, 2016) (Fig. 1).

In summary, the exchange of information takes place as follows: an institution sends a request for information to an Access Point (AP) within its own country through a National Application housed within the institution. This information is then routed from this AP through the Central Service Node to an AP in another country. This routing occurs via the sTesta network,[10] a hub and spoke topology, which connects the governments of Member States and is managed by the European Commission. From the latter AP, the request is delivered via the National Application in use by the institution to which it is addressed.

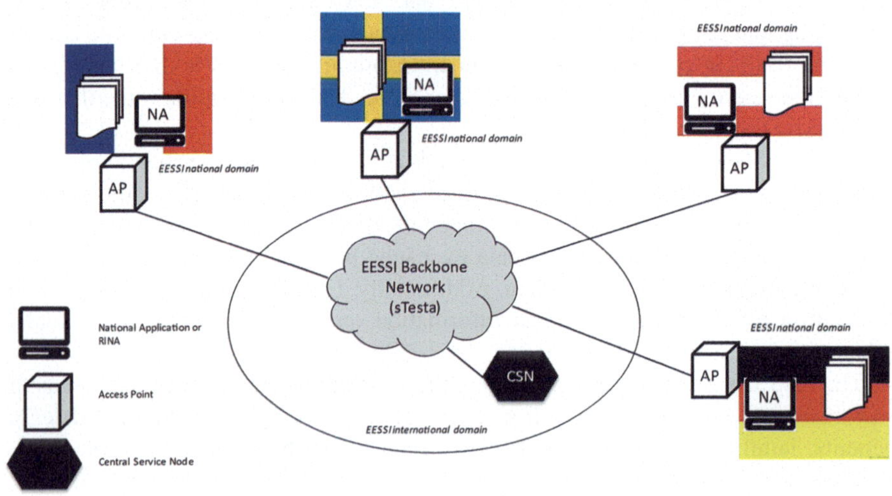

Fig. 1 High-level EESSI-architecture

ous institutes that act as liaison bodies.

[10] sTesta stands for secure Trans-European Services for Telematics between Administrations. These network services are managed by the European Commission. It is since more than 20 years a central infrastructure, separate from the Internet, used in many sensitive cross-border EU information services. Source : https://ec.europa.eu/isa2/solutions/testa_en/.

Many Member States and institutions use and manage the so-called RINA-software[11] as a National Application. This software is developed by the Commission but in a later stage of the project handed over to the Member States, a decision that stirred quite some discussion among the Member States. Some Member States, however, decided not to use RINA, but develop and use their own National Application. These National Applications had to go through a procedure of Conformance Testing before being allowed to connect to the central EESSI-system.

Next to this IT architecture it is important to outline the business architecture, consisting of 99 workflows, so-called business use case (BUCs). These BUCs can be processed through 300 structured electronic documents (SEDs) in 24 different languages. This business model mostly covers all the requirements laid down in the EC Regulations for the Coordination of the European Social Security. Although this business model is a crucial foundation in realizing the business needs of Member States organizations, the Commission has the final word when it comes to changes or adjustments in this model.

In this way the business model of EESSI was primarily based on a fulfillment of legal requirements, not necessarily the business logic and demands of the competent institutions at the national level. For this reason, several Member States considered this business model heavily "oversized," in the sense that a lot of BUCs had no relevance to them.[12] However, according to the EC implementation rules for EESSI, every Member State had to implement all the BUCs and the steps involved.

Governance

The EESSI governance has both an EU and a national dimension. At the EU dimension the European Commission and representatives of the Member States worked together in developing the EESSI-system and guiding its implementation. Directorate-General for Employment (DG Employment) had a central position, since it combined three crucial roles: Project Owner, Solution Provider, and Project Manager.

DG Employment engaged with Member States in the Administrative Commission (AC) on a strategic and steering level, and the Technical Commission (TC) on a directing level. The TC served as the "core" of the EESSI-program, where sometimes intense and heated discussions on the EESSI-system and its implementation took place between the Commission and Member States. The TC included representatives from ministries, implementing institutions, or national EESSI-programs of the Member States. The TC provided conclusions and recommendations for approval to the Administrative Commission (AC). Since DG Employment fulfilled

[11] RINA stands for Reference Implementation National Application.

[12] Estimates from some Member States were that 20% of the BUCs was sufficient to handle 90% of the EESSI data exchange.

the role of secretariat in both the TC and the AC, advice from the TC addressed to the AC was rarely criticized or rejected.

The AC involved policy representatives from the national ministries and focused on steering the main lines of the EESSI-program. EESSI was just one part of the AC's agenda, since its scope was the promotion of coordination in the field of social security in general. Occasionally, AC Working Parties were organized by the AC to delve further into the EESSI-program.

In addition to the AC and the TC, there were also occasionally high-level meetings, where the DG of DG Employment invited his counterparts of the national ministries to discuss EESSI matters, e.g., the handover of the RINA-software from the Commission to the Member States.

At the political level there was the EPSCO. The EPSCO Council brings together ministers responsible for Employment, Social Affairs, Health, and Consumer Policy from EU Member States. The status and progress of EESSI was a recurring topic on the EPSCO agenda. Although ministers occasionally made critical remarks about EESSI in EPSCO, this did not lead to extensive debates or additional decision-making. Also, from the EMPL Committee of the European Parliament no interventions took place on the EESSI implementation, although questions were directed to the Commission, like why such and such country was lagging behind in implementation and what measures could be taken to speed up the implementation?

The Member States were also formally represented by an Executive Board (EB). Contrary to its name, this body, composed of experienced participants from the Member States, also had little influence on the program's content and progress. In each TC-meeting, the EB was given the opportunity to express its views, which were then forwarded by the Chairmanship to DG Employment with thanks. DG Employment typically acknowledged these views but in general took little further action.

Next to the Executive Board, several other gremia were part of the EESSI-project, such as a Change Advisory Board, Security Expert Forum, Ad Hoc Groups (for business analysis), etc.

An overview of the EESSI governance in 2022 looked like this (Fig. 2):

At the national level, each country had its own national implementation program for EESSI. The challenge was to connect 32 different countries and 10,000–15,000 institutes in these countries, varying from small regional institutes run by a couple of employees to large national operating institutes with their own IT departments and IT strategies. Moreover, private institutes had to connect to EESSI.[13]

Some countries adopted a more centralized model in their national implementation program, working from a common approach and/or technical structure to connect implementing institutions. This approach seemed to be preferred when there were many small institutions to be connected or when a country was organized strongly regionally. Austria was an example of such approach.

[13] For example, in the Netherlands 50 private health insurance companies had to connect to EESSI. This was done by a liaison body connecting to the EESSI-architecture, and routing the messages to the private institutes.

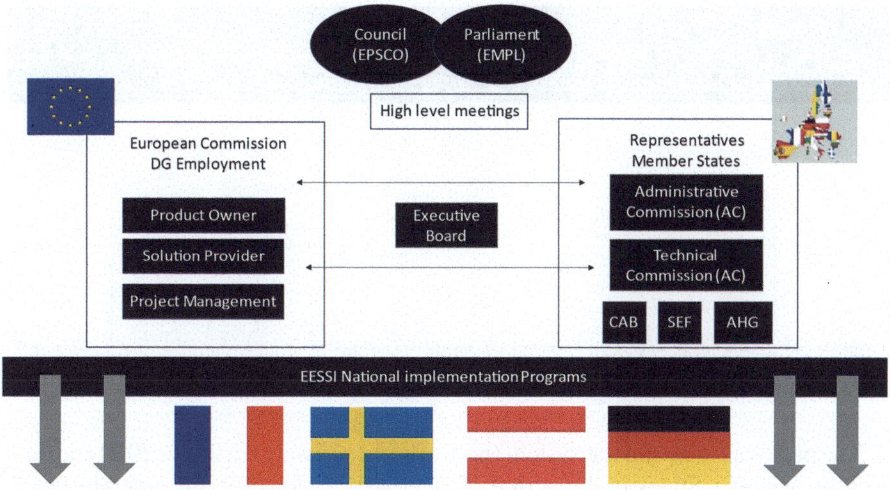

Fig. 2 EESSI Governance

On the other hand, some countries followed a more decentralized model, allowing implementing institutions relative freedom in their approach and/or technical structure for EESSI implementation. The Netherlands was an example of this latter approach, where there were four large national operating government agencies involved in the implementation of EESSI.

To facilitate the national implementation in an organizational way, Member States also had to appoint officials in mandatory functions, the so-called Single Point of Contact (SPOCs). These officials were national liaison for the EU on several topics.[14]

The Road to EESSI

The road to going live with the EESSI-system took considerably more time than initially anticipated. Below is an overview of the timeline of the project (Fig. 3):

Initially, there was a significant degree of an optimism regarding the implementation of the EESSI-system. The first implementation date was set for 2012, 2 years after the Regulations of 2010, which formed the basis for EESSI, came into force. The preparations began in 2007 with a feasibility study that yielded the system's architecture as a crucial result. An external vendor was awarded a contract for the development of the required software. DG Informatics developed the necessary infrastructure via the sTesta network.

[14]Governments had to install an EESSI Spoc (general national contact), IR Spoc (Institutional Repository), AP (Spoc) (Access Point), Security Spoc and Trainings Spoc.

2007-2008	2009-2010	2011-2012	2013-2014	2014-2017	2017-2019	2020-2022	2023-next
Preparation for the initial version of EESSI (architecture)	Development of the first version of EESSI	First attempt to connect Member States (unsuccessful)	Reflection period	SAFE pilot, resulting in Production Ready Release	National Implementation Programs in 32 Member States, (live July 2019)	Rina Handover	Finalizing and continuous improvement

Fig. 3 The road to EESSI

The plan was to install the system (network and software) in 2009–2010 and connect the Member States in the period of 2011–2012. However, this attempt failed. As one representative from a Dutch institute recalled, "the screen just went black."

2013–2014 was a reflection period. Furthermore, the entire business model was developed by defining all business use cases (BUCs) and structured electronic documents (SEDs) for all the domains of social security. Furthermore, a new external IT supplier was contracted.

In the subsequent years, efforts were made to identify improvements and alternative approaches. The Social Agencies for Europe (SAFE) program played a significant role in this regard, running from 2014 until 2017. Under Italian leadership, 13 countries worked on testing and further improving the EESSI-system. The result was acclaimed by the Commission as a "Production Ready Release."

A critical element of this Release was the Reference Implementation National Application (RINA), originally intended as an example for countries to develop their own National Applications and to handle low volumes of SEDs. Gradually, this RINA came to be seen by many countries as a production system, as it meant they did not have to develop their own National Application. This also suited the Commission, as Member States had fewer arguments to resist the implementation of EESSI. Later it became apparent that there was a (costly) drawback to this line of thinking.

Starting from 2017, the implementation could begin in the Member States, despite objections from some Member States that the release was not as production ready as expected. The criticism mainly targeted the decentralized RINA application, which was deemed not fit-for-purpose. These objections were disregarded, and in the period from 2017 to 2019, national efforts had to start by the Member States to implement the EESSI-system.

The target for all Member States was to be capable of handling all BUCs electronically by third July 2019, effectively ending paper-based exchanges. Being "EESSI-ready" for a particular BUC meant that the Member State concerned could both send and receive all messages in that BUC to and from other Member States. To emphasize the transition from paper to electronic, the term "transitional phase" was used for the period 2017–2019, possibly helping to forget the earlier failed implementation attempt.

Consequently, national programs were launched in all Member States from 2017 to implement EESSI. Under these national programs, implementing institutions had to develop implementation strategies for EESSI. To facilitate these implementations, Member States could use funds from the Connecting Europe Facility program.[15]

By 3rd July 2019, only one (small) Member State had successfully implemented EESSI in its entirety. The other countries were connected to the system, but there was significant variation in the level of EESSI readiness among them. Even within countries, there could be substantial differences in EESSI readiness among institutions. For instance, in the Netherlands, some institutions prioritized EESSI implementation due to a strong business case in their subdomain. Others however were more hesitant, as the business case was less compelling for them, or since they had little confidence in the quality of the EESSI-system, in particular the RINA.

Although most countries were not yet ready with the EESSI implementation, progress had to continue. Therefore, DG Employment introduced an executive decision:[16] if 80% of the Member States were live with a specific BUC, the remaining countries had 6 months to follow suit. This decision determined the subsequent implementation schedule.[17]

In 2020, DG Employment made a significant announcement: it would cease managing the RINA by the end of 2021, primarily due to the high costs involved for the Commission. This decision surprised Member States for several reasons. First, because it was taken unilaterally without approval or consultation with the Member States. Second, the RINA Handover would inevitably result in higher costs for Member States, being of manifold of the cost the Commission was spending on RINA. Third, it would make the EESSI-system more complex in operation and maintenance, and the timing of the proposal—amidst the critical implementation phase—was rather unfortunate.

The RINA Handover also introduced another complicating factor: finding a private entity willing to manage the RINA on behalf of the interested countries and institutions. This required additional time and effort. This was finally realized by a Joint Procurement Agreement (JPA), with a majority of the countries participating. The JPA also resulted in a successful selection of an (Italian) private party.

[15] The Connecting Europe Facility (CEF) is a key EU funding instrument to promote growth, jobs, and competitiveness through targeted infrastructure investment at European level. It supports the development of high performing, sustainable and efficiently interconnected trans-European networks in the fields of transport, energy, and digital services. Source: https://commission.europa.eu/funding-tenders/find-funding/eu-funding-programmes/connecting-europe-facility_en.

[16] This was the so-called EESSI E7 Executive Decision. Source: https://eur-lex.europa.eu/legal-content/EN/TXT/PDF/?uri=CELEX:32020D0306(01).

[17] The same decision stated also that all BUCs had to be implemented. The hope of some countries to be able to avoid implementing BUCs irrelevant to their context turned out to be idle.

With this last hurdle taken, Member States can finalize their national implementation and work on future improvement of the EESSI-system. The coming years it remains to be seen whether EESSI will indeed fulfill its promise of facilitating faster, more efficient, and error-free data exchange between institutions. Additionally, it will need to demonstrate its manageability and future viability, along with all its various components. In summary, the final verdict on EESSI is yet to be rendered.

Reflection on the EESSI-Case

We have not said too much that EESSI presents a rich basis for reflection. EESSI shows a particular way in which Europeanization can take place, not necessarily in the best possible way and with the best possible outcomes. Reflecting on EESSI is an exercise that can be done from several different angles and perspectives. From our position in the EESSI-project, as a national program coordinator, it feels best to stick to a bottom-up perspective, addressing the issues that were in particular relevant for Member States and their executive agencies. This is also in line with the call from scholars on Europeanization, who encourage a bottom-up or inside-out-approach (Radaelli, 2003).

In addition, a top-down perspective is relevant, to confront the bottom-up perspective, because we are sure that from the standpoint of the EC there will be other, complementary but possibly opposing positions on the EESSI-case. Also, we would like to repeat that our observations are made from the perspective of the Netherlands, a digitally advanced country that in a political sense supported the EU policies on social security coordination and welcomed the use of IT to modernize the cross-border data exchange. However, in the Netherlands there is also critical attitude toward IT projects, caused by various failures in the recent past and the political attention this has brought with it.

As said earlier, we will reflect on the strategy and the structure of EESSI.

EESSI Strategy

The design of the EESSI-system turned out to be a digital representation of legal requirements written down in two EU regulations. Translating these legal requirements to software code resulted in a one-size-fits-all system, which was quite "oversized," meaning Member States did not need all the BUCs to fulfill their business requirements. For agencies at the domestic level this resulted in mandatory efforts to implement a system which had partially no value to them, but nevertheless forced them to invest. Even worse, the quality of the RINA-software was a constant reason for discussion between the Commission and the Member States and frustrated the implementation to a certain degree. Discussion involved many IT topics, like functionality, security, performance, maintenance, etc., but also covered the IT strategy of the Commission. Why was there no better testing of software before it was released to the Member States? Why were complaints of the Member States not taken into consideration, etc.?

One wonders if the representatives of the Policy and the IT unit of DG Employment were up for the task to implement a system of this magnitude and complexity. Policy implementation by the Commission is most times of a normative—as opposed to operational—nature, enabling the uniform implementation of legislative acts through the adoption of implementing rules (Szapiro, 2013). This underestimation of the implementation effort at hand may be due to the "French DNA"[18] of the EC which includes a number of centralist traits. From this perspective it is tempting to conclude that EESSI was seen by the Commission more as an IT solution to enforce an EU policy, rather than an IT system that needed to be aligned with the business at the domestic level. Although the origins of the system undoubtedly were rooted in good and sound intentions, namely to replace paper forms and modernize data exchange, in the course of time the system became an aim in itself, and not an instrument to facilitate exchange which is necessary and useful for the Member States.

Regarding the substitution of inefficient paper exchange by digital means, and the strategy used in the implementation of EESSI, one may also wonder if the actors involved at the time of the start of the project did not suffer from "a car is a faster horse" reasoning. This relates to the "myth of substitution",[19] stating that when a new technology emerges, the widespread hope is that it will perfectly substitute the technologies that are currently in use. However, this rarely turns out to be true, "because a socio-technological transition is taking place, including a change in a cluster of aligned elements: artefacts, knowledge, user practices, cultural meaning, infrastructure, maintenance and supply networks" (Geels, 2005). All these elements need to be addressed when it comes to implementation, and this requires a proper strategy. One can wonder if the EESSI strategy at the EU level was sophisticated and encompassing enough to address all these issues. In a sense the focus was very much on technology, and not so much on the sociology of the system.

Structure of EESSI

Regarding the structure of EESSI, one central element for discussion is the pivotal role of the EC. The role of the EC fits in a rather centralistic picture we already painted and encapsulates a troublesome combination of responsibilities since DG

[18] The European Commission derives from one of the five key institutions created in the supranational European Community system, following the proposal of Robert Schuman, French Foreign Minister, on 9 May 1950. Source: https://en.wikipedia.org/wiki/European_Commission.

[19] The Substitution Myth is the term created by cognitive scientists David Woods and Eric Hollnagel to describe the pervasive (and wrong) assumption that a robot can seamlessly substitute for a human. Source: https://www.roboticsthroughsciencefiction.com/substitution-myth.

Employment was both project owner, project manager, and IT provider for EESSI. This could mean, for example, that flaws in software quality were ignored to avoid delays in the project, as happened during the fit-for-purpose discussion. One can argue that EU policy implementation, especially when it involves implementation of IT systems, should be much more subject of scrutiny. This is a lesson many governments in Europe have learned the hard way, because IT projects often present persistent challenges. They are not on-time, not on-budget, and fail to deliver on their initial promise. As a result, national governments, sometimes prompted by parliamentary inquiries, have stepped up their game in IT governance, introducing national CIO's, roadmaps, architectures, and risk management methodologies. One wonders if this also might not be helpful for the EC.

By adopting a one-size-fits-all implementation strategy, the Commission put more emphasis on legislative compliance than on meeting business needs. In an MLG setting this is something that should be given serious thought, in particular by the EC, as the hierarchically highest authority in a legal constitutional sense in this case. We agree with Milio (2010) that MLG cannot only be perceived as a model for EU policy implementation in a descriptive way, but also in a prescriptive way. This means successful policy implementation requires the input of all the relevant players involved. In the case of EESSI specific attention should be given to the interest of large executive agencies, since they have a lot to win and to lose with the implementation of such a Trans-European IT System. It is not enough for them to be heard, but they also should be listened to. This means formal representation of these agencies needs to be organized.

Last but not least, we want to address an institutional aspect of the EESSI-structure. The EU wide adage, that the EU is about the "what" in the policy process, and the Member States about the "how," seems to be subject to inflation when we look at the introduction of EESSI. With a decisive say in the business logic of EESSI, plus the RINA-software until this stage, it is difficult for the EC to maintain the standpoint that it does not interfere with the organization and operation of national administrations. Also, in this perspective it seems necessary to reexamine the formal governance structure of Trans-European IT Systems, since the administrative sovereignty of the Member States is at stake here.

Conclusions

With the presentation of the EESSI-case we have illustrated the IT dimension of Europeanization. The EESSI-case also shows that, from a bottom-up perspective, there is room for improvement in the way IT is used in the implementation of EU policies. In particular the role of the EC should be reconsidered, next to the governance structure of these kind of programs, where the voice of the Member States and their agencies should be heard much more.

This said, we would like to address the concept of Europeanization in a normative way. Not only is Europeanization a process in which "ways of doing things" at the domestic level become more European or EU-like. It is also a process that needs to meet certain requirements and follow specific conventions, when it is done in the digital way. Since Europeanization will increasingly be taking place with the use of IT the future years, it is time more scholars turn their attention to this subject.

References

Bache, I. (2012). Multi-level governance in the European Union. In D. Levi-Faur (Ed.), *The Oxford handbook of governance*. Oxford University Press.

EC. (2016). DG Employment. EESSI Presentation. 2nd ELRC Conference (Brussels).

EDPS. (2023). EDPS supervisory opinion on the role of the European Commission in the project Electronic Exchange of Social Security Information (EESSI) (Case 2023-0138).

Featherstone, K. (2003). Introduction: In the name of 'Europe'. In Featherstone & Radaelli (Ed.), *The politics of Europeanization*. Oxford University Press.

Geels, F. W. (2005). The dynamics of transitions in socio-technical systems: A multi-level analysis of the transition pathway from horse-drawn carriages to automobiles (1860–1930). *Technology Analysis & Strategic Management, 17*(4), 445–476.

Hamulák, O. (2018). La carta de los derechos fundamentales de la union europea y los derechos sociales. *Estudios constitucionales, 16*(1), 167–186.

Henderson, J. C., & Venkatraman, H. (1993). Strategic alignment: Leveraging information technology for transforming organizations. *IBM Systems Journal, 32*(1), 472–484.

International Labour Organization. (2010). Coordination of Social Security Systems in the European Union. An explanatory report on EC Regulation No. 883/2004 and its Implementing Regulation No. 987/2009.

Milio, S. (2010). *From policy to implementation in the European Union: The challenge of a multi-level governance system*. Tauris Academic Studies.

Peters, B. G., & Pierre, J. (2001). Developments in intergovernmental relations: Towards multi-level governance. *Policy & Politics, 29*, 131–135.

Pollitt, C., Van Thiel, S., & Homburg, V. (2007). *New public management in Europe: Adaptation and alternatives*. Palgrave Macmillan.

Radaelli, C. M. (2003). The Europeanization of public policy. In Featherstone & Radaelli (Ed.), *The politics of Europeanization*. Oxford University Press.

Schön, D. A. (1983). *The reflective practitioner*. Basic Books.

Szapiro, M. (2013). *The European Commission: A practical guide*. John Harper Publishing.

Evert-Jan Mulder works as an independent consultant in the Netherlands, focusing on IT strategy and digital transformation of the Dutch Public Sector, with a special emphasis on the EU context. He has worked with national, regional, and local governments, and executive agencies. His academic publications cover Multilevel Governance, eGovernment, Europeanization, and Digital Transformation. He is the founder and director of Red Plume Consultancy (www.red-plume.nl).

e-Justice Governance in the EU

Onţanu Elena Alina

Abstract Technology use has been seen as a way to make access to justice easier, faster, and more efficient. In the EU, e-justice actions have been centred around supporting activities leading to building up access to legal information, access to courts and extrajudicial procedures in a cross-border setting, and communication between judicial authorities. These actions have led to three main e-justice developments: the e-Justice Portal, the e-CODEX system, and the ODR Platform. All three are large complex systems of heterogeneous components managed by the European institutions with the collaboration and support of EU Member States, national and/or local authorities, professional bodies, and even private businesses. Due to EU's limited competencies in the area, developments depend significantly on the existence of national ICT systems and digital justice achievements, and the Member States' willingness to be involved in actions that enhance cross-border interoperability. This leads to multilevel governance structures with actors having different roles and competencies at national and European level. The e-Justice Portal, the e-CODEX system, and the ODR Platform are the first European models of e-justice architectural choices and governance. This chapter studies these systems' governance, the roles various actors play, the challenges encountered, and the existing interactions before looking towards future developments and solutions for the governance of large multilevel e-justice systems.

Introduction

Information and communication technology (ICT) is part of our daily lives and activities. The demand for 'faster, more efficient, and more accessible' justice is on the rise (Taal et al., 2019), and ICT deployment has been seen as the element that can 'significantly improve the administration of justice' (Velicogna, 2007) in a

O. Elena Alina (✉)
Department of Private, Business & Labour Law, Tilburg University, Tilburg, Netherlands
e-mail: e.ontanu@tilburguniversity.edu

D. Ramiro Troitiño (ed.), *E-Governance in the European Union*, Contributions to Political Science, https://doi.org/10.1007/978-3-031-56045-3_16

national and cross-border setting by promoting delay reduction, economy of judicial activities, effectiveness and efficiency of court procedures and resources used (e.g. staff, time), transparency and accountability, lowering users' costs, and supporting an increased quality of services offered (see also Ramiro Troitiño, 2023).

In the EU, technological developments to support justice services and access to justice can be grouped around the following activities:

1. building up access to information in the field of justice via a dedicated website (present e-Justice Portal) and interconnection of national registers;
2. facilitating access to courts and extrajudicial procedures in a cross-border setting (e.g. use of standard forms, ICT for communication and hearings, ODR Platform),
3. speeding up and guaranteeing secured communication between judicial authorities in civil, commercial, administrative, and criminal proceedings with the use of dedicated platforms such as e-CODEX and the e-Justice Portal.[1]

e-Justice has been used as an umbrella term for ICT developments in civil, commercial, and criminal matters (see Velicogna, 2018).[2] The actions undertaken to integrate ICT generally aim to facilitate access to justice and the functioning of judicial systems for citizens and businesses, legal practitioners, and judicial and security authorities while looking to preserve judicial independence and the separation of powers (Taal et al., 2019). The EU institutions and the Member States have worked together towards developing an e-justice strategy and synergies between existing projects and new initiatives to improve justice services and uphold fundamental values. Over the years, several Multi-annual European e-Justice Action Plans have been adopted—2009–2013,[3] 2014–2018,[4] 2019–2023,[5] and 2024–2028.[6] Each of these prioritises and looks to achieve several e-Justice goals: facilitating access to information via the e-Justice Portal, interconnecting national registries, accessing electronic procedural forms, using the e-CODEX system[7] for e-communication between judicial authorities and professionals, supporting court and out-of-court procedures in a cross-border setting (2014–2018), creating a European justice area via dematerialised procedures, offering direct justice services

[1] These actions have been identified based on Multi-Annual European e-Justice Action Plans 2009–2013 and 2014–2018. See Council (2009, 2014).

[2] The term was used for the first time during the Austrian EU Council Presidency who organised the first e-Justice conference in 2006.

[3] Council (2009).

[4] Council (2014).

[5] Council (2019a).

[6] Council (2019b).

[7] e-CODEX stands for e-Justice Communication via Online Data Exchange. It is a system designed to facilitate the cross-border electronic exchange of data for judicial cooperation in civil and criminal matters. Regulation (EU) 2022/850 on a computerised system for the cross-border electronic exchange of data in the area of judicial cooperation in civil and criminal matters (e-CODEX system), OJ L 150, June 1, 2022, 1–19.

to citizens and business via a dedicated e-Justice portal, and facilitating electronic collaborations between authorities (Hamulák, 2018). The upcoming action plan on European e-Justice emphasises the digitalisation process of cross-border judicial cooperation and access to justice, the legal data and dataset use, and artificial intelligence.[8]

The e-justice developments in the EU include the e-Justice Portal, the e-CODEX system, and the ODR Platform. They are multilevel governance structures with actors having different roles and competencies at national and European levels. In order to build of such large systems, as well as to manage and continue to develop them over time, the European institutions required the collaboration and support of Member States, national and/or local authorities within the Member States, professional bodies, and even private businesses. The EU e-Justice layer depends significantly on national ICT existence and achievements and the Member States' willingness to be involved in actions that enhance cross-border interoperability (Onţanu, 2020) because the EU has only limited competencies in this area.

In building such large-scale e-justice systems, technology is not sufficient. Actions need to be taken at various levels: legislative,[9] organisational, and

[8] Council (2023).

[9] The European Parliament adopted first a Resolution on e-Justice in 2008 (2008/2125 (INI) calling on legislation to be designed in a way that would allow its use in online applications. A series of legislative acts followed on: electronic identities, signatures, stamps, and payments (Regulation (EU) No 910/2014 on electronic identification and trust services for electronic transactions in the internal market and repealing Directive 1999/93/EC, OJ L 257, 28.08.2014, pp. 73–114); the interoperability between EU information systems in the field of police and judicial cooperation, asylum and migration (Regulation (EU) 2019/818 on establishing a framework for interoperability between the EU information systems in the field of police and judicial cooperation, asylum and migration and amending Regulation (EU) 2018/1726, (EU) 2018/1862 and (EU) 2019/816, OJ L 135, 22.5.2019, pp. 85–135); technology use for service of documents and taking of evidence (Regulation (EU) 2020/1784 of the European Parliament and of the Council of 25 November 2020 on the service in the Member States of judicial and extrajudicial documents in civil or commercial matters (service of documents) (recast), OJ L 405, 2.12.2020, pp. 40–78; Regulation (EU) 2020/1783 on cooperation between the courts of the Member States in the taking of evidence in civil or commercial matters (taking of evidence) (recast), OJ L 405, 2.12.2020, pp. 1–39); the use of a decentralised IT system for relevant communications between authorities of different Member States (Regulation (EU) 2022/850 on a computerised system for the cross-border electronic exchange of data in the area of judicial cooperation in civil and criminal matters (e-CODEX system), OJ L 150, 1.6.2022, pp. 1–19); easier and faster collection of e-evidence for law enforcement and judicial authorities from another Member State (Regulation (EU) 2023/1543 on European Production Orders and European Preservation Orders for electronic evidence in criminal proceedings and for the execution of custodial sentences following criminal proceedings, OJ L191, 28.7.2023, pp. 118–180; Directive (EU) 2023/1544 laying down harmonised rules on the designation of designated establishments and the appointment of legal representatives for the purpose of gathering electronic evidence in criminal proceedings, OJ L191, 28.7.2023, pp. 181–190); a Digital Package for all civil and commercial cross-border procedures (Regulation on the digitalisation of judicial cooperation and access to justice in cross-border civil, commercial and criminal matters, and amending certain acts in the field of judicial cooperation, European Parliament, PE-CONS 50/23, Brussels, 29 November 2023; Directive amending Directive 2011/99/EU and 2014/41/EU of the European Parliament and of the Council, Council Directive 2003/8/EC and

institutional, in order to secure the proper functioning of ICT for justice purposes. Funds need to be available and adequately sized to finance the development,[10] operation, and maintenance of ICT.

This chapter takes the most prominent e-justice systems that have been developed in the EU and studies their governance, the roles various actors play, the challenges encountered in their development, and the existing interactions between them before looking towards future developments and solutions.

The EU e-Justice Systems: Their Structures and Actors

The e-Justice Portal, the e-CODEX system, and the ODR Portal are the most significant European e-justice developments to date. They have shown that technology is not 'a passive tool that may support the justice service provision' (Velicogna, 2018). e-Justice is not only about technology[11] (e.g. technical characteristics of European and domestic architectures [where available] to digitise and/or digitalise justice police activities, use of AI software to support investigations, court-related transcription activities, etc.), but also about many other aspects: the legislative framework (e.g. diversity of national rules, the interaction between national and European legislation), the authorities and organisations involved (e.g. different structures of the authorities concerned, the dichotomy between the EU and national competencies, national and EU governance, governance of judiciary, governance of ADR bodies, governance of systems used), the users (e.g. their technology competences, their needs, ICT literacy, and skills), and upholding fundamental justice principles (e.g. independence of judiciary, impartiality, transparency, fair trial) (Onţanu, 2023a).

Council Framework Decision 2002/465/JHA, 2003/577/JHA, 2005/214/JHA, 2006/783/JHA, 2008/909/JHA, 2008/947/JHA, 2009/829/JHA and 2009/948/JHA, as regards digitalization of judicial cooperation); and latterly also for an AI Act that contains relevant norms for e-justice developments (Proposal for a Regulation of the European Parliament and of the Council laying down harmonized rules on artificial intelligence (Artificial Intelligence Act) and amending certain Union legislative acts, 14,954/22, Brussels 25 November 2022).

[10] The European Commission has financed the development, operation, and translations of information websites such as the European e-Justice Portal, and funded e-Justice projects (e.g. e-CODEX, ODR Platform) through a number of means such as DG Justice, the Connecting Europe Facility, the Interoperability Solutions for European public administrations, and the Competitiveness and Innovation Framework programmes.

[11] E-Justice Conference organised during the Dutch Council Presidency.

The e-Justice Portal

The European e-Justice Portal was developed by the DG Justice of the European Commission, with the support of the Member States and justice stakeholders.[12] The Portal was launched in 2010 with the aim to provide 'a single, multilingual, user-friendly access point'[13] ('one-stop cybershop for justice information') (Reading, 2010) to the whole European e-Justice system where legal information is available. In the first development phase, the focus was on providing information (especially for users not represented or not affording legal representation) on national and European procedural details and rights (Contini, 2013; Onţanu, 2020). Internet access and portals such as the E-Justice Portal are important instruments to provide access to justice by disseminating legal information at low cost for users and making it available at any moment (Reiling, 2009). The information provided by the Portal is made available with input from Member States, public authorities, and legal professionals and concerns: family and inheritance matters, monetary claims, court procedures, the possibilities of taking legal action in the EU (mediation or court procedures), and citizens' rights. This information has also expended over the years to include legislation and case law, finding legal professionals in the EU or competent courts, access to registers regarding business activities, land ownership and insolvency, and professional networks and agencies.[14] To support access to justice, a significant effort was made to integrate legal portals, wizards, and atlases (e.g. European Judicial Atlas).[15]

Besides its essential information component, since 2014, the e-Justice Portal has sought to expand its functionalities from an information provider to becoming a provider of services in the judicial area.[16] Thus, it supports the connection of various existing or developed services to one of the existing modules of the Portal (e.g. the interconnection of the national Insolvency and Land Registers through a web service specification to support the communication between the responsible national public bodies and registers with the Portal, the European Court Database containing information about national courts and their competences, the access to national case law with ECLI standard identifier, and support the Member States in joining the e-CODEX platform[17] as access point to the system).[18] The next functionalities to be made available to users envisage the interaction between the e-Justice Portal and the e-CODEX system (Fig. 1).

[12] Its contents incorporated information previously contained in two other websites: the Justice Atlas and the European Judicial Network in Civil and Commercial Matters. On the process, see Onţanu (2020); Onţanu (2019).

[13] Council (2013), Recitals 11 and 32.

[14] See https://e-justice.europa.eu/home?action=home

[15] On problematic aspects of some of these functionalities, see Velicogna (2018); Ontanu (2017).

[16] Commission (2018).

[17] On e-CODEX, see further Sub-sect. on e-CODEX.

[18] See, for example, Commission (2017).

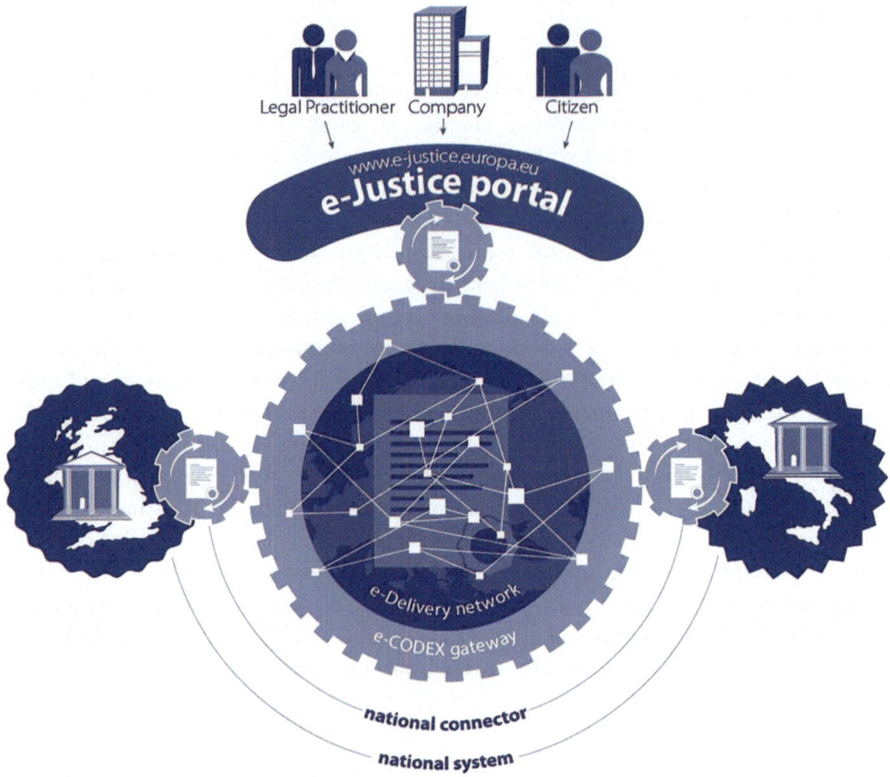

Fig. 1 Place of e-Justice Portal as access point to dematerialised cross-border court procedures (Figure available at Commission, 2020)

With these new functionalities, the Portal would become an e-CODEX access point interface to the infrastructure that will allow a complete dematerialisation of cross-border judicial procedures and communication between national authorities, practitioners, and parties in forwarding access to justice.[19] The infrastructural architecture is sought to make the interaction between the Portal and the national e-justice systems possible at various levels. It will enable even less digitalised national systems to communicate directly with e-CODEX.[20] In gaining these functionalities and providing an interface to the e-CODEX infrastructure, the e-Justice Portal will support a complete dematerialisation of cross-border procedures and communication between authorities, practitioners, and users. Hence, the e-Justice Portal will finally

[19] Proposal for a Regulation on Digitalisation of Judicial Cooperation and Access to Justice in Cross-Border Civil, Commercial and Criminal Matters, and Amending Certain Acts in the Field of Judicial Cooperation (Digitalisation of Judicial Cooperation Proposal), COM(2021)75. Onţanu (2020).

[20] The e-CODEX Gateway. See Pangalos et al. (2014).

develop into a complete 'one-stop-shop' in a cross-border environment looking to maximise the use and benefits of technology (Onţanu, 2020).

e-CODEX

The e-CODEX system—e-Justice Communication via Online Data Exchange—is a decentralised interoperable system for cross-border communication facilitating the electronic exchange of data in electronic format (text, audio, video) in a swift, secure, and reliable manner in the area of judicial cooperation in civil and criminal matters (Article 3(1) e-CODEX Regulation).[21]

e-CODEX started as a European Large-Scale Project (LSP) in December 2010.[22] The consortium included 22 Ministries of Justice or their representatives, and three other institutions: the Council of Bars and Law Societies of Europe, the Council of the Notaries of the European Union, and the National Research Council of Italy. The pilot phase started in 2013 as a decentralised service infrastructure. In building its infrastructure, the e-CODEX reused Connecting Europe Facility Digital Service Infrastructure (CEF DSI) (e.g. e-Delivery) to propose a gateway architecture that allowed existing national and EU solutions to be used and become interoperable through national access points connectors (Velicogna et al., 2020). The system uses a building blocks infrastructure (Fig. 2) with the technical objective of achieving 'interoperability between existing national judicial systems (i.e. for the cross-border transmission of judicial documents, decisions, information, etc.)' and securing the 'network for the judiciary and e-ID management of the different stakeholders (e.g. judges, courts, lawyers, etc.)' in order to 'rationalize and simplify judicial procedures (reduction of procedural deadlines and operating costs to the benefit of citizens, undertakings, legal practitioners and the administration of justice)'.[23]

Given the different levels of digitalisation of national justice systems, the European Commission is set to provide and maintain alternative back-end software components to secure the interoperability of national justice system to e-CODEX in transmitting and receiving judicial and extrajudicial documents. These alternative components for the adaptation of the national justice IT Systems are called Reference Implementation Software. This software has been piloted for the European Investigation Order (EIO) to exchange fully electronically the EIOs and related

---

[21] Regulation (EU) 2022/850 on a computerised system for the cross-border electronic exchange of data in the area of judicial cooperation in civil and criminal matters (e-CODEX system), OJ L 150, 1.6.2022, 1–19.

[22] It was launched in the Competitiveness and Innovation Programme (CIP) that became the Connecting Europe Facility (CEF), now CED 2.0 that will run until 2027. For CEF 2.0, see https://www.consilium.europa.eu/en/press/press-releases/2021/03/11/connecting-europe-facility-informal-agreement-with-european-parliament-on-the-post-2020-programme/

[23] Commission (2010).

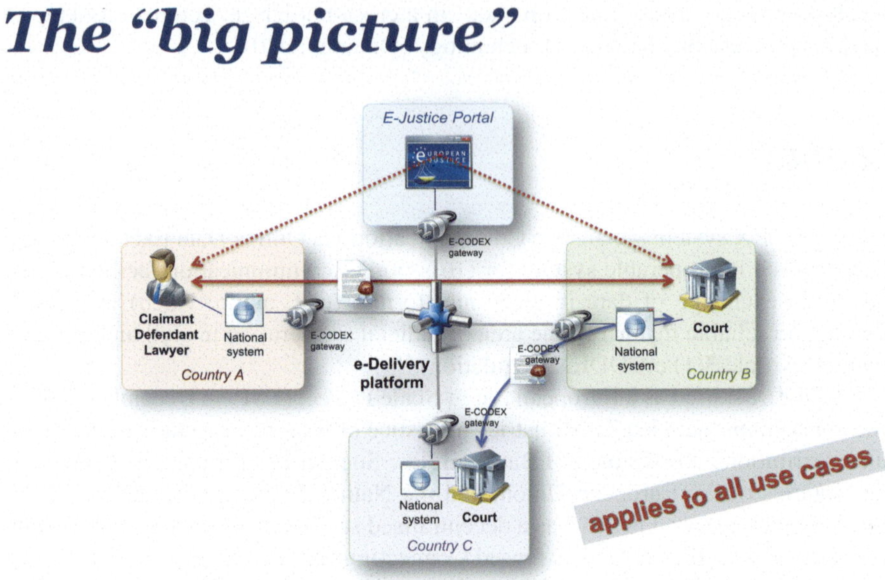

Fig. 2 e-CODEX overview (Commission, 2020, p. 5)

e-Evidence—e-EDES (e-Evidence Digital Exchange System) in e-CODEX.[24] A Reference Implementation System is now being built also for the service of documents—SoD (Reference Implementation Software for Service of Documents)[25] and taking of evidence—ToE (Reference Implementation Software for Taking of Evidence).[26]

The key non-technical component of e-CODEX is a Circle of Trust agreement (Velicogna & Steigenga, 2016).[27] This supports the legally valid communication between participants because it recognises e-Identification and e-Signature through

[24] See on this https://www.e-codex.eu/EXEC and https://www.e-codex.eu/EXECII

[25] Paragraph 1 Annex on Technical specifications, measures and other requirements of the decentralised IT system referred to in Article 1, Commission Implementing Regulation (EU) 2022/423 laying down the technical specifications, measures, and other requirements for the implementation of the decentralised IT system referred to in Regulation (EU) 2020/1784 of the European Parliament and of the Council, OJ L 87, 15.03.2022, 9. See also Onţanu (2023). On the first reflections on the creation of a Reference Implementation System for Service of Documents based on the Service Regulation (Regulation (EC) 1393/2007), see Steigenga et al. (2018).

[26] Commission Implementing Regulation (EU) 2022/422 laying down the technical specifications, measures and other requirements for the implementation of the decentralised IT system referred to in Regulation (EU) 2020/1783 of the European Parliament and of the Council, OJ L 87, 15.3.2022, 5–8.

[27] When the e-CODEX system was developed the legal framework on electronic communication and signature was not sufficient to support legally valid exchanges of legal documents or performing legal steps in cross-border procedures. This is why a Circle of Trust Agreement was created. The agreement allowed the mutual recognition of electronic data, documents, and signatures between Member States; if information was trusted in the Member State where it originated from

national systems across national borders. This gives the receiving party the 'trust' over the legal documents transmitted by the sending party (Velicogna & Steigenga, 2016).

The e-CODEX project ended on 31 May 2016, but its infrastructure was maintained via a series of projects—e-SENS (until April 2017), API for Justice (until June 2017), Pro-CODEX (until July 2018), and Me-CODEX[28]— and it is now in a phase of complete handover to the European Agency for the Operational Management of large-scale IT Systems in the Area of Freedom, Security and Justice (eu-LISA). The process was expected to be finalised by the end of December 2023 (Article 10(4) e-CODEX Regulation).[29] The symbolic handover of the e-CODEX system to EU-LISA took place on 29 February 2024 at the ME-CODEX Final Conference that took place in the Netherlands. With this, the last details of the system handover from the project consortium to the European Agency are approaching completion.

The ODR Platform

The ODR Platform was established as a single fully multilingual EU-wide platform infrastructure. The legal framework for its creation is the ODR Regulation.[30] The ODR Platform is managed by the European Commission DG JUST who is in charge of its development, operation, and maintenance. For the technical aspects, the European Commission is assisted by an expert group: national authorities, ADR entities, business and consumer representatives, and members of the European Disability Forum (Cortés, 2017). The infrastructure aims to facilitate the resolution of consumer disputes arising from e-commerce.[31] The platform guides consumers' complaint referral to nationally certified ADR bodies. However, if the national law where the consumer is habitually resident allows traders to bring complaints against consumers, the approved ADR entity will also be able to receive traders' complaints via the ODR Platform.[32]

The platform became operational in February 2016 and operates as a hub for consumers to submit a complaint online via standard forms and responses,

---

it was also trusted in the receiving Member States. Now, the eIDAS Regulation is providing the necessary legal framework.

[28] https://www.europarl.europa.eu/RegData/etudes/BRIE/2021/690667/EPRS_BRI(2021)690667_EN.pdf

[29] https://www.eulisa.europa.eu/Activities/Large-Scale-It-Systems/e-CODEX. The process of handover involved governance changes for eu-LISA because the agency did not initially deal with justice, see https://www.eulisa.europa.eu/Newsroom/News/Pages/eu-LISA-prepares-for-the-take-over-of-e-CODEX.aspx.

[30] Regulation (EU) No 524/2013 on online dispute resolution for consumer disputes (ODR Regulation), OJ L 165, 18.06.2013, 1–12.

[31] Article 5(6) ODR Regulation.

[32] Article 2(2) ODR Regulation.

supporting users in filling in some of the necessary information (e.g. finding the details of some major traders, drop-box systems for complaints types, category of dispute, and type of remedy sought) (Cortés, 2017). If parties involved cannot solve their dispute and agree to proceed, the Platform will forwarded their complaint to the competent national certified ADR entity.[33] An automated translation tool is available for users and is supported by human assistance to translate the outcomes and settlements (Cortés, 2017). The ODR Platform back-office has a number of ODR advisors per Member State who can help parties with queries. At the same time, Member States can choose to develop national portals, gateways and/or desks that can 'act as clearinghouses signposting complaints' to nationally certified ADR bodies (e.g. Belgium) (Cortés, 2017). If national platforms have been established, these have their own architecture and ICT system, but they are built to become more easily interoperable with the ODR Platform through the use of XML format for the web communication services.[34]

Since 2019, the Platform has also offered a direct-talks module that can bring consumers and traders in contact to allow them to negotiate a solution bilaterally. This development could be considered to be integrated with software technology that could transform it into an online assisted-negotiation tool that can structure the parties' interests, inform them on how far they are from reaching a solution, and in proposing direct solutions to the parties based on the information they provided and what can be retained to be legally just (van Gelder, 2022). However, for now, further developments in this direction are uncertain as the ODR Platform is set to be phased out due to its low performance in case handling—an average of 200 cases per year in the EU.[35] This does not justify the costs of its maintenance for the European Commission, national public administrations, and businesses.[36] Although the platform proved an 'important source of information' towards all the nationally certified ADR, its poor results have been linked to 'lack of prior information of visitors on how ADR works, the very limited interest of traders and the uneven completeness or relevance of the consumer complaints in relation with the eligibility criteria set by ADR entities'.[37] The information part of the ODR Platform aims to be maintained, and the e-Justice Portal could be a contender towards holding and making such information available to users in the future.

[33] Article 9(6) ODR Regulation.

[34] Commission (2015), p. 34.

[35] Proposal for a Regulation of the European Parliament and of the Council repealing Regulation (EU) No 544/2013 and amending Regulation (EU) 2017/2394 and (EU) 2018/1724 with regards to the discontinuation of the European ODR Platform, COM(2023) 647 final, 2.

[36] Ibidem.

[37] Ibidem 3.

The Systems and Their Actors

The experiences of the e-Justice Portal, the e-CODEX, and the ODR Platform have shown that all three are platform assemblages of heterogenous components (i.e. normative, organisational, and technological) that are 'loosely integrated' (Velicogna, 2023) through interfaces standardisation processes. They involve a multitude of actors (e.g. European authorities, national political authorities, technical agencies, public administrations, ICT providers, professional organisations, regulatory bodies, ADR bodies, research centres) with multiple authority structures who interact, 'display multiple logics', and 'where boundaries and linkages among administrative bodies cannot be unequivocally fixed' because they shift and change over time. Further, such platforms will likely need periodic 're-conceptualisation' (Lanzara, 2009) given the organisational, institutional, and legislative changes that happen over time.

The coordination and execution of administrative tasks in all three systems proved dependent on normative authority structures (i.e. dedicated legislation, formal agreements) '*and* on functional linkages and communication standards and protocols' as identified by Lanzara (2009). For example, for all three European e-justice systems, the European Commission is the owner of the structures jointly with the various DGs directly involved—DG Just for the e-Justice Portal with the Council providing the indications for its developments (Velicogna, 2018), DG Home for the e-CODEX together with the eu-LISA management (Taal et al., 2019), and DG Just for the ODR Platform. Together with formal owners of the systems, expert groups are used to support the governance of the platforms: for the e-CODEX there is an Advisory Group composed of Member States experts, stakeholders, members of the judiciary, legal practitioners and professional organisations, for the ODR Platform assistance is provided by an expert group comprising national authorities, ADR entities, businesses and consumer representatives, and members of the European Disability Forum. At policy level, the influence and steering of the e-Justice and e-CODEX platforms is exercised by the Justice and Home Affairs (JHA) Council together with the Working Party e-Law (e-Justice) as the Permanent Expert Group (PEG).[38] The European Judicial Network is also relevant for the steering of the e-Justice platform.[39]

Technology is no longer a simple tool for justice, but it develops into an environment (Reiling & Contini, 2022). ICT becomes 'formative of the cognitive and institutional context' (Lanzara, 2009) within which the e-justice activities are carried out and which influences the institutional configurations, links, and connectivity

[38] PEG was established by the European Commission and the Member States within the Working Party e-LAW (e-Justice) and consists of representatives of Member States (participating or not already in the e-CODEX related projects), the e-Justice unit of the European Commission and observes (especially representatives of European legal professional organisations—CCBE, CNUE, CEHR, UIHJ). See Taal et al. (2019).

[39] Council (2011).

(Lanzara, 2009). The systems' components are designed for different objectives (e.g. providing information, supporting legally valid and secure cross-border exchange of data and communications, bringing consumers and traders in contact and referring them to a competent certified ADR body). The digital infrastructures are constructed as decentralised platforms. CEF provides the systems' building blocks—digital service infrastructure—and these blocks are owned by the European Commission (DG Digit, DG Just) or the Member States. The Member States and the European Commission are responsible for the policy side as well as the functional side of the systems. At the same time, the digital service infrastructure providers are accountable for the building blocks design and the implementation of solutions in the form of specifications, software, and services (Taal et al., 2019).

The users of these platforms come from a variety of communities, with some of them overlapping for the three e-justice systems: professional organisations, judiciaries, public authorities, legal professionals, ADR bodies, and private users—citizens or businesses.

The Challenges of the European e-Justice Systems' Governance

Governance is a complex concept; and for the European e-Justice platforms this is 'not restricted to governmental institutions' (Schneider, 2012). The analysis revealed a multilevel governance structure divided between the EU and national governments and institutions, judiciaries, professional bodies and organisations, and private actors. The complexity of integrating judicial governance is given by its variety across Member States and the fact that it has to be addressed from the perspective of the responsibility of upholding fair procedures in the digital processes (Reiling & Contini, 2022). This will also require particular attention when legal datasets and artificial intelligence developments for justice will be considered and/or used in judicial or out-of-court procedures. Additionally, the e-justice assemblages involve not only a multilevel structure but also forms of collaborative governance bringing together actors with different perspectives (e.g. European institutions, European Agencies involved in the systems' management, Networks such as the European Judicial Network national judiciaries, ICT providers), knowledge (e.g. policymakers, legal professionals, software architects, IT technicians), and interests (e.g. European policymakers and national policymakers, national ministries and public administrations, professional bodies, police forces) that need to collaborate and find common ground. This can be done through agreeing on common standards and language for ICT developments, observing fundamental standards and principles (e.g. subsidiarity, independence of the judiciary) that could function in their own country's justice reality in order to further e-justice developments for facilitating access to justice and cooperation within a cross-border framework. Each actor would not be able to deliver this individually; thus, cooperation is necessary.

The e-Justice Portal, the e-CODEX, and the ODR Platform are systems that are each the first of their kind in Europe. Viable models were not available ex-ante and solutions and choices for e-architecture and governance had to be built on the way.[40] Failures exist (see ODR Platforms), but they can be learned from. The complexity of the European e-justice governance is not related only to the variety of roles, competencies, and relations between actors but also the variety of components with different objectives, procedures covered by ICT developments, and the need to maintain a dynamic adaptation of the technical part (redesign and reuse of technical components) which is at time required not only by the evolution of technology, but also by that of the law at national and/or European level, and occasionally organisational changes that are made.

An additional challenge also comes from the broad and diverse user community and the process of adding additional functionalities and procedures (e.g. the e-CODEX new digital procedures to be built for the service of documents communications and taking of evidence, the use of the e-Justice Portal as an access point for the e-CODEX). The e-CODEX pilots have shown that although the methodology used is identical, the approach to user communities involved in each of the supported procedures needed to be different, and the e-CODEX community had to get used to different modes of operations, cultures, and requirements regarding the data processing digital support (Taal et al., 2019). The procedures may require a learning process of the ICT solutions. This complexity will only increase in the coming period with more civil and criminal procedures being added to the e-CODEX platform (Taal et al., 2019) and with the governance structure of the various actors involved. The multilevel governance and coordination complexity will also increase, and this will call for new forms or governance arrangements in order to avoid unmanageable complexities (Taal et al., 2019). This experience will likely also be relevantals for AI systems for e-justice.

A final key challenge to address comes from the unique position of the judiciary and the need to maintain its independence as a fundamental principle for the rule of law in a democratic society. The ICT integration, and even more so AI developments, will have a positive value for justice only if the principle of judicial independence can be respected in the decision-making process and any external parties influence that can induce the judges to act partially prevented.[41]

Future Developments to Consider and Concluding Remarks

The experience of e-Justice Portal, e-CODEX, and ODR Platform shows that governance approaches to e-justice developments in Europe will have to find ways to keep complexity in governance manageable or even ways to reduce it. As remarked by Taal et al. (2019), this will inevitably reduce the competence of some of the

[40] On a national similar example, see Velicogna and Contini (2009). For e-CODEX, see Velicogna et al. (2020).

[41] Taal et al. (2019), pp. 46–47.

present actors in the identified governance practices for European e-Justice systems, but good governance, trust, and effective differentiation between governance roles will hopefully contribute to finding balanced solutions. The independence of the judiciary is a national responsibility, but in large ICT systems such as e-CODEX or the e-Justice Portal this could also be supported by the involvement of the judiciary (including professional bodies) in the design and decision-making on ICT integration and use, the internal work process, and the technology-enabled decision-making (Reiling & Contini, 2022). Judicial independence is a constitutive element in the fair administration of justice, and as technology is becoming a constitutive element, rising tensions must be solved and discretion maintained. The involvement of professionals knowledgeable about technology in the process as well as allowing them and other stakeholders to report improper coding of the law into ICT systems or identified dangers into e-Justice systems will allow early tackling of undesired effects and support good governance practices.

Diversity will remain a crucial component in the EU e-justice solutions, but this could be handled by building common understanding, common standards, and common interpretation in line with fundamental principles and values that are shared between Member States. A design that supports the co-evolution of e-justice systems over time, of the building blocks, and the legislation will have to be part of the European e-justice architecture and governance. Governance systems respond to changes in the environment, and they will seek to provide calibrated responses to those changes, adjusting, in this case, the European e-justice systems in subsequent rounds of decision-making.

Digital procedural standards will have to provide the same guarantees as procedural standards in paper-based procedures. Legal and technological flexibility will have to be built in, and common legal semantics for e-justice systems will contribute to keeping complexity manageable between European and national systems and procedures.

References

Commission. (2010). Competitiveness and Innovation Framework Programme (CIP), ICT Policy Support Programme, ICT PSP Work Programme, 2010, 30. Available at http://ec.europa.eu/information_society/activities/ict_psp/documents/ict_psp_wp2010_final.pdf

Commission. (2015). CEF-TC-2015-1: Connecting Europe facility (CEF) trans-European communication networks, Work Programme 2015.

Commission. (2017). CEF-TC-2017-1: European e-Justice Portal, Call for Proposals Concerning Projects of Common Interest under the Connecting Europe Facility in the Field of Trans-European Telecommunication Networks. Available at https://wayback.archive-it.org/12090/20180927165926/https://ec.europa.eu/inea/sites/inea/files/2017-1_calltext_european_e-justice_portal_superfinal_170217.pdf

Commission. (2018). Implementing decision on the adoption of work programme for 2018 and on the financing of connecting Europe facility (CEF)—Telecommunication Sector, Annex, C(2018) 568 final.

Commission. (2020). Commission Staff Working Document, Impact Assessment, Proposal for a Regulation of the European Parliament and of the Council on a Computerised System for Communication in Cross-Border Civil and Criminal Proceedings (e-CODEX system), and amending Regulation (EU) 2018/1726, SWD(2020) 541 final.

Contini, F. (2013). Let agency circulate: Architectures and strategies for pan-European e-Justice. In *The circulation of agency in e-justice: Interoperability and infrastructures for European transborder judicial proceedings* (pp. 331–353). Springer.

Cortés, P. (2017). *The law of consumer redress in an evolving digital market: Upgrading from alternative to online dispute resolution* (p. 117). Cambridge University Press.

Council. (2009). Multi-annual European e-Justice action plan 2009–2013 OJ C 75, 31.3.2009, pp. 1–12.

Council. (2011). Draft Council Conclusions, 5309/1, Brussels, 27 January 2011.

Council. (2013). Draft Strategy on European e-Justice 2014–2018 (2013/C 376/06) OJ C 376, 21.12.2013, pp. 7–11.

Council. (2014). Multi-annual European e-justice action plan 2014–2018, OJ C 182, 14.6.2014, pp 2–13.

Council. (2019a). 2019–2023 Action Plan European e-Justice, OJ C 96, 13.3.2019, pp. 9–32.

Council. (2019b). 2019–2023 Strategy on e-Justice, OJ C 96, 13.3.2019, pp. 3–8.

Council. (2023). European e-Justice Strategy 2024–2028—Approval, 15509/23 Bruselles 17 November 2023.

Hamulák, O. (2018). La carta de los derechos fundamentales de la union europea y los derechos sociales. *Estudios constitucionales, 16*(1), 167–186.

Lanzara, G. F. (2009). Building digital institutions: ICT and the rise of assemblages in government. In *ICT and innovation in the public sector: European studies in the making of e-government* (pp. 9–48). Palgrave Macmillan UK.

Ontanu, E. A. (2017). Cross-border debt recovery in the EU. A comparative and empirical study on the use of the European uniform procedures (November 2, 2017). In *Ius commune: European and comparative law series* (p. 159). Intersentia.

Onțanu, E. A. (2019). Adapting justice to technology and technology to justice: A coevolution process to e-justice in cross-border litigation. *European Quarterly of Political Attitudes and Mentalities, 8*(2), 54–74.

Onțanu, E. A. (2020, August). Encoding justice: A quest for facilitating access to justice by e-handling of cross-border litigation. The example of the European uniform procedures. In *The 50th anniversary of the European law of civil procedure* (pp. 473–506). Nomos Verlagsgesellschaft mbH & Co. KG.

Onțanu, E. A. (2023a). The digitalisation of European Union procedures: A new impetus following a time of prolonged crisis. *Law, Technology and Humans, 5*(1), 93–110. https://doi.org/10.5204/lthj.2706

Onțanu, E. A. (2023b). Article 27-reference implementation software. In *The European service regulation. A commentary* (p. 249). Edward Elgar Publishing Ltd..

Pangalos, G., Salmatzidis, I., & Pagkalos, I. (2014). Using IT to provide easier access to cross-border legal procedures for citizens and legal professionals-implementation of a European payment order E-CODEX pilot. In *IJCA* (Vol. 6, p. 43).

Ramiro Troitiño, D. (2023). Mapping e-governance in the EU. In *Digital development of the European Union: An interdisciplinary perspective* (pp. 303–317). Springer International Publishing.

Reading, V. (2010, July). Press Release *European e-Justice Internet Portal Offers Quick Answers to Citizen's Legal Questions* (Press Release), IP/10/956, Brussels. Available at https://ec.europa.eu/commission/presscorner/detail/en/IP_10_956

Reiling, A. D. (2009). Technology for justice: How information technology can support judicial reform.

Reiling, D., & Contini, F. (2022). E-justice platforms: Challenges for judicial governance. In *IJCA* (Vol. 13, p. 1).

Schneider, V. (2012). Governance and complexity. In *The Oxford handbook of governance* (pp. 129–142).

Steigenga, E., Taal, S., Medici, A. & Velicogna, M. (2018). *Exploring the potential for a service of documents e-CODEX use case in The Netherlands* (Pro-CODEX Report).

Taal, S., Kolitsi, Z., Velicogna, M., Groustra, J., & Steigenga, E. (2019). Connecting the European e-justice community: Towards a new governance model for e-CODEX. *Public Science and Policies, 5*(1), 34. https://doi.org/10.33167/2184-0644.CPP2019.VVN1/. pp. 33–51.

van Gelder, E. (2022). *Consumer online dispute resolution pathways in Europe*. Eleven.

Velicogna, M. (2007). Justice systems and ICT: What can be learned from Europe? *Utrecht Law Review*, 129–147.

Velicogna, M. (2018). e-Justice in Europe: From national experiences to EU cross-border service provision. *International E-Government Development: Policy, Implementation and Best Practice*, 39–72.

Velicogna, M. (2023, November). The rise of cross-border platforms in the European justice domain. Lessons from practice. In *Leila final conference - Towards an EU platform for judicial auctions and going forward.*

Velicogna, M., & Contini, F. (2009). Assemblage-in-the-making: Developing the e-services for the Justice of the Peace Office in Italy. In *ICT and innovation in the public sector: European studies in the making of e-government* (pp. 211–243). Palgrave Macmillan.

Velicogna, M., & Steigenga, E. (2016, September). Can complexity theory help understanding tomorrow e-justice? In *Conference on complex systems, law and complexity session, Amsterdam* (pp. 20–23).

Velicogna, M., Steigenga, E., Taal, S., & Schmidt, A. (2020). Connecting EU jurisdictions: Exploring how to open justice across member states through ICT. *Social Science Computer Review, 38*(3), 274–294.

SPRINGER NATURE

GPSR Compliance

The European Union's (EU) General Product Safety Regulation (GPSR) is a set of rules that requires consumer products to be safe and our obligations to ensure this.

If you have any concerns about our products, you can contact us on ProductSafety@springernature.com

In case Publisher is established outside the EU, the EU authorized representative is:

Springer Nature Customer Service Center GmbH
Europaplatz 3
69115 Heidelberg, Germany

The manufacturer's authorised representative in the EU is Springer Nature Customer Service Centre GmbH, Europaplatz 3, 69115 Heidelberg, Germany. If you have any concerns regarding our products, please contact ProductSafety@springernature.com

Printed and bound by CPI Group (UK) Ltd, Croydon, CR0 4YY

01/10/2026

02225898-0017